What's Wrong
with Morality?

What's Wrong with Morality?

A Social-Psychological Perspective

C. Daniel Batson

OXFORD
UNIVERSITY PRESS

OXFORD
UNIVERSITY PRESS

Oxford University Press is a department of the University of
Oxford. It furthers the University's objective of excellence in research,
scholarship, and education by publishing worldwide.

Oxford   New York
Auckland   Cape Town   Dar es Salaam   Hong Kong   Karachi
Kuala Lumpur   Madrid   Melbourne   Mexico City   Nairobi
New Delhi   Shanghai   Taipei   Toronto

With offices in
Argentina   Austria   Brazil   Chile   Czech Republic   France   Greece
Guatemala   Hungary   Italy   Japan   Poland   Portugal   Singapore
South Korea   Switzerland   Thailand   Turkey   Ukraine   Vietnam

Oxford is a registered trademark of Oxford University Press
in the UK and certain other countries.

Published in the United States of America by
Oxford University Press
198 Madison Avenue, New York, NY 10016

© C. Daniel Batson 2016

Library of Congress Cataloging-in-Publication Data
Batson, C. Daniel (Charles Daniel), 1943–
What's wrong with morality? : a social-psychological perspective / C. Daniel Batson.
pages cm
Includes bibliographical references and index.
ISBN 978–0–19–935554–9 — ISBN 978–0–19–935557–0   1. Ethics.   2. Values.
I. Title.
BJ1063.B37 2015
170—dc23
2015007028

3 5 7 9 8 6 4 2
Printed in Canada on acid-free paper

CONTENTS

INTRODUCTION

Morality is often celebrated as the bright star that shines at the pinnacle of human evolution. Indeed, at the pinnacle of all evolution. It's what separates us from the rest. We're the species that curbs selfish impulses, cooperates with one another, builds cities and civilizations. The ones created in the image of God.

To be sure, much can be said for morality. We probably couldn't survive without it. If it were suddenly taken away, we'd scramble desperately to regain it—as did Ralph and Piggy in *Lord of the Flies* (Golding, 1954). But all too often our morality doesn't serve us well. We walk inescapably in the shadow of religious wars, witch hunts, oppressions, and genocides. How can this moral animal act in ways that are so character-denying, so inhumane?

The problem isn't simply that there are bad people who act immorally—criminals and psychopaths. Trouble lies closer to home. Even the most stable, secure society is afflicted with moral maladies, as Jane Austen reminded us in the first few pages of *Sense and Sensibility* (1811/1995). There, the very wealthy Mr. John Dashwood and his wife are discussing how he should fulfill the promise to his dying father to "do everything in his power" (p. 3) to care for his stepmother and three stepsisters, whose financial situation is now dire. (John's father's entire estate was entailed to him.) "When he gave his promise to his father, he meditated within himself to increase the fortunes of his sisters by the [annual] present of a thousand pounds apiece. ... Yes, he would give them three thousand pounds; it would be liberal and handsome!" (p. 3).

But John soon sees his moral responsibility more clearly. His wife reminds him of their son: "How could he answer it to himself to rob his child, and his only child too, of so large a sum?" (p. 6). He cuts the planned annuity to five hundred pounds apiece, affirming, "I would not wish to do anything mean. . . . One had rather on such occasions do too much than too little" (p. 7).

With further reflection, John abandons the idea of an annuity altogether. "Whatever I may give them occasionally will be of far greater assistance than a yearly allowance, because they would only enlarge their style of living if they felt sure of a larger income and would not be sixpence the richer for it at the end of the year" (p. 9). His wife goes further, "I am convinced within myself that your father had no idea of your giving them any money at all. . . . They will be much more able to give you something" (p. 9). Finally, John settles on a plan that will "strictly fulfill my engagement":

"When my mother removes into another house [he's evicting her from the one that has been her home] my services shall be readily given to accommodate her as far as I can. Some little present of furniture too may be acceptable then. ..." He finally resolved that it would be absolutely unnecessary, if not highly indecorous, to do more for the widow and children of his father. (p. 10)

John Dashwood is very concerned about doing what's morally right. He feels he has done right. Yet what he does badly misses the mark set by his own standards. Something's wrong.

In raising the prospect that something is wrong with morality, I'm not suggesting that it's wrong to be moral—to be fair, kind, honest, and so on. Of course, we could debate over what's moral in certain cases. Is it moral to be totally honest about a friend's disastrous new hairstyle, or about the hiding place of a pursued innocent? Is it right to sacrifice the life of one person to save the lives of two? Of ten? Of ten thousand? Is it right to be more attentive to the needs of those close to you than to the needs of strangers? What if someone in authority tells you to do something you think wrong, ought you obey or refuse? What's right on issues like abortion, affirmative action, capital punishment, and gun control? I bypass these vexing normative questions to focus instead on moral psychology. So doing, I attempt to answer some equally vexing questions: When we embrace some moral principle or ideal, why do we often fail to act in accord even when we know we should? And how do we still manage to believe we succeeded? How can we act in ways that if done by someone else we would consider quite wrong? How is it that we too can be John Dashwoods?

Our potential for moral failure isn't news. It has been recognized since antiquity. But unless we want to settle for blaming human frailty or original sin, the cause remains controversial. Some experts believe the problem is lack of character. They argue that we haven't learned to value our moral standards and ideals sufficiently—or in the right way. Others say we're victims of poor judgment. If we could but discern what's morally right through careful reasoning, through tuned intuition and a keen moral sense, or through feeling and sentiment, we would act accordingly. Still others say the problem is that we're knocked off course by strong situational forces that overpower our good intent. Implicit in these different views is the assumption that if we can grow up properly, if we can think and feel as we should, and if we can keep a firm hand on the tiller despite the shifting winds of circumstance, all will be well. We can realize our moral potential.

Many of our best writers of fiction—Austen included—are less optimistic. She and other astute observers of the human condition such as Balzac (1834/1962), Dickens (1843–1844/1982), Dostoyevsky (1879–1880/1950), Eliot (1861/1962, 1874/1956), Hugo (1862), Stendhal (1830/2003), Tolstoy (1886/2009), and Twain (1884/1959) suggest that our moral psychology is more complex. We may care deeply about doing right, we may feel we know what's right, we may not be unduly pressured, and we may even believe we've done right—yet still do wrong. Nor is it simply a matter of good intentions gone astray, or being overpowered by self-interest. Our moral life is fertile ground for rationalization and deception, including self-deception. Not only do we often fail to live up to our moral principles and ideals, whatever they are, but we also manage to overlook our failures or to see them as successes. As a result, our morality becomes impotent. Like John Dashwood, we can fulfill a sincerely felt responsibility with some little present of furniture.

Writers like Austen encourage us to look more closely at our motives, emotions, and values, at what we really care about in the moral domain. That's what I want to do in the chapters that follow, doing so as a social psychologist rather than a novelist. My concern isn't to claim that we never act morally any more than to claim that we always do. Rather, I want to look behind both moral and immoral behavior to understand how and why each occurs. I want to consider the interplay of values, emotions, and motives that produce our behavior. It's in this interplay that I believe much of the problem lies.

Such an approach to moral psychology is different from most approaches in three ways. First, it considers morality not only as a solution but also as a problem. Second, it focuses on moral action rather than moral judgment. My concern is not how we decide what's moral, but how our morals affect our behavior. And third, it looks at the range of motives and emotions, many not intrinsically moral, that can lead us to act morally.

OVERVIEW

Chapter 1 begins with some reminders of the nature and scope of our moral maladies—our failures to live up to standards we embrace. Then it sets up a conceptual framework for exploration of possible causes. The framework includes, first, some reflection on the dictionary definition of morality, which I shall adopt. The dictionary defines morality in terms of principles of right and wrong conduct. "Principles" in the definition is a broad, umbrella term that covers principles, standards, rules, norms, commandments, ideals, and virtues. I emphasize this breadth because in both moral psychology and moral philosophy it has become common to use "principles" to refer specifically to Kantian (1785/1898) deontological (duty) principles. The dictionary doesn't intend so restricted a use, nor do I. The second element of the framework is an analysis of the way value, emotion, motivation, and behavior interact as we pursue our goals. Threats to valued states evoke emotions, which amplify goal-directed motives, which depending on circumstances produce behavior.

Completing the framework, I apply this analysis to the moral domain, highlighting the range of motives that can lead us to act morally. In addition to being motivated by a desire to uphold some moral standard, principle, or ideal (I call such a motive *moral integrity*, or *principlism*), moral behavior can be motivated by a desire to increase our own welfare (self-interest, or *egoism*), to increase another person's welfare (*altruism*), or to increase some group's welfare (*collectivism*). For these last three classes of motivation, acting morally isn't an ultimate goal valued for its own sake. Instead, it's either an instrumental means to reach a nonmoral ultimate goal or an unintended consequence of doing so. As a result, the link between the motive and morality is tenuous and can easily fail. In this regard, altruism and collectivism,

which are often thought to be intrinsically moral, stand on the same ground as egoism. Nor is acting on principlism, which *is* intrinsically moral, problem free. Rather,
each of these four types of motivation has its unique strengths and weaknesses as a
source of moral behavior. Recognizing the nature of the underlying motivation can
shed important light on when we're likely to adhere to our principles and when not.
This conceptual framework undergirds the rest of the book.

Standard scientific accounts of our moral failures haven't focused on motivation.
The focus has been on either personal deficiency or situational pressure, each of which
is also important for understanding our moral psychology. Chapter 2 considers deficiency accounts. These include not only classic characterological and social-learning
analyses that address the inculcation of moral standards and values but also analyses
that focus on moral judgment, including judgment based on reason, intuition, and
sentiment. Problems with either the acquisition of moral values or with their wise
application can lead to moral failure.

Chapter 3 considers the array of situational pressures that can keep us from acting morally. These include pressures that prevent us from recognizing the moral
relevance of events, that undermine or overpower our moral motivation, and that
thwart our good intentions. Such pressures can be especially pernicious when
applied over time in organizations or in society at large. They, too, are important
contributors to our moral ills.

Although there's much truth in the standard accounts reviewed in Chapters 2
and 3, neither one, nor the two combined, provides a complete diagnosis of what's
wrong with morality. Chapter 4 probes deeper by looking closely and critically at
the nature of moral motivation. Specifically, it explores the possibility that much
behavior thought to be directed toward the ultimate goal of promoting some
moral principle or ideal may instead be directed toward appearing moral while,
if possible, avoiding the cost of actually being moral. This form of motivation
has been called *moral hypocrisy*. It's a subtle form of egoism in which doing right
is only an instrumental goal on the way to the self-serving goal of seeing ourselves and being seen by others as moral. So motivated, even those who strongly
endorse moral standards and who aren't under pressure often fail to act morally.
Remember John Dashwood.

If moral hypocrisy is to realize its full potential, self-deception is required. To get
self-rewards for being moral (e.g., enhanced esteem) and avoid self-punishments for
not (e.g., guilt), yet still pursue self-interest, we must manage to convince ourselves
we've been moral when we haven't. Recent research provides empirical evidence that
many of us can do just that. Research also provides evidence that moral hypocrisy
isn't simply an after-the-fact phenomenon, whereby we rationalize our moral lapses.
It's a goal-directed motive that can produce them.

By taking a look at the way moral motivation is acquired in childhood, Chapter 5
addresses the question of why moral integrity is rare and hypocrisy common.
I suggest that hypocrisy is especially common in interpersonal morality situations, those in which our personal interests conflict with the interests of others.
Observational research suggests that we don't internalize standards that curb our

self-interest—standards of fairness, kindness, honesty, and the like—without resistance. As a result, these standards rarely become core, intrinsic values. We experience them as oughts but not wants.

Interpersonal interest conflicts are often considered to be what morality is all about, and they're certainly central. But morality extends beyond interest conflicts to also include matters of propriety. Propriety morality specifies how we should act if we're to maintain the natural and social order. It specifies, for example, right and wrong sexual practices, proper treatment of other beings, and the respect owed to certain institutions, traditions, and people. At least initially, propriety morality is more easily and fully internalized than interpersonal morality. As a result, adherence to our propriety principles is more likely to be motivated by moral integrity (principlism).

Chapter 6 turns to moral emotion. From the perspective of the value→emotion→motivation→behavior framework introduced in Chapter 1, many of what are commonly called moral emotions have been mislabeled. Rather than being evoked by threat to some moral principle or ideal, these emotions are evoked by the threat a moral violation poses to our own welfare (think of feelings of anger and guilt), to the welfare of a cared-for other (think of sympathy and compassion), or to the welfare of a cared-for group (loyalty, esprit, and patriotic fervor). That is, these emotions are related to egoistic, altruistic, or collectivistic goals, respectively. They promote moral goals only indirectly as instrumental means or unintended consequences, which makes their link to moral behavior unreliable. This weak link is another important contributor to our moral failures.

To illustrate, think about anger at unfairness (often called moral outrage). If another person's unfair behavior makes me angry, am I responding to the unfairness per se—that is, to the moral violation—or to the harm the behavior inflicts on me or on some person or group I care about? Recent research suggests that often our response is to the harm rather than to the unfairness itself. As a result, the emotion is not truly *moral* anger. A lack of moral anger is very much what would be expected if, as suggested in Chapters 4 and 5, appeals to fairness in interpersonal interest conflicts are likely to produce motivation to appear fair (moral hypocrisy) rather than actually be fair (moral integrity).

The distinction between interpersonal and propriety morality is as important for emotions as for motives. In contrast to our emotional response to interpersonal violations, research indicates that propriety violations may evoke truly moral emotion, especially feelings of disgust. Again, this finding is consistent with the developmental analysis in Chapter 5, which suggests that we're more likely to fully internalize and intrinsically value our propriety standards. A new understanding of our moral failures is beginning to take shape, one that takes account of motivational and emotional factors.

Chapters 7 and 8 consider some implications of this new understanding. If, as suggested, our concern in interpersonal interest conflicts is rarely to adhere to our moral standards except either as means to other ends or as unintended consequences, why do we so proudly proclaim such standards? What function do they serve? Chapter 7 addresses this question, suggesting that we often invoke our inter-personal moral standards to guide and direct other people's behavior rather than our own. At the same time, others invoke their standards to guide and direct our behavior. Both sides thrust and parry. Moral combat.

Even propriety morality may be a weapon of social control more than self-control. We rarely need our propriety standards to prod us to act as we feel we should regarding the natural and social order. It's difficult not to act as we think right when it comes to religious practices, incest, littering, poisoning stray cats, and so on. But not everyone shares our view of the way things ought to be, so we proclaim propriety standards to get others to act as we think they should. They, in turn, proclaim their standards to get us to act as they think we should. Again, thrust and parry.

Chapter 8 addresses the challenging question of how to treat our moral mala-dies. That is, how to induce us to act more reliably as our moral principles specify, especially in interest-conflict situations. A number of efforts based on the standard analyses—personal deficiency and situational pressure—have been proposed. But these efforts often fail to effectively address the problem. The present analysis, with its focus on motivation and emotion, suggests a different approach. It suggests that we try to orchestrate motives in a way that allows the strength of one motive to over-come the weakness of another.

Motivation to act morally (principlism) is directed toward promoting a moral principle or ideal. This is an important strength. But interpersonal, interest-con-flict principles are rarely fully internalized and intrinsically valued. As a result, their violation is unlikely to evoke moral emotion. And motivation to promote these principles is likely to be vulnerable to pretense and rationalization. These are serious weaknesses. Various forms of egoism, altruism, and collectivism are unreliable. They promote morality only as an instrumental goal or unintended consequence. An important weakness. But each has a strong emotional base and can be quite powerful. Clear strengths. Moreover, the ultimate goals of altruism and collectivism align with the goals of two frequently espoused interpersonal moral principles—care for the welfare of other individuals and care for the com-mon good. More strength. By evoking motivation to act morally along with one or more of these nonmoral motives, it may be possible to capitalize on the unique strengths of each to produce potent and reliable motivation to promote some interpersonal principle or ideal. It may be possible to transform adherence to our standards from something we feel we ought to do into something we want to do—that is, from an instrumental to an ultimate goal.

And through this process we may ourselves be transformed. Our moral stan-dards may become more integral to our character, to who we are as persons. If so, we should be less susceptible to moral maladies in the future. Of course, such a trans-formation doesn't guarantee that the standards we uphold are ones that someone else would judge right. Such a judgment is normative not scientific, and beyond the scope of the present analysis.

CONFESSION AND ACKNOWLEDGMENTS

Given that this book is about morality, I should be honest and admit up front that I'm not sure my analysis is right. Indeed, I think it's almost certainly wrong, at least in spots. Unfortunately, I don't yet know where those spots are. Both skepticism about the argument and calls for clearer evidence are warranted. My attention to the vast relevant literature is selective. The issues are complex and controversial. The conclusions rather cynical. Evidence to date, although supportive, isn't nearly as extensive and systematic as I would like. I present the analysis as a work in progress, counting on others and on future research to make it better. It's closer to a first sketch than a finished canvas.

The analysis has already benefited considerably from a number of critiques, insights, and suggestions. Especially useful have been comments by or conversations with Nadia Ahmad, Aaron Ancell, Karl Aquino, Max Bazerman, Paul Bloom, Hannah Bondurant, Jana Schaich Borg, Tommaso Bruni, Daryl Cameron, Nancy Carter, Vlad Chituc, Elizabeth Collins, Phil Costanzo, John Darley, Alexandra DeForge, Richard Dew, Nancy Eisenberg, Ernst Fehr, David Fisher, Lowell Gaertner, Francesca Gino, Jesse Graham, Josh Greene, Jon Haidt, Paul Henne, Lydia Eckstein Jackson, Meagan Kelly, Diane Kobrynowitz, Frank Lambert, Jeff Larsen, Mel Lerner, Christine Little, Peter McCutcheon, Jim McNulty, Heidi Maibom, Josh May, Christian Miller, Benoit Monin, Joe Nelson, Lawrence Ngo, Martha Nussbaum, Luis Oceja, Michael Olson, Erin O'Mara, Keith Payne, Jesse Prinz, Brenda Sampat, Jani Sherrard, Peter Sherrard, Garriy Shteynberg, Walter Sinnott-Armstrong, Nina Strohminger, Jesse Summers, Abraham Tesser, Lisa Thompson, Jo-Ann Tsang, Sandra Varey, Larry Ventis, and Jamil Zaki. Among these, I owe a particular debt of gratitude to members of the Duke University Moral Attitudes and Decision-Making (MAD) Lab. They dedicated an entire weekend to discussing the chapters, one by one. And special thanks also to students in Lydia Eckstein Jackson's undergraduate seminar at Allegheny College, who class-tested the manuscript. I doubt that any of the people listed will fully agree with what follows. Some may fully disagree. But all deserve credit and thanks for trying to make it better.

Thanks as well to Abby Gross of Oxford University Press for her interest and guidance at a time when this book was not all she was bringing to life. Finally, as always, loving thanks to Judy, my wife. She repeatedly encouraged me to keep going and consistently moved me in the direction of smoother prose. For the latter if not the former she deserves your thanks as well.

AUDIENCE

Naturally, I hope lots of people want to read this book. And I hope they find it enjoyable, informative, and thought-provoking. Given that I'm writing as a social psychologist, it should be of particular interest to others in that field. Many moral philosophers also have an active interest in moral psychology. I hope that they too will find the book relevant to their work. And I hope it will be of interest to undergraduate and graduate students in both social psychology and moral philosophy. Depending on the course, the book could serve as either a primary or a supplementary text. More generally, I hope the analysis will be of interest to anyone who puzzles over what's wrong with our morality, whether from another academic perspective or from outside academia. And who hasn't wondered what's wrong with morality? At least other people's.

PART I

What's Wrong

1

MORAL MALADIES

Most of us unhesitatingly affirm our allegiance to moral ideals such as fairness, honesty, and not harming innocents. Most of us also consider ourselves above average in adherence to these ideals (Alicke & Govorun, 2005; Epley & Dunning, 2000; Sedikides & Strube, 1997). Being moral is central to how we see ourselves (Aquino & Reed, 2002). And by-and-large we act accordingly. We don't lie, cheat, or steal whenever we can. We don't kill—at least not other humans—except in extreme circumstances. We don't simply use other people as instruments for our own pleasure or knowingly inflict pain without provocation. We wait our turn. We share. We're polite and nice. We try to be thoughtful and kind. Yet, it's logically impossible for most of us to be above average in morality. William Saroyan (1951) touched on this wry fact in the opening lines of *Rock Wagram*, "Every man is a good man in a bad world . . ., as he himself knows."

Unfortunately, our problems with morality go deeper than overly optimistic self-perception. That's but one comparatively mild symptom. The moral atrocities of the modern age remind us that horrendous things aren't done only by monsters. People who sincerely value morality, who firmly believe they shouldn't put their own rights and interests ahead of the parallel rights and interests of others, who think it's wrong to cause anyone pain—these people can act in ways that show blatant disregard for ideals and standards held dear. Our moral ills are widespread, as a brief look at the record shows. The symptoms extend well beyond biased self-perception.

SOME SERIOUS SYMPTOMS

A few examples may help orient us to the scope of the problem and the need to understand what's wrong.

Participation in the Final Solution

Early on the morning of July 12, 1942, and less than 3 weeks after arriving in occupied Poland, the approximately 500 middle-aged and predominantly working-class men of German Reserve Police Battalion 101 were addressed by their commander, Major Trapp. He informed them that their assignment for the day was unpleasant and demanding. They were to remove the 1,800 Jews from the village of Józefów. Jewish men of working age, about 300, were to go to a work camp. The 1,500 women, children, and elderly were to be shot. After explaining the orders—and after reminding the battalion that back home in Germany women and children were being killed by Allied bombs and that Jews were opponents of the Third Reich—Major Trapp said that if any of the older men felt they couldn't carry out these orders, they should step forward and would be given other duties. About a dozen men accepted this highly unusual offer. The rest of the battalion set about the gruesome task. It proved extremely difficult for many. Some of the men sought to evade the actual shooting. Others started but stopped, saying they found it unbearable and couldn't continue. Alcohol was provided to steady nerves. By the end of a long day, the job was done. The men returned to barracks "depressed, angered, embittered, and shaken. They ate little but drank heavily" (Browning, 1998, p. 69).

July 12 was only the beginning. Over the next 16 months, Battalion 101 shot more than 38,000 Jewish men, women, and children and rounded up another 45,000 to be sent to die at Treblinka. For most in the battalion, mass killing of Jews became routine. Browning (1998) estimated that only 10 to 20 percent remained nonshooters. Although some of the men were eager killers, the majority neither looked forward to nor celebrated the killing. Still, they killed.

> Increasingly numb and brutalized, they felt more pity for themselves because of the "unpleasant" work they had been assigned than they did for their dehumanized victims. For the most part, they did not think what they were doing was wrong or immoral because the killing was sanctioned by legitimate authority. Indeed, for the most part they did not try to think, period. As one policeman stated: "Truthfully, I must say that at the time we didn't reflect about it at all. Only years later did any of us become truly conscious of what had happened then. ... Only later did it first occur to me that had not been right." (Browning, 1998, p. 72)

You and I may judge what the men of Battalion 101 did to be horribly wrong. But through it all, if asked, they would almost certainly have described themselves as good and moral—good men in a bad world.

So would the SS doctors who carried out the selections at Auschwitz that sent over four million to the gas chambers. These doctors had sworn to live by the Oath of Hippocrates:

> I will use treatment to help the sick according to my ability and judgment, but never with a view to injury and wrongdoing. I will keep pure and holy both my life and my art. In whatsoever houses I enter, I will enter to help the sick, and I will abstain from all intentional wrongdoing and harm.

But they had also sworn an oath of "obedience unto death" to the Führer and had embraced the Nazi ideology that Jews were—in the words of Dr. Fritz Klein—a "gangrenous appendix in the body of mankind," specifically, in the body of the Aryan race (Lifton, 1986, p. 16).

According to Lifton (1986), Nazi doctors resolved the healing-killing paradox they faced by the "medicalization of killing" (p. 14). They viewed the mass extermination of Jews as the necessary response to a public health crisis.

> The only genuine "culture-creating" race, the Aryans, had permitted themselves to be weakened to the point of endangered survival by the "destroyers of culture," characterized as "the Jew." The Jews were agents of "racial pollution" and "racial tuberculosis," as well as parasites and bacteria causing sickness, deterioration, and death in the host peoples they infested. (Lifton, 1986, p. 16)

Framed in this way, not only was it possible for SS doctors to prescribe lethal injections, conduct grotesque experiments, and gas millions but also it was possible to see doing so as a moral duty—however personally difficult and distressing. Sending women and children to the gas chambers was the humane solution to the Jewish problem.

Eduard Wirths, chief doctor at Auschwitz, epitomized this way of dealing with the healing-killing paradox. A competent and dedicated physician and a loving husband and father, Wirths was kind, conscientious, and decent in his personal dealings both with his peers and with inmates of the camp. He used his medical authority to improve camp conditions in order to save lives. At the same time, he remained a loyal Nazi and oversaw the entire mass killing project that he said he opposed. Depressed and conflicted, Wirths finally committed suicide. Years later, his daughter remembered being told by her mother that "he was a good man and a really good father"—a judgment that matched her own memory of him and prompted the daughter to ask that persistent question, "Can a good man do bad things?" (Lifton, 1986, pp. 410–411).

What about the concentration camp guards? Surely they were morally deficient sadists. In his highly sensitive and probing analysis, Tzvetan Todorov (1996) said no:

> We cannot understand the evils of the concentration camps by interpreting them in terms of abnormality, unless we define abnormality—tautologically—as the behavior in question: nothing about the personalities or actions of the authors of evil, apart from this behavior, allows us to classify them as pathological beings— in other words, as monsters, whatever our definition of the terms *pathological* and *normal*. . . . Guards who committed atrocities never stopped distinguishing between good and evil. Their moral faculty had not withered away. They simply believed that the "atrocity" was a good thing. (pp. 121, 129, italics in original)

Other Crimes Against Humanity

The Holocaust is but the extreme of a long list of crimes against our own species that we humans have perpetrated. Remember My Lai, where US soldiers beat, shot, and bayoneted Vietnamese women, babies, children, and old people (Kelman & Hamilton, 1989; Lifton, 1973). Afterward, one of the soldiers explained, "We all thought we were doing the right thing. At the time it didn't bother me." Only later did he have second thoughts:

> The kids and the women—they didn't have any right to die . . .. They didn't put up a fight or anything. The women huddled against their children and took it. They brought their kids real close to their stomachs and hugged them, and put their bodies over them trying to save them . . .. It didn't do much good. (Hersh, 1969)

Remember also the genocides in Turkey, Cambodia, Rwanda, and Bosnia. And the disappearings in Argentina (Staub, 1989). Remember the ETA bombings in Spain, the 9/11 attack on the World Trade Center towers in New York, the prisoner abuse at Abu Ghraib, and the seemingly endless procession of suicide bombers in Israel, Iraq, Afghanistan, and Pakistan. More examples could be cited, many more (see Glover, 2000, for some). As every new one comes to light, we're aghast and appalled. Yet I suspect that the perpetrators—almost without exception—manage to see themselves as highly moral people responding to the dictates of conscience.

Bystanders

Interlocked with these sins of commission are sins of omission. For each of the foregoing atrocities, there were people who knew what was happening and did nothing. There were those who took no part in smashing the windows of Jewish-owned shops on Kristallnacht in November 1938, but who out of fear or indifference raised no objection. There were those who witnessed the round-ups, forced marches, and deportations. There were those—themselves uninvolved—who were aware of a planned bombing or suicide attack.

In hindsight and from afar, we can say that these bystanders weren't innocent. They had a moral obligation to intervene or at least voice opposition. But at the time, the bystanders likely focused on the fact that they did no active wrong rather than on the possibility that doing nothing might have been wrong. The thought that they should object and oppose may never have occurred. Even in retrospect, bystanders often say that although somebody should have done something, not them. After all, what could *they* do? As Todorov (1996) reflected,

> For evil to come into being, the actions of a few are not sufficient; it is also necessary that the vast majority stand aside, indifferent; of such behavior, as we know well, we are all of us capable. (p. 139)

Not only individuals but also nations can stand aside. In 1943, the British, US, and Canadian governments all were concerned that if they objected to Nazi extermination policies, Hitler might send them several million unwanted Jewish refugees.

Even if one can find exceptions to the rule, most onlookers, whether close or distant, let events take their course. They knew what was happening and could have helped but did not. . . . Germans and Russians, Poles and French, Americans and English—all were equal in this respect. They might not all bear the same responsibility because circumstances in each country were different, but all of them allowed things to happen. The misfortune of others, it seems, leaves us cold if in order to alleviate it we have to sacrifice our own comfort.

Of course, we need not have looked as far as the concentration camps to learn this truth. Acts of injustice take place all around us every day and we do not stop them. . . . The reasons are always the same: I didn't know, and even if I had, I couldn't have done anything about it. (Todorov, 1996, pp. 252–253)

Most of us are fortunate enough never to have faced circumstances as extreme as those that existed in Nazi Europe, or at My Lai or Abu Ghraib. Not having been put to the test, it's easy to affirm that we would never have succumbed. And the facts are on our side—we've no atrocities on our record. You and I are good people in a bad world, as we both know. Of course, if Soroyan was right, the same is true of those who did succumb. The distance between us and them shrinks. One way to assess this distance is to look at how well morality fares in the less extreme circumstances of our relatively comfortable and secure lives. As Todorov suggested, there too moral maladies are apparent.

Hometown Immorality

Moral failures permeate the news day after day.

Making Headlines

This morning, my local newspaper had five stories on the front page. The first was about whether the city government should address its budget crisis by cutting pensions for local public employees. You need not look far beneath the surface to find moral issues lurking. Who's to be held responsible for formally proposing the cuts? Should pensions be cut to address the crisis or should taxes be increased? If the latter, whose? City Council members say they want to do what's right. Unspoken is—as long as it doesn't cost them personally or politically.

Moral implications of the other four stories are even more obvious. As on most days, one front-page story was about a murder. I'll skip it because I assume you know such stories all too well.

The third story reported that 6 months earlier the Sutties, a cohabiting lesbian couple, had their house destroyed by fire. The word "Queers" was spray painted on the detached garage. Neither local nor federal investigators had brought charges against anyone, although the Sutties reported that their next-door neighbor repeatedly threatened their lives and home. They claimed that in one interchange he belligerently remarked, "Do you know what is better than one dead queer? Two dead queers."

[A postscript on this story. Two months after I wrote the preceding paragraph, another story appeared on page one. It reported that a lawsuit filed by their insurance company said the Sutties set the fire themselves and blamed the neighbor as a cover-up. The company was refusing to pay the Sutties' claim. So, is the moral malady here a malicious hate crime, or is it a false accusation?

I suspect there may be more chapters in this saga. Moral vigilantism has a long history in the county where the Sutties lived. My wife, who spent part of her childhood there, remembers seeing the Ku Klux Klan in white robes and carrying torches as they walked beside the road on their way to contribute money to a local church. And her aunt, who taught in a school nearby, told of a young girl who was absent for several days after the Klan dragged her and the rest of her family from their home and horsewhipped them for failure to attend church—where, I can't resist adding, they would be told to "Love thy neighbor".]

Here's the fourth story. Two US Army pilots, one local, were killed in a Kiowa helicopter crash while serving in Iraq. A lawsuit had now been filed, claiming that these highly advanced helicopters had an unsafe Full Authority Digital Electronic Control (FADEC) and its failure caused the crash. The suit said the manufacturers were negligent in not correcting or removing defective and dangerous equipment about which they should have known. Another suit recently filed in federal court in Indianapolis also charged that Kiowa equipment failures led to loss of lives. In that suit, a former senior official for the manufacturer claimed that the company sacrificed careful product regulation to increase profit, then concealed information about likely defects from the army.

This story called to mind similar reports over the years: The inadequate brakes provided to the Air Force for the A7-D by B. F. Goodrich. The Ford Pinto gas tank that was vulnerable to rupture in a rear-end collision. The shipyard executives who had employees continue to work with asbestos long after they knew it was carcinogenic. The tobacco industry's defense of cigarettes. It also brought to mind stories about accountants who easily slip into shading the truth in favor of their clients (Arthur Anderson), corporate executives who misrepresent the bottom line (Enron), and hedge-fund operators who mislead and ultimately defraud clients with Ponzi schemes (Bernie Madoff). (See Bazerman & Tenbrunsel, 2011, for more detail on these cases.)

The fifth story reported that an esteemed local judge would resign today. He had been found to be a drug addict and to have illegally bought prescription drugs from a felon he had placed on probation. The judge's attorney was now trying to plea-bargain his immediate resignation for reduction of the charge to "misconduct." This would keep a conviction off the judge's record and allow him to still receive a pension.

The judge is but one in the long line of public figures in the United States who seem to stand on high moral ground only to fall in disgrace. Most obvious are the politicians. Richard Nixon looked straight into the camera and said, "I am not a crook," shortly before he was forced to resign for his role in the Watergate break-in and cover-up. Ronald Reagan couldn't remember any involvement in the

Iran-Contra affair, in which his administration traded arms for hostages. And when he was reminded of involvement, his self-assessment was unaffected: "A few months ago I told the American people that I did not trade arms for hostages. My heart and my best intentions still tell me that's true, but the facts and evidence tell me it is not." Bill Clinton claimed, "I did not have sex with that woman." His presidency never recovered. Some objected to the sex, others to the falseness of his claim.

There are also the religious leaders. At the time of the 2004 John Jay Report, a total of 4,392 Catholic priests had been accused of engaging in sexual abuse of a minor between 1950 and 2002—10,667 allegations overall, of which 80 percent were substantiated. Many abusing priests continued in their role as moral guides and models for years before finally being charged and dismissed. Cases are still coming to light. If the Catholic Church has its pedophile priests, evangelical Protestants have their promiscuous preachers—Jimmy Swaggart and Ted Haggard to name but two. These religious sex scandals attract special attention because of the sharp discrepancy between what's preached and what's practiced. Priests solemnly vow celibacy. Evangelical Christians fervently espouse marital fidelity and family values.

Scientists too can act immorally with seeming equanimity. Recall the infamous Tuskegee experiment, the Piltdown Man hoax, and Sir Cyril Burtt's falsification of data. More recently, my discipline of experimental social psychology has had its own cases of research fraud and deceit, as reported by Carey (2011), Medin (2012), and Strobe, Postmes, and Spears (2012).

Not Making Headlines

Front-page stories are only the tip of the iceberg. Most moral failures don't make the news. Upstanding citizens can cheat on their taxes, exaggerate injuries and property losses for insurance claims, illegally download, shoplift, and fiddle situations to their personal advantage. With the possible exception of a few card-carrying Kantians, we all tell lies (DePaulo & Kashy, 1998). Many of our lies could be called moral. We assure a friend who has kept us waiting for 30 minutes that it's no problem and that her new outfit looks great. We tell our children that the barely edible birthday breakfast they struggled to fix is perfect. Each gift is just what we wanted. But it's easy for these white lies to morph into darker ones. Research indicates that most lies are self-benefiting (DePaulo, Kashy, Kirkendol, Wyer, & Epstein, 1996). If it helps us, we are apt to say that we didn't know when we actually did, that we didn't do what we actually did.

Lying is a close cousin of cheating, which is common in sports, in school, and on taxes (Ariely, 2012). In sports, drug-enhanced performance and stretching the rules is found in football, baseball, and even cycling. In school, the percentage of college students who have cheated is reported to be somewhere between 50 and 70 percent. For students in professional schools—business, education, engineering, and law—the rate is about 50 percent. The 2008 Josephson Institute of Ethics survey of almost 30,000 students at 100 randomly selected secondary schools across the United States found that 64 percent reported cheating on at least one test during the past year, and 38 percent reported cheating on two or more. Thirty percent (35 percent of boys, 26 percent of girls) reported stealing from a store. Eighty percent admitted lying to a parent. At the same time, 93 percent said they were satisfied with their personal ethics. And 77 percent marked either Agree or Strongly Agree to "When it comes to doing what is right, I am better than most people I know." The 2010 Josephson survey with a sample of over 40,000 students produced virtually identical results.

David Bersoff (1999) reviewed several surveys of everyday cheating and theft. In a random sample from a large metropolitan area in the southwestern United States, 25 percent of respondents reported having cheated on their taxes. Twenty percent had stolen something worth more than $20, and over half had stolen something of lesser value. One in three employees reported having stolen from their employers. The rate rose to close to 50 percent for those working in retail. Of 500 randomly selected shoppers observed on one visit to a store, almost 10 percent shoplifted. One particularly troubling variant of shoplifting is wardrobing, where a customer buys an item of clothing, wears it, and then returns it to the store for a refund. Wardrobing is said to cost retailers over $10 billion annually (Ayal & Gino, 2012).

How many of us, when given too much change, call the error to the clerk's attention—as opposed to when the error is in the opposite direction? Thinking of the environment, how many US citizens adjust their behavior because their homeland, with only 5 percent of the world's population, uses 30 percent of the atmosphere's capacity to absorb waste gasses? The list could go on and on. And through it all we see ourselves as highly moral, more moral than most.

Symptoms of Success

Symptoms of moral malady are numerous, but they aren't all the record shows. As noted at the start of this chapter, most of us act morally most of the time. We're fair, thoughtful, and kind. We don't break the law even when chances are good we won't get caught. Indeed, our moral successes can be quite spectacular. The very circumstances that produce the most chilling failures can also produce awe-inspiring triumphs. In Nazi Europe, there were those who endangered their lives and the lives of family members to rescue Jews (Hallie, 1979; Oliner & Oliner, 1988). At My Lai, US Army helicopter pilot Hugh Thompson Jr. and his two crew members took the initiative to oppose the soldiers under Lieutenant Calley's command. At great personal risk, they saved many Vietnamese women and children from slaughter and eventually stopped the massacre. In South Africa, there was the restraint and justice of Reconciliation at the end of apartheid.

Although it would be easy to cite as many examples of moral success as failure, that would lead us astray. The question isn't *whether* we're moral but *how* and *why* we are. If we can understand how and why, we may be able to predict when we'll be moral and when not. We may also be able to prescribe ways to treat our moral ills. But to address the how and why questions, we need to shift attention away from behavior—whether moral or immoral—and focus on the underlying psychology. In the third and fourth sections of this chapter, I offer a conceptual framework for such an approach. But before doing that, I need to say what I mean by the terms "moral" and "morality."

WHAT MAKES THESE FAILURES (AND SUCCESSES) MORAL?

As you have doubtless discovered, different people mean different things by these terms. I can only say what I mean by them. But if my definitions are to be taken seriously, they need to be in tune with common parlance. And they need to be heuristic. That is, they need to bring to the fore key issues and questions regarding what's wrong with morality.

My interest is in the role morality plays in the lives of ordinary people, not in the moral ideals of saints or philosophers or the behavior of psychopaths. So, perhaps the best place to look for definitions is the dictionary. Less than helpful, English dictionaries typically define "morality" by referring to "moral." *Morality* is, "moral quality or conduct" or "a doctrine of morals." Dictionaries do better with *moral*. Typically, the first two definitions are "1. of or concerned with principles of right or wrong conduct. 2. being in accordance with such principles" (e.g., *Webster's Desk Dictionary of the English Language*, 1990, p. 589). These statements certainly get us into the ballpark of morality. But like most definitions, they imply a lot that needs to be made explicit. Let me offer nine points of clarification and elaboration.

1. Morality Is About Conduct

According to the dictionary, morality is about conduct, not simply about the state of things. It's about people who are engaged in, have engaged in, have thoughts of engaging in, or have the potential to engage in intentional action (goal-directed behavior). Good and bad things happen. But when no one caused them or could possibly prevent them, they aren't moral events. Think of natural disasters such as tornadoes, earthquakes, and tsunamis. We may call such events bad and call other natural events—a beautiful spring day—good. But we don't call these natural events right or wrong unless we're using these terms as loose proxies for good and bad. On the other hand, we call moral and immoral action right and wrong, respectively. (We may call immoral thoughts bad or dirty, but we do so to say it's wrong to have them.) David Hume (1739–1740/1978, 1751/1975) spoke of the approbation (approval) and disapprobation (disapproval) felt in response to virtue and vice, to right and wrong conduct. A. J. Ayer (1936) said that good and bad—approval and disapproval—is all there is to morality. In the dictionary, morality and evaluation aren't the same. The former is a subset of the latter. Morality concerns right (good) and wrong (bad) *conduct*. The dictionary sides with Hume.

2. Moral Conduct May Be Specific or General

By suggesting that morality is concerned with conduct, I don't believe the dictionary means to restrict the term to specific acts in specific situations. Although the definition clearly applies to specific thoughts and acts, conduct can also refer to the way a person thinks and acts over time. That is, to the sort of behavioral pattern that we speak of as *character* or refer to with terms like *moral exemplar* (Colby & Damon, 1992; Walker & Hennig, 2004).

3. Morality Concerns Standards for Conduct

The reference to right or wrong in the dictionary definition implies the presence of a standard against which the conduct in question is judged. As already noted, the issue isn't simply whether we like the conduct (judge it good) but whether it's appropriate given the circumstances, right or wrong. A novel or other work of fiction can't be judged right or wrong, only good or bad. But characters in the novel can behave in ways considered right or wrong. And publication of the novel can be considered right or wrong. Further complicating matters, not all standards of appropriate conduct are moral. Solving a math problem, washing clothes, the way a soldier stands at attention, and how a soprano sings an aria—all involve conduct. And for each, there are standards of right and wrong. But these aren't typically considered moral acts.

4. Morality Concerns Standards for Conduct That Promotes or Thwarts Values and Interests Beyond the Actor's Own

Unfortunately, the dictionary definition gives no clue as to what's distinctive about *moral* standards. So we need some additional guidance to know which standards of conduct qualify. Casting a big net, let me suggest that moral standards, principles, and ideals are those that *apply to conduct that promotes or thwarts the values and interests of other individuals, groups, institutions, or systems of belief—especially when those values and interests are at odds with at least some of the actor's own.*

A distinction popular in recent years among those who study the moral development of children contrasts moral principles and social conventions. The former are said to be universal and unchangeable. Their violation is wrong even if an authority figure says it's OK. The latter are local, changeable, and can be violated if an authority says so. Some researchers have claimed that moral principles, so conceived, are a natural expression of biological preparedness and social experience and require no direct teaching (Turiel, 1983). Others say moral principles are culturally inculcated (Shweder, Mahapatra, & Miller, 1987). (See Kagan & Lamb, 1987, for a useful juxtaposition of these views.)

I suspect the key distinction isn't *whether* the principles are learned but *how* they're learned. Are violations of the principles always upsetting to others and consistently and strongly punished (as prohibitions against hurting and stealing often are)? Or does the child experience variation in observance of the principles and in reactions to their violation across people (as when a playmate from a different ethnic background dresses differently) or situations (as with the prohibition of talking in church)? If punishment is consistent and strong, the principles are likely to be treated as universal and noncontingent—moral. If observance and reactions to violation vary, they're likely to be treated as local and contingent—conventional. Principles of both kinds qualify as moral by my definition. (For a similar analysis of the moral vs. conventional distinction, see Prinz, 2007, 2008.)

Within the domain of morality as I'm using the term, I find it useful to distinguish two broad concerns: interpersonal interest conflicts and propriety. Moral principles exist regarding each. *Interpersonal principles* address the consideration an actor should give to the interests of others in situations in which the others' interests conflict with the actor's own. Fairness and justice principles, principles proscribing harm and prescribing care, and honesty principles form the core of interpersonal morality (Hoffman, 1984, 2000; Kohlberg, 1976). *Propriety principles* address the natural and social order. They specify conduct that promotes or violates the way things should be. To say that it's wrong to perform "unnatural" sex acts, to break the law, defile the sacred, disobey authority, disrespect elders, or act unpatriotically are propriety principles. Included within what I'm calling propriety concerns are issues that others have referred to as purity/sanctity, in-group/loyalty, and authority/respect (Graham et al., 2011; Haidt, 2012; Rozin, Lowery, Imada, & Haidt, 1999; Wilson, 1993). Although interpersonal and propriety principles can apply to the same conduct—many people think acting unfairly or harming innocents to benefit oneself violates the social order—the concerns addressed by these principles still seem distinct.

Principles that specify how to allocate scarce resources in interest conflicts run the gamut from "Look out only for Number One" (consider self-interest alone), through "Me first, but also think of others" (weight self-interest more heavily), to "Share and share alike" (weight everyone's interests the same), to "Go to the back of the line" (weight other's interest more heavily). Principles that prohibit killing also run a gamut: "Thou shalt not kill." "Don't kill humans." "Don't kill innocents." "Kill only in self-defense." "Kill to defend honor and property." So do principles that specify appropriate sex: "No sex outside marriage" "No casual sex." "Only consensual sex." Most of these principles could be invoked to address interpersonal interest concerns, propriety concerns, or both. All would qualify as moral principles by my usage.

5. Morality Includes More Than Principles

The dictionary speaks of the standards applied to moral conduct as "principles." Common parlance about morality employs three other terms in addition to principles and standards: rules, norms, and commandments. We also speak of moral ideals and virtues. "Principles," "standards," and "rules" are often used synonymously. Indeed, the dictionary defines them in terms of one another. A *principle* is "a general or fundamental rule." A *standard* is "a rule for making judgments." A *rule* is "a principle or regulation for governing conduct." *Norms* can be of two types, descriptive (specifying typical behavior) and prescriptive (specifying appropriate or required behavior). The reference to right or wrong indicates that moral norms are prescriptive. (When widely held, they're also descriptive.) *Commandments* usually refer to rules or principles that are religious in origin. The dictionary defines an *ideal* as "a standard of perfection," and a *virtue* as "a particularly good moral quality."

Some philosophers and psychologists use the terms "principle," "standard," "rule," and "norm" interchangeably. Lawrence Kohlberg made a distinction. For him, principles underlie and adjudicate conflicts between various rules and norms:

> When rules or norms conflict, a principle seems required. A moral principle, as distinct from a rule, implies two things. First, it is not a "thou shalt" or "thou shalt not" engage in a kind of action; it is a way of seeing, a way of choosing, when two rules are in conflict. It is a method of moral choice. Second, it is something underneath a rule, the spirit underneath the law rather than the rule itself; it is an attitude or idea that generates rules. It is more general and universal than a rule. Among ethical principles put forward by philosophers we may note particularly Kant's principle of justice and Mill's principle of utility. (Kohlberg & Candee, 1984, p. 62)

Kohlberg's description of a principle as a method of choice is largely idiosyncratic and seems unduly narrow. But the observation that principles are often relatively general and abstract seems right. In everyday use, rules, norms, and commandments tend to be more specific than principles and standards. Yet there are numerous exceptions. Most notably, the Golden Rule (Do unto others as you would have them do unto you.) is quite general. David Hume (1739–1740/1978) and Adam Smith (1759/1976b) both spoke of principles as "general rules."

Although I follow the dictionary and most often speak of moral principles, I use the terms "standard" and "principle" interchangeably and broadly. These terms provide an umbrella that covers rules, norms, commandments, ideals, and virtues. Principles include but aren't limited to Kantian deontological principles (Kant, 1785/1898).

6. Moral Principles Need Not be Explicit, Conscious, Rational, or Specific

For me, moral principles include more than explicitly stated, conscious, reason-based, act-specific principles. Concerning explicitness, a distinction is often made between laws and morals. Laws are formally stated and enforced. Moral principles are more informal. Laws are sometimes said to be a codification of moral principles, although the scope of morality is broader than the law. Indeed, morality comes to the fore most prominently in regard to conduct for which there are no formal laws—or when our principles and ideals conflict with laws. Moral principles are frequently shared with others in the culture or subculture, but they can also be atypical and idiosyncratic. Societies differ widely in the degree to which they tolerate a diversity of moral principles.

Concerning consciousness and rationality, people may apply principles of right or wrong conduct that they can't articulate and that aren't rational. Nor need they recognize the principles as moral. Concerning specificity, people can apply principles to their own or to another's conduct, and the principles can be quite specific or quite general. "Don't kill" is a moral principle. "Never break a promise," "Abortion is wrong," and "Masturbation is wrong" are all moral principles. So are "It's wrong to burn the US flag," "It's wrong to burn the Canadian flag," "It's wrong to burn a Bible," and "It's wrong to burn a Quran." These are relatively concrete, but principles can also be quite abstract. "Do your duty," "Be fair," "Do no wrong," "Be honest," "Don't covet," "Treat all humans as ends not only as means," "Do what's most right," "Never wish another person harm," "Follow the dictates of conscience," and "Do what will produce the greatest good for the greatest number" are all moral principles. One might even have a principle to "be moral" or to "act on principle," but few of us operate at so abstract a level. As philosopher Michael Smith (1994) has said, such a principle smacks of "moral fetishism." That is, of a concern for my personal goodness rather than for doing what's right.

Most people have a whole host of moral standards and principles. Although it seems unlikely that a person will simultaneously endorse two explicitly stated principles that are logically contradictory ("Women and children first" and "Everybody for themselves"), we can hold different principles for appropriate conduct regarding different people ("Women and children first" and "Every man for himself") and different situations ("Play fair" and "All's fair in love and war"). Even when not logically contradictory, principles can conflict in a given situation—as "Don't lie" and "Protect the innocent" conflicted when Belgian citizens were asked by the Nazis if they knew where Jews were hiding. Such conflicts can be resolved by allowing one principle to trump another ("It's right to lie to save lives"), by striking a compromise, by appeal to some higher-order principle, or by deciding that the conduct in question isn't morally relevant. Different principles can be weighted equally or arranged in a hierarchy. If the latter, location in the hierarchy can change depending on the situation.

7. Not Being Immoral Versus Being Moral

The dictionary definition is broad in yet another way. Philosophers sometimes make a distinction between *prohibitory* and *supererogatory* standards—between principles that proscribe what's morally wrong (duties of omission or perfect duties) and those that prescribe what's morally right (duties of commission or imperfect duties; Kant, 1797/1991). Those who make this distinction often add that although acting in accordance with supererogatory principles is desirable, it's not required. Only acting in accord with prohibitory principles is required.

You might think of this distinction as between the presence of a positive (being moral) and the absence of a negative (not being immoral). People differ in how much conduct, if any, they perceive to lie between these alternatives. That is, in how much thought and action is neither moral nor immoral. For some people, there's only one bar. Not to be moral is to be immoral. But many of us have a two-bar morality. Although we'd be pleased to clear the high bar and be moral, we're more concerned about clearing the low bar so as not to be immoral. The dictionary definition allows for principles and ideals relevant to both being moral and not being immoral—and to both one- and two-bar moralities. So shall I.

8. Moral Oughts Versus Moral Wants

One way in which the dictionary isn't as broad as it might be is in a focus on moral "oughts"—on being in accord with what our standards or principles say we ought to do. No consideration is given to moral "wants." That is, to a pursuit of right and avoidance of wrong that goes beyond the feeling of obligation. The dictionary isn't unique in this regard. Most discussions of morality—whether by philosophers, psychologists, sociologists, or anthropologists—focus on what we ought to do and not do. To consider moral wants is rare, although in recent years some virtue ethicists have done so (Louden, 2006). I consider the possibility of moral wants at several points in subsequent chapters. Still, I accept the dictionary's focus on oughts as the way we most often approach morality. Our moral principles tell us what we ought to do and be—or at least to what we ought to aspire.

9. The Definition Is Descriptive, Not Normative

Finally, the dictionary definition is descriptive, not normative. It concerns what moral principles are and how they function. It doesn't specify which principles are the right ones. I share this concern for description rather than prescription. I won't attempt to determine which moral standards are right, only how whatever moral standards we have function in our lives. As this goal implies, the term "descriptive" is used broadly to include not only description of what standards we have but also explanation of why we have these standards and how they affect our behavior (Gert, 2012; Hiadt & Kesebir, 2010). As said earlier, how and why are key.

Descriptively, it can be observed that most of us consider the principles we hold to be normative—to be the best ones, perhaps the only true ones. And we're likely to treat them as normative both for ourselves and for others—often especially for others. But this doesn't need to be the case. A person can perceive his or her moral standards to be subjective and relative and still feel that certain conduct is right or wrong for a given person in a given situation.

A FRAMEWORK FOR PSYCHOLOGICAL ANALYSIS

We humans are clearly concerned with principles of right and wrong conduct. Equally clearly, we can violate our principles, at times with terrible consequences. The moral maladies noted earlier leave little doubt that something's seriously wrong with our morality. If we're to hope for a cure, or even for improvement, we need to probe beneath the symptoms of malady and try to find the cause or causes of our problems. We need to consider what psychological processes underlie our moral and immoral behavior. Moreover, we need to understand what leads to such conduct in the various morally relevant situations we encounter every day, not simply what evolutionary functions moral behavior may serve or have served. Even if true, an evolutionary account—such as that morality serves to promote group cooperation and cohesion (Alexander, 1987; Bowles & Gintis, 2011; Haidt, 2012; Tomasello & Vaish, 2013; Wright, 1994)—is too general and too remote. It doesn't address the nuances, complexities, and contradictions that are apparent in our moral life. As is often true, the devil's in the details.

I believe that a particularly useful conceptual scheme to guide the search for our moral devils was provided by Kurt Lewin. His scheme is worth presenting in some detail for two reasons. First, it provides the framework for all that follows in subsequent chapters. Second, if you are like most people, you'll find it somewhat counterintuitive.

Lewin (1935) borrowed from Ernst Cassirer (1910/1921) a distinction between Aristotelian and Galilean approaches to science. *Aristotelian science* attempts to explain natural phenomena by beginning with observation of particulars. It proceeds to a conceptual ordering and classification of these particulars into types according to what are thought to be essential attributes. Finally, these attributes are used to explain the behavior of the particulars. (Cassirer's focus was on Aristotle's physics not his ethics.) In contrast, *Galilean science* begins with development of an explanatory model of underlying processes to account for natural phenomena. Then empirical predictions are derived from the model. And, finally, these predictions are tested through empirical observation. To provide an example from Galileo's own work, motion of objects is no longer explained in terms of essential attributes (light objects rise, heavy objects fall) but in terms of intangible yet still empirical concepts that focus on underlying processes (velocity and acceleration) whose relation can be clearly specified. Velocity is change in location over time (d/t). Acceleration is change in velocity over time (d/t^2).

Lewin (1935) thought that Aristotelian science was dominant in the psychology of his day. I think it's still dominant. I also think, as did he, that Galilean science is far more likely to provide insight and understanding.

Lewin called the intangible concepts that are at the heart of Galilean science *conditional-genetic* or *genotypic* because they specify the underlying conditions for generating observable, phenotypic events. As he explained,

> For Aristotle the immediate perceptible appearance, that which present-day biology terms the *phenotype*, was hardly distinguished from the properties that determine the object's dynamic relations. The fact, for example, that light objects relatively frequently go upward sufficed for him to ascribe to them an upward tendency. With the differentiation of phenotype from *genotype*, or more generally, of descriptive from conditional-genetic concepts and the shifting of

emphasis to the latter, many old class distinctions lost their significance. The orbits of the planets, the free falling of a stone, the movement of a body on an inclined plane, the oscillation of a pendulum, which if classified according to their phenotypes would fall into quite different, indeed into antithetical classes, prove to be simply various expressions of the same law. (Lewin, 1935, p. 11, italics in original)

Seeking a set of conditional-genetic concepts for psychology, Lewin (1951) turned his attention to three psychological constructs that underlie human behavior—motives, values, and goals—and to how they relate.

Relating Motives to Values and Goals

In Lewin's (1938, 1951) scheme, *motives* are goal-directed forces induced by opportunities or threats related to our values. *Values* are what we care about, not simply what we perceive, think, or believe. They're identified most generally by relative preferences. Mary values State A more than State B if she would consistently choose State A over State B—other things being equal. For Lewin, values include not only "capital-V" values such as Freedom, Justice, Loyalty, and Honesty but also more mundane ones like valuing clean clothes, quiet weekends, and Cabernet. If a negative discrepancy is perceived between a current or anticipated state and a valued state (we're down to our last bottle) then obtaining or maintaining the valued state is likely to become a *goal* (let's get another case). A goal-directed force, or *motive*, impels us toward this end. Some values are relatively stable, capable of producing a motive whenever threatened—such as the value of air to breathe. For others, an opportunity to obtain or maintain the state elicits a motive only under certain circumstances—the value of wearing a warm coat.

More formally, within his field theory, Lewin (1951) suggested that values have the status of *power fields*. They represent potential energy or potential desire. When activated by opportunity or threat, they produce goals. Goals have the status of *force fields*. They represent kinetic energy or actual desire. Goal-directed motives are *vectors* in a force field. They reflect the desire of the person to attain a positively valenced goal or avoid a negatively valenced one. Behavior is *movement* within the present set of force fields. Thus, the relations of the four constructs—values, goals, motives, and behavior—are specified. (For further discussion of these relations, see Batson, Shaw, & Oleson, 1992; Lewin, 1951; Verplanken & Holland, 2002.)

Distinguishing Ultimate Goals from Instrumental Goals and Unintended Consequences

In this framework, it's important to distinguish ultimate goals from both instrumental goals and unintended consequences (Heider, 1958; Lewin, 1951). *Ultimate goals* are the valued states we seek to obtain or maintain. Ultimate is not used here to mean "cosmic" or "most important." Nor does it refer to a metaphysical first or final cause. Nor to evolutionary function. It simply refers to the state or states a person is seeking at a given time. An ultimate goal defines a motive, and, conversely, each different motive has a unique ultimate goal. The ultimate goal of promoting some moral principle—be fair, tell the truth, care for the needy, and so on—defines what might be called a truly moral motive. But moral action can also be the product of motives that aren't themselves moral. That is, of motives with a different ultimate goal.

Instrumental goals are sought because they're stepping-stones to ultimate goals. If the ultimate goal can be reached more efficiently by other means, an instrumental goal is likely to be bypassed. A young boy who acts honestly in order to avoid being punished should feel free to cheat if he knows he won't get caught. The distinction between instrumental and ultimate goals shouldn't be confused with Milton Rokeach's (1973) distinction between instrumental and terminal values. All of the values named by Rokeach could induce either instrumental or ultimate goals depending on whether the value (e.g., a world at peace) is sought as an end in itself or as a means to some other end (e.g., personal safety). More applicable is Gordon Allport's (1961) distinction between intrinsic and extrinsic values. Intrinsic values (those valued as ends in themselves) induce ultimate goals. Extrinsic values (those valued as means to other ends) induce instrumental goals.

Pursuit of a goal—whether instrumental or ultimate—can produce effects that aren't themselves goals. These are *unintended consequences*. It's possible to act morally as an unintended consequence of pursuing some other goal. For example, a business executive motivated to maximize profit may move a factory into a depressed area to take advantage of the cheap labor. Quite unintentionally, this profit-driven action may promote the public good by providing jobs. We may, in turn, judge this result moral even though it wasn't morally motivated.

Focus on Motives, Not Behavior

A major implication that Lewin (1935, 1938, 1951) wished to draw from distinguishing ultimate goals, instrumental goals, and unintended consequences is the importance of focusing on goal-directed motives rather than on behavior or consequences. This focus is important even when we want to understand some behavior, including moral behavior. Behavior is highly variable. Occurrence of a particular behavior depends on the strength of the motive or motives that might evoke that behavior as well as on the strength of competing motives, how the behavior relates to each of these motives, and other behavioral options at the time. The more directly a given behavior promotes an ultimate goal, the more uniquely it does so among the behavioral options available, the more stable and important the underlying value, and the more vulnerable the value is to threat—the more likely the behavior is to occur.

Behavior that promotes an instrumental goal can easily change if either the causal association between the instrumental and ultimate goal changes or a less costly behavioral route to the ultimate goal arises. Unintended consequences can also easily change unless these consequences are a product of some behavior that directly and uniquely promotes the ultimate goal.

Motives Can Cooperate or Conflict, and Can Change

Often, an individual has more than one ultimate goal at a time, and so more than one motive. When this occurs, the different motives can either cooperate or conflict. Moreover, a person's goal-directed motives can change, sometimes quickly. The motives experienced in a given situation are a function of the strength and stability of the relevant values, and of the opportunities to promote them.

Motives as Current Goal-Directed Forces, Not as Dispositions or Needs

Lewin's goal-directed motives are current psychological states, not enduring personality types or dispositions. In this regard, his perspective on motivation differs from that of another pioneer in research on motivation, Henry Murray (1938). Murray and his followers treated motives as relatively stable dispositions or needs (need for achievement, need for affiliation, and so on). Thus, Murray's motives were similar to values rather than motives in Lewin's framework. Lewin emphasized the distinctions among instrumental goals, ultimate goals, and unintended consequences. Murray gave little attention to these distinctions. For Lewin, the list of our potential motives is long—as long as the list of states we value. Murray and his followers attempted to identify a relatively small number of primary motives.

Inserting Emotions

Lewin (1951) didn't include emotions in his conditional-genetic analysis of values, goals, motives, and behavior. I think they can and should be included. Emotions are typically felt when we experience some change in our relation to a valued state. Obtaining or losing a valued state produces *end-state emotions* such as happiness (if the valued state is obtained) or sadness (if it's lost). Awareness of a discrepancy between our current or future state and a valued state produces *need-state emotions* such as yearning or apprehension. (We can yearn to feel an end-state emotion such as happiness, but then happiness is a desired valued state, a goal, not what we're currently feeling.)

Why do we have emotions? What functions do they serve? Both end-state and need-state emotions provide information to us and others about what we value and where we are in relation to what we value. In addition, the physiological arousal component of need-state emotions amplifies the motivation to obtain or maintain the valued state. These emotions turn potential energy into kinetic. For example, fear of failure will amplify my motivation to study for an upcoming exam. Thus, need-state emotions can be inserted into Lewin's sequence after values (power fields) and before the goals (force fields) that produce motives (vectors within the force fields). Need-state emotions heat up the process. They take us beyond awareness of a value discrepancy to a felt desire to address it. More colloquially, they express our care.

For further discussion of the information and amplification functions of emotions, see Batson et al. (1992) and Schwarz and Clore (1983, 1988). For a review of neurological evidence related to the prosocial value→emotion→motivation→behavior sequence, see Moll, Oliveira-Souza, and Zahn (2008). (Given that the motivation at issue is always goal directed, from here on I omit "goal" when depicting this sequence.)

WHY ACT MORALLY? FOUR DISTINCT CLASSES OF MOTIVES

With this framework of value, emotion, motivation, and behavior in mind, let's consider the range of motives that might lead a person to act in accordance with principles of right or wrong conduct. In order to identify goal-directed motives that might produce moral action, we need to identify the values that induce these motives and the need-state emotions that might be aroused by threats to these values. We also need to consider the strengths and weaknesses of each motive as a source of moral action. I believe that at least four general classes of motivation deserve consideration. (For similar analyses see Batson, 1994, 2011; Jencks, 1990.) Motives from one or more of these classes may underlie any specific example of moral behavior. The weaknesses associated with each can help explain moral maladies such as those described in the first section of this chapter. The strengths provide clues to how we might treat our moral maladies.

The four classes are:

1. *Egoism.* Motivation with the ultimate goal of increasing our own welfare.
2. *Altruism.* Motivation with the ultimate goal of increasing another's welfare.
3. *Collectivism.* Motivation with the ultimate goal of increasing a group's welfare.
4. *Principlism (moral integrity).* Motivation with the ultimate goal of promoting some moral standard, principle, or ideal.

Motives in the first three classes are nonmoral. This is because the ultimate goal of each, the defining feature of the motive, is not to be in accordance with principles of right or wrong conduct. Still, motives in these three classes can produce moral behavior either as an instrumental means to reach the specified ultimate goal, or as an unintended consequence. But motives in these classes can also produce moral violations. For motives in the fourth class, accordance with some moral principle is the ultimate goal. So principlism can be considered truly moral motivation. But, as we shall see, even it can fail.

You may think that I should call motives in each class moral on those occasions when they produce moral behavior. After all, that's what most people do, including most scholars and researchers who study morality. I avoid this practice because it remains focused on the behavioral surface and ignores the underlying psychological process. That is, it ignores the distinction between ultimate goals, instrumental goals, and unintended consequences. To follow the common practice would be to slip from Galilean science back into Aristotelian.

Table 1.1 provides an overview of the values, need-state emotions, strengths, and weaknesses related to each of the four classes of motives. To flesh out the overview, let me say a little more about each class.

Egoism: Concern for Our Own Welfare

There's little doubt that we intrinsically value our own welfare. We feel upset and distressed when it's threatened, and we're motivated to increase it when opportunities arise. Jeremy Bentham's (1789/1876) opening sentence of *An Introduction to the Principles of Morals and Legislation* says it well: "Nature has placed mankind under the governance of two sovereign masters, pain and pleasure" (Chapter 1, paragraph 1).

Egoistic Motives for Acting Morally

Egoism can be a powerful motive for acting morally. A philanthropist may endow a hospital or university to gain recognition and a form of immortality. A capitalist motivated by relentless pursuit of personal fortune may promote the public welfare by providing needed goods and services. A student may volunteer at the local nursing home to add community service to her resume. The action of each may be judged moral given its consequences. And, for each, the motive is a form of egoism.

Egoistic motives for acting morally fall into two broad categories. We can act morally to gain material, social, and self-rewards (pay or prizes, recognition, esteem), or to avoid material, social, and self-punishments (fines, censure, shame, guilt). Acting in a way that I or others judge moral can be in the service of any and all of these egoistic goals. When it is, we have *instrumental moral motivation*. That is, motivation to act morally as a means to another end.

Nontangible self-benefits—often called *side payments* (Dawes, van de Kragt, & Orbell, 1990)—are particularly important egoistic goals of moral behavior. We may, for example, act in accordance with some moral principle as a means to avoid social censure or guilt. Long ago, John Stuart Mill (1861/1987) asked, "Why am I bound to promote the general happiness? If my own happiness lies in something else, why may I not give that the preference?" (p. 299). His answer was that we not only may but will give our own happiness preference until we learn the costs of doing so—social censure, divine censure, and pangs of conscience. To avoid these personal costs, we act morally. Freud (1930/1961) presented a similar view, as have most social-learning and norm theorists (see Chapter 2).

Side payments can be positive as well as negative. There are important nontangible rewards for doing good. People may act morally in order to get a "warm glow"

Table 1.1 Four Motives for Acting Morally

Motive	Ultimate goal/Valued state	Need-state emotions	Strengths	Weaknesses
Egoism	Increase our own welfare.	Many, including anticipated pride, fear, shame, guilt, embarrassment, etc.	Many forms; powerful; easily aroused; strong emotional base in anticipated pride, fear, guilt, etc.	Acting morally relates to egoistic motivation only as an instrumental means or an unintended consequence.
Altruism	Increase the welfare of one or more other individuals.	Empathic concern, including sympathy, compassion, tenderness, etc.	Powerful; can be easily aroused for cared-for others; strong emotional base in empathic concern.	Empathy-induced altruism is limited to cared-for others; altruistic motivation produces moral action only as an instrumental means or an unintended consequence.
Collectivism	Increase the welfare of a group or collective.	Group pride, esprit, loyalty, patriotism, collective shame, collective guilt, etc.	Powerful; can be easily aroused for cared-for groups; strong emotional base in group pride, loyalty, patriotism, etc.	Limited to cared-for groups; collectivist motivation produces moral action only as an instrumental means or an unintended consequence.
Principlism (moral integrity)	Promote some moral standard, principle, or ideal (e.g., fairness, justice, greatest good, do no harm, honesty).	Disgust, anger at violation of propriety principles; possibly anger at violation of interpersonal principles.	Focused on promoting moral principle as ultimate goal; often universal and impartial.	Moral principles can be abstract and varied, making them vulnerable to rationalization. True moral motivation is rare. Instrumental moral motivation is common but unreliable; it lacks a strong emotional base, and may be experienced as a motivational "ought" not "want."

(Harbaugh, Mayr, & Burghart, 2007). Or to see themselves and be seen by others as good, trustworthy, thoughtful people (Frank, 1988; Goffman, 1969). Pursuit of these side payments may produce behavior judged moral, but the underlying motivation is still egoistic. Again, instrumental moral motivation.

When we look beyond immediate gains to consider the long term, self-interest becomes *enlightened*. From an enlightened perspective, we may see that pursuit of immediate self-interest will lead to less long-term personal gain than will doing what's right. So we may act in accordance with principle as an instrumental means to maximize future self-benefit.

Appeals to enlightened self-interest are often used by politicians and preachers as they try to get us to do the right thing. They warn of the consequences for ourselves and our children of pollution or of underfunded schools. They remind us that an unchecked epidemic may reach our door. Or that if the plight of the poor becomes too severe, we may face revolution. Enlightened self-interest can also prompt adherence to standards of fairness and cooperation, such as reciprocity (Axelrod, 1984; Komorita & Parks, 1995). And it can prompt administration of sanctions to punish those who seek to free ride on the contributions of others (Bowles & Gintis, 2011; Fehr & Gächter, 2002).

Promise and Problems of Egoism as a Motive for Acting Morally

Egoistic motivation is potent, easily aroused, and has a strong emotional base in feelings of pleasure (e.g., pride) and pain (e.g., shame, guilt). But as a motive for acting morally, egoism has a major flaw. It's fickle. If an egoistically motivated person finds that self-interest can be served as well or better without acting in accord with principle, then principle be damned. If cheaper labor can be found overseas, a profit-minded capitalist is likely to shelve the plan to hire locally. The student whose ultimate goal when volunteering at the nursing home was to add community service to her resume isn't likely to last. Her goal has been reached the first time she enters the building.

Altruism: Concern for the Welfare of One or More Other Individuals

Altruism is motivation with the ultimate goal of increasing the welfare of one or more individuals other than myself. This motivation is aroused by threats to the welfare of cared-for others—including but not limited to spouses/partners, friends, progeny, and pets. If circumstances are right, we can also care for the welfare of a total stranger (Batson, 2011). Altruism as I am talking about it shouldn't be confused with either helping or moral behavior. This is true even though altruistic motivation often leads to action judged helpful and moral. Nor should it be confused with self-sacrifice, which concerns cost to self not benefit to other. These confusions result from a focus on consequences instead of motives and values. They reflect Aristotelian rather than Galilean science.

Promise

Research reveals that empathy-induced altruism—altruistic motivation evoked by feeling empathic concern for a person in need—can be a surprisingly powerful motive for benefiting that person (see Batson, 2011, for an extensive review). Feelings of empathic concern (sympathy, compassion, tenderness, and the like) provide a strong emotional base. (Note that empathic concern involves feeling *for* the person in need, not feeling *as* he or she feels.) Empathy-induced altruism can lead us to act in accordance with moral principles, especially interpersonal principles of fairness, justice, and care. When it does, we or others may judge our action moral. But the underlying motivation is still altruistic, not moral.

Problems

As a source of moral action, altruism also has problems. In many circumstances, it's not easily aroused. Altruism—at least empathy-induced altruism—is directed toward the welfare of specific other individuals. But the likelihood that the needs of different people will stir our empathic feelings isn't equal. We're more apt to feel empathic concern for those for whom we especially care and those whose needs are salient. Many of our most vexing moral issues—poverty, war, genocide, homelessness, population control, global warming, resource overconsumption, and so on—may evoke little empathic concern. This is because it may not be possible to feel empathy for an abstract social category such as people with AIDS, the elderly, or the homeless. Perhaps the most we can hope for is generalization of empathic concern felt for individual exemplars of these categories. Further, we sometimes actively avoid feeling empathy in order to forestall the resulting altruistic motivation, especially when we fear it will lead to personally costly action. We cross the street, change channels, close our eyes. Finally, like other emotions, empathic concern diminishes over time.

Even when aroused, empathy-induced altruism is limited in much the same way as egoism. If benefiting the person or persons for whom empathy is felt leads me to act in accord with principle, fine. But altruism and morality can be at odds. I may, for example, show partiality to those for whom I especially care, thereby violating my own standards of fairness and justice. (See Batson, 2011, for a review of research relevant to each mentioned promise and problem with altruism.)

Collectivism: Concern for the Welfare of a Group

Collectivism is motivation with the ultimate goal of increasing the welfare of a group or collective. The group may be small or large—from two to over two billion. It may be a marriage, a family, a sports team, a university, a neighborhood, a city, or a nation. It may be one's race, religion, sex, political party, or social class. It may be all humanity. Although the collectives we care about are typically those to which we belong, membership isn't required. We may, for example, care about the welfare of a disadvantaged or persecuted group without being in the group ourselves—homeless people, gays and lesbians, victims of genocide, orphaned animals. If we place intrinsic value on a group's welfare and this welfare is threatened or can be enhanced in some way, collectivist motivation should be aroused. This motivation can, in turn, promote action to benefit the group in ways judged moral.

A person who contributes to the local United Way in order to enrich his or her community is displaying collectivist motivation. So is the college student who becomes a Habitat for Humanity volunteer as a means to ease the plight of the poor. So is the rescuer of a Jewish family in Nazi Europe who acts out of love for all humanity (McFarland, Webb, & Brown, 2012). If the ultimate goal is to benefit some group, be it large or small, the motive is collectivism. Sometimes, we have an opportunity to benefit the group as a whole. More often, we can benefit only certain members—perhaps only one. Still, if promoting the group's welfare is our ultimate goal, the motive is collectivism. (If promoting the individual's welfare is our ultimate goal, the motive is altruism.) The ultimate goal not the number of people benefited determines the nature of the motive.

Promise

As a motive for acting morally, collectivism has some virtues that egoism and altruism don't. Egoism and altruism are both directed toward the welfare of individuals—self or another, respectively. Yet moral issues often transcend both self-interest and the interest of those individuals for whom we especially care.

Many contemporary moral challenges—including recycling, energy and water conservation, support for public TV, contribution to charities, and paying taxes—come in the form of *social dilemmas*. In a social dilemma what's best for each individual conflicts with what's best for the group as a whole. Research reveals that in such a situation, egoism and altruism pose threats to the collective good. They're likely to promote our own interests or the interests of cared-for others at the expense of the group (Batson, Ahmad et al., 1999; Batson, Batson et al., 1995). If we rely only on egoistic and altruistic motivation to address social dilemmas, the prognosis looks bleak.

Enter collectivism. There's considerable evidence that when faced with a social dilemma, whether in a research laboratory or in real life, many people show at least some concern for the welfare of the group (e.g., Alfano & Marwell, 1980; Brewer & Kramer, 1986; Dawes, McTavish, & Shaklee, 1977; Yamagishi & Sato, 1986). The most common explanation for this concern is collectivist motivation. It's assumed that individuals can and do act with an ultimate goal of increasing the group's welfare (e.g., Brewer & Kramer, 1986; Dawes et al., 1990). It's also assumed that this motive has a strong emotional base in feelings of loyalty, esprit, patriotism, national pride, and team spirit (Petrocell & Smith, 2005; Smith, Seger, & Mackie, 2007). If these assumptions are correct, then collectivism can produce behavior judged moral, even though accordance with principle (don't be selfish, do what's best for all) is an unintended consequence.

Problems

Collectivist motivation is less effective in addressing moral issues that concern the rights and interests of individuals who aren't members of the cared-for group. If acting morally toward nonmembers serves to promote the group's welfare, fine. If not, forget it. And, as noted above, we're most likely to care about collectives of which we're members—an *us*. Identifying with a group or collective usually involves recognition of an out-group—a *them* who's not us. (Tajfel & Turner, 1986, suggested that a them–us contrast is necessary to define a collective, but Gaertner, Iuzzini, Witt, & Oriña, 2006, presented data that suggest otherwise.) Within a them–us dichotomy, concern for our group's welfare may lead to callous indifference to the welfare of theirs. *They* may be placed outside the community of those to whom our moral principles apply, a perceptual reframing called *moral exclusion* (Staub, 1990; see Chapter 3). When AIDS was initially labeled as a gay disease, many outside the gay community felt little obligation to help. It was *their* problem.

Principlism: Concern to Promote Some Moral Standard, Principle, or Ideal

I suggested earlier that motivation with the ultimate goal of promoting some moral standard, principle, or ideal can be called truly moral motivation. It's aroused by threats to or violations of intrinsically valued moral principles. I call this form of motivation principlism simply to have a fourth "ism," (*Moralism* had been taken.) Because it has promotion of one or more of the person's moral principles as an intrinsically valued ultimate goal, I—like others—also call it moral integrity.

It's perhaps not surprising that most moral philosophers have argued for the importance of a motive for moral action other than egoism. But most since Kant (1785/1898) have also had doubts about altruism and collectivism, largely because of the problems already noted. They reject appeals to altruism, especially empathy-induced altruism, because feelings of empathy, sympathy, and compassion are too circumscribed. Empathic concern isn't felt to the same degree for everyone in need. They reject appeals to collectivism because group interest is bounded by the limits of the group. Collectivism not only permits but may even encourage harming those outside the group.

Recognizing these problems with altruism and collectivism, many moral philosophers call for motivation with a goal of promoting universal and impartial moral principles or ideals. For example, John Rawls (1971) famously argued for a principle of justice based on imagining the allocation of goods and opportunities to the members of society that would be made from a position behind a Veil of Ignorance, where no one knows his or her place in society—prince or pauper, laborer or lawyer, male or female, black or white. Allocating from this position eliminates partiality and seduction by special interest.

Universalist views of morality haven't gone unchallenged. Writers like Lawrence Blum (1980, 1988), Carol Gilligan (1982), Nel Noddings (1984), Joan Tronto (1987), and Stephen Asma (2013) have called for recognition of forms of morality that allow for special attention to the welfare of certain others or for promotion of certain relationships. In opposition to an ethic based on fairness and justice, these writers propose an ethic of care. Sometimes, care is proposed as an alternative principle to justice, either as a substitute for justice or in dynamic tension with it. At other times, care seems to be an alternative to principled morality altogether (Stocker, 1976). If care is an alternative principle, then it too may evoke a form of principlism—motivation to promote a principle of care. But if care means intrinsic valuing of another individual, of oneself, or of a certain relationship, then it would be a form of altruism, egoism, or collectivism, respectively.

Some conceptual precision is needed to appreciate the distinctions between principlism and both altruism and collectivism. After all, all three take us beyond self-interest. And the ultimate goals of altruism and collectivism—another person's welfare, a group's welfare—are the basis for classic moral principles such as "Love your neighbor" and "Do what produces the greatest good for all." To pursue these ultimate goals is to act morally according to such principles. But remember that it's important to focus on motivation rather than behavior. First, consider care for another person's welfare. Such care can be motivated by either altruism or principlism.

One way to distinguish care based on altruism from care based on principlism is to consider Kant's (1785/1898) second formulation of the categorical imperative. This formulation states that we should never treat any person only as a means but always as an end. Now imagine that someone whose welfare I intrinsically value is in need, and I'm altruistically motivated to see this need removed. To act on this altruistic motivation—that is, to act to promote the cared-for other's welfare as an ultimate rather than an instrumental goal—is to treat that other as an end. If successful, my action accords with the persons-as-ends imperative. But, as Kant argued, such action isn't morally motivated because the altruistic ultimate goal is to increase the other's welfare, not to treat him or her as an end. For principlism, the action must not only be consistent with an intrinsically valued principle but also must be carried out to promote the principle. "Treat others as ends" must be why I promote the other's welfare. It must be the ultimate goal not simply a consequence.

We can also distinguish altruistic concern for another's welfare from concern based on a Utilitarian principle of promoting the greatest good for the greatest number. A person motivated to uphold such a principle would be concerned about the welfare of others. A person motivated by altruism is also concerned about the welfare of one or more others. But for the former person, a given individual's welfare will be sought only if it increases the overall good. The individual's welfare is an instrumental goal. For the person motivated by altruism, the cared-for individual's welfare is an ultimate goal, and the effect that increasing the individual's welfare has on the overall good is an unintended consequence.

Parallel distinctions can be made between principlism and both egoism and collectivism. Consider collectivism. Calls to act for the general welfare often appeal to principle rather than to the good of society (collectivism). We're told that it's our duty to vote, that it's not right to leave litter for someone else to clean up, that we should give our fair share to the United Way, and that we ought to serve the community in which we live. Although adherence may in each case increase the group's welfare, the call is to promote some standard or ideal, not the group's welfare. Principlism.

Promise

For principlism, promoting one or more moral principles is an ultimate goal rather than an instrumental goal or unintended consequence. This makes the principle–behavior link more reliable. Further, unlike egoism, altruism, and collectivism, principlism provides a motive for acting morally that transcends reliance on self-interest and interest in and feeling for the welfare of certain other individuals or groups. Moral principles that are universal and impartial don't play favorites. This is true of the Utilitarian principle of the greatest good for the greatest number (Mill, 1861/1987). It's true for Hume's earlier principle of utility directed toward "the happiness of mankind" (1751/1975, Appendix 1). It's true of any principle that satisfies the first formulation of Kant's (1785/1898) categorical imperative: the principle can be willed to be a universal law. It's true of Rawls's (1971) criterion for justice—allocation of goods and opportunities behind the Veil of Ignorance. It's true of a principle to do no harm (Baron, 1996). And it's true of the Golden Rule.

Problems

Along with these strengths, principlism has some serious weaknesses. Simply because I place intrinsic value on a principle doesn't guarantee that the principle is right—or right for the situation. Although this normative issue lies outside the scope of the present analysis, it shouldn't be forgotten.

Nor is principlism problem free within the present analysis. The major problem is its scarcity. Does truly moral motivation—acting with an ultimate goal of promoting some moral standard, principle, or ideal—even exist? Is principlism within the human motivational repertoire? (Parallel questions can be and have been asked regarding the existence of altruism and collectivism. For the former, the empirical evidence provides a tentative affirmative answer; see Batson, 2011. For the latter, the jury is still out.)

When Kant (1785/1898) briefly shifted his attention from what ought to be to what is, he admitted that behavior thought to be motivated by principle may actually be prompted by self-love (i.e., egoism):

> Sometimes it happens that with the sharpest self-examination we can find nothing beside the moral principle of duty which could have been powerful enough to move us to this or that action and to so great a sacrifice; yet we cannot from this infer with certainty that it was not really some secret impulse of self-love,

under the false appearance of duty, that was the actual determining cause of the will. We like to flatter ourselves by falsely taking credit for a more noble motive; whereas in fact we can never, even by the strictest examination, get completely behind the secret springs of action. . . . A cool observer, one that does not mistake the wish for good, however lively, for its reality, may sometimes doubt whether true virtue is actually found anywhere in the world, and this especially as years increase and the judgment is partly made wiser by experience and partly, also, more acute in observation. (Section 2, paragraphs 2–3)

Conspicuous self-benefits arise from acting morally. We can gain the social and self-rewards of being seen and seeing ourselves as good people. We can avoid the social and self-punishments for failing to do the right thing. Are these self-benefits unintended consequences or are they our ultimate goal? Perhaps, as Freud (1930/1961) suggested, society inculcates moral principles in the young to bridle their antisocial impulses by making it in their own best interest to act in accord.

But even if moral principles are learned in this way as extrinsic values, perhaps they can come to function autonomously (Allport, 1961). Perhaps they come to be valued intrinsically and not simply as instrumental means to self-serving ends—at least by some people (see Colby & Damon, 1992, for possible examples).

At issue is the nature of the goal. Is promoting the principle an instrumental goal on the way to the ultimate goal of self-benefit? If so, the motive is a form of egoism. Is promoting the principle an ultimate goal, with the ensuing self-benefits unintended consequences? If so, we have princiPlism, a motive for acting morally that's distinct from egoism. And if we do, it's meaningful to speak of intrinsic moral value—Kant's "true virtue." Chapter 4 explores this issue in some detail.

For now, we're left with Kant's candid assessment. We don't know whether princiPlism is a distinct form of motivation, or only a subtle form of egoism. There's some empirical evidence, limited and weak, that endorsement of at least some moral principles can be associated with increased moral behavior (see Blasi, 1980; Eisenberg, 1991, for reviews). But the evidence is far from impressive, and it doesn't identify the ultimate goal.

Clearly, we need to look more closely at the nature of moral motivation. But first, we need to consider the two standard diagnoses for our moral ills. Each sheds important light on what's wrong with morality.

2

PERSONAL DEFICIENCY

Scientific explanations of our moral maladies tend to be of two types. One type focuses on the person, the other on the situation. Explanations that focus on the person—the topic of this chapter—can be further subdivided. Philosophers and psychologists who approach the problem from the perspectives of character development and social learning are likely to blame our moral ills on defective socialization that produces bad character. If a person's behavior isn't adequately controlled by his or her standards, the standards must not have been learned well enough or in the right way. Others are likely to blame bad judgment. The person must not have reached the level of moral reasoning necessary to appreciate the scope and intent of the standards. Or the person must have a deficient moral sense, failing to heed the guidance of moral intuition and sentiment. These two camps often draw swords in opposition. There are even fights within camps. But the different views needn't be seen as mutually exclusive. Each can contribute to understanding our moral ills, especially when related to the value→emotion→motivation→behavior framework from Chapter 1.

BAD CHARACTER

Our failure to act morally has been an abiding concern of Western philosophy for at least 2,500 years. Both Plato (427?–347 BC) and Aristotle (384–322 BC) thought that moral failures are due to a deficiency of character. In the *Republic* (c. 375 BC), Plato (1999) presented his well-known vision that good character is manifest in the temperate rule of reason over appetite and spirit. Aristotle's (1976) analysis in the *Nicomachean Ethics*, a compilation of his lecture notes from around 325 BC, was more systematically developed and has been even more influential.

Aristotle

Aristotle believed that good character consists of virtues, including the ideals of courage, temperance, patience, truthfulness, and justice. Virtues are initially acquired in childhood through practice and habit because

> like activities produce like dispositions. Hence we must give our activities a certain quality, because their characteristics determine the resulting dispositions.

So it is a matter of no little importance what sort of habits we form from the earliest age—it makes a vast difference, or rather all the difference in the world. (Aristotle, 1976, p. 92 [Bekker number 1103b])

But habit-based moral dispositions aren't all that's required. Excellence of character isn't fully expressed until adulthood, because only then does the virtuous person develop the practical wisdom to follow reason and enact the virtues appropriately. The morally right course of action can't be specified in general but must be discerned by wisely attending to specifics in each new situation.

According to Aristotle, a person who has acquired sufficient virtue and the wisdom to express it appropriately feels no conflict or constraint in doing so. Acting morally is a free expression of his or her character. It's also the source of true happiness because it fulfills the "function of Man" as a species. To be truly moral is a matter of bringing head and heart into harmony. It's a matter of who one is as much as what one does.

Moral failures can be of two types—vice and incontinence. First, Aristotle distinguished the virtuous person from persons given to the excesses or deficiencies that we call vices. Vices include, for example, rashness (an excess) or cowardice (a deficiency) rather than courage. Vices reveal both lack of good character and failure to understand the source of human happiness. Second, Aristotle distinguished the virtuous person from the person who feels a conflict between what he or she morally ought to do in a given situation and what he or she wants to do. For the conflicted person, reason isn't fully in control. He or she is apt to yield to nonvirtuous desire (show incontinence) due to weakness of will (*akrasia*). And even when doing what's right (being continent with virtue), the conflicted person hasn't reached the level of wisdom to know that human happiness lies in rational pursuit of moral excellence. Only with that level of understanding is virtue expressed freely without conflict.

The Greek emphasis on character, supplemented by Judeo-Christian religious teachings, held sway in moral philosophy through the Renaissance. With the Enlightenment, focus shifted from good character to right judgment, and from moral wants to oughts. By then, certainty—whether based on reason or on religion—about the function of Man, the natural order, and the harmony of happiness and goodness had begun to crumble. Still, modern skepticism not withstanding, the Greek emphasis resurfaced in the past century. Stimulated by Anscombe's (1958) criticism of the focus on duties and standards in modern moral philosophy, concern for character enjoyed a return to prominence in the form of virtue ethics (Annas, 2006; Foot, 1978; Hursthouse, 2013; MacIntyre, 1984). But not without doubters (e.g., Doris, 2002; Harman, 1999).

Freud

In the much briefer history of psychology as a discipline, development of good moral character during childhood, or failure to develop it, has been an abiding concern. But in psychology, good character isn't typically thought to consist of harmonious, free, reasoned expression of virtue, as Aristotle said. It requires coercion and constraint. Early on, Freud focused on the internalization of parental and societal standards. This internalization leads the child to censor and control his or her own behavior. The ego—that part of our psyche that brokers between our personal desires and the realities of the external world—is under internal scrutiny. As Freud explained in *A General Introduction to Psychoanalysis*,

> In the ego there exists a faculty that incessantly watches, criticizes, and compares, and in this way is set against the other part of the ego ... [It] measures his [the person's] actual ego and all his activities by an *ego ideal*, which he has created for himself in the course of his development. . . . We recognize in this self-criticizing faculty the ego censorship, the "conscience." (1917/1960a, pp. 435–436, italics in original)

Freud came to call this self-criticizing faculty the *superego*, in which parents' standards and demands are "introjected" into the psyche of the child. The superego "has a great share in determining the form taken by the ego and ... makes an essential contribution towards building up what is called its 'character'" (Freud, 1923/1960b, p. 18). Freud thought the superego provided an answer to those critics of psychoanalysis

> who have complained that there must surely be a higher nature in man: "Very true," we can say, "and here we have that higher nature, in this ego ideal or superego, the representative of our relation to our parents. When we were little children we knew these higher natures, we admired them and feared them; and later we took them into ourselves." . . . The role of father [and mother] is carried on by teachers and others in authority; their injunctions and prohibitions remain powerful in the ego ideal and continue, in the form of conscience, to exercise moral censorship. . . . As the child was once under a compulsion to obey its parents, so the ego submits to the categorical imperative of its superego. (Freud, 1923/1960b, pp. 26, 27, and 38)

The superego exercises its censorship through feelings of guilt and self-recrimination. Moreover, it judges thoughts and desires as well as deeds:

> The tension between the harsh superego and the ego that is subjected to it, is called by us the sense of guilt; it expresses itself as a need for punishment. . . . The distinction, moreover, between doing something bad and wishing to do it disappears entirely, since nothing can be hidden from the superego, not even thoughts. (Freud, 1930/1961, pp. 70, 72)

For Freud, moral failures are due to a weak superego. But, as we shall see in Chapter 7, he believed a strong superego produces problems as well. Morality isn't the source of happiness Aristotle thought, but a curb on happiness. Our personal

wants and society's oughts are fundamentally at odds. Our moral character is conflicted and fragile.

The Character Education Inquiry

Along with Freud's psychoanalytic reflections, the 1920s and 1930s brought considerable empirical research on moral character. Much of it was part of an effort by the
Religious Education Association and the Institute of Social and Religious Research
to understand how children learn to think and act morally. Most notable of these
projects—and most ambitious—was the Character Education Inquiry conducted by
Hugh Hartshorne and Mark May under the general supervision of E. L. Thorndike,
one of the leading experimental psychologists of the day.

Assisted by a team of researchers, Hartshorne and May conducted numerous
studies of schoolchildren's honesty and generosity. Over a 5-year period they tested
more than 11,000 children, observing their behavior in a range of situations in
which the children could cheat, steal, or lie for personal gain—and in situations that
allowed for engagement in various service activities. The children were observed
not only in their classrooms but also while doing homework, competing in sports,
and playing party games. In addition, Hartshorne and May studied self-control by
assessing how long the children persisted on difficult problems or on dull tasks when
more interesting activities were available. Of primary interest was the children's
behavior in these situations. But Hartshorne and May also assessed knowledge of
and attitudes toward widely accepted moral standards. And they collected peer and
teacher ratings of the children's honesty and service. Results of this massive project
appeared in three volumes—*Studies in Deceit* (Hartshorne & May, 1928), *Studies
in Service and Self-Control* (Hartshorne, May, & Maller, 1929), and *Studies in the
Organization of Character* (Hartshorne, May, & Shuttleworth, 1930). (See Burton &
Kunce, 1995, for a useful overview.)

The Character Education Inquiry revealed considerable cross-situational variation in a child's tendency to uphold moral standards. Most children acted morally
in some situations and failed to do so in others. But cross-situation variation isn't all
that was found. When Hartshorne and May aggregated responses across measures
and situations, they discovered evidence of an underlying unidimensional factor of
honesty that was moderately associated with resistance to temptation across situations. (Burton, 1963, and Rushton, 1980, found the same in subsequent analyses of
the Inquiry data.). Further, "total character" scores across 37 behavioral tests correlated moderately positively ($r = .34$) with "reputation" based on ratings by teachers
and peers (Hartshorne et al., 1930, p. 230).

Overall, the research indicated that there is a relationship between moral character and moral action, but it's far more complex than suggested by a simple notion
that some children are moral and others aren't . Rather than a general character trait
of honesty, many children seemed to have more nuanced standards tuned to specific
circumstances. Instead of "Thou shalt not cheat," the behavior of many was more
consistent with, "Thou shalt not cheat unless you need to in order to succeed and can

be certain you won't get caught." Instead of "Thou shalt not steal," there was more consistency with, "Thou shalt not steal from your friends." The children's standards left much room for questionable behavior and moral rationalization.

Findings like these of Hartshorne and May led to a shift in level of analysis in empirical research on moral character. Rather than attempting to measure the acquisition of general traits or virtues, attention turned to how children acquire or fail to acquire specific regulatory standards of right and wrong conduct in situations of particular concern to parents, teachers, and society at large: How does the child learn to take turns, share, tell the truth, not hit or steal, and so on? Immoral behavior wasn't attributed to a general lack of character but to failure to properly learn specific self-regulatory standards. This shift was apparent in social learning theory.

Social Learning Theory

Social learning theory sought to bridge the divide in early 20th-century psychology between the stimulus-response patterns of classic learning theory and psychoanalytic notions such as superego, character, and conscience. John Dollard and Neal Miller pioneered the development of social learning theory (e.g., Miller & Dollard, 1941). In *Personality and Psychotherapy*, a volume they dedicated to both Freud and Pavlov, Dollard and Miller (1950) provided an insightful integration of psychoanalytic thought and learning theory. The integration involved translation of Freudian concepts into more operational and testable learning theory terms. To this end, Dollard and Miller (1950) employed the concepts of stimulus, response, and reinforcement, as well as the theoretical perspective of Clark Hull. Based largely on studies of learning in laboratory rats, Hull (1943) had argued that the tendency of an organism to respond in a given situation is a multiplicative function of habit strength and relevant drives. Both must be present for a response to occur. Reflecting Thorndike's (1898) famous Law of Effect ("pleasure stamps in; pain stamps out"), habits are learned products of our reinforcement history. Drives are internal stimuli derived from innate physiological needs.

In order to deal with the complexities of human social behavior addressed by Freud, Dollard and Miller (1950) found they had to go beyond Hull and give attention to higher cognitive processes. These included learning by imitation, modeling, and through verbal instruction, as well as decision-making, expectation, and interpretation. Dollard and Miller emphasized that we not only acquire behavioral responses and habits. We also acquire drives, values, and goal-directed motives:

No two people are exactly alike because each has learned different combinations of motives and values under the different conditions of life to which he has been exposed. Freudian theory contains many assumptions about how drives are changed by experience and how these changes affect the personality. . . . An important part of what has often been called Ego strength, or strength of character, is the ability of socially learned drives to compete with primary ones. (Dollard & Miller, 1950, p. 63)

Included among learned motives and values are those related to moral sanctions and standards acquired from parents, teachers, and society at large.

Dollard and Miller themselves didn't give much attention to the acquisition of moral standards, but subsequent social learning theorists did. Albert Bandura's social cognitive theory is perhaps the best known example. Bandura (1977) emphasized that rewards and punishments provided by parents, teachers, and peers are important sources of moral behavior. So are self-rewards and self-punishments.

> Many forms of behavior are personally advantageous but are detrimental to others or infringe on their rights. Without some consensual moral codes people would disregard each others' rights and welfare whenever their desires come into social conflict. Societal codes and sanctions articulate collective moral imperatives as well as influence social conduct. However, external sanctions are relatively weak deterrents because most transgressive acts can go undetected. But people continuously preside over their own conduct in countless situations presenting little or no external threat. So the exercise of self-sanction must play a central role in the regulation of moral conduct. (Bandura, 1991, p. 46)

As this passage makes apparent, Bandura's goal was to provide an empirically based social-learning analysis of much the same socialization process that Freud had sought to explain with his concepts of the ego ideal and superego. For Bandura, our moral maladies arise from failure to acquire and employ the social and self-sanctions needed to control our behavior.

Early Steps in Moral Socialization

From a social learning perspective, we can identify several steps in early moral socialization. It's no surprise to any parent that by the second year of life, when the child becomes mobile, a war of wills ensues in which the parent seeks to control the child's behavior, often against the latter's wishes. Statistics presented by Martin Hoffman—another prominent social learning theorist of morality—reveal the extent and effect of these parental efforts: "In the 2- to 4-year-old range children experience pressures from mothers to change their behavior on the average of [once every] 6 to 8 minutes throughout their waking hours, and in the main they end up complying" (Hoffman, 1977, pp. 87–88). In addition to parental reward and punishment, imitation and modeling are extremely important in early moral development, including imitation of parental responses to the behavior of others (Forman, Aksan, & Kochanska, 2004).

Initially, the young child is rewarded and punished for specific behaviors. But as cognitive skills develop—and especially after the acquisition of language—socializing agents give increased attention to standards that apply across a range of behaviors and situations. In the words of Walter and Harriet Mischel,

It is essential for a mother to prevent young Johnny from injuring his sibling, even when she does not have the time, and Johnny does not have the capacity, to reason about the moral bases of this constraint; therefore she must rely on specific admonitions and punishments. Later in socialization, when the child's cognitive and verbal skills expand, the justification for right and wrong courses of action tends to be increasingly based on rules—first of an arbitrary authority-oriented type but gradually of a more abstract and reasoned nature. (Mischel & Mischel, 1976, p. 95)

The transition to abstract rules (i.e., principles) is crucial if the child's behavior is to be controlled in relatively novel situations. Although the effects of reward and punishment in one situation can be expected to generalize to highly similar situations—such as Johnny hitting his sister Suzie today and hitting her tomorrow—generalization gradients for specific learned behaviors are steep. If, rather than learning "Don't hit Suzie when Mommy is watching, you'll get spanked," Johnny learns "Don't harm others, you wouldn't want them to harm you," the situations to which his learning is relevant expand enormously.

But this transition also has a downside. The more abstract the learned standard or principle—"Be a good boy." "Be nice."—the less likely it is to be recognized as relevant to any given situation. In addition, its guidance is more likely to be ambiguous and vulnerable to rationalization. Is stealing apples for my friends being a good boy or bad?

Especially effective in the transition from inhibition of specific behaviors to inhibition based on general standards and self-regulation is a shift from control strategies based on physical restraint, reward, and punishment (Sheikh & Janoff-Bulman, 2013) to what Hoffman (1977, 2000) called *inductive discipline*. In inductive discipline, the effects of the child's behavior on other people are pointed out and the relevant rules or principles stated: "You've taken Suzie's truck. How do you think she feels? How would you feel? It's important that we try not to make others unhappy. What can you do to make her feel better? Can you take turns?" There's some evidence that parental disappointment at the child's misbehavior conveyed by such statements plays a particularly important role in making induction effective (Krevans & Gibbs, 1996). And at least in the early years, this form of discipline seems to be more commonly used and more effective with girls than with boys (Smetana, 1989).

Internalization of Self-Regulatory Standards

The transition to more abstract and reasoned standards sets the stage for internalization of these standards. That is, for the shift from control by external, socially administered rewards and punishments to control by internal, self-administered ones. The child becomes sensitive to the self-praise and self-censure expressed in feelings of pride and guilt (Campbell, 1964). There are sizable individual differences in the degree to which we internalize moral standards and in the degree to which they effectively control our behavior. These individual differences are reflected, at least in part, by self-report personality measures such as the Agreeableness and Conscientiousness items of the Five-Factor model (Fleeson & Gallagher, 2009; McCrae & Costa, 2003) and the Importance of Moral Identity scale (Aquino & Reed, 2002). Internalization of self-regulatory moral standards is greatly facilitated if the parent–child relationship is close, so that the child loves, wants to be loved by, and wants to emulate the parent (Berkowitz, 1964). Hoffman (1977, pp. 85–86), like Bandura, considered Freud's superego to be an attempt to describe this regulation of our behavior by self-rewards and punishments.

Illustrating the importance of internalization in promoting moral behavior, research by Joan Grusec (1991) and her colleagues showed that providing children who have acted generously with an attribution to their personal standards and values rather than to external pressure increased generosity in subsequent novel situations. For example, Grusec, Kuczynski, Rushton, and Simutis (1978) told some 7- to 10-year-old children who had just been induced to share with poor children, "You shared quite a bit. I guess you shared because you're the kind of person who likes to help other people." These children subsequently shared more pencils with another child than did other children told, "I guess you shared because you thought I expected you to," or children given no interpretation for their initial sharing.

Complicating Internalization—The Role of External Pressure

Research stimulated by Leon Festinger's (1957) theory of cognitive dissonance adds three complicating factors to the transition from external to internal control of moral behavior. These complications arise from the effect of external pressure on the acquisition and maintenance of internal standards. They extend the possibilities for moral failure.

Overly Sufficient External Pressure Can Inhibit Internalization

First, dissonance theory suggests that if strong and salient external incentives to comply with moral standards are provided—either in the form of promised reward or threatened punishment—internalization is less likely to occur. As Festinger and Jonathan Freedman (1964) explained,

> Imagine the following kind of situation. A parent may discover that his four-year-old son stole something. The parent regards such behavior as wrong and consequently, punishes the child in an endeavor to teach the child that stealing is bad and in order to prevent a recurrence of the act. If the child has been punished very severely, and the same treatment is threatened explicitly or implicitly if there is a recurrence, it will undoubtedly affect the child's behavior. The next time the child has an impulse to steal something he will probably refrain. There will, however, be little or no attitudinal consequences for the child [i.e., little internalization of a standard that stealing is wrong]. (p. 229)

The idea is that after severe punishment the child thinks that his decision to refrain from stealing is based on the threat of more punishment rather than on a personal belief that stealing is wrong. But a mild threat, as long as it's sufficient to inhibit the proscribed behavior, will lead the child to think that his decision to refrain is a product of personal values, encouraging internalization.

Freedman (1965) provided data that support these predictions. Boys 8 to 10 years old, run individually, were told by a male experimenter that although they could play with four less interesting toys, they shouldn't play with an especially expensive and attractive remote-controlled robot: "Do not play with the robot. It is wrong to play with the robot." Some of the boys were threatened with severe punishment if they broke this rule. The experimenter said, "If you play with the robot I'll be very angry and will have to do something about it" (high threat). Others were told only that it was wrong (low threat). For half of the boys in each threat condition, the experimenter stayed in the room during the play period, providing surveillance, a second form of external pressure to comply with the rule. For the other half, the experimenter explained that he had to run an errand and would be gone for about 10 minutes, leaving the boy alone in the room. All of the boys included in the experiment refrained from playing with the robot (2 of 23 in each of the experimenter-absent conditions played with it, but these four boys were excluded prior to analysis).

Three weeks later, each boy was again given a chance to play with the five toys. This time a new experimenter, who was female, pointed to the toys and said that while she was doing some work, the boy could play with "any of the toys" that someone had left in the room. Consistent with predictions based on dissonance theory, only boys in the low-threat/experimenter-absent condition showed evidence of having internalized the standard that playing with the robot was wrong. Less than 30 percent of the boys in that condition played with the robot in the second session. In each of the other three conditions, over 60 percent did.

These and similar results in related studies (e.g., Aronson & Carlsmith, 1963; Lepper, 1973) led Mark Lepper (1983) to propose a *minimal sufficiency principle* of internalization:

> Techniques of social control that are successful in producing compliance, but are at the same time sufficiently subtle (rather than obviously coercive) to prevent the individual from viewing such compliance solely as a function of those extrinsic controls, will be most likely—other things being equal—to promote subsequent internalization. (p. 305)

Insufficient External Pressure Can Also Inhibit Internalization

Second, dissonance theory suggests a further complication—one that turns moral socialization into a high-risk, high-stakes enterprise. What if the external pressure isn't sufficient to produce compliance? As Festinger and Freedman (1964) pointed out,

> Maximal internalization of the culturally desired moral value should occur if the person resists temptation under conditions of high motivation to succumb and low threat for yielding. If the person yields to temptation, however, value changes occur in a direction opposite to that which, presumably, the culture is attempting to inculcate. (p. 234)

That is, if I yield to the temptation, the weaker my desire to yield—and the stronger the threat of punishment for yielding—the more likely I am to internalize an *immoral* standard. Imagine a child who asks himself, "Why, after being told I'll be punished if I steal, did I shoplift this CD that I don't especially like?" He may well conclude that it's because he really sees nothing wrong with shoplifting. Clearly, if we're to promote internalization, we must make sure that external pressures are sufficient to make the child uphold the moral standard. If not, the attempt will backfire. But if the pressures are too strong, the attempt will simply fail. The window of opportunity is narrow.

External Pressure Can Erode Internalization

Third, consider the effect of external pressure once internalization has occurred. Self-perception theory (Bem, 1967) and attribution theory (Lepper, 1983) suggest that unnecessarily powerful or salient external incentives can erode internalization that has already occurred, producing moral regression. Consistent with this overjustification prediction, Batson, Coke, Jasnoski, and Hanson (1978) found that if undergraduates were given a monetary inducement when asked for help, they subsequently rated themselves as less helpful and cooperative than did participants in three other conditions—those who helped without inducement, those who were informed about being paid only after they had agreed to help (so the payment couldn't be viewed as an incentive, only as a reward), and those who were not asked for help. Similarly, Batson, Harris, McCaul, Davis, and Schmidt (1979) found that, compared with undergraduates led to attribute their initial willingness to help to a desire to do what's right, those led to attribute their initial willingness to social pressure saw themselves as less helpful and generous, and were less likely to agree to a second, unrelated request for help. So, erosion of standards that have been internalized is yet another way moral socialization can fail.

Moral Disengagement

These complications due to external pressure not withstanding, by late childhood internalized self-sanctions come to operate anticipatorily for most of us. We act in accord with moral standards in order to get the self-rewards for compliance (praise, esteem) and avoid the self-punishments for violation (censure, shame, guilt).

Add another complication. Feeling good about standard compliance is often not our only motivation. In many situations, we can anticipate benefits for violating moral standards, such as when we think it would be fun or profitable. The result is moral conflict and, potentially, motivation to temporarily deactivate the standards. Imagine that I think cheating's wrong but also think that it's the only way I can win some game or pass some test. I may employ strategies to disengage my self-regulatory standards regarding cheating so that I can violate them. As Bandura (1991) explained,

> Development of self-regulatory capabilities does not create an invariant control mechanism within a person, as implied by theories of internalization that incorporate entities such as conscience or superego as continuous internal overseers of conduct. Self-reactive influences do not operate unless they are activated, and there are many processes by which self-sanctions can be disengaged. (p. 71)

Disengagement Strategies

In his theory of moral disengagement, Bandura (1990, 1991, 1999) identified a number of strategies for deactivating self-regulatory moral standards: I can reframe or reinterpret a standard-violating action in a way that makes it seem moral rather than immoral. Or I can convince myself that someone else is responsible for the violation. I was given orders. I'm only a small cog on a big wheel. Or I can convince myself that what I'm contemplating isn't *that* bad. Or that those harmed by my action deserve it because they brought it on themselves. Situational factors to be discussed in Chapter 3 can facilitate each of these perceptions.

Disengagement of Standards, or of Anticipated Censure/Guilt?

Bandura (1990, 1991) assumed that for moral disengagement to work, I must deactivate the relevant self-regulatory standards themselves. But there's a second possibility. Perhaps all that's necessary is for me to disengage my concern over the negative consequences of violating the standards. If relevant standards are still active but I experience no alarm bells about impending censure and guilt, is that enough to inhibit my moral self-regulation and allow standard violation?

At least for the freshmen psychology students who participated in a clever experiment on cheating conducted by Richard Dienstbier and Pamela Munter (1971), the answer seemed to be yes. During the waiting period in a study of the effect of a vitamin supplement on vision, participants took a difficult vocabulary test (ostensibly to provide standardization data for researchers in the Educational Psychology Department). The test was said to be highly predictive of college success, and each of the freshmen was told that anyone who performed poorly would be contacted about the implications for their college career. Unknown to participants, the test was so difficult that everyone did poorly. Once they learned of their performance, participants were given an apparently inadvertent opportunity to improve their score by cheating. After seeing the correct responses, they had a chance to change answers in a way that seemed likely to go undetected.

Before taking the vocabulary test, participants had been given a capsule that supposedly contained the vitamin supplement (actually, it was a gelatin placebo). All were told that the supplement had some side effects, which were mild and harmless. Half of the participants (misattribution condition) learned that the side effects they might experience were "a pounding heart, hand tremor, sweaty palms, a warm or flushed face, and a tight or sinking feeling in the stomach." These symptoms are ones generally associated with arousal of the sympathetic nervous system, which occurs when feeling fear or anxiety. The other half (no-misattribution condition) learned that the side effects were "an increased tendency to yawn, a lessening of eye blink rate, and 'tired eyes,'" symptoms irrelevant to either fear or anxiety.

Dienstbier and Munter (1971) reasoned that the participants led to expect irrelevant symptoms as a result of the vitamin supplement should interpret any sympathetic arousal produced by the thought of changing answers as due to fear of self-censure and guilt, which should inhibit their cheating. In contrast, participants led to expect symptoms of sympathetic arousal as a result of the supplement should interpret arousal produced by anticipated self-censure as due to the capsule. This misattribution would disengage their fear about the consequences of cheating, making it easier to cheat. Consistent with this reasoning, 49 percent of participants in the misattribution condition cheated, whereas only 27 percent in the no-misattribution condition did. (The difference was somewhat greater for men than women, suggesting that it may have been harder to mislead the women about the true source of their feelings of fear and anxiety about cheating.)

Also consistent with the possibility that moral standard violation can be due to disengagement of anticipatory affect rather than disengagement of the standards themselves are results of a study by Stanley Schachter and Bibb Latané (1964). These researchers found that prior administration of a drug that depresses sympathetic nervous system response—the tranquilizer chlorpromazine—led to more cheating than did administration of a placebo. Once again, suppression of anticipatory fear and anxiety made cheating more likely.

So it seems that internalized moral standards can be deactivated, allowing us to violate them, by disengaging either the standards themselves or the negative affect that considering standard violation evokes. Two more sources of moral maladies.

Beyond Social Learning of Instrumental Morality

Social learning theorists typically assume that adherence to internalized moral standards is an instrumental not an ultimate goal (recall this distinction from Chapter 1). Self-regulated moral action "depends on expected consequences, although the consequences are often temporally distant, are not in the immediate external environment, are not easily identified, and reside in the actor himself rather than in social agents" (Mischel & Mischel, 1976, p. 98; also see Bandura, 1990,

1991). I toe the moral line not because I intrinsically value the standard but in order to avoid self-censure/guilt and to gain self-esteem/pride. My motivation is a form of egoism.

Is it possible for internalization to go beyond this instrumental morality? As suggested at the end of Chapter 1, perhaps we can come to value moral standards as ends in themselves rather than simply as means to gain self-rewards and avoid self-punishments. Intrinsic valuing of this kind is what I believe Aristotle had in mind when speaking of moral excellence and good character.

Deci, Eghrari, Patrick, and Leone (1994) provided a useful discussion of this possibility from the perspective of self-determination theory (Assor, 2012; Deci & Ryan, 1985, 1991; Ryan & Deci, 2000). Deci et al. adopted the term that Freud used when describing formation of the superego—*introjection*—to speak of internalization of moral standards valued extrinsically. They used *integration* to speak of internalization to the level where moral standards are valued in their own right, that is, intrinsically:

> Introjection refers to partial or suboptimal internalization . . . in which the person "takes in" a value or regulatory process but does not identify with and accept it as his or her own. Instead, it becomes an inner control—a rule for action that is enforced by sanctions such as threats of guilt or promises of self-approval. In a metaphorical sense, when a regulation is merely introjected, it is as if the regulatory process and the person being regulated were still separate even though both are "within the same skin."
>
> Integration, in contrast, refers to internalization in which the person identifies with the value of an activity and accepts full responsibility for doing it. . . . As such, one's behavior emanates from one's self; it is self-determined. One does the behavior wholly voluntarily . . . .. With integrated regulation, the person would not experience the conflict and tension associated with introjection. (Deci et al., 1994, pp. 120–121)

For similar ideas about internalization to the level of integration, see the discussions of moral identity by Blasi (1984) and Glover (2000).

Relating the introjection-integration distinction to an earlier point, it might be said that introjection produces moral oughts whereas integration produces moral wants. Even though accepted as part of who we should be, introjected moral values aren't fully a part of who we are. They're in conflict with more core values and personal desires. Integrated moral values aren't in conflict with personal desires; they *are* personal desires. They produce truly moral motivation, or principlism (again, see Chapter 1). Of course, integrated moral desires may still conflict with other personal desires—unless Aristotle was right that human nature is harmonious and all conflict disappears for the truly virtuous and wise person.

Not only can forms of internalization differ but also the place of internalized standards in our value hierarchy can differ. Some moral values, whether introjected or integrated, may allow for negotiation or compromise when they conflict with other interests. Others may be *sacred* in the sense that they're at the top of the value hierarchy and nonnegotiable. Sacred values need not be religious, but they often are (Tetlock, Kristel, Elson, Green, & Lerner, 2000). Consider, for example, Huguenot Pastor André Trocmé of Le Chambon-sur-Lignon in France. In the face of Nazi and Vichy demands to turn over Jewish refugees, Trocmé steadfastly refused any compromise of his religious principles to provide care for the needy and to harm no human. This led him to save many lives at great personal risk (Hallie, 1979). Linda Skitka (2012) has spoken of this level of valuing as *moral conviction*.

Summary

Two major themes run through this overview of thinking and research on the development of more or less moral persons. First is the theme of general charac-ter traits versus more specific self-regulatory standards. Empirical research sug-gests that most people tend to operate at the level of relatively specific standards. This doesn't mean that it's impossible to develop moral traits that are consistently but sensitively applied to produce virtuous behavior attuned to different circum-stances, as Aristotle thought. Such moral excellence may be possible even if not common. What it does mean is that most of us find ourselves faced with more complex challenges in the moral realm than simply deciding how best to express our harmonious virtue. We find ourselves listening to a cacophony of moral voices—some counseling this, others that—and these voices may contradict one another. Rather than an angel on one shoulder and a devil on the other, there are multiple angels and multiple devils, all in debate. Some speak to the immediate consequences of our actions. Others speak to long-term consequences that are harder to anticipate and appreciate. Social and self-sanctions often fall in the latter category. It's easy to be led astray.

The second major theme is the degree to which moral standards are integrated into our personal value structure. For Aristotle's person of good character, moral and intellectual virtue stands at the top of the value hierarchy. It's the fulfillment of our true nature as humans. Modern psychological research on the inculca-tion of moral values doesn't focus on harmonious expression of our true nature. Instead, the focus is on regulation of personal desires and behavior that are prob-lematic for our life with others—both in the family and in society. Morality takes us beyond control by external sanctions and rewards to control by self-sanctions and -rewards that can regulate our behavior even when we're alone. The capacity to acquire moral self-regulation is clearly within the genetic repertoire of nor-mal humans. But equally clearly, our self-regulatory standards are acquired not inborn. And we don't acquire them without a fight. For the young child, the right thing to do is often not what he or she wants to do. The same is true for many of us adults.

Those with whom we interact have good reason to want us to learn to be moral. Through careful use of external control, modeling, and tutelage about social expec-tations, moral standards can become part of our personal value structure. But there are different forms of internalization with different motivational consequences.

Introjection leads us to act in accord with moral standards as an instrumental means to reach the egoistic ultimate goal of seeing ourselves and being seen by others as a good person (or at least not bad). With integration, standard compliance is valued intrinsically as an end in itself. It's an ultimate goal. Introjection produces a more tenuous link between endorsement of the standard and actual behavior than does integration. These two forms of internalization have very different value→emotion →motivation→behavior trajectories.

We've moved from a general diagnosis that our moral maladies are symptoms of bad character to a more fine-grained, dynamic analysis with many sources of moral failure. Failure can occur because I haven't learned the specific standards and principles relevant to a given moral issue. Or I haven't internalized them. Or, although internalized, they've been undermined by the imposition of unnecessary external pressure to act in accord. Or they've been disengaged, or the anticipated censure for their violation has. These possibilities are especially likely if my standards are internalized only to the level of introjection. But even integrated standards, unless sacred and nonnegotiable, can be overpowered by competing desires. Any of these possibilities can lead me to violate my moral principles.

Nor are these possibilities the only ones. Over the past half century, it has become increasingly common to suggest that our moral maladies arise from problems with the way we use our standards to decide what is right and wrong in specific situations. The deficiency is in how we make moral judgments.

BAD JUDGMENT

Bad moreal judgment has been blamed on poor reasoning, deficient intuition, and absence of sentiment. Let's consider each possibility.

Judgments Based on Reasoning

Both Jean Piaget and Lawrence Kohlberg focused on deficient moral reasoning as a key source of our moral ills.

Piaget

In *The Moral Judgment of the Child* (1932/1965), Piaget extended to the moral realm the same perspective he earlier applied to the child's understanding of the physical world. Central to this perspective is the view that cognitive development involves more than changes in what the person knows and believes. It also involves changes in cognitive structure. Structural changes reflect new assumptions about the nature of reality and new ways of thinking about experience. Adaptation to new information can take two forms. *Assimilation* involves fitting new experience into existing cognitive structures—as when we store the memories of a friend's home after a first visit. *Accommodation* involves changing existing cognitive structures to fit a new understanding of experience—as when we learn that rotation of the earth rather than movement of the sun produces day and night and, more generally, that appearance and reality aren't always the same (Piaget, 1926, 1953).

Applying this perspective to moral reasoning, Piaget (1932/1965) made a sharp distinction between two types of moral judgments. Some are based on standards and principles acquired through assimilation from parents and other authority figures—internalization. Others are based on accommodation to self-discovered standards that emerge through social interactions, especially with peers. Morality of the first type he called *heteronomy*. He called the second type *autonomy*. Heteronomy is the morality of duty, a product of constraint. Autonomy is the morality of cooperation, a product of mutual respect.

Piaget believed he saw these two forms of morality in the judgments made by children growing up in and around Geneva as they responded to questions that he and his colleagues posed. Many of the questions were about the rules of games—especially marbles. What's allowed? What's cheating? Can the rules be changed? There were also questions about responsibility for accidents, about stealing, about lying (in particular, lying to protect someone), and about fairness, justice, and retribution.

Although Piaget insisted that heteronomy and autonomy don't constitute "definite stages" (1932/1965, p. 195), he found that younger children (6 to 8 years old) were far more likely to make heteronomous judgments. They treated rules as absolute and unmodifiable obligations ("moral realism"). They tended to assign blame for accidents on the basis of consequences without considering intent. And they defined what's morally right as adherence to the dictates of authority figures. In contrast, older children (10 to 12 years old) were more likely to make autonomous judgments based on reciprocal relations and mutual respect for the parties involved. They saw rules as modifiable consensual conventions and took intention into account in assigning blame. They defined what's right as what promotes harmonious social relations and solidarity, not simply as following rules.

Piaget recognized that rules or principles can become independent of concern about punishment yet still remain obligatory (heteronomous). Such rules can also be generalized beyond the immediate context of application to become "universal and absolute."

> But even though they are generalized in this way, rules are none the less heteronomous. The child, it is true, takes the particular command that has been given him and raises it to the level of a universal law. This rational process of extension is probably already due to cooperation. But the rule may nevertheless persist in the form of an imperative that is external to the child's own conscience. (Piaget, 1932/1965, p. 170)

Deci et al. (1994) would say the universal law has been introjected rather than integrated. I would add that heteronomy and autonomy reflect two different moral values: Obey the rules. Show mutual respect.

Those who judge right and wrong based on heteronomous principles may adhere to the letter of the law, but their morality is rigid. Their principles are a response to coercion and based on unilateral respect for authority. This morality is likely to fail in the face of complexities, qualifications, and novel circumstances. Those who judge autonomously operate with principles directed toward cooperative social interaction. Their principles are responsive to nuance. Autonomy is an "ideal equilibrium, dimly felt on the occasion of every quarrel and every peace-making, [which] naturally presupposes a long reciprocal education of the children by each other" (Piaget, 1932/1965, p. 318). Piaget thought autonomous morality promotes thoughtful, responsive, and responsible moral action across a range of situations. Heteronomous morality doesn't.

Kohlberg

Kohlberg continued Piaget's focus on sound moral thinking as the basis for sound moral judgment and action. He also continued Piaget's focus on qualitative differences in the cognitive structure underlying moral judgments. But Kohlberg deviated from Piaget by claiming clear evidence for discrete stages in moral reasoning. And he deviated in his depiction of the most mature form.

Kohlberg (1969, 1976) claimed to find six stages of moral reasoning grouped by pairs into three levels. Pre-Conventional morality is based on immediate consequences for self. It includes Stage 1 (do what avoids punishment) and Stage 2 (do what works to your best advantage, as others do). Conventional morality is based on social norms, rules, and laws. It includes Stage 3 (do what's expected of you by yourself and those close to you) and Stage 4 (do what you ought to do to promote society and its institutions). Post-Conventional or Principled morality is based on universal moral principles that at once transcend and undergird the moral conventions of society. It includes Stage 5 (uphold the social contract and the universal values it embodies) and Stage 6 (follow self-chosen universal principles that prescribe respect for the dignity of all individuals).

Kohlberg thought that each of these six stages involves a qualitatively distinct way of thinking about moral issues. He also thought that the six stages are universal, that they are hierarchically arranged, and that movement from one stage to the next occurs in an invariant sequence. We all begin at Stage 1. In our lifetime, many of us progress through Stage 2 only as far as Stage 3 or—more likely—Stage 4. Stage 5 is unusual. Stage 6 extremely rare. The moral principle that Kohlberg considered most central to Post-Conventional morality was a neo-Kantian principle of justice. According to this principle, each individual should be given equal rights in a Kingdom of Ends where no person is treated as a means only but is always intrinsically valued. (Principled reasoning could, of course, be based on some other principle, such as the Utilitarian principle of the greatest good/happiness for the greatest number, as suggested by Greene, 2013.)

Piaget would likely have objected that Kohlberg's principled reasoning can still be heteronomous unless it arises out of day-to-day negotiation in an atmosphere of mutual respect and solidarity. In turn, Kohlberg would likely have objected that Piaget's autonomous negotiation smacks of Conventional morality. Kohlberg might have added that his principled morality isn't simply received from authority figures. It emerges from a concern to identify and adhere to the universal moral principles on which a good and just society must be based. Thus, Kohlberg—like Piaget—felt that mature morality emerges from the individual's social experience. It isn't merely a product of internalizing parental standards. But Kohlberg's concern was for mature morality at a societal level instead of at the face-to-face interpersonal level that concerned Piaget.

Over time, Kohlberg's research came to focus more on the considerations that shape a person's moral judgments than on the nature of the experience from which the judgments arise. He attempted to identify individuals' level of moral reasoning by use of an extensive standardized interview in which a series of hypothetical moral dilemmas is presented. For each dilemma, respondents make a judgment about the right thing to do, then explain in detail the basis for their judgment. A coding system is used to classify the level and stage of moral thought displayed. Illustrative of the dilemmas is Kohlberg's classic, "Heinz and the Drug":

> In Europe, a woman was near death from a special kind of cancer. There was one drug that the doctors thought might save her. It was a form of radium that a druggist in the same town had recently discovered. The drug was expensive to make, but the druggist was charging ten times what the drug cost him to produce. He paid $200 for the radium and charged $2,000 for a small dose of the drug. The sick woman's husband, Heinz, went to everyone he knew to borrow the money, but he could only get together about $1,000, which is half of what it cost. He told the druggist that his wife was dying, and asked him to sell it cheaper or let him pay later. But the druggist said, "No, I discovered the drug and I'm going to make money from it." So Heinz got desperate and began to think about breaking into the man's store to steal the drug for his wife.
>
> Should Heinz have broken into the store to steal the drug for his wife? Why or why not? (Kohlberg, 1981)

Pre-Conventional answers to this dilemma focus on the immediate consequences for Heinz: He shouldn't steal the drug because he'll be put in prison. He should steal it because he'll feel good about saving his wife. Conventional answers focus on living up to the rules and expectations of society: He shouldn't steal the drug because stealing is against the law. He should steal it because that's what is required of a good husband. Post-Conventional answers appeal to universal moral principles: He shouldn't steal it because others may need the drug as much as his wife does and their lives are equally important. He should steal it because saving human life is a more fundamental value than the right to property.

Based on his stage model, how would Kohlberg explain moral failures? He believed that good behavior is predicated on good thought—good in the moral stage it reflects: "To act in a morally high way requires a high stage of moral reasoning. ... Moral stage is a good predictor of action" (Kohlberg, 1976, p. 32). Poor (low-stage) moral thinking produces poor judgment. Poor judgment produces poor moral behavior.

Subsequently, Kohlberg and Candee (1984) elaborated on the relation of moral judgment to moral action in several ways. First, they argued that two kinds of moral judgment are necessary for moral action. I must make a *deontic judgment* that the action is right and obligatory based on some moral principle, standard, or rule, and a *responsibility judgment* that I should follow through and perform this right action. Without the responsibility judgment, I may reason my way to the right thing to do, yet still do nothing. Kohlberg and Candee (1984) claimed: "The stage generates a judgment of what action is right in a particular situation" (p. 54). Further, this judgment "is increasingly likely to be acted on at higher moral stages" (p. 54) because the necessary responsibility judgment is increasingly likely at higher stages (pp. 57–58). (For a similar view of the motivating power of mature moral judgment, see Falk's, 1947, description of motivational internalism in moral philosophy.)

Second, Kohlberg and Candee (1984) argued that the stage-behavior relation is even more complicated because in addition to judgments based on reason, we must take account of judgments based on intuition. Intuitive judgments lack an articulated rational basis. To take account of intuition required a modification of Kohlberg's original stage model. The modification was to distinguish between "Type A" and "Type B" judgments at the lower stages. According to this distinction, some judgments (Type A) are intuitively more oriented to following concrete rules and to personal welfare. Other judgments (Type B) are intuitively more oriented to underlying principles. Type B judgments are "more prescriptive, more reversible, and more universalistic" (p. 63). As a result, Type B judgments produce responsibility judgments more like those at higher stages and so are more likely to produce moral action. But they do this on the basis of intuition rather than principled (Post-Conventional) reasoning. Therefore,

> If we are going to look for a relationship between moral thought and moral action, we should look to those persons who judge that it is right to perform the more moral behavior either by virtue of their Stage 5 [principled] reasoning or the Type B intuitions. (Kohlberg & Candee, 1984, p. 64)

Kohlberg's stage model of moral reasoning has generated much interest but also much criticism. First, evidence that moral reasoning develops universally in the invariant sequence of stages that Kohlberg described has been equivocal at best (Kurtines & Greif, 1974). Second, research to date indicates that the link between level of moral reasoning and moral behavior is far less clear than Kohlberg suggested (see Blasi, 1980; Eisenberg, 1991; Kurtines & Greif, 1974, for reviews). And adding the Type A–Type B distinction has done little to improve matters (Krebs & Denton, 2005, 2006). Third, in addition to Kohlberg's focus on an ethic of justice and fairness, Carol Gilligan (1982) has called for recognition of an ethic of care. Although Gilligan believed that both men and women display reasoning based on justice and reasoning based on care, she claimed that a justice perspective is more characteristic of men and a care perspective more characteristic of women. Subsequent research has supported Gilligan's argument that moral dilemmas can be approached from a perspective of care rather than justice (Gilligan, Ward, & Taylor, 1988; Walker, 1991). But evidence for the claimed sex difference in use of perspectives of justice and care has been limited and weak (Jaffee & Hyde, 2000; Walker, 1991).

Thinking about Kohlberg's analysis of moral judgment and action from the perspective of the value→emotion→motivation→behavior sequence, it seems apparent that the different forms of moral reasoning that Kohlberg categorized into his levels and stages reflect different motives and, in turn, different underlying values. Pre-Conventional reasoning reflects egoistic motivation to promote self-interest without regard for moral considerations. Conventional reasoning reflects egoistic motivation to gain social and self-benefits by adhering to societal standards, a form of instrumental moral motivation. Such reasoning is based on internalization to the level of introjection. Post-Conventional reasoning reflects principlism and intrinsic moral values. It's based on integration. These observations prompt a question: Instead of Kohlberg's focus on differences in reasoning, would increased attention to the different motives, values, and forms of internalization permit better prediction of when moral behavior will and will not occur? I suspect it would.

Judgment Based on Intuition or Sentiment

Psychologist Jonathan Haidt and philosopher Jesse Prinz have also concerned themselves with moral judgment. But their accounts differ sharply from the reason-based accounts of Piaget and Kohlberg. Haidt has focused on intuition, Prinz on sentiment.

Haidt

Kohlberg came to believe that good moral judgment—the kind that leads to right action—can be based on intuition (Type B) as well as on articulated, principled reason. Still, intuition remained a minor theme for him. For Haidt, the emphasis was reversed. In an influential paper entitled, "The Emotional Dog and Its Rational Tail: A Social Intuitionist Approach to Moral Judgment," Haidt (2001) appealed to David Hume's famous dictum, "Reason is and ought only to be the slave of the passions, and can never pretend to any other office than to serve and obey them" (Hume, 1739–1740/1978, p. 415). Haidt argued that most moral judgments are made intuitively. Judgments based on reason are rare:

> Moral judgments appear in consciousness automatically and effortlessly as the result of moral intuitions. . . . People may at times reason their way to a judgment by sheer force of logic, overriding their initial intuition. In such cases reason truly is causal and cannot be said to be the "slave of the passions." However, such reasoning is hypothesized to be rare, occurring primarily in cases in

which the initial intuition is weak and processing capacity is high. (Haidt, 2001, pp. 818–819)

Haidt (2001) argued that reason does play a role in morality, but a very different one from that claimed by either Piaget or Kohlberg. Instead of producing moral judgments, reason functions primarily to provide post hoc justification and rationalization for intuition-based judgments: "Moral reasoning is an effortful process, engaged in after a moral judgment is made, in which a person searches for arguments that will support an already made judgment" (Haidt, 2001, p. 818). Haidt (2001) also saw a role for reason when personal reflection is necessary to adjudicate between conflicting intuitions.

The role of intuition in moral judgment is dramatically illustrated in cases of what Haidt called *moral dumbfounding*. These are cases in which people make quick and confident moral judgments, yet when pushed to explain the reasoning behind their judgment find that they can't. Prototypic, and now almost as famous as Kohlberg's dilemma of Heinz and the Drug, is the case of Julie and Mark:

> Julie and Mark are brother and sister. They are traveling together in France on summer vacation from college. One night they are staying alone in a cabin near the beach. They decide that it would be interesting and fun if they tried making love. At the very least it would be a new experience for each of them. Julie was already taking birth control pills, but Mark used a condom too, just to be safe. They both enjoyed making love, but they decide not to do it again. They keep that night as a special secret, which makes them feel even closer to each other. What do you think about that? Was it OK for them to make love? (Haidt, 2001, p. 814)

Other scenarios that often produce moral dumbfounding include: a family that eats its pet dog after the dog was hit by a car and killed; a woman who cuts up an old flag and uses it to clean her toilet; and a man who cooks and eats a chicken after having used the dead chicken to masturbate (Haidt, Koller, & Dias, 1993). Each scenario is carefully constructed so that no harm is done to anyone. Yet Haidt et al. (1993) found that in both the United States and Brazil many research participants said these actions were wrong. Participants said this, but couldn't give clear reasons why.

Intuition as Affectively Valenced Cognition

Haidt emphasized that the moral intuition he was talking about is a form of cognition. But unlike moral reasoning, it's not based on either deductive or inductive logic. Moral intuition is instead similar to aesthetic judgment in being "affectively valenced" (Haidt, 2001, p. 818). I see or hear about some conduct, and immediately feel positively or negatively toward it. The judgment is often accompanied by an emotional response—a feeling of awe, disgust, or anger if the conduct is someone else's, a feeling of pride, shame, or guilt if it's my own. Haidt et al. (1993) found that affective reactions to the dumbfounding scenarios were better predictors of moral judgments about the behaviors described than were ratings of how much harm was done.

To further explain what he meant by moral intuition, Haidt (2001) appealed to Thomas Jefferson's assertion in the Declaration of Independence that certain truths are self-evident. Haidt claimed that people grasp self-evident moral truths by a process "akin to perception" (p. 814; for a similar view, see Wilson, 1993). He also appealed to the intuitive process in dual-process models of cognition (e.g., Chaiken & Trope, 1999; Zajonc, 1980). But Sinnott-Armstrong, Young, and Cushman (2010) have provided a philosophical analysis of the nature and function of moral intuition that offers a useful cautionary perspective on any claim of self-evident truth, including Haidt's.

Moral Judgment as a Culturally Shaped Innate Evolutionary Adaptation

Haidt (2001) also departed from the assumption of Piaget and Kohlberg that moral judgment is a product of social interaction and conflict resolution. Instead, he suggested that it's an evolutionary adaptation that is "better described as emergent than as learned yet that requires input and shaping from a particular culture. Moral intuitions are therefore both innate and enculturated" (p. 826). But despite his appeal to innate evolutionary adaptation rather than learning, Haidt (2001, p. 828) relied heavily on social learning principles to explain the acquisition of moral intuitions. His doubts about the role of learning in acquiring moral intuitions appeared to be directed toward explicit instruction rather than toward conditioning, modeling, and other forms of social learning.

In a later paper, Haidt and Bjorklund (2008a) took a stronger stance on innateness. They described moral development as an example of "assisted externalization," which they contrasted to internalization: "The basic idea is that morality, like sexuality or language, is better described as emerging from the child (externalized) on a particular developmental schedule rather than being placed into the child from outside (internalized) on society's schedule" (Haidt & Bjorklund, 2008a, p. 206; also see Haidt, 2012; for more on the comparison of moral development to language development, see Hauser, 2006; Mikhail, 2007, 2011; and Rawls, 1971).

What exactly did Haidt and Bjorklund (2008a) mean by assisted externalization? It's hard to know, but they offered some clues. First, they asserted that "moral beliefs and motivations come from a small set of intuitions that evolution has prepared the human mind to develop" (p. 181). Second, they noted that "there are a great many ways to think about innateness" (p. 204). Third, they placed their own view of innateness between what they called the "mildest" extreme (genetically based preparedness to learn a few specific associations, such as fear of snakes) and the "other" extreme (hardwired predisposition to acquire specific abstract cognitive content and responses in many domains—what has been called "massive modularity of mind"). Finally, in the end, Haidt and Bjorklund (2008a) contented themselves with saying that morality is modularized (that is, our brains are genetically prepared to make certain moral judgments) "to some interesting degree" (p. 205).

Where this leaves them on preparedness and externalization remains unclear. (See Carruthers, Laurence, & Stich, 2005, for a range of possibilities.) It seems clear that we humans have a genetically based capacity to think and act morally. Evolution has prepared us in this sense. Of course, we have a genetically based capacity to do anything we can do. It also seems clear that we have some genetically based values, preferences, and desires. We value air to breathe. We value food, drink, sex, moderate temperatures, stable and safe surroundings, pleasure not pain, and so on. We also have social and moral values.

But the degree to which social and moral values are innate in the same way as physical ones—or the degree to which they emerge through assisted externalization as Haidt and Bjorklund (2008a) claimed—is far from clear. Occasionally, Haidt has gone so far as to suggest that moral preparedness "is akin to a kind of taste bud producing affective reactions of liking and disliking when certain patterns are perceived in the social world" (Haidt & Graham, 2007, p. 104). Or that it's an "evolved first draft" which is edited by experience (Haidt, 2012; also see Graham et al., 2013, and Graham et al., 2009). These analogies seem quite loose and fanciful—and highly questionable.

The analogies seem questionable because there's a conspicuous alternative. Social and moral values may emerge as a result of experience and learning as we use our general cognitive skills and personal attributes (gender, temperament, etc.) to pursue basic values and desires within the constraints of our physical and social environment. Prinz (2008), in his argument against the claim that morality is innate, stated this alternative succinctly:

> Most cultures have fire, weapons, religion, clothing, art, and marriage. Many also have taxes, vehicles, and schools. It is unlikely that any of these things are innate. Humans the world over face many of the same challenges, and they have the same cognitive resources. If these two are put together, the same solutions to challenges will often arise. (p. 372)

Add to these two features (same challenges, same cognitive resources) the innate organismic values that we all share, and the room for doubt about the innateness of any specific moral content is apparent—even content that's widespread within and across cultures. To provide but one example, there are good reasons for the children of each new age to rediscover the value of cooperation, as Piaget (1932/1965) observed.

Further, as Darwin pointed out long ago, early learning can produce intuitive responses:

It is worthy of remark that a belief constantly inculcated during the early years of life, whilst the brain is impressible, appears to acquire almost the nature of an instinct; and the very essence of an instinct is that it is followed independently of reason. (Darwin, 1871/1913, p. 124)

The combination of genetically based values, general cognitive skills and personal attributes, environmental demands, internalization via social learning, and emergence based on social interaction (Piaget, Kohlberg) provides a conspicuous alternative to innateness and assisted externality as the source of moral intuition.

Deficient Intuitions May Account for Our Moral Failures

Haidt (2001) said little about moral action and failures to act morally, but what he did say (pp. 824–825) suggests that he shared Kohlberg's assumption that bad moral judgment leads to bad action. Of course, for Haidt it wasn't lack of good thought but lack of good intuition that accounted for bad judgment. To provide support for the assumption that affectively valenced intuitive moral judgment is needed for moral action, Haidt turned to Antonio Damasio's (1994) research on neurological patients with lesions in the ventromedial prefrontal cortex. These brain-lesion patients have trouble knowing what action is best in many everyday situations, including moral ones. Damasio attributed this difficulty to a lack of affective/emotional response to potentially dangerous or socially inappropriate behavioral options.

Damasio's (1994) description of one of these lesion patients, Elliot, is dramatic. Elliot was unable to make effective plans and decisions in his personal life, and he didn't learn from his mistakes. He had these deficiencies despite normal to superior performance on a range of intelligence and personality tests, on tests of his ability to come up with alternative solutions to hypothetical social problems, and even on a Kohlberg measure of moral reasoning. As Elliot himself put it at the end of a session in which he had successfully generated a number of possible ways to act in a given situation, "And after all this, I still wouldn't know what to do!" (Damasio, 1994, p. 49). Damasio concluded that, "The cold-bloodedness of Elliot's reasoning prevented him from assigning different values to different options, and made his decision-making landscape hopelessly flat" (Damasio, 1994, p. 51). From Haidt's (2001) perspective, patients such as Elliot have lost access to moral intuition. They have therefore lost the major basis for moral action.

... or maybe not

But Haidt and Bjorklund (2008b) presented a quite different view of the role of intuition-based judgment in producing moral behavior. They claimed that for most people, moral judgment and moral decision-making aren't closely related. The former concerns evaluation of others' actions, whereas the latter involves selecting our own course of action. And although moral intuitions play an important role in judging the behavior of others, they play little role in producing our own behavior. With something at stake for the self, we rely on reason to weigh the pros and cons of possible actions and to adjudicate among conflicting intuitions (Haidt & Bjorklund, 2008b).

Whether Haidt and Bjorklund (2008b) are right that moral intuition plays little role in producing moral behavior, it certainly seems right that the extensive research inspired by Haidt's ideas about intuitive moral judgments has tended to disregard the role of intuition in guiding our own actions. The focus of the research has been on judging others' behavior. As a result, this research says little about the source of our moral failures. Damasio's (1994) earlier analysis—which accords well with the value→emotion→motivation→behavior sequence from Chapter 1—seems far more pertinent: Lose emotional response to possible value violations and you lose the motivation to act morally.

Prinz

Like Damasio, Prinz (2006, 2007) built a stronger link than Haidt and Bjorklund (2008b) between emotion-based judgment and moral behavior. Invoking Hume's (1739–1740/1978) sentimentalist theory of moral judgment, Prinz claimed, first, that "To believe that something is morally wrong (right) is to have a sentiment of disapprobation (approbation) towards it" (2006, p. 33), and second, that this sentiment is motivating.

To clarify what he meant by a sentiment, Prinz (2006) explained, "As I will use the term, a sentiment is a disposition to have emotions" (p. 34; also Prinz, 2007, p. 84). He also offered an example:

> If you love chocolate, you will feel delighted when you see chocolate cake on the menu, and you will feel disappointed if the waiter then reports that they have run out. Sentiments of approbation and disapprobation are, likewise, constituted by different emotions on different occasions. (Prinz, 2006, p. 34)

This characterization of the relation of sentiments and emotions recalls the discussion in Chapter 1 of the relation between values and emotions—with Prinz's sentiments equated to what I am calling values. Prinz illustrated with the sentiment that killing is morally wrong:

> Can one sincerely attest that killing is morally wrong without being disposed to have negative emotions towards killing? My intuition here is that such a person would be confused or insincere. To support this intuition, we might imagine a person who knows everything non-emotional about killing. She knows that killing diminishes utility and that killing would be practically irrational if we universalized the maxim, thou shalt kill. Would we say of this person that she believes killing is wrong? It seems not. She could believe all these things without having any view about the morality of killing or even any comprehension of

what it would mean to say that killing is wrong. Conversely, if a person did harbor a strong negative sentiment towards killing, we would say that she believes killing to be morally wrong, even if she did not have any explicit belief about whether killing diminished utility or led to contradictions in the will. These intuitions suggest that emotions are both necessary and sufficient for moral judgment. (Prinz, 2006, p. 32)

I would only add that values (sentiments) are necessary for the emotions. As suggested in Chapter 1, need-state emotions evoked by events that threaten our moral values—our standards, principles, and ideals—are motivating. They amplify goal-directed motives, which can lead to behavior to promote our moral values.

Prinz considered his sentimentalist view to be quite compatible with views that make intuition the basis of moral judgment. But he thought his emphasis on the role of emotion provided a more plausible explanation of the self-evident nature of moral judgments than did most intuitionist accounts:

> It is evident to me that Buster Keaton is funny, because he makes me laugh. It is evident to me that chocolate is delicious because it induces pleasure when I taste it. It would be somewhat perverse to demand more evidence than this. .... The judgment that killing is wrong is self-justifying because killing elicits the negative sentiment expressed by that judgment and having the power to elicit such negative sentiments is constitutive of being wrong. (Prinz, 2006, p. 37)

From whence did Prinz think the love of various forms of right or wrong conduct—analogous to the love of chocolate—arise? Not from our evolutionary heritage, at least not in any direct way. Reviewing the relevant research, he found no convincing evidence that we are congenitally disposed to embrace certain moral precepts or even, as Haidt (2012) claimed, to embrace precepts in certain moral domains (Prinz, 2007, 2008). Rather, he suggested that we learn to value culturally transmitted moral standards that provide effective solutions to the problems and challenges of social living we all face. This suggestion takes us back to the earlier sections of the chapter—to the internalization of moral standards and values through social learning and interaction.

How did Prinz account for our moral failures? They're products of deficiencies of moral sentiment and emotion. If we fail to care about (i.e., value) what happens to others and about how they feel, we won't experience the emotions of approbation and disapprobation that motivate us to act morally toward them. To reveal the effects of such emotional deficiency, Prinz (2006, 2007) turned to research on psychopathy. Because of problems learning reinforcement contingencies and internalizing the principles behind these contingencies, psychopaths seem remarkably insensitive both to the distress of other people and to whether causing others distress is morally wrong (Blair, 2009; Blair, Jones, Clark, & Smith, 1997). As a result, Prinz suggested,

I think that psychopaths behave badly because they cannot make genuine moral judgments. They give lip-service to understanding morality, but there is good reason to think that they do not have moral concepts—or at least they do not have moral concepts that are like the ones normal people possess. (Prinz, 2006, p. 32)

What about the moral failures of those of us who aren't psychopaths? Unless psychopathy is far more widespread than all evidence indicates, it's time to ask again how people like you and me—people who seem quite capable of caring about the feelings of others—can violate moral principles we hold dear. Is my distaste for killing so much weaker than my love of chocolate? Have I not internalized my moral standards in the right way? Once again, we're back to issues of character development and social learning.

Summary

I've sketched three different accounts of how we employ our standards, principles, and ideals to make judgments about what conduct is right and wrong in specific situations. We can rely on one or another form of moral reasoning, as argued by Piaget and Kohlberg. We can rely on relatively automatic, gut-level intuitions, as argued by Haidt. We can rely on our emotional reactions and the sentiments (values) that lie behind them, as argued by Prinz. Of the three, Prinz's account aligns most closely with the value→emotion→motivation→behavior sequence from Chapter 1—and with the social learning analysis in the first half of this chapter. Reason-based and intuition-based accounts focus more on the type of cognition involved in making judgments about others' actions and on how those judgments are justified than on how our own moral actions are shaped by underlying moral values. Still, even for these accounts, values lie just below the surface.

CONCLUSION

The social learning tradition in psychology has used empirical data to address questions similar to those raised by Freud—and much earlier by Aristotle—about the development of moral character. Not only do we learn to act morally out of fear of social censure and to garner praise but also we seek to avoid self-censure and gain self-esteem. Principles internalized to the level of introjection are valued extrinsically as instrumental means to the egoistic ultimate goal of seeing ourselves and being seen by others as a good person. Principles internalized to the level of integration are valued intrinsically as ends in themselves. The link to moral action is more tenuous for the former than the latter.

The way we think about and apply our principles can also differ. As young children we're likely to think in terms of concrete, specific rules. But, as Piaget observed, our understanding may be deepened by social encounter, debate, and negotiation with our peers. Over time we come to recognize broader, more fundamental principles that underlie the specific rules. This development enables us to move toward more context-sensitive, reason-based moral judgments and actions. But moral judgments aren't simply the product of reason. Our emotional responses, which reflect our underlying values, also play a central role. They not only prompt intuitive judgments about what's right and wrong but also trigger motivation to promote those values.

Development of character and internalization of moral standards on the one hand, and moral judgment on the other, are often portrayed in opposition. They're cast as alternative sources of moral action. But it seems more appropriate to view them as allies. Character and social learning provide an account of how we acquire our moral values or sentiments. Moral judgment concerns the application of these values to particular events and issues. These judgments assess the rightness of past actions and motivate future ones. Personal deficiency caused by failure to forge either link in this acquisition-application chain can account for moral failures.

And personal deficiency isn't the only cause of our failures. Even if the acquisition-application chain is strong, it can be broken by situational pressure.

3

SITUATIONAL PRESSURE

Moral action—behaving in accordance with our moral values—always occurs in a specific situation. The previous chapter focused on acquisition of moral values and on the psychological processes needed to apply them appropriately. It considered ways that deficiencies of character and judgment can cause moral maladies. This chapter turns to the second standard diagnosis for our moral ills, situational pressure.

PRESSURES THAT CAN PRODUCE MORAL MALADIES

A moral disposition is necessary for moral action but not sufficient. To bring some order to the myriad ways in which characteristics of a situation can keep us from acting morally, it may be useful to identify the steps needed to progress from disposition to action. Then we can consider situational factors that make each step difficult.

Generalizing from the decision sequence for bystander intervention provided by Bibb Latané and John Darley (1970), five steps seem necessary. These steps map easily onto the value→emotion→motivation→behavior sequence from Chapter 1.

1. Perceive one or more personally held moral values (standards, principles, ideals) to be relevant to the current situation.
2. Perceive the situation to provide an opportunity to act in accordance.
3. Experience motivation to uphold the principle(s).
4. Decide to act on this motivation.
5. Act morally.

Failure to take any one of these steps leads to inaction. And situational pressure can make each step difficult if not impossible. Here are some of the pressures that can inhibit each.

Step 1. Perceive Moral Relevance

The first step from principle to action is to recognize that one or more of my moral principles is relevant to the current situation. I need to perceive that my standards of right and wrong conduct have been violated, may be violated, or may be promoted. If I have relevant principles, recognition of that fact might seem inevitable, but it isn't. I can fail to recognize the relevance if I'm overloaded, preoccupied, or if I frame the situation in a way that keeps me from thinking about its moral implications.

Overload

Reflecting on the experience of living in cities, Stanley Milgram (1970) provided his interpretation of the 1964 murder of Kitty Genovese. News media at the time reported that despite her repeated pleading screams, Kitty's neighbors in the Kew Gardens area of Queens, New York, failed to intervene or even summon the police until after she had been fatally stabbed by her attacker. Commentators spoke of apathy and alienation (Rosenthal, 1964, but also see Manning, Levine, & Collins, 2007).

Milgram disagreed. He thought that urban environments bombard us with so much information that we experience overload. To cope, city dwellers employ strategies to limit the amount of information they take in. One strategy is to distinguish between high and low priority information and attend only to the former. Another is to spend less time on each piece of information. A third is to dampen the intensity of information by limiting involvement with other people to sporadic and superficial interaction. An unintended consequence of these strategies can be that what in retrospect is recognized as a morally relevant event—such as Kitty Genovese's cries—isn't recognized as such at the time. Afterward, we may lament, "If only I'd known!"

Consistent with Milgram's analysis, there's evidence that helping a stranger in need is less likely in cities than in towns (Amato, 1983; Korte, 1981; Steblay, 1987). And a series of field studies conducted in the Netherlands found that a city-town difference in helping could indeed be accounted for by differences in information load (Korte, Ypma, & Toppen, 1975). In a more direct test of the effect of information load, Ferne Weiner (1976) had research participants perform a task that involved dealing with two different streams of information. Some dealt with the two streams simultaneously (high-load condition). Others dealt with them sequentially (low-load condition). While participants were performing their task, a young woman entered the room, tripped, and fell. Weiner found that the high-load participants, trying to deal with both streams of information at once, were less likely to offer aid.

Even more subtle forms of overload such as mental fatigue can keep us from perceiving moral relevance (Gino, Schweitzer, Mead, & Ariely, 2011). So can feeling pressed for time. In a study modeled on the Parable of the Good Samaritan, Darley and Batson (1973) found that theological students told to hurry because they were late for an appointment were less likely to try to help a rather scruffy looking young man slumped and groaning in a doorway along their route than were those told they had extra time. Some of the hurried seminarians said afterward that they simply didn't notice him.

Preoccupation

Preoccupation with an ongoing task, even if not overloading, can lead us to miss the moral implications of events. In a clever experiment, David Bersoff (1999) provided possible evidence of such an effect. After participants completed a test for recall of geographical information, they were sent to a disbursement office to collect their payment of $6.25, the amount ostensibly determined by their recall performance. When they arrived, the young woman in the office counted out $8.25, overpaying each participant by $2.00. (Participants had been given a receipt to present to her, and she apparently misread a poorly written 6 as an 8.) Only 20 percent of participants returned the overpayment unless either (a) issues of fairness or care had been made salient (in which case, 45 percent and 50 percent, respectively, returned it) or (b) the participant was directly asked by the woman after she counted out the money, "Is that right?" (in which case, 60 percent said it wasn't, and returned the $2.00).

What accounted for the low return rate in the absence of something to make the moral implications apparent? Bersoff (1999) attributed the low rate to participants' ability to convince themselves that keeping the overpayment was acceptable. But it seems at least as likely that without a prompt many failed to think of the overpayment as a moral issue. Instead, they may have considered it personal good luck—or a mistake to which they shouldn't call attention.

Framing

Situational factors can powerfully affect how we frame events. When something unexpected or ambiguous happens, the way other people interpret it is likely to affect the way we do. Others can call attention to moral aspects of a situation or to its nonmoral aspects, leading us to frame it accordingly. (For examples, see Bazerman & Tenbrunsel, 2011; Gino, Ayal, & Ariely, 2009; Mazar, Amir, & Ariely, 2008.)

Even if others say nothing, they can affect our framing. Imagine you're having breakfast in a coffee shop when suddenly you hear a crash and scream from the back. Is someone hurt? Should you rush to the rescue? Or would that be a foolish overreaction? Unsure, you sit tight and furtively glance to see how the other customers are responding. They're responding just as you—sitting tight. Each of you interprets the inaction of the others as evidence that everyone else thinks nothing needs to be done. The result is a state of *pluralistic ignorance* (Miller & McFarland, 1987) in which you all conclude the situation isn't morally relevant. Classic bystander intervention studies (e.g., Latané & Darley, 1968; Latané & Rodin, 1969) showed that if you had been alone when the crash occurred your conclusion would likely have been quite different.

As described in Chapter 2, both Damasio (1994) and Prinz (2007) suggested that recognition of moral relevance is a product of emotion-based judgment. But what if I'm led to believe that the emotional arousal evoked by a potential moral violation was instead caused by nonmoral aspects of the situation? This misattribution should inhibit my recognition of moral relevance. Results of the emotion-misattribution study by Dienstbier and Munter (1971), also described in Chapter 2, are quite consistent with such a possibility. Participants were more likely to cheat if they believed their feelings of fear and anxiety were a side effect of a vitamin supplement they had taken rather than a reaction to the thought of cheating. Research has also provided evidence of a reverse misattribution effect. If I misattribute emotional arousal produced by nonmoral aspects of the situation to its moral aspects, that can enhance my perception of moral relevance (see the studies by Schnall, Benton, & Harvey, 2008, and Schnall, Haidt, Clore, & Jordan, 2008, described in Chapter 6).

In cases of pluralistic ignorance and misattribution of emotion, situational factors subtly influence how we frame events. In other cases, the situation comes with an explicit frame that leads us to think morality isn't relevant. Some areas of life seem to carry a *moral exemption*. Standards applied elsewhere are set aside. It's said, for example, that "All's fair in love and war." When in love, we may indeed feel free to forego moral niceties of fairness and honesty as we pursue our heart's desire. And a war frame can produce especially dramatic exemptions. In war, many who consider it horribly wrong to kill or abuse other human beings do just that.

To the list of domains in which "all's fair," we may need to add business. Nunner-Winkler (1984) observed that espoused principles of fairness and care often have little effect on business decisions. To take advantage of others is seen as "a legitimate pursuit of business interests, based on the assumption that all market partners can take care of themselves and look out for their own interests" (p. 360). Consider two oft-quoted statements from Adam Smith's *The Wealth of Nations* (1776/1976a):

> It is not from the benevolence of the butcher, the brewer, or the baker, that we expect our dinner, but from their regard to their own interest. (I, p. 18)

> I have never known much good done by those who affected to trade for the public good. It is an affectation, indeed, not very common among merchants, and very few words need be employed in dissuading them from it. (I, p. 478)

A person guided by such texts may feel that moral concerns should be tempered if not set aside entirely when doing business. The Golden Rule takes a new form, "Do unto others as you know they're trying to do to you." Research supports this possibility. Several studies have found that US undergraduates are more likely to act competitively rather than cooperatively toward a peer if the situation is framed as a business transaction instead of as a social exchange (Batson & Moran, 1999; Ross & Ward, 1996).

In addition to a moral exemption for certain domains of behavior, there's *moral exclusion* of certain individuals (Opotow, 1990; Staub, 1990). We may feel that we should behave morally toward some people—kin, comrades, countrymen—but not others. These others are outside our moral circle, beyond the reach of our principles of justice, care, and the like. Stated so bluntly, this exclusion may seem quite incompatible with the universalizing character of many moral principles. But it needn't be. I can hold standards that apply to all people yet still exclude some if I don't consider those excluded to be truly people (de Waal, 2006; Nussbaum, 2014; Vaes, Paladino, Castelli, Leyens, & Giovanazzi, 2003; Zimbardo, 2007). As Peter Singer (1981; also see Pinker, 2011) has emphasized, even though our moral circle has expanded over the centuries, many humans may still lie outside. Their plight isn't seen as a moral issue.

And our moral circle can contract as well as expand. Bernard Weiner (1980) found that if a fellow undergraduate asking to borrow class notes skipped to go to the beach, the request is likely to provoke anger not pity and to arouse no moral concern. Needing the notes is his fault, so we feel no obligation (Weiner, 1995).

The consequences of moral exclusion can be severe. As I discuss at the end of this chapter, in periods of extreme economic difficulty it can spiral into genocide. People who've been inside the moral circle can be pushed out, as were Jews in Nazi Europe. Once outside, their pain, exploitation, humiliation—even extermination—are facts, but no longer facts with moral relevance (Staub, 1989, 1990). The power of situational factors to alter the moral landscape looms large.

Step 2. Perceive an Opportunity to Act Morally

"There was nothing I could do" comes readily to our lips when we fail to act morally. Sometimes it's only a convenient excuse, but not always. Simply because I feel that life or some specific event in life isn't fair doesn't mean that I can see a way to set matters right. In some cases, there really is nothing I can do. History is littered with events that violate our moral standards. Think of slavery, cultural oppression, displacement of indigenous peoples, death marches, and witch burnings. Think of destruction of sacred objects and places. Of rapes, murders, and purges. But history is past. We weren't there and can't rewrite it. There's nothing we can do. Of course, to see some heinous practice as in the past may well prevent us from recognizing similar practices in the present, another example of a failure to perceive relevance (Step 1). Slavery is a case in point.

Present-day moral violations also may be beyond our reach. This can be due either to distance or to the expertise and resources required for effective action. But the line between what's impossible to do and what's possible yet difficult can be both fine and fuzzy. Singer (1999) reminds us that the personal cost involved may lead us to perceive effective action as impossible even when there is something useful we could do were we willing to pay the price.

An effectiveness-driven perception of impossibility may help explain what has been called the *identified-victim effect*—the greater willingness to assist one needy individual than to assist many in need (Kogut & Ritov, 2005; Slovic, 2007; Small, Lowenstein, & Slovic, 2007). Surely, moral prescriptions to help the needy apply regardless of number. Yet the number may affect what we see as possible and, so, affect our response. With many in need, we feel our assistance would be an ineffective drop in the bucket. Such a perception may also help explain the greater willingness to respond to an acute need than to a chronic one. For example, to reach out to the victims of a once-in-a-lifetime tsunami but not to victims of starvation caused by climate change (cf., Miller, 1977).

Finally, we may feel there's nothing we can do because we're already doing something. As noted earlier, one reason for the failure of theological students in a hurry to stop and help a slumped, groaning young man may have been because they failed to notice him as they rushed along. But a follow-up experiment by Batson, Cochran et al. (1978) found that a more likely explanation for the hurry effect is competing responsibility. Their research participants in a hurry were less willing to stop and help a student in apparent need only if the participants knew that the experimenter who sent them to another building really needed them to reach their destination quickly. If prompt arrival wasn't essential, hurry didn't inhibit helping. Rushing to campus to teach a class, I give no thought to whether I should stop and help a stranded motorist. I'm already engaged.

Step 3. Experience Moral Motivation

To take the first two steps—perceive moral relevance, perceive opportunity—brings us to the point of experiencing motivation to act morally, either as an instrumental or as an ultimate goal. But the progression from perception to motivation isn't automatic. As discussed in Chapter 1, if a moral standard we value is violated or threatened, we're likely to feel one or more need-state emotions. These emotions, in turn, inform and amplify our motivation to uphold the standard. But the research of Dienstbier and Munter (1971) and Schachter and Latané (1964) described in Chapter 2 indicates that situational pressure can short-circuit the information and amplification functions of need-state emotions. So, in addition to inhibiting recognition of relevance, either misattribution or suppression of emotional arousal can diminish motivation to act morally.

Thinking back, misattribution and suppression of emotion may have played important roles in the mass killing of Jews by the members of German Reserve Police Battalion 101 (Browning, 1998) and by the Nazi doctors at Auschwitz (Lifton, 1986), described in Chapter 1. Drink and distraction—two sources of suppression of emotion—were prominent features of each situation. And it may have been relatively easy to misattribute any remaining moral feelings. Aversion and disgust at the killing of women and children could be attributed to those being killed rather than to the killing itself. "*They're* the cause of these feelings, the dirty, disgusting, vermin!" Far from serving as alarm-bells that killing is wrong, the feelings could increase motivation to kill.

Our past behavior also can bring pressure to bear. If we've internalized our moral standards only to the level of introjection (see Chapter 2), then we should be motivated to act morally in order to gain the social and self-benefits that come from displaying our moral goodness. But what if we've recently displayed our goodness? As with the effect of a hearty meal on appetite, to have acted morally at Time 1 should diminish our motivation to do so at Time 2.

Consistent with this reasoning, Benoit Monin and Dale Miller (2001) suggested that having recently provided evidence of my moral credentials can reduce my desire to avoid acting in a way that might appear sexist or racist. In a series of experiments, they found evidence of such *moral licensing*. Research participants who had recently acted in a nonprejudiced way were more willing to express politically incorrect and potentially prejudicial opinions. Importantly, a licensing effect was found even when the audience to whom participants expressed these opinions didn't know about the previous display of lack of prejudice. This finding indicates that self-evaluation as moral was at issue, not just evaluation by others. Subsequent research has provided evidence of moral licensing in a range of other settings. For example, charitable contributions are lower after people have written about their moral attributes (Sachdeva, Iliev, & Medin, 2009). Fairness is reduced and cheating increased after "buying green" (Mazar & Zhong, 2010).

Finally, for me to know that others also know about the need for moral action can create a *diffusion of responsibility* (Darley & Latané, 1968). Knowing others know, I may assume that one of them has already addressed the issue—or should. Such assumptions undermine my motivation to act. Darley and Latané suggested that such diffusion could have been an important factor in the lack of response to Kitty Genovese's pleas.

Step 4. Decide to Act on My Moral Motivation

The most frequently discussed situational pressures preventing moral action are those at Step 4. These are pressures that lead me to not act on my moral motivation even when experienced. As with any goal-directed motive, there are both benefits and costs of acting on moral motivation. The major benefit is that my principles are promoted, either as an ultimate goal or as an instrumental means to reach some other goal. Major costs include the time, expense, risk, and effort involved. When the costs outweigh the benefits, I'm likely to decide not to act.

In addition, as suggested by the framework in Chapter 1, moral motives often conflict with other motives. When they do, failure to reach the goals of these other motives is a cost of acting morally. Most obviously and most often, doing what's moral conflicts with my self-interest—my egoistic motives. But acting morally can also conflict with altruism and collectivism when at odds with the interests of individuals or groups for whom I especially care. When such conflicts occur, I'm forced to choose. Depending on the relative strength of the different motives, I may decide that doing what is morally right isn't worth the cost. As mentioned in Chapter 2, Aristotle (1976) spoke of this as weakness of will (also see Hare, 2001). Considerable research has provided data consistent with this motivational-conflict analysis (e.g., Batson, Ahmad et al., 1999; Batson, Batson et al., 1995).

Situational factors that decrease the cost of acting on self-interested motives can tip the scales against morality in this me-versus-morality conflict. Consider the effect of anonymity or a sense of deindividuation (Diener, 1980; Zimbardo, 1970).

As demonstrated by Edward Diener and colleagues (Diener, Fraser, Beaman, & Kelem, 1976), the likelihood is greater that children will take more than their fair share of Halloween candy when in a group and anonymous than when alone and identified—what might be called the *unidentified-actor effect*. Moreover, knowing that others are watching doesn't guarantee that I'll act morally. In fact, public scrutiny too can tip the scales away from acting morally when, for example, I'm concerned that others may attribute my action to ulterior motives such as ingratiation (Jones & Pittman, 1982; Ratner & Miller, 2001).

Milgram's Obedience Studies

High costs and conflicting nonmoral motives aren't the only pressures that keep us from deciding to act on our moral motives. Situational pressure can also pit one moral motive against another. Recall Milgram's (1963) famous obedience studies, in which research participants in the role of Teacher were instructed by the experimenter to continue to deliver seemingly harmful shocks to a Learner, Mr. Wallace (actually a confederate), despite his protests. Many participants complied and continued. Milgram (1974) believed that this compliance was a result of participants having entered an *agentic state* and, so, having shifted moral motives. Both this research and Milgram's interpretation are worth considering in some detail.

The Research

In Milgram's (1963) initial study, research participants were men between the ages of 20 and 50 who responded to a newspaper ad to take part in a memory experiment. Ostensibly assigned randomly to the role of Teacher, their job was to administer a shock whenever the Learner gave a wrong response, each time moving to the next higher shock level across a panel of 30 switches. Voltage designations on the panel ran from 15 volts to 450 volts, and the switches were labeled in groups of four from left to right, "Slight Shock," "Moderate Shock," "Strong Shock," "Very Strong Shock," "Intense Shock," "Extreme Intensity Shock," "Danger: Severe Shock." The last two switches beyond 450 volts were marked "XXX."

For most participants, to continue administering the shocks was extremely difficult after—at 150 volts—Mr. Wallace cried out, "Experimenter, get me out of here! I won't be in the experiment any more! I refuse to go on!" (Milgram, 1974, p. 23). Still, when the experimenter told participants they should continue, most did. At 300 volts, Mr. Wallace shouted in desperation that he would no longer give answers. Hearing this, the experimenter instructed participants to treat no answer as an incorrect answer and to deliver the next level of shock. In his initial report of the research, Milgram (1963) described the tension these events produced in many participants: "Profuse sweating, trembling, and stuttering were typical," and occasionally "nervous laughter" occurred, which in some participants "developed into uncontrollable seizures" (p. 371).

This research wasn't about deficiencies of moral character but about obedience to authority. The participants weren't sadists who enjoyed delivering shocks. They wanted to stop. But the experimenter used a sequence of prods, as needed, to keep them going:

Prod 1. Please continue, *or*, Please go on.
Prod 2. The experiment requires that you continue.
Prod 3. It is absolutely essential that you continue.
Prod 4. You have no other choice, you *must* go on. (Milgram, 1974, p. 21, italics in original)

Two more prods were used in response to specific concerns raised by many participants:

Although the shocks may be painful, there is no permanent tissue damage, so please go on.
Whether the Learner likes it or not, you must go on until he has learned all the word pairs correctly. So please go on. (Milgram, 1974, pp. 21–22)

Thus prompted, 26 of the 40 men in the original study (65 percent) continued delivering shocks to the level marked "XXX." They did so even though Mr. Wallace had long before quit responding and all that was heard from him was ominous silence.

Milgram's Interpretation

Milgram (1974) defined an agentic state as "the condition a person is in when he sees himself as an agent for carrying out another person's wishes." He contrasted this agentic state with an *autonomous state*, "when a person sees himself as acting on his own" (p. 133). Milgram thought that the shift from an autonomous to an agentic state changes the target of responsibility. It transforms our morality.

The most far-reaching consequence of the agentic shift is that a man [or woman] feels responsible *to* the authority directing him [or her] but feels no responsibility *for* the content of the actions that the authority prescribes. Morality does not disappear, but acquires a radically different focus. . . . Language provides numerous terms to pinpoint this type of morality: *loyalty, duty, discipline*, all are terms heavily saturated with moral meaning and refer to the degree to which a person fulfills his obligations to authority. They refer not to the "goodness" of the person per se but to the adequacy with which a subordinate fulfills his socially defined role. (Milgram, 1974, pp. 145–146, italics in original)

Most participants in Milgram's experiments seem to have experienced moral motivation. Indeed, they experienced two conflicting moral motives: I ought to end the Learner's suffering. I ought to follow the experimenter's instructions. Those who shifted to the agentic state were, Milgram believed, more sharply attuned to their responsibility to obey the experimenter. The rights and interests of the Learner faded into the background.

Consider the responses of one obedient participant, a 39-year-old social worker whom Milgram (1974) called Morris Braverman. After giving a few shocks, Braverman began to snicker as he flipped the switches. Soon, Mr. Wallace's screams triggered nervous, uncontrolled laughter. Braverman later explained that this was a reaction to the "totally impossible situation ... of having to hurt somebody. And being totally helpless and caught up in a set of circumstances where I just couldn't deviate and I couldn't try to help" (Milgram, 1974, p. 54). When told he must treat a failure to respond as an error, Braverman dutifully relayed this instruction, "Mr. Wallace, your silence has to be considered as a wrong answer." And he continued to administer shocks with only mild protest but considerable tension. Here are the experimenter's notes on Braverman's last few shocks: "Almost breaking up now each time gives shock. Rubbing face to hide laughter. ... Clenching fist, pushing it onto table" (Milgram, 1974, p. 53).

In the interview immediately after the experiment, Braverman was asked about his reaction.

Experimenter. At what point were you most tense or nervous?

Mr. Braverman. Well, when he first began to cry out in pain, and I realized this was hurting him. This got worse when he just blocked and refused to answer. There was I. I'm a nice person, I think, hurting somebody, and caught up in what seemed a mad situation ... and in the interest of science, one goes through with it. At one point, I had an impulse to just refuse to continue with this kind of a teaching situation.

Experimenter. At what point was this?

Mr. Braverman. This was after a couple of successive refusals and silences. This is when I asked you a question as to whether I have a choice in my teaching method. At this point my impulse was to plead with him, talk with him, encourage him, try to ally myself with his feelings, work at this so we could get this through together and I wouldn't have to hurt him. (Milgram, 1974, pp. 53–54)

On a follow-up questionnaire a year later, Braverman reflected on what he had learned from being in the experiment:

"What appalled me was that I could possess this capacity for obedience and compliance to a central idea, i.e., the value of a memory experiment, even after it became clear that continued adherence to this value was at the expense of violation of another value, i.e., don't hurt someone else who is helpless and not hurting you. As my wife said, 'You can call yourself Eichmann.' I hope I can deal more effectively with any future conflicts of values I encounter." (Milgram, 1974, p. 54)

Here's a summary of Milgram's conclusions based on the behavior of Mr. Braverman and other participants in the obedience experiments:

> Although a person acting under authority performs actions that seem to violate standards of conscience, it would not be true to say that he loses his moral sense. Instead, it acquires a radically different focus. He does not respond with a moral sentiment to the actions he performs. Rather, his moral concern now shifts to a consideration of how well he is living up to the expectations that the authority has of him. In wartime, a soldier does not ask whether it is good or bad to bomb a hamlet; he does not experience shame or guilt in the destruction of a village: rather he feels pride or shame depending on how well he has performed the mission assigned to him. (Milgram, 1974, p. 8)

Not only Milgram's Teachers who went all the way, but also many of the soldiers at My Lai seemed to switch to an agentic state, as did many of the Nazi doctors at Auschwitz. They resolutely pursued one moral course—obeying orders, even orders to kill. Pressure from above trumped any conflicting moral desire to not harm innocents.

To bring the agentic state closer to day-to-day life, Milgram (1974) offered an example:

> Those who are skeptical of this effect might observe the behavior of individuals organized in a hierarchical structure. The meeting of a company president and his subordinates will do. The subordinates respond with attentive concern to each word uttered by the president. Ideas originally mentioned by persons of a low status will frequently not be heard, but when repeated by the president, they are greeted with enthusiasm. There is nothing especially malicious in this; it reflects the natural response to authority. (p. 144)

Natural, but also pernicious when it leads one moral motive—to obey—to overpower all others.

The Stanford Prison Experiment

Social roles often carry with them both implicit and explicit rules for expected behavior. These rules put pressure on people who occupy the roles. In Milgram's studies the role of Teacher was in itself relatively benign. It required participants to help the Learner perform better on a memory task. Of course, the help involved punishing wrong responses with increasingly strong electric shocks. This cast a shadow over the benign purpose and set the stage for pressure from authority and for the moral dilemma that ensued. Other roles make explicit demands on the occupant to inflict harm and duress. Think of the role of soldier or prison guard. People in these roles receive orders not just instructions. And even without direct orders, the roles require that occupants be ready to "do what's necessary" to defeat, to restrain, to subdue. In such cases, the role itself can produce pressure to act against our moral values in the line of duty.

Philip Zimbardo (2004) and his collaborators dramatically illustrated the effect such a role can have in what has come to be called the Stanford Prison Experiment. To get participants, they placed an ad in the local newspaper asking for young men between the ages of 18 and 30 to take part in a simulated prison experience last-ing two weeks. From almost a hundred responses to the ad, the 24 men evaluated as most normal and healthy were selected to participate. These 24 were randomly assigned to be either prisoners or guards, 12 to each role. The 12 prisoners were to remain in a simulated prison set up in the basement of the psychology building at Stanford University day and night for two weeks. The 12 guards were to work 8-hour shifts, with three guards on duty at a time. The guards were responsible for keeping the prison secure and the prisoners under control.

To start the experiment, prisoners were subjected to a realistic surprise arrest by officers from the Palo Alto Police Department. They were then booked at the police station and taken to the prison, where each was dressed in a loose-fitting smock with a prison ID number. The guards, when on duty, wore military-style uniforms and silver-reflecting sunglasses to enhance anonymity. At any one time, nine prisoners were on "the yard," three to a cell.

Although scheduled to go 2 weeks, the simulated prison was shut down after just 6 days. Zimbardo (2004) explained why:

> Pacifistic young men were behaving sadistically in their role as guards, inflicting humiliation and pain and suffering on other young men who had the inferior status of prisoner. Some "guards" even reported enjoying doing so. Many of the intelligent, healthy college students who were occupying the role of prisoner showed signs of "emotional breakdown" (i.e., stress disorders) so extreme that five of them had to be removed from the experiment within the first week. (p. 40)

Their role as guards, and the pressure this role placed on them, led young men who could just as easily have been assigned to be prisoners to inflict harsh and cal-lous treatment on their peers. And it happened very quickly. What might be the effects of longer-term situational pressure on moral action? Before addressing this question, we need to consider Step 5.

Step 5. Act Morally

Even the decision to act on moral motivation doesn't ensure moral action. We can't always achieve what we intend. Insurmountable obstacles or other more pressing demands sidetrack the planned course of action.

"The road to hell is paved with good intentions." Stumbling on Step 5 isn't the sort of failure to which this quip refers. It refers to a willingness to be satisfied with wishing good rather than doing good. Acting morally, although desired, isn't worth the cost. This is a failure at Step 4. But even if you decide to act morally, situational pressures can intervene. You may arrive too late. Or what's needed may turn out to require skills or resources you don't have. Or your plans may be thwarted by circumstances, or by the action of others. When such things happen, we may blame ourselves for our failure to act, and others may blame us too. But, although failure at this final step can be tragic, it doesn't raise doubt about the nature and function of morality. Rather, it points to our fallibility and lack of omnipotence.

SITUATIONAL PRESSURE OVER TIME

We've already seen some indication of the effect of situational pressure over time. In Milgram's obedience studies, participants were under pressure from the experimenter for less than an hour. Still, Milgram (1974) felt the sequential nature of the action was important. The shocks gradually rose in intensity. The first was only 15 volts. There was no indication that it caused any harm or even discomfort. By the time Mr. Wallace began to protest, participants had delivered a number of increasingly intense shocks. To stop at that point would call into question what they had already done. It was easier to minimize or rationalize and keep going. Imagine the internal monologue: "The shocks are in a good cause, research on memory. . . . The experimenter says there's no tissue damage. . . . He says we must continue, and he's in charge. He must know it's OK. . . . This next shock is only a little stronger than the one I just gave. . . . Surely the shocks aren't as bad as they seem. Wallace must just be a wimp."

Not able to anticipate how events would unfold, participants were well down the path before discovering that it led to a moral precipice. Had the experimenter sat participants in front of the shock machine and told them to begin with the switches marked "Danger: Severe Shock" or had Mr. Wallace protested vehemently from the outset, the number of participants willing to proceed would likely have dropped considerably. But neither was true. By the time most participants started to worry that what they were doing was wrong, they had a history of self-incriminating behavior.

> If he [the participant] breaks off, he must say to himself: "Everything I have done to this point is bad, and I now acknowledge it by breaking off." But, if he goes on, he is reassured about his past performance. Earlier actions give rise to discomforts, which are neutralized by later ones. (Milgram, 1974, p. 149)

Participants who continued sought to justify doing so in order to bring it in line with their moral self-image. Justification can involve any of the processes that Bandura (1991, 1999) listed as sources of moral disengagement (see Chapter 2). But in the case we're considering now, the justification is sought after the person has acted questionably rather than before. It sets the stage for even more questionable future action and for more justification. The twig is bent, and the tree begins to grow.

Guards in the Stanford Prison Experiment weren't given explicit orders or prods to humiliate and abuse. But they were under role-related pressure for days not minutes. And once again, gradual escalation of morally questionable behavior was apparent. Harsh treatment of the prisoners that would have been thought wrong at the outset was commonplace by the end.

Milgram's (1974) participants were under situational pressure for less than an hour. Zimbardo's (2004) guards for several days. Extend the parameters of time and space, and the escalation amplifies. Imagine you're a member of German Reserve Police Battalion 101. You're in Poland, many kilometers from home without the support and guidance of family and friends, under pressure from your superiors and peers to do your part to help the battalion complete its difficult mission. And you live in this world all day every day for months. Imagine you're a Nazi doctor or guard at Auschwitz. You know that if you don't perform your distasteful duties, you're apt to be demoted, disgraced, or—far worse—deployed to the Eastern front, where what awaits is discomfort, danger, and quite possibly death. Imagine you're a soldier under Lieutenant Calley's command at My Lai, in hostile territory. You've seen buddies wounded and killed. You're angry and afraid. Moreover, you know that refusal to obey orders in combat can mean court martial.

John Darley (1992) summarized the psychology involved:

> The essence of the process involves causing individuals, under pressure, to take small steps along a continuum that ends with evildoing. Each step is so small as to be essentially continuous with the previous ones; after each step, the individual is positioned to take the next one. The individual's morality follows rather than leads. Morality is retrospectively fitted to previous acts by rationalizations involving "higher goods," "regrettable necessities," and other rationalizations mentioned by Bandura and others. (p. 208)

Situational Pressure in Organizational Settings

Darley (1992) didn't stop with this summary. He took our analysis of the effects of situational pressure an important step farther by turning attention to organizational settings. Organizations play a major role in modern society. Most of us work, study, play, and perhaps pray in such settings. They add an extra layer of pressure. Relevant organizations include military and police forces; corporations; manufacturers; accounting and investment firms; government agencies; political, educational, research, and religious organizations—even sports teams, fraternities, and sororities.

Some Features of Organizational Life

Organizations typically share several important features. First, most have a hierarchical structure. Whether in the military or in manufacturing, higher-ups provide directives—sometimes explicitly stated, sometimes only implied—to those closer to the ground. And the higher-ups have the power to punish those who fail to do as directed. Second, the organizations we join, whether by choice or by birth, almost always already exist. They come with roles, rules, and norms in place, some clearly defined but many not. We must learn to fit in and function effectively within this preexistent organizational reality. Whether as a US soldier in Viet Nam, a Nazi doctor at Auschwitz, or a new hire at a brokerage firm, the newcomer faces strong pressure to learn the ropes and get up to speed. Scrambling to do so, we rarely think of challenging or changing the reality. And if we do, the attempt is likely to be summarily dismissed. It may even lead to summary dismissal. The way things are is the way they will be. We try to find our place, often with a sense of desperation. In the process, we take an important initial step of commitment to the organization and its practices.

Third, if the organization is of any size, the newcomer likely has only a limited understanding of how the organization as a whole works and what it does. My responsibility is to install the water pump on each frame as it comes down the assembly line, not to build an entire auto. The brakes aren't my responsibility. Indeed, even the water pump isn't, only that it's correctly installed. Defects can creep into the brakes—or the water pump—and I won't know for months, perhaps years. Trying to do my job as best I can, I'm not likely even to think about possible defects. And once I learn the routine, I'm even less likely to think about them. My job becomes automatic, mindless.

Fourth, by coordinating the resources and efforts of many, organizations can accomplish tasks that individuals can't. But in pursuit of their grand long-term goals, organizations incur substantial costs. These *sunk costs* (Staw & Ross, 1987) produce inertia. They can prevent people in the organization from changing course even when it's clear the present course isn't leading to the desired end. It's hard to admit a mistake, especially a very costly one.

These four features of organizational life may seem innocent enough. Yet they can create an environment that, quite unintentionally, breeds bad results. Those who designed the Pinto gas tank never intended for it to rupture in low-speed rear-end collisions. Those who installed the gas tanks and those who sold the cars likely never knew this was even a possibility. Yet it happened, and people died in flames. And that was only the beginning.

Such a tragedy brings those in the organization abruptly to a point of awareness. The deaths can't be denied. And in retrospect it may seem that there was at least some forewarning of the possibility. Darley (1992) again summarized,

> The moral essence of the situation is this: An organization has unforeseeably, carelessly, or in some sense willfully harmed others. In the clear light of hindsight, to the organizational higher-ups, it must seem, as it seems to the potential outside observers, that the negative outcomes were at least foreseeable and perhaps, in the complex sense that an organization can be said to intend something, "intended." There may be internal evidence that all the information was available within the organization to know that the effects would be harmful. Thus, were they to publicly or privately admit to the existence of the outcomes, or

their role in producing them, they would be publicly convicted of harm doing and internally faced with feeling shame and guilt. These are negative outcomes, which do not fit in with the people's dim memories of the paths that led them to the present predicament. At this point, it must be extraordinarily tempting to "cover up" the evidence if it is possible to do so. (Darley, 1992, p. 215)

A key phrase in this summary is "at least foreseeable." Research suggests that it's not necessary to have foreseen the negative consequences of my actions for these consequences to produce cognitive dissonance—in this case, dissonance between cognitions such as "I'm a well-intentioned, good, moral person" and "I've contributed to causing serious harm to innocents." All that's necessary is that I see the consequences as foreseeable, as something I should have been able to anticipate (Wicklund & Brehm, 1976; also see Tavris & Aronson, 2007).

How do I deal with such dissonance? I have several options. I can accept that I was culpable and revise my beliefs either about my own goodness and morality or about my competence. Alternatively, I can deny that I was a party to the harmful action. I was out of the loop; *they* did it. Or I can minimize the consequences, denying that what seems harmful really is. There's no good evidence that cigarettes cause cancer. Or I can conclude that the victims are to blame. Careless driving caused the gas tank ruptures.

Here we encounter a fifth feature of institutional life. Its momentum. The personal, social, and material costs argue strongly against admitting I did wrong. Denial is far less costly, at least in the short run. But denial leads almost inevitably to attempts at cover-up. A cover-up usually starts by the withholding of information. But this soon leads to destroying and falsifying it. Denial and cover-up also lead to continuing the harmful practices because, as was true for Milgram's participants, to stop now would be tantamount to confession. I find myself violating principles held dear to save my own honor and dignity, as well as the honor and dignity of the organization. Acting immorally in the name of morality.

Diffusion of responsibility and fragmentation of responsibility, both of which are common in organizations, make denial and cover-up easier (Darley, 1996; also see Dana, Lowenstein, & Weber, 2012). Earlier, I noted that the responsibility to do right can diffuse. So can the responsibility to stop wrong. Organizations involve collective action, and there are almost always others to whom I can point. They should have done something. They're as much to blame as I.

Fragmentation of responsibility occurs when the left hand doesn't know what the right hand is doing—or when I can convince myself this is the case. I did my job. Others did theirs. Together, our efforts may have produced great harm, but I wasn't responsible for that, only for doing my job. Consider Adolf Eichmann's explanation at his trial:

> With the killing of Jews I had nothing to do. I never killed a Jew, or a non-Jew, for that matter—I never killed any human being. I never gave an order to kill either a Jew or a non-Jew. I just did not do it. (Arendt, 1963, p. 22)

Jo-Ann Tsang (2002) interprets.

> The nature of the Nazi killing machine enabled Eichmann to make this claim;
> the labor was in fact divided up, and he never really did have to kill anyone with
> his own hands or give direct orders to kill. Instead, he gave orders for shipments
> of Jews to be moved to concentration camps, where, although death was certain,
> he was not the one who directly caused the death. In fact, the work was divided
> up such that the individuals directly involved in killing were Jewish prisoners
> themselves. (p. 41)

Organizational Pressure in Action

Some organizations intend to inflict harm, like the one carrying out the Final
Solution. Such organizations usually work to make it possible for the people within
them to maintain a moral self-image. This is achieved not only by fragmenting
responsibility but also by, on the one hand, presenting the harm as a necessary
means to achieve a moral end and, on the other, dehumanizing, derogating, and
blaming those harmed. "The Jews are to blame; they brought it on themselves." Far
less extreme but sufficient to bring financial ruin to many, stockbrokers at Salomon
Brothers were encouraged to think of their clients as sheep to be fleeced. This made
it easier to dupe the clients into buying bonds the company knew were about to drop
in value and wanted to unload (Lewis, 1989; also see Smith, 2012).

Fortunately, most organizations don't intend harm. Yet the features described
can still produce it. To provide a concrete illustration, Darley (1996) took advantage
of Kermit Vandivier's (1972) first-hand report of the sequence of events that led B. F.
Goodrich to provide defective brakes to Ling-Temco-Vought Corporation (LTV) for
the US Air Force A7-D light attack airplane. At the time, Vandivier worked as a
data analyst and technical writer at Goodrich. The case is especially telling because
Goodrich employees had no desire to do wrong. But the features of organizational
life pushed them inexorably in that direction.

According to Vandivier, the process began when John Warren, a highly competent but prickly design engineer, made a calculation error that led him to propose a brake design for the A7-D that required only four disks not five. The less
expensive four-disk design enabled Goodrich to submit a highly competitive
bid and win the coveted LTV contract. Warren was made project engineer, and
a young engineer named Searle Lawson was assigned to finalize the design for
production. Lawson's job was to find the best material for the brake linings. After
testing a number of materials, all of which overheated and failed, Lawson went
back to Warren's calculations and found the error. Correcting it showed that a
four-disk brake had too little surface area to stop the aircraft without overheating.
"The answer to the problem was obvious but far from simple—the four-disk brake
would have to be scrapped and a new design, using five disks, would have to be
developed" (Vandivier, 1972, p. 8).

Powerful forces resisted this move. To switch to a five-disk brake would be costly and would put the project badly behind schedule. Moreover, having assumed that a workable lining material would be found, people at Goodrich had already reported to LTV that preliminary tests on the four-disk brake were quite successful. How could they go back on their claim? At a more personal level, Warren would have to admit a serious design error and, worse, that a rookie caught his mistake. Despite Lawson's clear evidence, Warren refused to accept that the four-disk brake was inadequate.

Lawson took his evidence one step up the corporate ladder to projects manager Robert Sink. But Sink was the person who had prematurely assured LTV that the four-disk system would work. He sent Lawson back to try more linings. As the date for flight tests approached, others at Goodrich became aware of the problem. In Vandivier's (1972) words, "It was no longer possible for anyone to ignore the glaring truth that the brake was a dismal failure and that nothing short of a major design change could ever make it work" (p. 11). Darley (1996) described the plight of those involved: "To their dismay, they saw the Goodrich organization marching toward delivering a brake that would inevitably fail when it was flight tested, causing acute danger for the test pilots" (p. 30).

More pressure. A team of LTV engineers visited Goodrich to see the brake in action. Presumably out of organizational loyalty, Goodrich engineers managed to hide the looming crisis and prevent the LTV team seeing any tests. In so doing, there was a shift from not volunteering troubling information to actively withholding it in order to mislead the LTV engineers. The cover-up quickly escalated.

When the brake entered its qualification-test phase prior to flight tests, procedures were adjusted to hide failure. Lawson, the original whistleblower, had by now yielded to pressure from above—from Sink he said—and instructed a technician to miscalibrate a pressure gauge so that it gave inaccurate but more favorable readings. Vandivier (1972) reports that Lawson told him, "Regardless of what the brake does on test, it's going to be qualified" (p. 15). Vandivier repeated this remark to Ralph Gretzinger, the test lab supervisor, who responded, "No false data or false reports are going to come out of this lab" (Vandivier, 1972, p. 16).

As organizational pressure for a positive report increased, Gretzinger angrily objected to his boss Russell Line, the senior executive in the section. According to Vandivier (1972), Gretzinger returned from his meeting with Line shaken and talking of the two sons he needed to put through college. Gretzinger had agreed to a compromise in which the test lab would do the graphic presentation for the report, but "someone upstairs will actually write the report" (Vandivier, 1972, p. 17). Reframing his moral obligation by fragmenting responsibility and narrowing perspective, Gretzinger explained, "We're just drawing some curves, and what happens to them after they leave here, well, we're not responsible for that" (Vandivier, 1972, p. 17). Vandivier recalls his thoughts on hearing Gretzinger's words:

He was trying to persuade himself that as long as we were concerned with only one part of the puzzle and didn't see the completed picture, we really weren't doing anything wrong. He didn't believe what he was saying, and he knew I didn't believe it either. It was an embarrassing and shameful moment for both of us. (p. 17)

At this point, Vandivier went to Line and raised the prospect of a test pilot being injured or killed when the brakes failed. Line replied, "I have no control over this thing. Why should my conscience bother me? . . . I just do as I'm told, and I'd advise you to do the same" (Vandivier, 1972, p. 19). Now thinking of his own seven children and the house he had recently bought—and knowing that if he refused to "do the same" he would either be fired or have to resign—Vandivier agreed to join Lawson in drafting the graphic presentation in a way that included changing and occasionally fabricating data to hide the fact that the four-disk brake had failed qualification. He thought he'd done all he would have to do.

But when the draft was sent on to the chief engineer for narrative to be added, it was bounced back with instructions to write the complete report, including the narrative. Vandivier complied.

As far as I was concerned, we were all up to our necks in the thing anyway, and writing the narrative portion of the report couldn't make me any more guilty than I already felt myself to be. (Vandivier, 1972, p. 23)

He wrote the narrative. But to salve his conscience added a sentence in the conclusion stating that the four-disk brake assembly "does not meet the intent or the requirements of the application specification documents and therefore is not qualified" (Vandivier, 1972, p. 24). He expected this sentence would be changed by somebody else, as it was. Vandivier, Lawson, and Warren all refused to sign the report, so it was forwarded without signature.

The report was finalized and submitted to both LTV and the Air Force. Four-disk brakes were delivered to LTV, and flight testing began. Fortunately, no pilots were injured during testing. But after a number of flight tests that included two low-speed lockups on landing—reportedly, in one case the plane skidded along the runway for nearly 1,500 feet before stopping—it was clear that the four-disk brakes weren't adequate. Still, Goodrich tried to hold the line. Vandivier and Lawson didn't. They secretly consulted an attorney, who referred them to the FBI, which began an undercover investigation.

After the brake's failure, the Air Force rescinded approval of the qualification report and insisted on seeing the testing raw data. At Goodrich, Sink called a meeting where he said that they were going to level with LTV and tell them the whole truth. Vandivier (1972) says he asked, "Isn't it going to be pretty hard for us to admit to them that we've lied?" (p. 26). Sink's reply was, "We're not really lying. All we were doing was interpreting the figures the way we knew they should be. We were just exercising engineering license" (Vandivier, 1972, p. 27).

Several months later, Vandivier and Lawson resigned. In another ten months, a congressional hearing was convened, at which Sink denied any wrongdoing on the part of Goodrich and explained that changing data on qualifying reports was normal procedure. Goodrich had by that time supplied a workable five-disk brake to LTV at no additional cost. The company received no sanctions, but the day following the hearing the Department of Defense made sweeping changes in its inspection, testing, and reporting procedures.

Darley (1996) reviewed the interplay of organizational pressure and psychological process that step-by-step produced this sad sequence of events:

> Poor calculations [by Warren], made under time pressure, caused the corporation to commit to manufacture a product that was soon discovered to be bound to fail, and fail dangerously. Costs were incurred that would be sunk costs if that realization of failure were allowed. The costs were not only literal costs spent on subassemblies but—perhaps more powerfully—costs of loss of individual and corporate face. In this hierarchical organization, the possibilities of lost jobs must have been apparent. With these considerations in place, all the concrete decisions taken were tilted in the direction of continuation of the flawed course of action. Loyalties to the immediate group were mobilized. The possible harm caused by possible product failure was probabilistic and remote, and only unknown others were at risk. Under hierarchical pressures, individual responsibilities were redefined and narrowed, so that each person would continue to participate in the flawed course of action. Superiors simultaneously arranged "not to know" of the flaw and reinforced the hierarchical pressures to continue to fragment the responsibility of the individuals. These intertwined processes inevitably led to the production of a product that would certainly fail. (p. 34)

That such a sequence could occur among well-intentioned engineers and technical staff at a respected corporation like Goodrich underscores how pervasive organizational pressure can be. It isn't limited to the police, prison guards, and the military. Every organization is vulnerable.

Situational Pressure in Society at Large

Ervin Staub (1985, 1989) sought to identify situational factors that contribute to society-wide and government-sanctioned mass killing of innocents in cases of genocide, including the Holocaust. He pointed to many of the same organizational pressures noted by Darley (1992). But Staub broadened his perspective to also include pressures coming from the economic and historical context. Among the pressures already discussed, he placed special emphasis on three.

Three Familiar Pressures

First is a powerful hierarchical political structure that demands unquestioned loyalty and allegiance. The government takes a strong stand and assumes responsibility for ensuing events, pressuring the populace to adopt a mindset akin to Milgram's (1974) agentic state.

Second is the behavior of others in the society. Staub distinguished two main types of others whose behavior produces pressure. There are the *active supporters of and participants in the mass killing*. They create pressure by providing a model for "appropriate" behavior in the situation. They also provide evidence of popular support for government policy. And they extend the power of the government by creating fear that any opposition to policy will be reported and punished.

There are also the *bystanders*. Staub (1989, pp. 86–88, 151–158, 164–166) considered their behavior especially important. Early in the chain of events that lead to genocide, active participants may be visible and vocal, but they're usually a small minority of the populace. The majority are bystanders who only witness—perhaps with surprise and concern—the behavior of active participants. Most in Germany in 1938 were well aware of the broken shop windows, looting, and destruction of Kristallnacht but took no part. They were quite innocent. Yet, as Staub (1985) pointed out, to be aware yet do nothing is to do something:

> Even limited participation in cruelty—such as boycotting Jewish stores in Germany as demanded by the Nazis, or passivity in the face of cruelty . . .—can lead to acceptance and justification of, and even direct participation in, the mistreatment of others. (p. 78)

An outcry of protest when unfair, unjustified, and immoral actions first appear can be very effective in stopping the escalation toward genocide. Staub (1989, p. 87) cited as examples the success of the protests in Denmark, Bulgaria, and parts of Italy against the Nazi treatment of Jews. But to protest requires courage, especially when you don't know how other bystanders feel about the mistreatment and persecution, and when speaking out can provoke anger because it threatens the moral self-image of those who remain silent (Monin, Sawyer, & Marquez, 2008). As a result, "In a totalitarian system usually no dissenting opinions are publicly expressed, and any that are tend to come from discredited minorities or political groups" (Staub, 1985, p. 73).

Bystanders may oppose the mistreatment but be uncertain whether others also oppose. So they wait and watch to see how the people around them respond. Those around them do the same. The result is pluralistic ignorance, as discussed earlier. No one is objecting to the mistreatment, so each bystander concludes that others must not be troubled by it. The consequences can be deadly:

> Lack of reaction by people at home and of protest by people in the outside world can confirm perpetrators' faith in what they are doing. Hitler took the limited response, both in Germany and in the outside world, to his persecution of the Jews as evidence that the whole world was in favor—though he was the only one who had the courage to act. (Staub, 1985, p. 79)

This situation leads us to Staub's third emphasis, one we already heard from both Milgram (1974) and Darley (1992). There's a gradual step-by-step escalation of mistreatment and persecution in which each step taken makes the next more likely. Staub (1989) called this "the continuum of destruction" (p. 17, also see pp. 116–127). Kristallnacht is a step toward the round-ups and seizure of property, which is a step toward deportation and the death camps. Importantly, Staub pointed out that not only active participants but also bystanders experience the pressure of their past action pushing them toward the next step. Failure to object to Kristallnacht made it harder to object to the round-ups, and so on. Passive acquiescence escalates among bystanders, paralleling the escalation of mistreatment and persecution among active participants. But, conversely and again importantly, moral action can escalate as well. As noted in Chapter 2, early protest evolved step-by-step into a major rescue effort in the French village of Le Chambon-sur-Lignon (Hallie, 1979).

Four Novel Ones

Staub (1985, 1989) highlighted four additional sources of society-level pressure. First, societies that engage in genocide have typically faced a period of unusually *difficult life conditions* (Staub, 1989, pp. 35–50). The difficult conditions aren't only economic but also psychosocial. They include feelings of frustration and anger at the economic difficulties and of wounded national and cultural pride. People sense that things have gone badly wrong and something must be done to set them right.

National and cultural history is a second novel source of pressure. It can provide a context in which to understand the difficult conditions and what should be done. History can contribute at both an interpretative and a factual level. Interpretatively, if a society views its history in terms of what might be called a *resurrection myth*, this view is likely to contribute to the sense of need to have something done. Resurrection myths frame the national and cultural history as a progression from a past time of grandeur and superiority to the present decline into difficulty and thwarted greatness due to corruption by alien forces, which is to be followed by a return to former glory by purging the nation of the corrupting forces. Such myths lead to a search for what or who must be removed to rise again.

Factually, if there are groups within the society that are seen as historically different from the majority—especially groups that have been targets of prejudice and persecution in the past—these groups are prime suspects. They're likely to be seen as contributing to if not creating the current difficulties. *They* display the traits and behaviors that have brought *us* low. *They* are the cancer that must be removed. Freed from their corrupting influence, our return to glory is assured.

These historical forces are likely to produce a third societal pressure—*scapegoating the target group or groups* as the cause of any new difficulties. Staub quoted Tertullian's description of the scapegoating of Christians by the Romans in the third century:

> They take the Christians to be the cause of every disaster to the state, of every misfortune to the people. If the Tiber reaches the wall, if the Nile does not reach the fields, if the sky does not move or if the earth does, if there is a famine, or

if there is a plague, the cry is at once, "The Christians to the Lions." (Staub, 1989, p. 49)

In discussing scapegoating, Staub (1985, 1989, pp. 79–80, 163) pointed out that when action is taken to purge the society by persecuting and killing innocents, this action threatens the widely held belief in a just world (Lerner, 1980). You might think that such a belief would inhibit these acts, but it may instead encourage them. The sense of order and security I get from my belief that "people get what they deserve and deserve what they get" can lead me to blame innocent victims for their fate. If I can convince myself that they deserve to suffer, then their suffering is just and my belief secure.

A fourth situational pressure that often contributes to the movement of a society toward genocide is the *presence of a charismatic, fanatical leader*. Staub (1989, pp. 23–24) argued that a fanatical leader is neither necessary nor sufficient to move a society to mass killing. But within the context of the other situational pressures described, such a leader can have major impact. Hitler is the obvious example.

Under the influence of these combined pressures, "at the extreme, a complete reversal of morality may take place, so that the murder of some human beings becomes what's morally good, a service to humanity" (Staub, 1985, p. 77). To illustrate this reversal, Staub turned to testimony at the Nuremburg Trials by a Nazi who worked at Belzec, one of the extermination camps. This man recalled a conversation about whether burying the bodies might be unwise because it would leave evidence of what had been done. When another man asked, "Wouldn't it be more prudent to burn the bodies instead of burying them? Another generation might take a different view of these things," the man proudly responded:

"Gentlemen, if there is ever a generation after us so cowardly, so soft, that it would not understand our work as good and necessary, then, gentlemen, National Socialism will have been for nothing. On the contrary we should bury bronze tablets saying that it was we, we who had the courage to carry out this gigantic task." (Staub, 1989, pp. 83–84)

History provides far too many examples of such courage.

CONCLUSION

The steps leading from moral dispositions to moral action are several, and it's easy to trip. These steps occur at different points in the value→emotion→motivation→ behavior sequence. First, under the pressure of overload, preoccupation, pluralistic ignorance, misattribution of emotion, moral exemption, moral exclusion, and other framing effects, we may fail to recognize the relevance of our moral values to events around us. Second, even if we recognize their relevance, we may fail to see any way to promote them in the particular situation. Perception of impossibility is especially likely when what we could do is personally costly or when we're already committed elsewhere. Third, even if we see that something can be done, situational factors may sap the strength of our motivation. Or may lead us to feel that we need do nothing, that others will or should act. Our sense of responsibility is diffused.

If we manage to take these first three steps, we find ourselves motivated to act morally. But we may decide not to act on this motivation for a number of reasons. The costs outweigh the benefits, conflicting motives are stronger, we defer to the wishes or orders of others, or we feel the pressure of role expectations. Finally, even if we decide to act, our good intentions may be thwarted by a lack of resources or ability, or by circumstances beyond our control.

The power of situational pressure to inhibit the expression of our moral values increases dramatically when the pressure is applied over time in organizations and in a larger political and historical context. In these settings, situational pressure can not only inhibit moral action, it can push us toward immorality in the name of morality. It can transform into a praiseworthy moral act behavior that, were it not for the setting and persistent pressure, we would consider deeply wrong. It can change our moral values themselves. As Bandura (1991) summarized, "It requires conducive social conditions rather than monstrous people to produce heinous deeds. Given appropriate social conditions, decent, ordinary people can be led to do extremely cruel things" (pp. 89–90).

Recognition of the pervasive and persistent power of situational pressure has led many social and behavioral scientists to shift their focus from efforts to understand what makes people good or bad to what makes situations good or bad. But by itself neither focus seems sufficient. Moral failures can result from either personal deficiency or from situational pressure. The challenge is to understand the role of each, and to understand the way the two interact. Considering each in the context of the value→emotion→motivation→behavior sequence provides a framework for such understanding.

And this framework does more. It draws our attention to the need for a closer look at the motives and emotions that lie behind moral action, and moral failure.

PART II
What's More

4

MORAL MOTIVATION

The standard scientific diagnoses considered in Chapters 2 and 3 offer important insight into sources of our moral ills. They shed light on the general processes whereby we acquire our moral standards, principles, and ideals, as well as the processes whereby we access our principles to make judgments about what's right and wrong in specific situations. And they place our moral life in the context of the many pressures that can inhibit expression of our moral values. These are necessary insights if we're to understand what's wrong with morality.

Still, neither a personal deficiency account nor a situational pressure account nor the two combined is sufficient. Keeping both of these diagnoses in mind, I think we need to follow the lead of novelists and look more closely at the psychological dynamics of morality. The conceptual framework presented in Chapter 1, which specifies the relation of values, emotions, goal-directed motives, and behavior, seems quite useful in this regard. Although the symptoms and consequences of our moral ills are manifest in behavior, we need to examine the motivational and emotional processes that underlie the behavior to understand its causes. If we can better grasp why we act morally, we should be in a position to predict when we will fail to do so. And we can move beyond handwringing at the manifestations of malady to consider strategies for treatment.

The place to begin is by looking more closely at moral motivation. This is because goal-directed motives reveal underlying values. To start, let's review some terms and conceptual relations from Chapter 1. There, I noted that a goal-directed motive is defined by its ultimate goal, the valued state we are seeking to obtain or maintain. To reach an ultimate goal, we may pursue one or more instrumental goals. Instrumental goals aren't valued in their own right but as means to ultimate goals. (Of course, if we have multiple motives—as we often do—a given goal may be ultimate for one motive and instrumental for another.) Further, pursuit of a valued state may lead to unintended consequences, to foreseen or unforeseen outcomes that aren't what we're after either as an end or as a means.

Acting morally—behaving in a way that promotes some moral standard, principle, or ideal—can be an ultimate goal or an instrumental goal. If promoting morality is an ultimate goal, it seems appropriate to say the motive is truly moral. Although I used two terms in Chapter 1 to speak of truly moral motivation, "principlism" and "moral integrity," I primarily used "principlism" because it provided a parallel to three other motives that might lead us to act morally: egoism (seeking personal welfare), altruism (seeking another's welfare), and collectivism (seeking a group's welfare). In the present chapter, I'll use "moral integrity" instead of "principlism" because I want to emphasize that promotion of some moral value is the ultimate goal of this motive.

When acting morally as a means to some other end, it's appropriate to speak of instrumental moral motivation. In Chapters 1 and 2, I identified a number of forms of egoism for which moral action can be instrumental. Especially for young children, right conduct can be a means to gain material rewards (treats) and avoid material punishments (time-outs). As the child matures, doing right becomes a means to gain social and self-rewards (praise, esteem) and avoid social and self-punishments (censure, guilt). Moral action isn't often instrumental for either altruistic or collectivistic motives, so I won't consider those possibilities. (Let one example of instrumental moral motivation to promote an altruistic end suffice: Doing what's right to please a parent you love.) When I speak of instrumental moral motivation, I mean instrumental in pursuit of egoistic ends.

Acting morally can also be an unintended consequence. When it is, the motivation shouldn't be called moral at all. It should be labeled to reflect the intended goal. Egoistic, altruistic, and collectivistic motives can all lead to moral action as an unintended consequence. I provided a number of examples when discussing these types of motivation in Chapter 1. Even though the motive isn't moral, we may call the result moral if it accords with our moral values.

It's easy to think of moral actions that fall into each category—ultimate goal, instrumental goal, and unintended consequence—and even to think of cases in which the action is the same across categories. Consider a robber who divides the loot equally with his accomplices. If he does so because he wants to be fair and preserve honor among thieves, he displays truly moral motivation. If he divides equally to avoid the inevitable fight an unequal division would produce, he displays instrumental moral motivation. And if he divides equally as the best way to manage a successful escape, he provides a moral result as an unintended consequence. Simply to observe a moral act tells us little about the nature of the underlying motivation. (For a similar analysis of moral motivation, see Blasi, 2004.)

MORAL HYPOCRISY: A SUBTLE FORM OF INSTRUMENTAL MORAL MOTIVATION

In this chapter, I want to contrast moral integrity with one specific form of instrumental moral motivation. Setting aside the harsh connotations of the term, I call this motive *moral hypocrisy*. In contrast to moral integrity—motivation to promote some moral principle as an ultimate goal—moral hypocrisy is egoistic motivation with the ultimate goal of gaining the self-benefits of being moral with minimal cost. Said more pointedly, moral hypocrisy is *motivation to appear moral while, if possible, avoiding the cost of actually being moral.* As discussed in Chapter 1, *Webster's* (1990) defines "moral" as "1. of or concerned with principles of right or wrong conduct.

2. being in accordance with such principles" (p. 589). *Webster's* defines "hypocrisy" as "a pretense of having desirable or publicly approved attitudes, beliefs, principles, etc., that one does not actually possess" (p. 444). (For reviews of Western thought on moral hypocrisy, see Crisp & Cowton, 1994: Kittay, 1992; McKinnon, 1991.)

Some clarification about moral hypocrisy. It should be apparent that I mean more by this term than either a discrepancy between our moral standards and our behavior (Lammers, Stapel, & Galinsky, 2010; Lerner & Clayton, 2011) or a tendency to judge our own moral lapses more leniently than other people's (Valdesolo & DeSteno, 2007, 2008). Although each of these conditions has been called moral hypocrisy, either could occur for a number of reasons other than a desire to appear moral yet, if possible, avoid the cost of being moral. Most obviously, a behavior-standard discrepancy could arise because of the overpowering strength of other motives. Self-leniency could be the result of our insider knowledge of intent and extenuating circumstances.

Reflecting the dictionary's emphasis on pretense, moral hypocrisy is concerned with appearance. Sometimes, the only way to appear a certain way is to be that way—the only way to appear moral is to be moral. At such times, hypocrisy will promote morality. But if being moral involves personal cost, which it often does, and if it's possible to appear moral yet avoid the cost, a person motivated by hypocrisy should do just that. Then hypocrisy will promote only the appearance of morality, not the real thing.

For people who consider any act of pretense immoral, "moral hypocrisy" may seem to be an oxymoron. I use the adjective to specify that the domain of pretense is morality rather than, for example, science, politics, or religion. Not to claim that hypocrisy is moral.

Moral hypocrisy is an especially important form of instrumental moral motivation for two reasons. First, its goal is to masquerade as moral integrity in order to get the social and self-benefits associated with being truly moral. So hypocrisy can lead us to believe that a person is motivated by moral integrity when he or she is not. Indeed, that's its goal. Second, because its goal isn't to actually be moral, moral hypocrisy is likely to lead seemingly good, moral people to fail to act morally. Specifically, it's likely to do so when such action is personally costly and the person can still manage to appear moral. If provided sufficient "wiggle room," a person motivated by hypocrisy may strongly endorse moral principles, may judge these principles relevant to matters at hand, and may be under no particular situational pressure, yet still fail to act morally. This possibility certainly has a ring of familiarity—and plausibility. Again, remember John Dashwood.

Why Be a Moral Hypocrite?

There's good reason to want to appear moral without actually being moral. Morality is lauded by parents, preachers, and society at large. Immorality is castigated. As noted in Chapter 2, both Freud and social learning theorists suggested that society inculcates moral principles in us when young in order to bridle our selfish impulses by making it in our best interest to act morally even when unobserved. We become constrained by conscience and self-regulatory standards.

But unless we have internalized our moral values to the level of integration, the bridle chafes. Especially in interpersonal interest conflicts, to act morally is likely to involve personal cost. We yearn to break free, to pursue what we want rather than what we ought. Freud (1930/1961) spoke of this as our discontent with civilization. One way to deal with the discontent is to make a show of morality but only a show. If successful, we can avoid the social and self-punishments for failing to be moral. We can even garner the social and self-rewards for being moral. Better yet, we can get these benefits without paying the price.

Note that the internalization of moral self-regulatory standards described in Chapter 2 adds an important requirement if moral hypocrisy is to fully succeed. It's a requirement that takes us beyond Plato's analysis of moral deceit in *The Republic* (1999). If we are to get the self-benefits of seeing ourselves as moral, we need a Ring of Gyges that makes our moral lapses invisible to ourselves not just to others. Our masquerade must deceive both us and them.

Although I have defined moral hypocrisy as motivation to appear moral, I use this definition to cover two versions of this motive. The two versions reflect a distinction made in Chapter 1. In what might be called the high-bar version, the goal is to appear moral, to obtain the rewards of virtue—the social and self-esteem for doing right. In the low-bar version, the goal is to not appear immoral, to avoid social and self-censure—the criticism and guilt for doing wrong. The full benefits of moral hypocrisy accrue only to those who make it over the high bar and appear moral. But it's easier to clear the low bar, and many of us seem satisfied with that (see Janoff-Bulman, Sheikh, & Hepp, 2009).

How Is Moral Hypocrisy Possible?

Rationalization is an important contributor to moral hypocrisy, but hypocrisy involves more. Before turning to the more, a few words about rationalization.

Rationalization

Many moral philosophers consider the generality and abstractness of universal moral principles such as those of fairness, justice, and the greatest good for the greatest number to be major strengths (e.g., Kant, 1785/1898; Mill, 1861/1987; Rawls, 1971). Universal principles expand our moral circle beyond the narrow partialities of self-interest, kinship, friendship, and group membership. But from the perspective of moral motivation, generality and abstractness can be an Achilles heel. The more general and abstract a principle is, the more vulnerable it is to rationalization (Tsang, 2002; Uhlmann, Pizarro, Tannenbaum, & Ditto, 2009). Indicative of such rationalization, Valdesolo and DeSteno (2007, 2008) found that when people thought back on a morally questionable act they committed, they judged their behavior more moral than they judged the same behavior committed by someone else (also see Messick, Bloom, Boldizar, & Samuelson, 1985; Shu, Gino, & Bazerman, 2011).

Self-Deception

There's more to moral hypocrisy than retrospective rationalization of past acts. As defined, moral hypocrisy is a goal-directed motive that can lead us to act. But how can we believe that what we're about to do is moral when it really isn't? Economist Robert Frank (1988) built on biologist Robert Trivers's (1971) ideas about reciprocal altruism to argue that people are motivated to present themselves as passionately committed to moral principles in order to gain the self-benefits that the ensuing trust provides—a form of moral hypocrisy. Frank further argued that shamming this commitment is difficult due to humans' highly developed ability to detect deception. The more evolutionary stable strategy is genuine commitment. Our ancient ancestors may have taken up morality lightly as part of a masquerade, but over time natural selection came to favor those whose appearance of morality is genuine because only they get the rewards of being moral. For Frank, primordial hypocrisy has bred modern moral integrity.

Trivers himself (1985, pp. 415–420; von Hippel & Trivers, 2011) argued for a less sanguine scenario, one in which primordial hypocrisy has bred a more subtle form of hypocrisy (also see Alexander, 1987, pp. 114–125). If we can deceive ourselves into believing that we have acted morally when we haven't, we don't need to sham. We can honestly appear moral, giving off no signals of deceit. So self-deception may be a major asset in hypocrisy's moral masquerade. It can provide access to all the social and self-benefits that being moral offers—free of charge.

But perhaps this cynical scenario is wrong. Perhaps Frank (1988) and others from Plato and Aristotle on who have argued for the existence of moral integrity are right. Our principles may be inculcated in childhood through appeals to reward and punishment. Yet once the principles are properly internalized, upholding them may become an ultimate goal not just an instrumental means. Perhaps by the time we reach late adolescence, most of us are motivated not simply to appear moral but to actually be moral. Perhaps moral integrity is one of the goal-directed motives we acquire as we mature.

THE NATURE OF MORAL MOTIVATION: INTEGRITY OR HYPOCRISY?

So, what's the nature of our moral motivation? Is it integrity, hypocrisy, both, or neither? To address this question empirically, a research strategy is needed that reveals the ultimate goal of some moral action. Following the same logic used over the past four decades to test for the existence of altruistic motivation (Batson, 1991, 2011), I think a two-step strategy is required.

First, it's necessary to give people a chance to act morally. In so value-laden an area as morality, we can't trust either people's self-reports of what they have done in the past or their judgments about what they would do in hypothetical situations. We need to infer motivation from behavior. This is especially true given that hypocrisy may involve self-deception. But moral action by itself only tells us there's some motivation, not the nature of that motivation. Therefore, second, it's necessary to vary the circumstances under which the moral act can occur. The circumstances need to vary in a way that reveals whether the actor's ultimate goal is to actually be moral (integrity) or only to appear that way (hypocrisy).

Using a Procedural-Fairness Dilemma to Unmask Moral Hypocrisy

To implement this two-step strategy, Batson, Kobrynowitz, Dinnerstein, Kampf, and Wilson (1997) confronted undergraduate research participants with a moral dilemma. The dilemma involved a straightforward zero-sum conflict. The conflict pitted self-interest against the interest of another individual rather than against the interest of a hallowed institution such as church or state so responses would not be affected by institutional affiliation or allegiance. The dilemma was mundane and bland rather than stereotypically moral and dramatic (e.g., stealing or killing) in order to avoid scripted responses. It required a real decision, not a hypothetical one, in order to observe actual behavior. The dilemma was simple, not complex, so there would be no problem understanding what was at stake, and so variations could easily be created to disentangle goals. Finally, it was a dilemma with broad consensus about the morally right course of action, not one where opinions differed, so there would be widespread agreement on what action was right.

The dilemma concerned procedural fairness. It involved having participants assign themselves and another participant (actually fictitious) to tasks. There were two tasks, a positive-consequences task on which each correct response earned a raffle ticket for a $30.00 gift certificate and a neutral-consequences task on which each correct response earned nothing and which was described as rather dull and boring. One person had to be assigned to each task. Participants were told that they would never meet the other participant, and that the other thought the assignment was being made by chance. Participants were left alone to make the assignment decision, then indicate which consequences each participant would receive—positive or neutral—by entering an S (for Self) and an O (for Other) in the two blanks on an assignment form. Batson, Kobrynowitz et al. (1997) explained their reason for using such a dilemma:

> Compared with the dilemmas posed by Kohlberg (1976) . . . , ours was simple, pedestrian, even banal. . . . Not the kind of decision that immediately leaps to mind when one thinks of moral dilemmas. One may not even think of it as moral, although virtually all of our participants did [when asked afterward]. No doubt, had we posed a choice between getting raffle tickets and saving someone's life, we would have seen a very different pattern of results; everyone would have

immediately recognized the moral dimension of the decision and would have acted to achieve a moral outcome. But such a finding would tell us nothing about the nature of their motivation. (p. 1346)

Conflict between Self-Interest and Morality

Documenting a clear preference for the positive-consequences task, Batson, Kobrynowitz et al. (1997, Study 1) found that most research participants faced with this simple dilemma assigned themselves the positive consequences (80 percent). This was true even though when later asked on an open-ended questionnaire item ("In your opinion, what was the most morally right way to assign the task consequences?"), very few said that assigning themselves the positive was the most moral way (5 percent). And when asked in another part of the questionnaire to rate the morality of their own action, "Do you think the way you made the task assignment was morally right?" (1 = not at all; 9 = yes, totally), the 80 percent who assigned themselves the positive consequences rated the morality of their assignment relatively low (M = 4.38) compared with the 20 percent who assigned the other person the positive consequences (M = 8.25). Batson, Thompson, Seuferling, Whitney, and Strongman (1999, Study 3) replicated this pattern. Results of these two studies are summarized in Table 4.1.

In each of these studies, the action of most participants failed to match their retrospective judgments about the most moral thing to do. But this behavior-standard discrepancy wasn't necessarily evidence of moral hypocrisy. As mentioned earlier, an egoistic desire for the raffle tickets may have overpowered moral integrity. Or participants may simply have failed to think about the moral implications of their decision until asked about it afterwards.

Table 4.1 Task Assignment and Subsequent Reflections When Moral Standard Not Salient

Study	Assign self to positive consequences	Perceive self to positive as most moral	Participant's rated morality of the way he/she assigned the tasks	
			By those who assigned self to positive	By those who assigned other to positive
Batson, Kobrynowitz et al. (1997, Study 1)	80%	5%	4.38	8.25
Batson, Thompson et al. (1999, Study 1)	71%	0%	5.40	8.00

Note: Participants' ratings of the morality of the way they assigned the tasks were on a 1 (not at all morally right) to 9 (yes, totally morally right) scale.

Adding Salience and Wiggle Room

Two procedural changes were necessary to test the nature of participants' moral motivation. First, it was important to make sure the moral relevance of the decision was salient. Second, there needed to be sufficient wiggle room—ambiguity—so it would be possible to appear moral without having to actually be moral. (Snyder, Kleck, Strenta, & Mentzer, 1979, introduced a classic method of producing moral wiggle room; for more recent examples, see Dana, Weber, & Kuang, 2007; Shalvi, Dana, Handgraaf, & De Dreu, 2011.)

If participants were motivated to actually be moral (integrity), they should be no more likely to favor themselves when provided wiggle room. They should remain steadfast in their pursuit of fairness. But if they were motivated to appear moral (hypocrisy), then those provided wiggle room should take advantage of the appearance-reality slippage to favor themselves. Only when the appearance-reality connection is tight should moral hypocrisy produce a moral result.

Across studies, Batson, Kobrynowitz et al. (1997) used two techniques to provide wiggle room. One was to give participants who were alone in a research cubicle a coin to flip if they wished. This allowed them to flip the coin, a fair assignment method, but not necessarily abide by the outcome. The second technique was to allow participants to accept a "random" assignment that participants knew had given them the positive-consequences task. (Participants in a different experimental condition knew the random assignment had given them the neutral task.)

Initial Tests of the Nature of Moral Motivation

Results with each technique were much the same, so let me focus on the first and present results of the second only briefly.

Using the Coin Flip

To make sure the moral standard of fairness was salient, Batson, Kobrynowitz et al. (1997, Study 2) included the following statement in the task-assignment instructions:

> Most participants feel that giving both people an equal chance—by, for example, flipping a coin—is the fairest way to assign themselves and the other participant to the tasks (we have provided a coin for you to flip if you wish). But the decision is entirely up to you. (p. 1341)

Wiggle room was—as already mentioned—provided by participants being alone when they made their task assignment decision. This allowed them to flip the coin but not follow it.

Under these conditions, virtually all participants said in retrospect that using a fair method such as the coin flip was the most moral way to assign the tasks. Yet only about half chose to flip it. Of those who chose not to flip, 90 percent assigned themselves the positive-consequences task. This is quite similar to what is found in Table 4.1 for participants not given the sentence about fairness and not given the coin. More interesting and revealing, the same was true among those who flipped the coin—90 percent assigned themselves the positive consequences. This percentage is significantly higher than the 50 percent expected from a fair coin flip. Clearly, either the coin was very charitable, or some who flipped it failed to abide by the outcome. Batson, Thompson et al. (1999, Study 2) replicated these findings. Results of these studies are summarized in Table 4.2.

Although the pattern of assignment was the same in these studies for participants who flipped the coin and those who didn't, Table 4.2 shows one notable difference. Participants who assigned themselves the positive consequences after flipping the coin rated the morality of the way they assigned the tasks considerably higher (Ms = 7.11 and 7.82 for the two studies, respectively) than did those who made this assignment without flipping (Ms = 3.56 and 4.00). Even though many who flipped didn't abide by the outcome, they seemed to see themselves as having acted morally.

The pattern of results reported in Table 4.2 has proved very robust. In study after study, the percentage of participants who assign themselves the positive consequences after flipping the coin (always in private) has been significantly greater than the 50 percent expected from an unbiased coin flip. This pattern provides evidence of motivation to appear fair yet avoid the cost of being fair (moral hypocrisy). For example, the pattern was found in a study in which the less desirable consequences were more negative, uncomfortable electric shocks (Batson, Tsang, & Thompson, 2001,

Table 4.2 Task Assignment and Subsequent Reflections When Moral Standard Salient

Study	Assign self to positive consequences	Perceive self to positive as most moral	Participant's rated morality of the way he/she assigned the tasks	
			By those who assigned self to positive	By those who assigned other to positive
Participants Who Did Not Flip the Coin				
Batson, Kobrynowitz et al. (1997, Study 2)	90%	10%	3.56	8.00
Batson, Thompson et al. (1999, Study 2)	85%	8%	4.00	9.00
Participants Who Did Flip the Coin				
Batson, Kobrynowitz et al. (1997, Study 2)	90%	0%	7.11	9.00
Batson, Thompson et al. (1999, Study 2)	85%	0%	7.82	9.00

Note: Participants' ratings of the morality of the way they assigned the tasks were on a 1 (*not at all morally right*) to 9 (*yes, totally morally right*) scale.

Study 3). The prospect of shocks led a smaller percentage of participants to flip the coin (30 percent, down from around 50 percent when the less desirable consequences were neutral). But the prospect of shocks didn't reduce the percentage of those who, after flipping, assigned themselves the positive consequences (100 percent).

The pattern was also found in a study in which participants were told that the other participant knew they were assigning the tasks (Batson, Thompson, & Chen, 2002, Study 1). Being told this instead of that the other believed the assignment was made by chance led a much larger percentage of participants to flip the coin (90 percent), but it didn't noticeably reduce the percentage who, after flipping (in private), assigned themselves the positive consequences (89 percent). And the pattern was found in a study in which, at the top of the form on which they made the task assignment, participants indicated both the importance of their making the assignment in a fair way and whether or not they had flipped the coin (Batson, Sampat, & Collins, 2005). Virtually all participants said it was very important to them to make the assignment in a fair way. Reporting this at the top of the form and reporting whether they had flipped led more participants to flip the coin (83 percent). But it didn't noticeably reduce the number who, after flipping, assigned themselves the positive consequences (93 percent).

Nor has the evidence of moral hypocrisy been limited to those scoring relatively low on measures of the personal importance of morality. Quite the contrary. Batson, Kobrynowitz et al. (1997, Study 2) found that an index of personal commitment to moral values correlated positively with choosing to flip the coin ($r = .40$). But after flipping, those who scored high on this index were as likely as those who scored low to assign themselves the positive consequences. Thus, those with greater self-reported commitment to morality didn't show signs of greater moral integrity. They showed signs of greater hypocrisy. They were more likely to appear moral by flipping the coin. But no more likely to be moral by allowing the flip to determine the task assignment. Batson et al. (2002, Study 2) replicated this finding.

Using Prior "Random" Assignment

Study 3 reported by Batson, Kobrynowitz et al. (1997) provided wiggle room in the second way. In addition to being given a chance to flip a coin, participants could accept a previously made random assignment of the tasks. Some participants knew the random assignment benefited them. Some knew it benefited the other. Prior random assignment that benefited the self provided wiggle room. Participants could appear fair by deferring to a random method, yet be assured of getting the positive consequences. In contrast, to accept the prior assignment that benefited the other would allow participants to appear fair, but only at the cost of giving up the positive-consequences task.

Results of this study again provided evidence for moral hypocrisy. More participants were willing to defer to the random assignment when they knew in advance that it gave them the positive consequences (85 percent) than when it gave them

the neutral consequences (55 percent). And those who accepted the random assignment that they knew favored themselves reported afterward that they considered
their action to be quite moral (M = 7.06 on a 1–9 scale), not significantly less moral
than did those who accepted the assignment that favored the other (M = 7.91). (In
each condition of this experiment, everyone who didn't accept the random assignment gave themselves the positive consequences—either with or without flipping
the coin.)

Taken together, these studies provide considerable evidence of moral hypocrisy
but very little evidence of moral integrity. The results consistently conform to the
pattern expected if the goal of many who flipped the coin or accepted the favorable
random assignment was to appear moral rather than actually be moral.

The Role of Self-Deception in Moral Hypocrisy

How did participants in these studies manage to negotiate the task-assignment
dilemma so as to appear moral yet still unfairly favor themselves? They don't seem
to have distorted or disengaged their moral standards (Bandura, 1990, 1999). When
(after they assigned the tasks) participants were asked about the morally right way
to make the assignment, by far the most common response was that one should
use a random method such as flip a coin. Next most common was that one should
give the other participant the positive consequences. Participants' moral standards
were still there. And for many, so was the appearance of morality. But real morality
was rare.

Nor is self-presentation—trying to look good in other people's eyes—a sufficient
explanation (Jones & Pittman, 1982). Participants were alone when they made the
assignment decision. No one but they would know whether or not they flipped the
coin, so there was no need to flip to impress others.

But if they didn't flip the coin to impress others, then why? If participants were
to gain the self-rewards for being moral and perhaps more importantly to avoid the
self-punishments for being a hypocrite, they needed to appear moral to themselves.
How is this possible when violating their moral standards to serve self-interest? As
discussed earlier, it's possible if participants can self-deceive.

Self-deception is a concept that has been used with varying meanings in both
philosophy and psychology. So it's important to consider what form of self-deception
is implied by the motive of moral hypocrisy. Sometimes self-deception has been
thought to require that a person simultaneously hold two contradictory beliefs,
being unaware of one (e.g., Gur & Sackheim, 1979). Or that a person believe what
at some level he or she knows is not so (e.g., Demos, 1960). Such paradoxical forms
of self-deception aren't required for moral hypocrisy. It's sufficient that a person
engage in what philosopher Alfred Mele (1987) called "ordinary self-deception" or
"desire-influenced manipulation of data" (p. 126; also see Mele, 1997, 2001). The goal
of appearing moral to myself can be reached if I can manage to manipulate matters
so as to avoid confronting the discrepancy between my self-serving behavior and my
moral standards.

How might I manage to avoid this discrepancy? Assuming that I have behaved in a way that violates my moral standards (e.g., by failing to abide by the result of the coin flip) and responsibility for my action can't be denied, ordinary self-deception strategies that would serve moral hypocrisy can be classed into two types. First, I might misperceive my self-serving behavior as being in line with my moral standards even though it actually isn't. Second, I might avoid comparing my behavior to my standards, thereby overlooking the discrepancy and maintaining the illusion of morality. The first of these two strategies, if available, seems preferable because the second leaves me vulnerable to anything that draws my attention to the behavior-standard discrepancy. If I can employ the first strategy and convince myself that I've acted morally, then I can scrutinize my behavior from the perspective of my moral standards with impunity—even pride.

Could participants in the studies providing evidence for moral hypocrisy have been able to perceive their self-serving behavior as in line with their standards? Could they, for example, have perceived their coin flip as fair even when it wasn't? It seems possible. Participants were left alone to decide whether to flip the coin and, if so, how to interpret the outcome. Some—perhaps many—may not have decided the consequences of heads and tails in advance. Rather, once they saw that the flip produced heads [or tails] they may have "remembered" that this result assigned them the positive: "It's heads [tails]. Let's see, that means I get the positive task." In this way, they could enjoy both the positive consequences and the knowledge that they made the assignment fairly by using the coin.

Labeling the Coin to Eliminate the First Type of Self-Deception

If participants relied on this kind of self-deception, it should be relatively easy to diminish if not eliminate the moral-hypocrisy effect. All that's required is to specify in advance who gets which task when the coin comes up heads or tails. Accordingly, Batson, Thompson et al. (1999, Study 1) placed participants in the task-assignment dilemma, but now there was a blue sticker on each side of the coin. One sticker said "SELF to POS," and one said "OTHER to POS." If, when using this labeled coin, the hypocrisy effect disappeared (i.e., there was no longer a significant deviation from 50 percent in the direction of giving oneself the positive consequences), we would have evidence that the effect is due to the first self-deception strategy—perceiving self-serving behavior as standard consistent. If the hypocrisy effect remained, we would need to seek another explanation.

As can be seen in the top half of Table 4.3, adding labels did nothing to reduce the effect. Once again, the percentage of those assigning themselves the positive consequences after flipping the coin (86 percent) was much like the percentage doing so without flipping the coin (83 percent), and was significantly greater than the 50 percent expected from a fair coin flip. Moreover, once again, those who assigned themselves the positive consequences after flipping the coin rated the morality of the way they assigned the task higher ($M = 7.42$) than did those who made this assignment without flipping the coin ($M = 3.90$).

Table 4.3 Task Assignment and Subsequent Reflections When Coin Is Labeled

			Participant's rated morality of the way he/she assigned the tasks	
Did participant flip coin?	Assign self to positive consequences	Perceive self to positive as most moral	By those who assigned self to positive	By those who assigned other to positive
Coin with Labels (Batson, Thompson et al., 1999, Study 1)				
No	83%	17%	3.90	8.50
Yes	86%	0%	7.42	9.00
Coin with Different Colored Labels (Batson et al., 2002, Study 2)				
No	75%	0%	3.89	8.00
Yes	84%	0%	6.33	8.80

Note: Participants' ratings of the morality of the way they assigned the tasks were on a 1 (*not at all morally right*) to 9 (*yes, totally morally right*) scale.

Could it be that the labels failed to clarify who won the flip? Apparently not. When asked afterward whether it would make a difference if the coin had no labels, all participants said the labels made things clear. Most also said the labels eliminated the possibility of the first form of self-deception. Typical comments were, "It would be easier to pick me if the coin wasn't labeled. You could fool yourself and say, 'No, I meant that side.'" "Without the labels you'd be more likely to change your mind after the flip." "People would probably cheat their way out and take the positive for themselves." "You could fudge it." "You could play mind games until you came to the conclusion that you get the positive." Despite these assertions, labeling the coin didn't noticeably reduce the hypocrisy effect.

Identifying Who Fiddled the Flip

After the study just described had been run, Batson et al. (2002) realized that labels on the coin could provide additional useful information if the two labels were of different colors. There was a small window in the door of the research cubicle in which participants sat to make the task-assignment decision. The window was covered with paper. By making a small hole in the paper, it would be possible for the experimenter to peek in and see not only whether participants flipped the coin but also which color label came up. So, with different colored labels it would be possible to know which participants won the flip fair-and-square and which did not. Comparing ratings of the morality of their task assignment by those who assigned themselves the positive consequences after losing the flip with the ratings by those who assigned themselves the positive without flipping the coin would shed light on a question raised by the results of previous studies: Was the higher rating among those who flipped the coin before assigning themselves the positive consequences simply a product of those who honestly won the flip (after all, half should) or was the charade of a dishonest flip sufficient to produce higher ratings of morality?

Accordingly, Batson et al. (2002, Study 2) placed a yellow "SELF to POS" sticker on one side of the coin and a blue "OTHER to POS" sticker on the other side. As can be seen in the bottom half of Table 4.3, the pattern of task assignment was much the same as in the previous labeled-coin study and in the studies where the coin wasn't labeled.

But now, surreptitious observation permitted classification of task-assignment behavior into four categories. *Category 1*. Assign the other participant the positive task (of the 44 participants in the study, 8 did this—3 without flipping the coin, 5 with). *Category 2*. Flip the coin, get SELF to POS, assign self the positive task (11 participants did this). *Category 3*. Not flip the coin, assign self the positive task (9 participants did this). *Category 4*. Flip the coin but either ignore the result or "fiddle" the flip, assign self the positive task (16 participants did this). Of the 16 participants in the final category, five flipped the coin once and got OTHER to POS, yet assigned themselves the positive consequences. Seven used the coin, but rigged the flip so they won. For example, several participants who lost the initial flip, flipped the coin again until it came up SELF to POS, then stopped and made their assignment. Four didn't flip the coin at all, but reported on a subsequent questionnaire and in a postdecision interview that they did. Perhaps they flipped mentally.

Table 4.4 presents mean ratings of the morality of the way participants made the task-assignment decision separately for each of the four categories. As can be seen, those in Category 1, who assigned the other the positive task, rated the morality of the way they made the decision quite high ($M = 8.50$). So did those in Category 2, who flipped the coin, won, and assigned themselves the positive task ($M = 7.45$). In contrast, participants in Category 3, who didn't flip the coin and assigned themselves the positive task, rated the morality of the way they made the task-assignment decision relatively low ($M = 3.89$). Most important, participants in Category 4, who fiddled the coin flip and then assigned themselves the positive task, rated the morality of the way they made the decision moderately high ($M = 5.56$), significantly higher than participants in Category 3. And the higher rating among Category 4 participants wasn't a function of only one type of fiddler (e.g., those who rigged the flip). A comparison of rated morality among the three types didn't approach statistical significance.

So, even though the coin had no more effect on the fiddlers' decisions than it had on the decisions of those who didn't claim to use the coin at all, the fiddlers said they thought the way they made the task-assignment decision was more moral. Their sham use of the coin seems to have provided sufficient appearance of morality that they could claim to have acted at least moderately morally. They cleared the low bar. And by fiddling the flip, they made sure that they got the more desirable task. They were able to appear moral without incurring the cost.

This pattern of responses couldn't be explained by the first type of self-deception because the consequences of the coin coming up each way were clearly labeled. But

Table 4.4 Mean Rated Morality of the Way They Assigned the Tasks by Participants in Four Task-Assignment-Behavior Categories (Batson et al., 2002, Study 2)

Task-assignment behavior	N	M	SD
Assign other the positive task	8	8.50	0.76
Flip the coin, win, and assign self the positive task	11	7.45	1.37
Not flip the coin, assign self the positive task	9	3.89	1.45
Fiddle the coin flip, assign self the positive task	16	5.56	2.37

Note: Ratings were on a 1 (*not at all morally right*) to 9 (*yes, totally morally right*) scale.

it didn't address the second type, avoid comparing my immoral behavior (unfairly assigning myself the positive consequences) with my moral standards (be fair).

Using a Mirror to Eliminate the Second Type of Self-Deception

How might the second type of ordinary self-deception operate in the task-assignment situation? Consistent with notions of motivated reasoning (Ditto, Pizarro, & Tannenbaum, 2009; Kunda, 1990; Tenbrunsel & Messick, 2004) and with Baumeister and Newman's (1994) claims about the role of strategically interrupted thought in enabling self-deception, those who ignored or fiddled the flip may have reasoned to the point, "I flipped the coin, which is fair," and stopped without adding, "But I fiddled the result, which is not." In this way, they may have managed to avoid assessing their behavior in light of the salient moral standard.

Self-awareness manipulations, such as looking at your face in a mirror, have been found to heighten awareness of discrepancies between our behavior and our salient personal standards, creating pressure to act in accord with standards (Wicklund, 1975). For example, Diener and Wallbom (1976) used being in front of a mirror to induce self-awareness in research participants who had the opportunity to cheat on a test. Those who were in front of the mirror cheated significantly less often than those who were not (also see Gino & Mogilner, 2014, Experiment 3).

If people motivated to appear moral yet avoid the cost of actually being moral rely on not comparing their immoral behavior to their moral standards, then making them self-aware should reduce or eliminate the hypocrisy effect. It should draw attention to the behavior-standard discrepancy, creating pressure to act in accord with the standard. Pursuing this logic, Batson, Thompson et al. (1999, Study 2) once again placed participants in the task-assignment dilemma, gave them the statement that made the fairness standard salient, and provided a coin (unlabeled). But now, a large mirror that was ostensibly for use in another study was sitting on the participant's desk. (The mirror was leaning against the wall to make clear it wasn't a one-way mirror.) Participants in a high self-awareness condition were seated facing themselves in the mirror as they made the task assignment. Those in a low self-awareness condition were also seated facing the mirror, but it was turned to the wall so they saw only the nonreflecting back. A notice in the corner of the mirror (or its back) said, "ANDERSON STUDY—DON'T TOUCH PLEASE." Participants were asked not to move the mirror, and none did.

As can be seen in the top half of Table 4.5, results in the low self-awareness condition were much as in previous studies. Even among those who flipped the coin, well over half assigned themselves the positive consequences (85 percent). But results in the high self-awareness condition were dramatically different. Those who flipped the coin while facing themselves in the mirror showed no bias; 50 percent assigned themselves the positive consequences (see the bottom half of Table 4.5). Reflecting their fair use of the coin, these participants rated the morality of the way they assigned the tasks very high ($M = 8.80$ on the 1–9 scale). This assignment difference across conditions was precisely what would be expected if self-awareness induced by the mirror rendered the second type of self-deception ineffective, forcing participants to actually be moral in order to appear moral to themselves. It suggested that the second type of self-deception—avoiding comparison of my immoral behavior and moral standards—plays an important role in moral hypocrisy.

Summary

Research using the task-assignment paradigm has provided considerable evidence of moral hypocrisy. With sufficient wiggle room, apparent evidence of moral integrity such as choosing to assign the tasks by flipping the coin is often, it seems,

Table 4.5 Task Assignment and Subsequent Reflections When Not Facing or Facing Mirror (Batson, Thompson et al., 1999, Study 2)

Did participant flip coin?	Assign self to positive consequences	Perceive self to positive as most moral	Participant's rated morality of the way he/she assigned the tasks	
			By those who assigned self to positive	By those who assigned other to positive
Not Facing Mirror				
No	85%	8%	4.00	8.00
Yes	85%	0%	7.82	9.00
Facing Mirror				
No	62%	0%	3.50	8.00
Yes	50%	0%	8.80	8.00

Note: Participants' ratings of the morality of the way they assigned the tasks were on a 1 (*not at all morally right*) to 9 (*yes, totally morally right*) scale.

a masquerade in the service of hypocrisy. By flipping the coin but ignoring or fiddling an unfavorable result, research participants seem able to maintain the appearance of morality even to themselves without having to pay the price of actually being moral.

But we shouldn't overgeneralize these findings. The task-assignment situation addresses only one type of fairness, procedural fairness. At issue is whether both participants are given a fair chance to be assigned the positive-consequences task. Yet, no matter how fair the procedure, one person is going to receive a more desirable task than the other. A second important type of fairness in many interest-conflict situations is distributive fairness. When resources are divisible, is the division fair (equal or equitable)? Rather than a fair chance, the issue is whether each person gets his or her fair share.

MORAL MOTIVATION WHEN MAKING A DISTRIBUTIVE-FAIRNESS DECISION

It's important to ask the same question about distributive fairness that we asked about procedural: What's the nature of the underlying motivation? Is it integrity, hypocrisy, both, or neither? Although much less evidence is available, what there is suggests that here too, when provided sufficient wiggle room, behavior that appears motivated by moral integrity often proves to be motivated by hypocrisy instead. The evidence comes from a study that used privileged information to provide wiggle room. The basic idea for the study was suggested by a call to National Public Radio's *Car Talk* on May 24, 2003.

Mary from Minneapolis Wants to Sell Her Honda

Mary, who lived in Minneapolis, wanted to sell her 1994 Honda Accord. Before putting an ad in the classifieds, she had a local dealer give the car a thorough 40-point inspection. The inspection revealed that the car was in good shape except for a leaking water pump and an aging timing belt. Both would soon need to be replaced at a cost of about $500. To her credit, Mary rejected the advice of a nondealer mechanic who suggested that the water pump wasn't really leaking only "seeping," and that she sell the car without making the repairs or telling prospective buyers. She also rejected the deceptive strategy of appearing fair and honest by pointing out a scratch on the fender requiring a $25 touchup while keeping quiet about the looming $500 repairs. Apparently, Mary wished to be moral. At the same time, she wished to sell the car. Her question for Click and Clack, the Tappet Brothers who hosted *Car Talk*, was how to appear most honest and, therefore, be most likely to attract a buyer. Mary wanted to solve what Robert Frank (2003) called the commitment problem. Should she have the repairs made before selling the car? Or should she inform prospective buyers and offer to reduce the price by $500?

After a lengthy, humorous discussion that included on-the-air consultation with Max Bazerman of Harvard Business School, consensus was that the most trust-inducing strategy was a third option. Mary should inform prospective buyers, and allow the buyer to have the repairs made at her expense. This plan certainly seems moral by virtually any standard you can imagine, including the Golden Rule ("Do unto others . . . ."). Were the roles reversed, Mary would doubtless have been happy to be so treated.

Issues of the sort raised by Mary's call arise almost every time a sale takes place, whether sale of a used car, bicycle, boat, or house, sale of a brand-new product, of real estate, or of a corporation. One party, perhaps each, knows things relevant to the sale that he or she knows the other doesn't know. And similar issues arise in other interest-conflict situations. How do I advertise a product I know has risks or limitations? Should I reveal my true bottom-line in contract negotiations? Should I point out what isn't covered by an insurance policy (instead of burying that information in the fine print)? What if I have access to insider investment information? How much should I reveal in the annual report to stockholders? Even a child dividing sweets with a sibling may know which ones are best. Do people in such situations pursue moral integrity as eagerly as Mary seemed to? Or are they motivated by moral hypocrisy? Do they really want to be fair, or only to appear that way and still take advantage of their knowledge to serve self-interest?

Using Privileged Information to Provide Wiggle Room

Mary's situation suggested a new paradigm in which to study the nature of moral motivation. The idea was to have research participants divide differentially valued resources between themselves and another person. In one experimental condition, participants would have information that the other person didn't have about which resources were more valuable. In other conditions, participants wouldn't have this information. If participants were motivated by moral hypocrisy rather than integrity, they should take advantage of the special knowledge, substituting an appearance of fairness for true fairness.

Batson, Collins, and Powell (2006) reported a study by Batson et al. (2004) that employed this logic. In each session of the study, 12 raffle tickets were to be divided between two participants who would never meet, the research participant and another undergraduate (actually fictitious). Ostensibly, the purpose of the study was to assess reactions to receiving various types of rewards. So some of the tickets were good for one chance at a $5 gift certificate at the store of the winner's choice, while others were good for one chance at a $30 gift certificate. Each ticket had a number and a place for the ticket holder to write his or her name. The ticket numbers were in sequence, 6 odd and 6 even.

Participants were told that how many of the tickets for each gift certificate they and the other participant received would be determined either by chance or by one of the two participants. Supposedly as the result of a random drawing, participants were always selected to divide the tickets. They were given all 12 tickets and left alone in a small research cubicle to make their division. Any tickets they wished to give the other participant were to be sealed in an envelope and slipped under the cubicle door for delivery. They were to write their name on the remaining tickets for entry in the raffle. If a ticket with their name was drawn, they would win a gift certificate good for either $5 or $30 depending on whether the winning ticket was low value ($5) or high value ($30).

There were three different experimental conditions. In one condition, participants were informed that neither they nor the other participant would know which tickets were low value and which were high value (no-information condition). In a second condition, they were informed that both they and the other participant were being told which tickets, odd or even, were for the $5 certificate and which were for the $30 certificate (shared-information condition). Participants in this condition had all the information needed to benefit themselves. But they had no wiggle room to do so and still appear moral. In a third condition, participants were informed that, although the other participant had been told that neither participant would know which tickets were of low and high value, it was necessary that participants be told the values because they had been randomly chosen to divide the tickets (privileged-information condition). Participants in this condition had both information and wiggle room. (To control for any possible effect of odd vs. even numbers, half of the participants in each of the last two conditions were told that odd-numbered tickets were for the $5 certificate and even-numbered tickets were for the $30 certificate. The other half were told the reverse.)

Predictions

If participants in this study were motivated only by material self-interest, they should keep all 12 tickets for themselves regardless of experimental condition. If they were motivated only by a desire to promote distributive fairness (moral integrity), those in each condition should divide the tickets evenly, 6 for self, 6 for other. Further, in the two conditions in which they knew which tickets were for which gift certificate (shared-information, privileged-information), they should divide both the 6 low-value and 6 high-value tickets evenly, 3 for self, 3 for other.

If research participants were motivated only by moral hypocrisy, they should still divide the tickets evenly in each condition in order to appear fair. But privileged information should affect the number of high-value tickets among the 6 kept. In the shared-information condition, in which both they and the other participant knew which tickets were for which gift certificate, participants should divide both the low-value and the high-value tickets evenly. This was the only way to appear fair. But in the privileged-information condition, in which only they knew which tickets were for which certificate, they had wiggle room. So they should keep a disproportionate number of high-value ($30) tickets, sending the other participant what appeared to be a fair allotment—6 tickets—but was actually of less value. In this condition, moral hypocrisy should show its face.

Note that this ticket-allocation procedure focused on other-deception rather than self-deception. The attention needed to select the high-value tickets would make self-deception difficult, although with some creative rationalization it might still be possible. Some participants might think, "What she doesn't know can't hurt her."

Results

The mean number of tickets given by research participants in each of these experimental conditions is presented in Table 4.6. The means suggest that more than one motive was operating. Reflecting material self-interest, the total number of tickets given regardless of value (bottom row) shows that participants on average gave less than half of the 12 tickets (overall $M = 4.78$), keeping more for themselves ($M = 7.22$). But the division approached equality in the shared-information condition (Ms = 5.45 and 6.55, respectively). Clearly, there was some concern either to be or to appear fair. Also reflecting a concern for fairness, the most frequently occurring split in each condition was 6–6.

On average, participants in the no-information condition were significantly less willing to give away tickets ($M = 4.07$) than were those in the two conditions in which they knew the values ($M = 5.11$). Not knowing which tickets were of which value, no-information participants appeared loath to give away what might turn out to be high-value tickets. They seemed to experience a conflict between material self-interest and either moral integrity or moral hypocrisy. But in this condition, where participants had no information about ticket value, it was impossible to know which.

Behavior in the other two conditions provided considerable evidence of moral hypocrisy, little of moral integrity. Even participants in the shared-information condition—who lacked wiggle room because the other also knew the ticket values—gave away more low-value tickets ($M = 3.33$) than high ($M = 2.12$) and kept fewer low-value tickets ($M = 2.67$) than high ($M = 3.88$). Once again, this reflected material self-interest. Importantly, participants in the privileged-information condition, who knew the values and knew the other participant didn't, were even more likely to give away low-value tickets ($M = 3.38$) than high ($M = 1.38$) and less likely to keep low-value tickets ($M = 2.62$) than high ($M = 4.62$). This finding suggests that

Table 4.6 Mean Number of $5 (Low-Value) and $30 (High-Value) Tickets Given to the Other Participant in Each Experimental Condition (Batson et al., 2006)

Tickets given to other	Experimental condition		
	No information	Shared information	Privileged information
$5 tickets	2.10	3.33	3.38
$30 tickets	1.97	2.12	1.38
Total	4.07	5.45	4.77

the main motive operating along with material self-interest was moral hypocrisy. As in the task-assignment paradigm, evidence of moral integrity was limited.

After dividing the 12 tickets, participants were asked about the most moral way to allocate the tickets. By far the most common response in the two information conditions was to divide both low-value and high-value tickets equally. Yet, many participants failed to live up to this standard. When given the opportunity in the privileged-information condition, many displayed the trademark of moral hypocrisy. They adhered to the appearance of morality by dividing the number of tickets close to equally, but favored themselves by keeping almost twice as many high-value tickets. Other studies have found similar results using privileged information to provide moral wiggle room (e.g., Pillutla & Murnighan, 2003; Steinel & De Dreu, 2004).

ANOTHER SOURCE OF WIGGLE ROOM: COST-BASED JUSTIFICATION FOR SETTING MORALITY ASIDE

To see moral hypocrisy in action, wiggle room is needed. Without it, there's no way to appear moral yet not be moral. We've seen that wiggle room can be provided by allowing participants to flip a coin in private, by giving them a chance to accept a random assignment they already know favors themselves, or by giving them privileged information. In one task-assignment study briefly mentioned earlier, a fourth source of wiggle room seemed to be operating, although it wasn't part of the research design.

The study is the one in which the alternative to a positive-consequences task wasn't a dull and boring neutral task. The alternative was a negative-consequences task in which incorrect answers were to be punished with electric shocks. Faced with the prospect of getting shocks, only 30 percent of the participants flipped the coin. And everyone in this 30 percent assigned themselves the positive-consequences task. Apparently, many who flipped took advantage of the wiggle room provided by the coin—the first source of wiggle room just noted.

The fourth source appeared among the 70 percent in this study who didn't flip the coin. The vast majority of them assigned themselves the positive consequences (86 percent). Further, they seemed quite ready to admit that the way they assigned the tasks wasn't morally right. They also seemed quite untroubled by this.

How did these participants deal with the discrepancy between their standards of fairness and their action in this relatively high-stakes dilemma? Comments made during debriefing suggested that many felt that the cost to self introduced by the prospect of getting shocked was sufficient justification for not using a fair procedure. They said such things as, "If it had been anything but shocks," or "I just can't take shocks." Employing a two-bar morality, these participants didn't claim to have cleared the high bar of being moral. But they seemed to feel that the cost associated with being moral in this situation carried them over the low bar. To assign the other the shocks may not have been especially praiseworthy, but it was excusable. The high cost of doing what was moral provided sufficient wiggle room to allow them to take advantage of the situation without self-recrimination.

A cost-based justification for failing to uphold our moral principles is quite understandable. It's no surprise that participants didn't want to be shocked. But a cost-based justification for moral failure carries troubling implications. Just think. If personal cost is sufficient to justify setting aside our principles, then we can set them aside when considering whether to stand by or intervene as perpetrators of hate crimes pursue their victims. Or when considering our own position of wealth while others are in poverty. Or considering whether to recycle or to contribute our fair share to public TV. In each of these cases, to act morally carries personal cost. Yet isn't it in precisely such situations that moral principles are supposed to do their most important work?

If—as is often assumed—the role of morality in interest-conflict situations is to keep us from placing our own interests ahead of the parallel interests of others, then cost-based justification poses a serious problem. A principle that says, "Don't give my interests priority unless there's clear personal cost," turns morality into a luxury. It becomes something I would love to have, but given the price am happy to do without.

OVERPOWERED INTEGRITY: ANOTHER SOURCE OF MORAL FAILURE

Before concluding that moral hypocrisy accounts for the failure of many participants to actually be moral in the research I've described, it's important to consider another possibility. In interpersonal interest conflicts of the sort studied, motivation to uphold our moral standards is at odds with egoistic motives and may be overpowered by them. Think about the task assignment. Perhaps at least some of those who flipped the coin did so with a genuine intent to be fair. Their motivation was moral integrity. But when they discovered that the flip went against them, which meant that to be fair would cost them the positive consequences, self-interest may have overpowered their initial intent. As a result, they appeared moral (flipped the coin), yet still served self-interest. If this is what happened, they didn't display moral hypocrisy but *overpowered integrity* (another name for what philosophers have called weakness of will). Rather than casting doubt on the existence of moral integrity, such a process casts doubt on its strength. In the words of the Biblical lament, "The spirit is willing, but the flesh is weak" (Matthew 26: 41).

Evidence of Overpowered Integrity

Greene and Paxton (2009) used a clever procedure to provide evidence suggestive of overpowered integrity in a functional magnetic resonance imaging (fMRI) scanner. Ostensibly as part of a study of paranormal ability, participants tried to predict the outcome of computer-randomized coin flips under a variety of conditions. On key trials, they could earn from $3 to $7 if they accurately predicted the outcome. Further, on some of these trials they recorded their prediction in advance (no chance to cheat). On other trials they reported their prediction after knowing the outcome (chance to cheat). An accuracy rate significantly ($p < .001$) above chance (50 percent) when the participant "predicted" after knowing the outcome was considered evidence of dishonesty. Of the 35 participants in the study, 14 were classified as dishonest by this criterion.

When given the chance to act dishonestly for substantial gain, these 14, unlike the remaining participants, deliberated longer (relative to other trials) and exhibited increased neural activity in cortical areas associated with motivational conflict (e.g., anterior cingulate cortex) and with cognitive control (e.g., dorsolateral and ventrolateral prefrontal cortex). To explain these results, Greene and Paxton (2009) suggested, "This activity may reflect the process of actively deciding whether to lie, independent of the choice made" (p. 12,509). Instead of being motivated by self-deceptive hypocrisy—which wouldn't involve conflict—these 14 participants seem to have been conflicted about whether to honestly report their prediction or to lie and take the money. Sometimes they went one way, sometimes the other. Perhaps they were motivated to be honest. But when they guessed wrong, conflict arose and their honest intent was trumped by desire for the money. Overpowered integrity.

Instead of or In Addition to Moral Hypocrisy?

Looking back at the research claimed to provide support for moral hypocrisy, it certainly seems possible that some research participants initially intended to flip the coin and abide by the result. Then when the coin came up against them, this intent was overpowered by their desire for the positive consequences. But, although this seems possible, the research also provides considerable evidence of hypocrisy that can't be explained as overpowered integrity.

Evidence that can't be explained as overpowered integrity includes, first, the behavior of participants who fiddled the coin flip by flipping until they won. If their integrity has been overpowered, why bother to flip again? Even harder to explain is the fact that these fiddlers rated the way they assigned the tasks as more moral than did participants who assigned themselves the positive consequences without going through the charade of flipping the coin (see Table 4.4). If the fiddlers' integrity was overpowered, there should be no difference in these ratings. So, both the fiddled flip and the subsequent ratings are consistent with a hypocrisy explanation, but not with overpowered integrity.

Second, there's the effect of sitting in front of a mirror on the fairness of assignment after flipping the coin (see Table 4.5). Unless we assume that the mirror strengthened the standard instead of, as in other self-awareness studies, made salient the impending standard-behavior discrepancy, this finding also is hard to explain in terms of overpowered integrity. But it's quite consistent with hypocrisy. Third, there's the behavior of participants who took advantage of privileged information to give the other participant more low-value tickets while keeping more high-value tickets for themselves (see Table 4.6). Once again, this result is difficult to explain in terms of overpowered integrity, but quite consistent with hypocrisy.

On the other hand, some evidence is more indicative of overpowering. First, as already noted, there's the evidence of motivational conflict in the Greene and Paxton (2009) study. Further, in the distributive-fairness study, the tendency to keep more than half of the tickets for oneself that was apparent in the no-information condition (where participants didn't know which tickets were high-value and which were low) could be due to overpowered integrity. Alternatively, this tendency could be due to the overpowering of a desire to appear moral rather than a desire to actually be moral. That is, it could be due to *overpowered hypocrisy*. We don't have clear evidence that the moral motive being overpowered in this condition was integrity instead of hypocrisy. Nor do we have clear evidence that it was not. We need more research.

DOES MORAL INTEGRITY EVEN EXIST?

Returning to Kant's (1785/1898) candid assessment at the end of Chapter 1, is there any evidence that moral integrity even exists? Perhaps the most suggestive evidence in the reviewed research is that in virtually all of the task-assignment studies, 10 to 20 percent of participants assigned the other person the positive consequences. This was true whether they flipped the coin or not (see Tables 4.1 through 4.5). And in the privileged-information condition of the distributive-justice study (Table 4.6), 32 percent distributed both the low-value and high-value tickets fairly, 3 tickets of each value to self and 3 to other (down from 48 percent in the shared-information condition). The behavior of this 32 percent is consistent with integrity.

These findings are suggestive but not conclusive. The reason they aren't conclusive is that individuals differ in what's needed to provide them wiggle room. Some of us have a more strict set of self-regulatory standards than others. For those with strict standards, the opportunity to ignore or fiddle a coin flip, or to distribute raffle tickets equally but not equitably, may not have provided sufficient wiggle room to allow them to appear moral to themselves without actually being moral. If so, like those facing themselves in the mirror, these participants could have acted fairly yet still have been motivated by moral hypocrisy. Consistent with this possibility, there are several studies in which dispositional or situational restriction of wiggle room seems to have produced an appearance of integrity (see Carpenter & Marshall, 2009; Fernandez-Dols et al., 2010; List, 2007; Lönnqvist, Irlenbusch, & Walkowitz, 2014; Mazar et al., 2008; and Shalvi, Eldar, & Bereby-Meyer, 2012). Going in the other direction, Gino and Ariely (2012) presented provocative evidence that more creative people may be better able to provide *themselves* the wiggle room needed to appear yet not be moral (also see Vincent, Emich, & Goncalo, 2013).

At this point, the existent research suggests that moral integrity is less prevalent and powerful than often assumed. There may well be people whose moral standards are sufficiently integrated into their core self to be intrinsically valued and provide pervasive, potent guides to action. But at least among the undergraduates studied thus far, these people seem rare—even among those scoring high on measures of moral dispositions. And the examples in the first section of Chapter 1 suggest that such people may be rare among nonundergraduates as well. Rare but, as I shall argue in the next chapter, not nonexistent.

PERSPECTIVE TAKING: A STIMULUS TO MORAL INTEGRITY?

Perhaps in order to be more prevalent moral integrity needs to be stimulated. Many religious teachers and moral philosophers have suggested that perspective taking is a way to do just that.

Arguably, some form of the Golden Rule, "Do unto others as you would have them do unto you" (Matthew 7:12), is the world's most popular interpersonal-morality principle. It's found in all major religions and cultures. The Golden Rule implies an act of perspective taking in which you mentally place yourself in the other's situation. How you would want to be treated provides a standard for how you should treat others.

Philosopher Mark Johnson (1993) made the importance of this act of perspective taking explicit in his analysis of moral imagination. He argued that moral sensitivity requires the ability to imagine ourselves in others' shoes.

> Unless we can put ourselves in the place of another, unless we can enlarge our own perspective through an imaginative encounter with the experience of others, unless we can let our own values and ideals be called into question from various points of view, we cannot be morally sensitive. . . . It is not sufficient merely to manipulate a cool, detached "objective" reason toward the situation of others. We must, instead, go out toward people to inhabit their worlds. (Johnson, 1993, pp. 199–200)

Johnson's argument suggests that if we can be induced to take the perspective of another with whom our interests conflict, this will stimulate moral integrity.

Two Different Perspectives on Another's Situation, Two Different Motives

In his classic studies on empathy, Ezra Stotland (1969) identified two different forms of perspective taking. He found that imagining what your own thoughts and feelings would be if you were in the situation of a person in need (an imagine-self perspective) and imagining the thoughts and feelings of the person in need (an imagine-other perspective) both lead to increased emotional arousal compared to adopting a cool, objective perspective. But he also found that the emotions aroused by the two imagine perspectives aren't the same. An imagine-self perspective produces a mix of self-oriented personal distress (feeling tense, upset, etc.) and other-oriented empathic concern (feeling sympathetic, compassionate, etc.). An imagine-other perspective produces relatively pure empathic concern. Batson, Early, and Salvarani (1997) and Lamm, Batson, and Decety (2007) provided further evidence of this difference in the emotions produced by these two forms of perspective taking.

Imagine-Self

The Golden Rule and philosopher Johnson seem to agree that it's an imagine-self perspective that stimulates moral integrity. To actually be moral, a person should first imagine him or herself in the other's place. This suggests that research participants in the task-assignment paradigm should be induced to imagine themselves in the other participant's situation prior to making the assignment decision. They would then be more likely to flip the coin, and among those who flip the outcome would be fair. After all, that's how they would like to be treated were the other assigning the tasks.

Imagine-Other

As just mentioned, adopting an imagine-other perspective toward a person in need evokes empathic concern for that person. And, as discussed in Chapter 1, empathic concern leads to increased altruistic motivation—motivation with the ultimate goal of relieving the empathy-evoking need—not to increased moral motivation (also see Batson, 2011; Batson, Klein et al., 1995). So, in the task-assignment paradigm, participants induced to imagine the other's feelings prior to making the assignment shouldn't become more fair. Instead, they should be more likely to give the other participant the positive consequences directly without flipping the coin—much as those motivated by material self-interest would take the positive consequences for themselves without flipping.

Effects of Perspective Taking on Task Assignment

To test these predictions, Batson et al. (2003, Experiment 1) had some participants who were about to make the task-assignment decision first perform a brief imagination exercise. Other participants did not. Among those who performed the exercise, half were asked to "imagine yourself in the place of the other participant" for one minute, then write down what they had imagined (imagine-self condition). The other half were asked to "imagine how the other participant likely feels," then write (imagine-other condition).

As can be seen in Table 4.7, the imagine-self perspective had only a limited (and not statistically significant) effect on the fairness of the task assignment. It somewhat reduced the percentage assigning themselves the positive consequences after flipping the coin (67 percent) compared with the percentage doing this when not asked to do an imagination exercise (85 percent), and it somewhat increased this percentage among those who didn't flip (89 vs. 64 percent). The imagine-other perspective also had little effect on the fairness of the task assignment after

Table 4.7 Percentage Assigning Self to Positive Consequences in Each Perspective Condition (Batson et al., 2003, Experiment 1)

	Perspective condition		
Did participant flip coin?	No Perspective	Imagine self	Imagine other
No	64% (7/11)	89% (8/9)	27% (4/15)
Yes	85% (11/13)	67% (10/15)	67% (6/9)

flipping the coin, 67 percent of those who flipped the coin assigned themselves the positive-consequences task.

What's striking in Table 4.7 is the percentage of participants in the imagine-other condition who, without flipping the coin, assigned themselves the positive consequences. It was 27 percent—by far the lowest that had been seen in any study using the task-assignment procedure. Typically, 70 to 90 percent of those who don't flip the coin assign themselves the positive. But after imagining the other's feelings, almost three-fourths who didn't flip assigned *the other* the positive consequences. Consistent with the idea that an imagine-other perspective produces empathy-induced altruistic motivation and not increased moral integrity, this direct other-favoring assignment was significantly positively correlated with reported empathic concern felt for the other ($r = .60$), whereas choosing to flip the coin was significantly negatively correlated with reported empathic concern ($r = -.53$).

Symmetrical and Asymmetrical Moral Dilemmas

Why did an imagine-self perspective, widely touted as a stimulus to moral integrity, have such a small effect? Are those who have extolled the virtues of this form of perspective taking simply wrong? Perhaps not. The zero-sum nature of the task assignment poses a particular type of moral dilemma, one in which the preassignment plight of both participants is exactly the same. Each faces the prospect of being assigned to either the more desirable or the less desirable task. In a symmetrical dilemma such as this, to imagine myself in the place of the other participant may not lead me to focus on the other's interests, stimulating moral integrity. It may lead me to focus even more on my own interests.

If the inability of an imagine-self perspective to stimulate moral integrity was due to the symmetrical nature of the dilemma, then this perspective should be more effective when the other's initial situation is worse than my own. When the other is clearly disadvantaged, to imagine myself in his or her place may provide insight into what it's like to be in such a position. In this case, an imagine-self perspective may stimulate moral integrity. For example, when considering whether to vote for an increase in my own taxes in order to fund a job-training program for the unemployed, to imagine myself in the place of someone without work may stimulate moral action.

Pursuing this logic, Batson et al. (2003) ran a second experiment with only the imagine-self exercise and no-imagination-exercise conditions. In this experiment, participants were told that they had been randomly assigned to an asymmetrical-reward condition. They would receive two raffle tickets for each correct response on their task, whereas the other participant would receive nothing for a correct response. Participants were also told that if they wished, they could switch to a symmetrical-reward condition in which each participant would receive one raffle ticket for a correct response.

Participants who made the decision about whether to switch to the symmetrical condition after imagining themselves in the place of the other participant were far more likely to make the switch (83 percent) than were participants who made the decision without an imagination exercise (38 percent). So, in this asymmetrical dilemma an imagine-self perspective may indeed have stimulated moral integrity. (Alternatively, it may have stimulated moral hypocrisy by eliminating wiggle room and rendering it necessary to opt for the switch in order to appear moral. Once again, we need more research to know.)

Results of these two experiments suggest that an imagine-self perspective may have a limited but important role in stimulating moral integrity. Imagining oneself in the other's place may provide a corrective lens for the specific moral myopia to which those in a position of advantage are prone. This myopia is legendary. People who—like Voltaire's (1759/1930) Candide—live in the best of all possible worlds aren't likely to trouble themselves thinking about the worlds in which others live. Those born with a silver spoon in their mouth aren't likely to ask whether it's morally right to keep it there. If introducing an imagine-self perspective can effectively stimulate the moral sensitivity of persons of privilege, it has done important work.

But this very effectiveness may lead to a less salutary development. Persons of privilege, aware of the motivational consequences of imagining themselves in the place of the less advantaged, may not simply neglect to adopt such a perspective. They may actively resist it. That is, they may be motivated to avoid imagining themselves in the place of the less fortunate so as to avoid stimulating moral integrity. If so, admonition or instruction to imagine themselves in the other's place may fall on deaf ears. We may hear them say, "The peasants have no bread? Let them eat cake instead!"

Distinct from moral hypocrisy, avoidance of perspective taking may be another important reason for the scarcity of moral integrity. Yet again, we need more research. (For evidence of a parallel motive to avoid empathy-induced altruism, see Cameron & Payne, 2011; Shaw, Batson, & Todd, 1994.)

CONCLUSION

Psychologists have given relatively little attention to the nature of moral motivation. Those who consider moral motivation at all focus on its strength and power to stand up to temptation—or not (e.g., Bandura, 1991; Hartshorne & May, 1928; Hartshorne et al., 1929; Mischel, 2014; Mischel & Mischel, 1976). Even if weak, moral motivation has been thought pure in intent. Its goal has been assumed to be to act in accord with our moral standards, principles, or ideals (moral integrity). To propose that the goal of at least some moral motivation is to appear moral yet, if possible, avoid the cost of actually being moral (moral hypocrisy) casts doubt on this optimistic assumption. It also suggests that something other than insufficient inculcation or application of moral standards (Chapter 2) and situational pressure (Chapter 3) contributes to our moral failures. If we aren't motivated to actually be moral but only to appear that way, then whenever we can manage the appearance without incurring the cost of being moral we should.

Research reviewed in this chapter provides considerable evidence for the proposed hypocrisy motive. Apparently, moral motivation can indeed be deceptive. What's thought to be moral integrity can be hypocrisy instead. And if we're motivated by hypocrisy, then when there's sufficient wiggle room we should pursue the social and self-benefits of moral integrity without the accompanying price. We should fail to be moral.

The goal of moral hypocrisy isn't reached without skill. To gain the full benefits, we must be adept not only at retrospective rationalization and deceit of others but also at self-deception. Many of us seem to be.

The chapter also provided some evidence that moral integrity is vulnerable to being overpowered by self-interest. And some evidence that integrity isn't as easily stimulated as has been thought. On both of these points, more evidence is needed.

To recognize the existence of moral hypocrisy and the role that self-deception plays in our moral life complicates our understanding of moral motivation. Yet this recognition seems essential if we're to unravel the mysteries of why we act morally. And why we so often don't.

5

WHY IS MORAL INTEGRITY RARE, HYPOCRISY COMMON?

The previous chapter presented evidence that motivation to actually be moral isn't as prevalent as often thought. Motivation to appear moral yet, if possible, avoid the cost of being moral is common. This chapter considers how each of these conditions might arise. The answers proposed are admittedly speculative. They rest on some intriguing observational research on moral experiences and dialogues in childhood. This research builds on and extends the work on moral development described in Chapter 2.

WHY IS MORAL INTEGRITY RARE?

Before attempting to answer this question, it's important to point out that motivation to actually be moral is neither nonexistent nor always weak. Anne Colby and William Damon (1992), in *Some Do Care: Contemporary Lives of Moral Commitment*, reported a project in which they sought to identify exemplars of moral excellence in modern American society. Their nomination procedure produced 84 likely exemplars. Of these, 28 agreed to be interviewed, and 23 interviews were completed. Ages of those interviewed were from 35 to 86, with the majority over 65. There were 10 men and 13 women.

Although Colby and Damon's (1992) research design made it impossible to determine what motives were at work, the behavior and personal histories of their exemplars suggest that moral integrity often played an important role. Colby and Damon certainly thought it did. A key criterion for nomination was "personal integrity—that is, not merely a belief in certain noble moral principles but also a pervasive consistency between those principles and one's conduct" (Colby & Damon, 1992, p. 314). For the exemplars, morality was a want not just an ought:

> They were not setting their moral interests in opposition to their personal ones. ... The exemplars were starting from the assumption that their own interests were synonymous with their moral goals. ... None saw their moral choices as an exercise in self-sacrifice. ... In the end, it is this unity between self and morality that makes them exceptional. (Colby & Damon, 1992, pp. 299–301, italics omitted)

To indicate the sort of people who would qualify as moral exemplars by their crite-ria, Colby and Damon pointed to Mahatma Gandhi and Andrei Sakharov.

Even though their goal was to highlight the existence of moral integrity, Colby and Damon (1992) also wished to underscore its rarity. "Morality and the self grow closer together during the course of normal development, but they still remain rela-tively uncoordinated for most (but not all) individuals" (p. 308). Instead of qualify-ing as exemplars of moral integrity, many of us may resonate more with the morality reflected in an interchange reported by Damon in an earlier book (Damon, 1988, pp. 44–45). Seven young hockey players had stopped at a local pizza parlor after practice. When presented with their pizza, each took a piece. Then the question arose of what to do with the eighth piece. The oldest boy immediately offered a fair solution, "The guy who's the oldest should get it." The boy who got the smallest piece proposed instead, "What about giving it to the one with the small piece?" The oldest countered with a compromise, "C'mon, let's cut it. The oldest kid will get one piece and the kid with the smallest piece will get one piece." Not surprisingly, none of these solutions sat well with the other five boys. One of them began to pick cheese off the top of the extra piece. Others joined in pulling off chunks, and the eighth piece was quickly gone. Morality had been invoked to serve self-interest, a strategy that—given its transparency—failed. The result was unrestrained grabbing.

Look Not to Our Genes but to How We Acquire Moral Standards

So why is moral integrity rare? In recent years, it has become popular to appeal to our genetic makeup to explain our moral proclivities (e.g., Alexander, 1987; Bloom, 2013; Haidt, 2012; Haidt & Bjorklund, 2008a; Hauser, 2006; Wilson, 1993; Wright, 1994). But most of these appeals are designed to account for our moral capacities not our moral weaknesses. And there's disagreement about what it means to say that our moral capacities are genetically or biologically based.

Jerome Kagan (1987), for example, spoke of a "biologically based preparedness to judge acts right or wrong" that is manifest by the time the child is two (p. x). But what's the nature of this preparedness? Are we genetically programmed to adopt cer-tain moral standards and principles? Or only to have general attributes that allow us to acquire morality? That is, are humans, and perhaps some other species, prewired to care about fairness and not harming others, as some claim (e.g., Bloom, 2013; de Waal, 2006; Haidt, 2012; Haidt & Bjorklund, 2008a)? Or is the 2-year-old's—or brown capuchin monkey's (Brosnan & de Waal, 2003)—concern about these mat-ters a product of the interaction between (1) prewired biological desires for food, comfort, security, and so on; (2) personal attributes such as gender and tempera-ment; (3) problems posed by living with others in a world of finite resources and many dangers; and (4) cognitive capacity to learn reinforcement contingencies, form expectations, infer intentions, and "keep score"?

I don't believe we yet know. But my guess is that the interaction of the four factors just described accounts for the cross-cultural and even cross-species consistencies that are taken as evidence of biological preparedness to embrace certain moral content. Based on this guess, I'll assume that our moral standards and principles aren't inbred but are products of experience. Virtually all humans embrace principles of fairness, honesty, and the like, not because these principles are prewired but because we all have similar basic biological desires and cognitive skills, and we live with others in a world with insufficient resources to fully meet the desires of all. As suggested in Chapter 2, to face similar problems with similar resources is apt to produce similar solutions.

Problems That Produce Morality: Coherence and Conflict

At a very general level, the problems we face that lead to morality might be grouped into two types, coherence problems and conflict problems. *Coherence problems* concern the need to make sense of the world in which we live and to find our place in that world. Along with a need to understand how our physical and social world works, we want to make sense of our present experience in the context of past and future. We want to know where we've come from and what lies ahead. This includes an account of the past that recognizes and makes sense of the regularities we encounter in life and, ideally, the irregularities as well. It also includes an account of the future that tells us what to expect and how to produce change. To this end, we need to understand cause-and-effect relations. We need to know where we fit in—especially in our social world. And because others also have a sense of where both they and we fit, we need to reconcile our perception with theirs or face the consequences.

Without a sense of coherence, we're powerless. There's no reason to act. Idiosyncratic, individual solutions to coherence problems are possible, but at least among humans, solutions are typically shared. They're embodied in social institutions, mores, and a worldview. A shared solution—often in the form of religion—is one of the key defining features of a culture. Actions that promote or maintain the cultural worldview are seen as moral. Actions that cast doubt or disparage it, immoral. In Chapter 1, I called morality that promotes the natural and social order *propriety* morality.

Conflict problems concern the distribution of resources among interested parties when resources are insufficient to fully meet the needs of all. The resources at issue aren't simply material ones such as food, drink, possessions, mates, and money. They also include activities (Jane wants to talk but John wants to sleep), attention ("Look at me, Mom!"), affection ("It's *my* turn to sit on your lap"), and more. In families, interest conflicts can arise between parents, between children, and between parents and children. Friends also often face interest conflicts as they debate what to do, with whom, and when. Employees compete and negotiate over salary, work load, space, recognition, and promotions. Groups within society face conflicts over the distribution of power, wealth, opportunities, and benefits.

A host of sometimes contradictory moral standards, principles, and ideals specifies how we should act in various interest-conflict situations: Treat everyone the same. Divide equally. No, divide equitably. Reward success. Be kind. Take turns.

Care for the needy. Turn the other cheek. Don't tease. Be honest. The young hockey players in the pizza parlor faced an interest-conflict problem. Moral principles were invoked even if to no avail. In Chapter 1, I called morality that specifies how to deal with interest conflicts *interpersonal* morality.

Acquiring Propriety Morality

Compared with the acquisition of interpersonal morality, childhood acquisition of propriety standards and ideals is likely to be smooth and largely tension free. There can be some consternation if the child fails to control bowels and bladder as the parents and society deem appropriate. But toilet training is among the few areas—along with eating habits and table manners—in which the acquisition of propriety principles requires the child to change an existing pattern of behavior. In most areas, the child accepts the proprieties of his or her parents without any reason to question or object. Alternatives aren't considered until later if at all. For example, the child is typically dressed as the parents see fit with no question or complaint until the child sees a sibling or friend dressed differently. Even then, telling the child that people like him/her dress this way (e.g., gender-typical clothing) usually settles the issue.

Despite the questionable logic of inferring ought from is (Hume, 1751/1975), what the child learns about the way things are is likely to become the way they ought to be. This is especially true if the way they are provides coherence and helps the child fit in. Along with principles of natural and social order—The sun in the morning and the moon at night. No school on weekends.—he or she learns principles of right and wrong conduct—"Don't say that word!" Pray five times a day. These propriety principles can be imbued with as much reality and inviolability as natural laws.

Modeling plays an important role in learning propriety principles. The child follows the lead of parents and older children, trying to walk as they walk, talk as they talk, and think as they think. After all, it works for them, so it must be right. Similarly, the explanations received in response to the child's seemingly endless questions about the natural and social world must be right. If the parents are trusted and reasonably knowledgeable, their explanations are likely to be confirmed by experience and taken as gospel. Unless actively encouraged to do so, the child has no reason to doubt what's said. This is true when told about why it gets dark at night, when told about what happens after death, and when told about God. It's also true when the child is told about the way *we* think and when observing the way *we* act. The child easily becomes a follower and an enforcer of these truths (Schmidt & Tomasello, 2012).

In time, experience and exposure to alternative views may cause doubts. But there's little incentive to doubt initially. The child may delight in playing with the constraints of natural and social reality. Young Johnny may laughingly say, "I'm not Johnny; I'm Sam!" But except in pathological cases, the play is clearly make-believe. It doesn't challenge the natural and social order. Were his parents to accept and adopt the name change, Johnny would likely not think it funny at all.

Learning general principles of right and wrong conduct should be distinguished from learning the special way the child is supposed to act in certain situations—such as at bedtime or at school. In these situations, the local order often conflicts with the child's desires to hear another story or to play, laugh, and shout. It also conflicts with what's acceptable at other times and places. Faced with these conflicts, the child may resist and question. Internalization of these situation-specific standards is far from automatic. As noted in Chapter 1, some call these standards social conventions and distinguish them from moral standards (Smetana, 1989; Turiel, 1983). Some even consider all propriety principles conventional. But because propriety principles specify right and wrong conduct, they qualify as moral according to the dictionary, as discussed in Chapter 1.

By puberty, propriety conflicts may well appear, produced both by more diverse experiences and by developmental changes. Most obviously, new sexual interests and desires can lead the individual to violate his or her own propriety principles such as, "Thou shalt not masturbate." or "Thou shalt not have premarital sex." Some societies try to prohibit such violations. Others create institutionalized, ordered ways of handling them. A society may, for example, offer a ritualized sequence of temptation, violation, guilt, confession, and penance that can be repeated many times. Such a ritual may allow the propriety standard and its violation to coexist, producing considerable guilt.

In sum, initial acquisition of propriety morality occurs largely through practice, modeling (imitation), and didactic instruction. The carrot and stick of reward and punishment play a minor role. Given that the child wants to understand the way things are and to find his or her place in the world—and given that society wants this as well and has such understanding prepackaged and readily available in the form of a cultural worldview—initial acquisition is likely to go smoothly.

At least in a homogeneous society in which everyone shares the same solutions to coherence problems, most propriety standards are likely to be internalized to the point of integration. They become part of the core self and aren't subject to question. Should an adult in such a society be asked why he or she embraces a given propriety standard, the answer is likely to be a blank look and rather unsatisfactory, "Because it's right!" These are the hallmarks of what Haidt (2001) called moral dumbfounding. Not surprisingly, all Haidt's dumbfounding scenarios involve propriety violations—sibling incest, masturbating with a dead chicken, using the national flag to clean a toilet, and so on (Haidt et al., 1993; see Chapter 2).

Resistance to Propriety Changes

Once beliefs and practices that make sense of the child's world and life are in place, whether beliefs that the world is flat and was created in six days, that homosexuality and incest are sins, or that it's immoral to eat pork, they can be highly resistant to change. Three social-psychological theories speak to why.

The Need to Believe in a Just World

Melvin Lerner (1970, 1980, 1981; Lerner, Miller, & Holmes, 1976) hypothesized that most people develop a need to believe they live in a just world. They need to live in a world in which people get what they deserve and deserve what they get, or at least a world in which terrible things don't happen to good people. How does this need to believe in a just world come to be? Lerner argued that it arises in response to a basic coherence concern. Very early in life, we must make a contract with ourselves if we are to pursue anything more than immediate pleasure. This *personal contract* is of the form, "If I do this now, I'll get that later." Without faith that we'll eventually get our due, why pursue long-term goals? Why engage in any future-oriented action at all? Our personal contract makes possible delay of gratification (Mischel, 2014; Mischel & Mischel, 1976). It also enables development of goal-directed motivation. It's fundamental and nonnegotiable. To void it would send us tumbling into an abyss of helplessness and depression.

Of course, belief in a just world isn't easy to maintain. It's continually challenged by examples of injustice and innocent suffering. Such challenges may lead to a probabilistic view, "Yes, undeserved suffering occurs, but even if I don't always get what I deserve I usually do, so it's still worth investing in the future." Or the challenges may lead to a them-me distinction, "*Their* world may not be just, but mine is." Although such compromises may complicate the belief in a just world, they don't eliminate it. Only surrender of the personal contract would do that.

Implications of the just-world hypothesis are extremely broad. For example, it led Zick Rubin and Anne Peplau to predict that young men in the United States who learned that they had "lost" in the 1969 Vietnam War draft lottery—their birthday was drawn early, meaning that they were certain to be drafted—would, as a result, consider themselves to be less worthy people as indicated by lower ratings of self-esteem. A dramatic prediction, but one supported by their data (Rubin & Peplau, 1973). Lower self-esteem following innocent misfortune suggests how desperate can be the need to believe in the moral order. "For me to lose in the lottery and be drafted isn't unfair; I kinda deserve it." In like manner, we may come to believe that other innocent victims deserve their suffering as well. As discussed in Chapter 3, the just-world hypothesis applies to others' fate not only ours.

Belief Intensification in Response to Disconfirming Information

One of the more dramatic predictions of Leon Festinger's (1957) theory of cognitive dissonance is that a coherence-providing belief to which a person is publicly committed is likely to be intensified rather than weakened in response to information that contradicts the belief. Unwilling to discard a cherished belief, we attempt to drown the dissonance by reaffirmation. Festinger and colleagues (Festinger, Riecken, & Schachter, 1956) applied this principle to religious beliefs. As already noted, religious beliefs are one of the most important sources of a coherent worldview and of propriety morality. Subsequent research has supported Festinger et al.'s

prediction of intensification of religious beliefs in the face of disconfirming information (Batson, 1975; Hardyck & Braden, 1962).

Managing the Terror of Death

Building on Ernest Becker's (1973) analysis in *The Denial of Death*, Sheldon Solomon,
Jeff Greenberg, and Tom Pyszczynski (1991) proposed terror-management theory.
They suggested that both our cultural worldview and our personal sense of goodness and self-worth are responses to coherence problems created by the disturbing
awareness that we're going to die. Our worldview and self-worth each give meaning to life in the face of this reality. And because they do, we resist challenges or
threats to them. Much as we might pull a coat more tightly around us on a cold
windy night, reminders of our impending death lead us to cling more tightly to
both. Once again, research supports this prediction. When our mortality is made
salient, we judge more harshly those who violate cultural propriety standards for
sexual behavior, patriotism, and so on, and an ordered, proper life assumes more
meaning (Greenberg, Solomon, & Pyszczynski, 1997).

Propriety Morality and Integrity

I've suggested that propriety moral principles are relatively easily, innocently, and
uncritically acquired. And once acquired, they're likely to be automatically followed
and diligently defended. Of course, if you and I have different views about the natural and social order, I'm likely to judge your propriety standards wrong and you're
likely to judge mine the same. But when it comes to adherence to our own sense of
propriety, what we feel we ought to do and what we want to do are likely to coalesce.
Because of the coherence they provide, the way they're acquired, and their resistance
to change, propriety principles are likely to be valued intrinsically. So valued, they're
also likely to be a source of truly moral motivation. With regard to propriety, then,
moral integrity isn't rare. It's common.

Acquiring Interpersonal Morality

Acquisition of interpersonal morality is different. It requires a more detailed analysis. During the first few months of life, the child's moral world is quite limited if it
can be said to exist at all. This is because the child hasn't yet developed standards for
right and wrong conduct. The infant expresses distress and frustration when basic
desires aren't satisfied—desires for nourishment, security, stimulation, warmth,
and personal contact—and expresses pleasure when they're satisfied. The infant also
becomes quite attentive to who brings pleasure and who doesn't. A sense of good
and bad exists. But a sense of right and wrong doesn't begin to appear until around
8 to 12 months (Bloom, 2012, 2013; Hamlin, Wynn, Bloom, & Mahajan, 2011).

Still, even within the first year the child is likely to be part of interest-conflict
situations that raise moral issues for parents and siblings. A parent may struggle

with what's the right thing to do when the baby cries and wants to be held but the parent desperately needs sleep. An older brother or sister may feel it's not right that the baby gets so much attention when "I was here first!" The infant may not like the results of these conflicts and may make this displeasure known. But he or she doesn't judge the results morally wrong.

Especially if caregiving interactions are regular, tender, and responsive to needs, the infant develops expectations for what will happen. By playing with toys that can be moved and manipulated, he or she learns about physical cause and effect. Nurturant parental response to the child's cries provides early lessons in social cause and effect. The child learns how important other people can be in meeting his or her needs. Early drafts of the personal contract described by Lerner (1981) are taking shape.

Around the end of the first year, a fundamental change brings interest-conflicts to the fore in a much more dramatic way. The child begins to crawl, then toddle, and soon to run, jump, and roll. With mobility, the child can do more that others want, and that they don't want. Parents begin to expect more of the child, and to use reward, punishment, restraint, and instruction to control the child's behavior. These developments are apparent in research reported by Robert Emde, William Johnson, and Ann Esterbrooks (1987). They observed interactions between normal infants from middle-class US families and the infants' parents in a laboratory play setting. Here are typical observations:

> Parents of 12-month-olds in our sample frequently attempted to get their child to help in putting away the toys at the conclusion of their visit to our playroom. They often instructed their child to say "thank you" or "goodbye" upon leaving. (p. 263)
> An 18-month-old took several tissues and proceeded to dust the room. The parents praised him and he beamed; they smilingly told the interviewer that he often imitated his mother as she did housework. (p. 264)

But, as parents well know, the child isn't always compliant. Again, from Emde et al.'s (1987) observations:

> Parents of a 12-month-old girl report that their child will not stop a behavior when told "no." They need to remove the child's hand from the object, and she may repeatedly "test them." (p. 265)
> Parents report that when they say, "no" to their 18-month-old daughter, she ignores them, stares at them, occasionally will smile, and usually repeats the prohibited behavior. (p. 265)
> In our playroom, an 18-month-old boy played with a hammer on the pounding bench. When he hammered the chair, both parents said, "no," and mother unsuccessfully attempted to take the hammer. The child hammered the chair again, and the parents at first ignored this; the mother later grabbed the hammer and laid it on the floor. The child took the hammer again and hit the chair. Mother then retrieved the hammer. (p. 265)

One 18-month-old boy banged on the radiator when reminded by dad not to touch the tape recorder. Another 18-month-old boy in our playroom hit a baby doll in his mother's lap following his parents telling him to replace the magazines on the table. Still another 18-month-old, after replacing a vase on the table, subsequently banged on the table vigorously with the toy hammer. (p. 268)

Resistance, opposition, and tension are apparent.

Internalization of Interpersonal Principles

Even though all of their observations took place with parents present, which meant that social control was most common, Emde et al. (1987) included some examples of the child's first steps toward internalization and self-control:

Parents of an 18-month-old boy describe instances in which "we can't even see what he is doing, and he will run into the room we are in and say 'no,' and drag us back into the room, wanting confirmation that he did something wrong." (p. 267)

On a home visit, another 18-month-old girl was fascinated by the video taping equipment brought into her home. She remained near it, saying "no, no, no, no," to herself but did not touch. (p. 267)

Developmental psychologist Roger Burton (1984) provided an illuminating account of the evolution of his own daughter Ursula's response to interest conflicts over candy and other possessions. It shows her progression from external to internal control. Burton's account, which I quote at length, begins when Ursula was 18 months old. After her first experience of Halloween trick-or-treating, she was

admiring all the candy she and her sisters had been given. When putting it away, Ursie started to put some of her sisters' candy into her bag. "No, Ursie, that's mine!" said one of the sisters, and I explained that she should put only her own candy into her bag.

A week later, when most of the candy was gone, the sisters found that some of their candy was in Ursie's bag. Hearing the fuss about "Not going to let you come into my room," and "That's stealing, Ursie," my wife intervened to see to it that Ursula returned the purloined loot and again explained about not taking her sisters' things. The next day, however, when my wife saw Ursula with her hand in a sister's candy bag, she said, "No, Ursula! You know you're not to take your sister's candy. Come out of her room now." Later, I saw Ursula in her sister's room looking at the candy bag, and she looked up and said, "No, this is Maria's, not Ursula's," and walked out of the room to me. "Good girl, Ursie. You know you're not to take candy that's not yours."

About the age of 3, there was an episode in which a plastic toy was taken from a store, and Ursula had to return it immediately to the manager and say she was sorry. I again explained that taking it without paying was stealing and that she was not to do that. A few weeks after starting first grade, Ursula brought home a cartoon-character mechanical pencil with another child's name on it. After a painfully circuitous discussion at the dinner table, it finally came out that Ursula had "borrowed" the pencil, although the owner did not know it yet. We then explained about temptations, honesty, and how she would feel if it had been her pencil and another child had taken it, and her sisters talked about how no one likes to be a stealer.

Seven years later in Yellowstone Park, Ursula saw a wallet on the ground with money blowing out of it, frantically ran around gathering up the $20 bills, and finally mailed the wallet and its $485 to its owner in Montreal. When asked later if she had been tempted to keep any of the money, she looked nonplussed and said, "Dad! That would be stealing!" (Burton, 1984, pp. 199–200)

Discipline Encounters

In these observations we have examples of the discipline encounters referred to in Chapter 2, in which parents attempt to change a child's behavior against the child's will. Such encounters occur with increasing frequency once the child begins to toddle. Martin Hoffman (2000) estimated that, on average, there's one every 11 minutes when the child is between 12 and 15 months old. At this age, most concern safety and preventing damage to breakable objects. But soon, encounters that concern interest conflicts and the child harming another person come to the fore.

> By the end of the second year fully two-thirds of all parent-child interactions are discipline encounters. . . . Children in the 2- to 10-year age range experience parental pressure to change their behavior every 6 to 9 minutes on average, which translates roughly into 50 discipline encounters a day or over 15,000 a year! (Hoffman, 2000, p. 141)

Hoffman considered encounters over harming others essential for the internalization of interpersonal morality:

> Whether the harm done by the child is accidental or intentional and whether the victim is a parent or a peer, it is only in discipline encounters that parents are likely to make the connection, necessary for guilt and moral internalization, between children's egoistic motives, their behavior, and their behavior's harmful consequences on others—and to put pressure on children to control their behavior out of consideration for others. . . . The type of discipline that can do this is induction, in which parents highlight the other's perspective, point up the

other's distress, and make it clear that the child's action caused it. (Hoffman, 2000, pp. 142–143)

It certainly seems plausible that such discipline can produce internalization to the level of introjection (Deci et al., 1994). By her early teens, Ursie clearly felt that stealing was wrong. She would be ashamed even to contemplate it. But, as discussed in Chapter 2, it's not clear that such discipline can produce the full integration necessary for moral integrity in the face of interest conflicts. Perhaps playing games can.

Playing Games

Recall that Piaget (1932/1965) emphasized the importance of game playing for moral development (again, see Chapter 2). Games create social realities complete with rules and roles. If players ignore the rules, a game quickly falls apart. In this sense, cooperative play involves a social contract. The contract isn't a defensive, negative one of the sort depicted by Thomas Hobbes (1651), whereby I allow constraints on my power in order to assure constraints on yours. It's a more positive contract that allows each of us to enter into and enjoy a socially constructed world that we otherwise could not.

Important lessons in interpersonal morality can be learned from playing games. We learn to take turns, apply rules impartially, and be attuned to the effects of our actions on others. We learn to adopt the perspective of other players in order to understand and anticipate their moves. We come to recognize that others do the same with regard to us. Finally, we learn that events that are good for us can be bad for others, and vice versa.

But not all games teach these lessons to the same degree. Formal, adult-regulated games such as Little League baseball probably teach more about following externally imposed rules (Piaget's heteronomy) than about creating a socially constructed world, being fair, and perspective taking (his autonomy). Informal competitive games created on the spot with playmates tend to do the opposite. Even though competitive, such games are also necessarily cooperative, as Piaget (1932/1965) found was true of the game of marbles once players realized that the rules are largely arbitrary. Without mutual agreement on boundaries, turn taking, and so on, the game isn't possible. To satisfy our own interest in playing and winning we must give attention to the parallel interests of others.

These observations suggest that through games we may discover the value of fair play, respect for others, honor, courage, self-discipline, and self-sacrifice for the good of the collective (e.g., the team). These values may, in turn, provide the basis for moral principles, especially fairness principles that focus on giving equal consideration to the interests and desires of each person in interest-conflict situations. Does the motivation to adhere to these interpersonal principles remain instrumental in the service of avoiding accusations and getting ahead? Or does the game player learn to value fair play intrinsically as an ultimate goal? If the former, game playing is only another source of extrinsic moral value and instrumental moral motivation. If the latter, it's a source of moral integrity.

Piaget (1932/1965) clearly believed that the mutual cooperation of playing games produces autonomous moral standards with intrinsic value, standards that prompt moral integrity. But insofar as I know, this belief has never been adequately tested. At present it's only a promising possibility. To his credit, Piaget (1932/1965) was careful to point out that his own research didn't provide the needed test. Some subsequent research, to which I now turn, adds complications to Piaget's belief in the moralizing power of competition, negotiation, and mutual respect.

Acquiring Interpersonal Immorality

Judy Dunn (2006) characterized the conflict between the 2-year-old child's personal desires and the desires of others in a manner reminiscent of both Freud and social learning theorists:

> The driving self-concern in the face of powerful others within the family characterizes many of children's interactions with their parents and siblings in the early years, as they develop a more elaborate sense of themselves and an increased capacity to plan. This self-interest invests the understanding of other people and of the social rules of the family world with especial salience. (p. 336)

But Dunn and her colleague Penny Munn went beyond this characterization by providing a more in-depth look at the child's experience dealing with interest conflicts and interpersonal morality. Their in-depth look was based on extensive observations during the 1980s in middle-class homes in Cambridge, England, and surrounding villages.

Primary targets of these observations were second-born children in their second year of life. Sampling this population meant that Dunn and Munn could watch these children interact with their mother and with an older brother or sister—on average, about 2 years older than the child—as well as observe the interaction of all three. Conflicts were of particular interest (sibling conflicts occurred at a rate of 8.0 and 7.6 per observation hour when the child was 18 and 24 months old, respectively; Dunn & Munn, 1986a, p. 587). By going into the home multiple times and staying for an hour each time—and by using relatively unobtrusive, low-tech recording methods (audiotape, paper and pencil)—the observer was able to approach becoming part of the furniture, and so get a glimpse of unstructured, natural events and conversations.

Moral Conflicts

Dunn and Munn (1985) noted a significant increase between 18 and 24 months in the number of mother–child conflict incidents in which the mother referred to rules, standards, and expectations. Similarly, there was a significant increase over the same months in the number of sibling–child conflicts in which an older sibling attempted to control the child's behavior by reference to rules and standards (Dunn & Munn, 1985, p. 487).

> The moral order of their parents' world was conveyed to the children again and again in the repeated events of their daily lives . . . . Mothers make such messages explicit long before children are capable of verbally expressing their own under-standing of the forbidden behavior. (Dunn, 1988, p. 73)

The observations made clear that moral standards became highly salient to children during the second year. Morality was "a source of curiosity, distress, delight, and shared humor" (Dunn, 1987, p. 91). In addition to anger and distress at being told "no," expressions of shame, embarrassment, and guilt began to appear (Dunn, 2006, p. 337; see also Kagan, 1984). Dunn and Munn (1985) observed that children were likely to respond negatively to the implications of standards for their own behavior. But standard violations by the older brother or sister were more apt to evoke positive emotions, amusement, and imitation of the forbidden act (Dunn, 1988, p. 64). Dunn summarized the clash between the child and parent over conduct:

> Throughout the last three centuries doctors, diarists, and philosophers writing about children and childrearing have noted the growth of willful, disobedient, and contrary behavior in the second and third year of life. The passion and pleasure children show in resisting parental wishes is documented—often with anguish—by parents and by those concerned with the moral development of children. Our observations of the Cambridge children followed through the transition from infancy to childhood confirm the accuracy of the accounts given by these earlier writers. . . .
>
> The evidence for growth of assertive and resistant behavior shown by the children toward their mothers was striking. While exchanges in which the mother simply prohibited the child and the child complied without protest occurred at much the same frequency as the children grew from 14-month-olds to 3-year-olds (on average, around nine such exchanges for each two hours of observation), conflicts in which the child protested the mother's actions, resisted her demands, or—most irritating of all for mothers—repeated what they had just been forbidden to do all nearly doubled in frequency between 18 and 24 months. (Dunn, 1988, pp. 14–15)

Another Disturbing Development

The home observations of Dunn and Munn (1985) highlighted a development in response to sibling interest-conflicts that's quite different from the gradual internalization of moral standards depicted by social learning theorists. It's also quite different from the discovery of autonomous moral standards of cooperation and mutual respect described by Piaget.

> Although empathic responses to others do become more frequent in the second and third years there is also an increase in diametrically different behaviors: actions that reflect a practical grasp of how to upset others. Not only does this sophisticated behavior depend on understanding the feelings and wishes of the sibling; it also suggests that the intense emotional experiences of rivalry within the sibling relationship may well lead to the learning or development of *immoral* behavior. Behavior that is specifically intended to hurt or upset others takes place at least as early as *moral* behavior. And the pleasure and interest that children show in breaking rules echo this point. (Dunn, 1987, p. 107, italics in original)

Both physical aggression against and teasing of the sibling came to the fore in the second year: "The children showed, with increasing frequency, pragmatic understanding of how to annoy the sibling in family disputes. They not only perceived what would upset the sibling, but also acted upon this understanding" (Dunn & Munn, 1985, p. 485). And by watching the sibling, they learned ways to misbehave and get away with it. The children weren't only learning to adhere to interpersonal moral standards that curbed their self-interest. They were also learning how to pursue those interests more aggressively and creatively by bringing moral sanctions to bear on others. One way to do this was by tattling (Ross & den Bak-Lammers, 1998, discussed in Chapter 7). When the sibling was aggressive toward the child, teased the child, or took something that was the child's, the child appealed to the mother 65 out of 99 times. When the child was the initiator of the aggression, teasing, or taking, the child called the mother's attention to it only four out of 125 times (Dunn & Munn, 1985).

Summary

Although it seems likely that initial acquisition and internalization of propriety morality proceeds relatively smoothly even to the level of integration, the acquisition and internalization of interpersonal morality does not. Because interpersonal morality addresses situations of interest conflict, the child has reason to resist, ignore, and dissemble. This resistance can be overcome, but rarely without a struggle. Both material and social rewards and punishments are employed. Due to the resistance—and to the consequent reliance on reward and punishment—interpersonal moral standards are likely to be internalized only to the level of introjection. They function as extrinsic oughts rather than intrinsic wants.

I believe this is why we find moral integrity to be rare in interpersonal conflict situations. The child is taught to share, take turns, and play by the rules. He or she is also taught not to grab, steal, hit, bite, or lie. But the resulting standards and principles are apt to be experienced as constraints not desires. They are also experienced as weapons that can be used against others in conflict situations. The experience of constraint is reflected in neuroimaging evidence that cortical areas associated with self-control of self-interested impulses (e.g., regions of the prefrontal cortex and anterior cingulate cortex) are active when upholding fairness standards in an Ultimatum Game (Knoch, Pascual-Leone, Meyer, Treyer, & Fehr, 2006; Sanfey, Rilling, Aronson, Nystrom, & Cohen, 2003) and when faced with an opportunity to benefit from lying (Greene & Paxton, 2009).

WHY IS MORAL HYPOCRISY COMMON?

While following the bumpy road that must be traveled to reach interpersonal moral integrity, we've caught glimpses of a second road, one that leads to moral hypocrisy. The road to integrity runs uphill through conflict after conflict. When what the child wants is at odds with what the parents want, the parents first physically control the child's behavior. Later, they use verbal restraints, reward and punishment, instruction, explanation, and reason. Even later, parents appeal to general standards and principles. They explain what they expect of the child and why. And they express disappointment when the child fails to live up to expectations.

In time, the child comes to employ these methods to control his or her own behavior. Initially, a self-addressed "no" may be used to forestall conflict with parents and others. But once the child has internalized moral rules and standards to the level of introjection, he or she actively curbs desires so as to avoid self-censure, shame, and guilt. To reach moral integrity, we must travel beyond this internal conflict to a point where the oughts become wants. Moreover, these moral wants must be high enough in our value hierarchy that they consistently trump other wants. Few travel this far.

Along this road, the child learns that being immoral can be costly. Punishment, social censure, parental disappointment, and self-condemnation loom. But the child also learns that being moral can be costly. When he or she does what's right, pleasures are lost and desires thwarted. Having recognized how important it is to both others and self that I adhere to moral standards and principles, and having recognized the loss of personal pleasure that adherence brings, it's natural to seek a road that bypasses both sets of costs. This is the road to hypocrisy. If I can convince those wielding the standards that I've acted morally and yet can still do as desired, both sets of costs are avoided. Better yet, they're replaced with important benefits. In addition to the benefits of getting what's wanted, I get the social and self-rewards for doing what's right.

How do we manage to find this second road? Surely our parents don't point the way. They don't tell us to dissemble. They don't reward our attempts at hypocrisy when they discover them, nor do they preach it. Quite the opposite. Parents preach integrity and living up to our moral standards and ideals. Hypocrisy is castigated.

So how does the child acquire the hypocrisy motive? As far as I know, no developmental psychologist has explicitly addressed this question. (But Nietzsche, 1887/1967b, and Freud, 1930/1961, at least approached it—each from his own historical-cultural perspective; see Chapter 7.) Despite the lack of explicit attention, I believe we have some clues to the way children acquire hypocrisy. Most come from the observational studies already mentioned.

Starting on the Road to Hypocrisy

An early turn toward moral hypocrisy occurs when the child learns a truism of childhood: Undetected misbehavior goes unpunished. This inevitable lesson is good news. It reveals a way to pursue self-interest and still escape punishment. Even more important, it provides valuable information about parents and other control agents. They aren't omniscient. It makes a big difference whether I misbehave where others can see, as in the observations recorded by Emde et al. (1987). Or where they can't, as in Ursie's attempts to sneak candy (and in the tactic of a colleague's young son who, when playing the board game Trouble, intentionally rolled the dice where only he could see). From this truism, it's but a short distance to the discovery that other people—parents included—can be deceived. Initially, I deceive by withholding information, by hiding my actions and keeping quiet. But before long by providing it ("I rolled a 10, just what I needed!").

Childish Deceit

Dunn (1988) offered the example of 21-month-old Ellie (C), who wanted to play with a bar of soap. Having been told "no" several times by her mother (M), this interchange ensued:

M: Have a bath later, shall we?
C: Ba.
M: You put it in the bath, ready then?
C: (does so).
M: There you are. Now it's ready for you later when you have a bath. Come on.
C: Ba (points to soap).
M: No, we're not taking it. I said you can get in the bath later.
C: (lies down on floor in position for diaper change and gestures to diaper).
M: No, I'm not taking it off.
C: Cack (word for dirty diaper). [Ellie's diaper is quite clean]
M: No, you haven't.
C: Cack.
M: No you haven't. (p. 20)

Ellie's pretense of having a dirty diaper so she could get in the bath and play with the soap didn't work, but its cleverness can't be denied. Nor can the intent to deceive.

Dunn (2006) summarized her observations of young children as follows: "They both draw the attention of parents to forbidden acts (their own and those of others), and they make attempts to evade adult attention or to deceive adults increasingly during the second and third years" (p. 333).

Intriguing in this context is the previously mentioned account by the parents who reported that their 18-month-old son came to find them, said "no," and then led them to the evidence of his misdeed (Emde et al., 1987, p. 267; for a similar example, see Dunn, 1988, pp. 18–19). Perhaps this boy was firmly on the road to moral integrity. Or perhaps he had not yet discovered his parents' fallibility. But I wonder about a third possibility. Perhaps his proud parents had praised him in the past for such reporting. Perhaps they also forgave him the wrong. If so, I suspect they came to regret their behavior. Once the boy learned that to report wrongdoing paid, he could do wrong with impunity, and even to get praise.

Growing Sophistication

Over time, the child's deceptions gain sophistication. This development is nicely documented in a series of experiments begun by Lewis, Stanger, and Sullivan (1989). Three-year-old children were told not to peek at a toy while the experimenter was out of the room, they would get to play with the toy when the experimenter returned. Of the 33 children placed in this situation, 29 peeked. But when the experimenter returned and asked, "Did you peek?," 11 children denied doing so and another 7 didn't answer. Only 11 admitted peeking. Facial expression and body movement didn't differentiate those who lied about peeking from the truth tellers.

Using a similar procedure, Polak and Harris (1999) found that about half of both 3- and 5-year-olds touched a toy guitar while the experimenter was out of the room, after they had been told not to. Twenty-eight of 52 (54 percent) did so, with no reliable difference across age or gender. Of the 28 who disobeyed, 23 (82 percent) subsequently denied having touched the guitar. In a second experiment, both 3- and 5-year-olds were extremely likely to look inside a toy house to see the toy animal inside while the experimenter was out of the room, after being told not to. Fifty-seven of 60 (95 percent) did so. Of the 57, 48 (84 percent) denied having looked. Tellingly, those children who on independent tests showed a better understanding of how people can be misled into false beliefs were the ones more likely to falsely deny having looked. Apparently, they had learned what they could get away with.

Talwar, Lee, Bala, and Lindsay (2002) had 3- to 7-year-old children play a game in which the children tried to guess the name of different toys placed out of sight on a table behind them by listening to audio clues. After the child correctly guessed two toys, a third toy was placed on the table with an ambiguous musical clue playing. Before the child could guess, the experimenter was called out of the room to take a telephone call, leaving the toy (a Barney doll) behind the child with the music playing. The children were told not to turn around and peek at the toy while the experimenter was gone. They were also told that when the experimenter returned, if they guessed the toy correctly, they would get a prize. The experimenter left saying, "Remember, no peeking."

Across three experiments using this general procedure, 324 of 403 children peeked (80 percent). On returning, the experimenter asked, "When I was gone, did you peek to see who it was?" Of the 324 peekers, 216 lied and said no (67 percent). Older children were no less likely than younger ones to lie after peeking. This was true even though on an independent test using a hypothetical situation older children were more likely to say that they wouldn't lie about disobeying. Overall, a majority of the children said lying after disobeying was wrong. Again tellingly, those who lied about peeking were more likely to say this than were those who told the truth. With age and growing cognitive skills, we learn that what we say we've done needn't match what we actually do. Nor does what we say would be right to do.

Shifting from research on honesty to research on fairness, Shaw, Montinari, Piovesan, Olson, Gino, and Norton (2014) found that 6- to 8-year-old children given wiggle room to appear fair to the experimenter yet not be fair were significantly less likely to act fairly than those given no wiggle room. And, using a coin-flip procedure adapted from the task-assignment paradigm described in Chapter 4, Shaw et al. found that older children (9 to 11 years old) were much more likely than younger ones (6 to 8 years old) to appear fair (flip the coin) but no more likely to actually be fair (abide by the flip). These results suggest growing hypocrisy not growing integrity.

Modeling Hypocrisy

Another important clue to the development of hypocrisy is provided by the social learning research on modeling. It's well known that children will imitate the moral behavior of powerful and affectionate role models such as parents and older siblings (Dunn & Munn, 1986a, p. 589). For example, Rushton (1975) demonstrated long-term effects (over 2 months) on the charitable behavior of 7- to 11-year-olds after they observed an adult model play a game, win tokens, then donate some of the tokens to charity. But Rushton (1975) also found that inconsistency between what the model said was the right thing to do (give tokens) and what the model actually did (give none) was likely to lead children to model both responses—to say giving is the right thing to do but practice selfishness.

Most parents are well aware of this potential and try to practice what they preach "in front of the children." But most of us also make slips. When we do, our children may not be as troubled by the inconsistency as are we. Instead, they may embrace it as a way to appear on the side of right and still do what they want. Nascent hypocrisy.

Learning to Use Morality for Personal Gain

Instrumental use of moral standards to promote self-interest is common in children's negotiations over the use of toys, over who will play what role in pretend play, and over the allocation of scarce resources.

Interest Conflicts with Peers

The distributive-justice principle that "possession is nine-tenths of the law" is often invoked implicitly if not explicitly in interest conflicts, as in the following exchange reported by Eisenberg and Garvey (1981) in their observational study of 3- to 6-year-olds:

> Child 1: Annie, gimme that ladder.
> Child 2: No, I don't have to.
> Child 1: I wanna play with it.
> Child 2: Well, I got it first.
> Child 1: I gotta put it on here. Now you gimme it.
> Child 2 (offers truck): You can have this.
> Child 1: No, if you gimme ladder, I'll give you this if you gimme ladder (offers flashlight).
> (Child 2 drops ladder and picks up flashlight.) (p. 155)

In the preceding interchange, a possession conflict was resolved by appeal to a principle of reciprocity. In the next one, the appeal is to sharing:

> Child 1: I'm gonna play with the camper.
> Child 2: *I'm* gonna play with the camper.
> Child 1: I said I'm gonna play with that.
> Child 2: We'll share it. (Eisenberg & Garvey, 1981, p. 161, italics in original)

Without some attempt to justify one's own claim and, ideally, give some attention to the interests of the other child, matters are likely to end in a stand-off—much as in adult life.

> Child 1: You go in the back. Go in the back.
> Child 2: No.
> Child 1: You go in the back.
> Child 2 (moving away): No!
> Child 1: Why?
> Child 2: (no response)
> Child 1: My mommy told me to go here.
> Child 2: No.
> Child 1: My mommy told me to go here.
> Child 2: No.
> Child 1: Uh-huh.
> Child 2: No.
> Child 1: Yes.
> Child 2: No.
> (long pause—both sit and stare at each other) (Eisenberg & Garvey, 1981, p. 167)

As the years pass, right of possession is likely to be contested by each claimant appealing to a different moral principle. Each picks a principle that favors self. Consider this example of 10-year-old boys observed by Walton (1985):

Kerry: John, that's my seat.

John: How do you know?

Kerry: 'Cause that's my stuff. (He nods toward the papers on the table in front of John.)

John: How am I supposed to know that?

Kerry: It has my name on it. (He points to his name on the papers.)

John: How do you expect me to see that? (Kerry stands over John as if expecting him to leave the seat.)

John: Scott, were you saving his place?

Scott: No.

John: Were you? (He looks toward Omar.)

Omar: No.

John: I have every right to sit here. 'Cause no one is saving your place. Just as I thought.

Kerry: My paper was saving my place.

John: Your paper?! Your paper doesn't even have your name on it.

(Kerry sits down in the chair, forcing John to scoot over and the two boys share the chair.) (p. 735)

In negotiating conflicts of interest with peers, the child is almost certain to be exposed to unsuccessful attempts—both his or her own and other people's—to pursue moral hypocrisy. (If the attempt is successful, it won't be recognized as hypocrisy.) For example, among the young hockey players negotiating how to divide the extra piece of pizza, neither blatant attempt to appear moral yet benefit self worked, not that of the oldest boy nor that of the boy with the smallest piece. What lesson did these two boys and the other five learn from this failure? Perhaps they learned that hypocrisy doesn't pay. More likely, the take-home message was that *transparent* hypocrisy doesn't pay.

Moral Negotiations with Teachers

Moral dialogues also play a large role in the interaction of children with their teacher. In these conversations the child is usually on the defensive after having been charged by the teacher with doing something wrong. The child attempts to escape blame by use of the various strategies of denial of responsibility, reframing, and justification described in Chapters 2 and 3. First, an example from Much and Shweder (1978),

1. Diane, accused of "stealing" Sandra's chair, points out that since the chair was empty, she didn't steal it, she "sat in it." (p. 37)

And two from Walton and Sedlak (1982),

2. I got it out of your office so I could clean the sink. (p. 398)
3. My foot just did that by itself. (p. 398).

New Standards

With age, the standards invoked become more diverse and more attuned to the welfare of others. For example, Laursen and Hartup (2002) argued that standards followed in friendships "change from an emphasis on self-interest, to the matched exchange of material resources, to a matched exchange of emotional and psychological resources, and finally to a need-based exchange that emphasizes mutuality and collective concern" (p. 31; also see Damon, 1977; Selman, 1980; and Youniss, 1980). One might assume that this change facilitates progress toward moral integrity. Certainly, examples like the one above in which two children agree to share a camper are consistent with Piaget's (1932/1965) contention that autonomous morality develops in the negotiation of interest conflicts between peers showing mutual respect and pursuing cooperation.

But perhaps the new friendship standards are simply a product of differences in society's expectations regarding the behavior appropriate for children of different ages. Consistent with this possibility, the older siblings in Dunn and Munn's research were significantly more likely to share, help, and comfort than were their younger brother or sister. Dunn and Munn (1986b) attributed this difference not only to increased cognitive ability but also to new expectations and added instrumental moral motivation:

> The older siblings are under considerable pressure from their mothers to behave in a socially responsible manner. They are, for instance, three times as likely as the second-born to be reproved for conflict with the sibling, although the younger siblings are equally likely to be responsible for such conflict. (p. 280)

Expectations are doubtless even higher by the time the child approaches adolescence.

So, older children may still be using their more sophisticated moral rules and standards instrumentally in the service of self-interest. Cooperation is, after all, an effective strategy to use in the enlightened pursuit of what we want for ourselves when, without cooperation, we would end up with less. By adolescence, attention to a friend's needs is necessary if we want to keep the friend. Suggestive of an early move in this direction, Dunn and Munn (1986b) found that the 18-month-old children in their Cambridge sample were capable of sharing, helping, and comforting, and had some understanding of related standards. But the children rarely responded in these ways. In contrast, cooperative behavior as well as conciliation was frequently seen. Perhaps this was because cooperation and conciliation have more instrumental value. They produce immediate self-benefits.

Appearing in Court

Once the child learns that moral principles are tools that can be used to personal advantage, but are also tools that others can use to constrain the child's behavior, the stage is set for a move toward moral hypocrisy in yet another key context. This context is the adjudication by adults of conflicts among children over who misbehaved. Observational research in homes (Dunn, 1987, 1988; Dunn & Munn, 1986a, 1986b, 1987) and schools (Walton & Sedlak, 1982) provides a provocative glimpse of inadvertent but almost inevitable lessons in hypocrisy as each child tries to avoid blame.

Here's an example from Dunn (1988), in which Annie (C for Child), who is 30-months old, has been told not to play with the garden hose. She turns it on again and then attempts to blame her older sister Carol (S for Sibling).

> M (Mother) enters garden: Who's put the hosepipe out again?
> C to M: Carol.
> S to C: No, it was Annie.
> M to both: Why did any of you put the hosepipe out again? 'Cos I'd packed it all away to go in the shed.
> C to M: Umm. Carol did it.
> S: I didn't. She did it.
> C to M: Carol did it.
> S to C: No she didn't. (to M:) On no I didn't. She done it.
> C to M: Carol did. Carol did.
> S to C (shouts): *I did not!!*
> C to M: Umm. Carol—
> M to both: Well, whoever it was is a naughty girl.
> S to M: It was Annie. (Dunn, 1988, pp. 29–30, italics in original).

In this interchange, there's no reasoned defense by either sister. Only finger-pointing, denial, insistence, and a shout. But even this strategy succeeded in diffusing blame to the level of a tepid "whoever it was is a naughty girl."

Once language skills develop a little further, the mother, teacher, or other authority is called on to judge right and wrong in a proceeding that Thomas Shultz and John Darley (1991) compared to a courtroom trial (also see Darley & Shultz, 1990). As if in court, each child pleads his or her case before the adult. "She hit me first!" "Did not, he took my truck!" The adult then renders a verdict.

> Within this "trial," under the direction of the adult, the child learns that a moral challenge is an occasion for negotiating the meaning of the incident, and that there are a number of specific claims, that group under general rule headings, that are the basis for this negotiation. ... The child learns this for the best of

reinforcement reasons. Getting the rules right avoids punishment; getting them wrong leads to punishment. (Shultz & Darley, 1991, p. 270)

Shultz and Darley reflected on whether such experiences move the child toward valuing the rules intrinsically or only extrinsically:

> The question arises about whether the child learns to abide by these moral rules, or simply to use them. That is, whether the child internalizes the rules, and uses them prospectively to govern his or her behavior, or instead learns to use them, after the fact, to put the best face on transgressions he or she has committed. ... Certainly the transcripts provided by Dunn and others provide vivid examples that reveal that surprisingly young children can carry out these negotiations with a wily regard for their own self-interest, and at least occasionally a wily disregard for truth. (1991, p. 270)

In the observational accounts of children's misbehavior trials, the instrumental use of moral rules and principles is conspicuous.

Dunn's (1988) summary assessment of the moral development of the 2-year-olds she observed seems quite consistent with Shultz and Darley's courtroom analogy. She, too, pointed to the instrumental use of moral rules and principles:

> By 18 to 20 months, the children were taking part more explicitly in an active way, playing, teasing, contradicting, and insisting on their own way verbally. Justifications and excuses for defiant behavior were given more and more frequently .... Their arguments make it clear that at a practical level they have grasped the idea of prescriptivity and the possibility of breach and sanction. A closer look at children's comments, justifications, and excuses begins to give us a picture of their moral intuitions: their notions of harm or injury to others, of responsibility, of what exempts an individual from the application of a rule, and so on. Beyond this picture of the child as moralist, we can see in such conversations how the child *uses* this growing understanding in his family relationships, to get his way, to escape blame, to deflect punishment onto his sibling, to tease and joke—the child as psychologist. (Dunn, 1988, p. 26, italics in original)

Rather than "the child as psychologist," we might follow Shultz and Darley (1991) and say, "the child as defense attorney." Nor is this depiction new. As Dunn (1988, p. 42) noted, James Sully reached much the same conclusion over a century ago:

> One cannot say that these first incursions into the domain of logic do Master C. [the child] particular credit. Perhaps we may see later on that he came to use his rational faculty with more skill and precision and to turn it to nobler uses than the invention of subterfuges whereby he might get his willful way. (Sully, 1908, p. 449)

Shultz and Darley's (1991) courtroom analogy highlights the fact that moral issues are brought to the child's attention not in the abstract but in interpersonal interest conflicts where someone else's interests are at odds with the child's own. The result is that "children are likely to most quickly learn those moral principles that will work to their advantage in actual moral disputes" (Shultz & Darley, 1991, p. 269). At least in Western society, principles of possession and ownership probably come first, followed by fairness in the form of turn-taking and distributive justice ("No fair, your piece is bigger!"). Children are also likely to "learn that moral rules, like the rules of games and other interpersonal endeavors, are to some extent flexible, and that that flexibility can be exploited by interested parties" (Shultz & Darley, 1991, p. 274). Echoes of Piaget (1932/1965)—but with a twist.

Crucial in the courtrooms of childhood, whatever can be made to appear true to the adult, even if not actually true, decides the case. No doubt the child is shocked and confused the first few times he or she, although innocent, is judged guilty because a brother, sister, or playmate was more adroit at juggling the evidence: "This *is* my fair share. I'm bigger so I should get more." Here again, the truism about lack of omniscience comes into play. Those who hear these disputes and dispense justice in the form of rewards and punishments can be deceived. From such experiences, it's only a short, natural step to convert any inclination to be moral into a desire to appear moral while, if possible, avoid the cost. The hypocrisy motive is born.

Self as Judge and Self-Deception

I've suggested that often the most we can hope for with regard to interpersonal morality is internalization to the level of introjection, where the individual uses principles to constrain his or her own behavior. Integration of interpersonal standards and principles into the core self as intrinsic values is likely to be rare. Many of the observations above seem to point in this direction. But internalization even to the level of introjection poses a problem for moral hypocrisy.

The problem is this: Once moral standards and principles are internalized, reaping the full benefits of hypocrisy becomes difficult, especially when one of the standards internalized is that moral hypocrisy is wrong. As noted earlier, trying to appear moral yet avoid the cost of being moral is castigated and censured by society. Once we've internalized this standard, we're called on to do more than simply juggle evidence and arguments to convince others that we acted morally or at least not immorally. We must also stand before ourselves as judge. We can no longer pursue hypocrisy in a blatant, premeditated way without incurring the costs of self-censure, shame, and guilt. This is a major roadblock. Unless we can manage to escape self-condemnation, moral hypocrisy ceases to be a way to have our cake and eat it too. It loses much of its appeal.

Here's where self-deception becomes so important. If I can manage to appear moral to myself by hiding my true motivation under the cloak of moral integrity, the roadblock is removed. Indeed, not only is the troubling self-censure gone, it's replaced with the approbation that is integrity's due. Instead of meting out self-punishment in my role as judge, I can bestow rewards. Imagine, for example, the righteous pride and pleasure experienced by John Dashwood once he convinced himself that he had with a little present of furniture strictly fulfilled his engagement to his father and that to do more would be absolutely unnecessary if not highly indecorous (Austen, 1811/1995, p. 10).

As the research reported in Chapter 4 reveals, this kind of self-deception isn't simply the stuff of fiction. By late adolescence many of us seem able, if given sufficient wiggle room, to violate our moral standards yet still appear moral even to ourselves. With this ability, we can reach the goal of a fully developed hypocrisy motive. We can avoid the costs of being moral and still receive the social and self-benefits that morality provides.

Implications

The lessons that teach the child hypocrisy are neither explicit nor intentional. They're the product of direct experience and discovery not instruction. As a result, our hypocrisy motive can operate outside the realm of language, cognitive awareness, and rational control. Moreover, unlike integrity, hypocrisy has the virtue that it still serves self-interest. Little surprise, then, that much behavior that appears to be a product of moral integrity turns out on closer inspection to be a product of moral hypocrisy. Also little surprise that we're prone to keep this truth even from ourselves. And little surprise that the hypocrisy motive is an important source of moral failure.

CONCLUSION

The nature of moral motivation seems to differ depending on whether the principle in question specifies right conduct in interest-conflict situations or in maintenance of the natural and social order. Because interpersonal standards and principles clash with self-interest, whereas propriety ones don't, interpersonal and propriety morality are acquired in different ways. The result is a difference in level of internalization and in the manner in which the principles are valued. These differences, as well as their motivational and emotional consequences, are summarized in Table 5.1.

At the start of this chapter, I said that my answer to the question of why moral integrity is rare and hypocrisy common would be speculative. Sadly, in this regard I've been unable to disappoint. I've provided no more than examples to support many key points in the argument. I would like to offer more and better data, but insofar as I know such data don't yet exist. The presented argument may seem plausible, but it's badly in need of more direct empirical tests. Specifically, we need to test

- the suggestions that propriety principles are relatively easily acquired, are learned primarily through practice, modeling, and didactic instruction with reward and punishment playing a minor role, and are likely to be fully internalized to the level of integration. In contrast, interpersonal principles are acquired despite conflict and resistance, are learned primarily through reward and punishment, didactic instruction, and guilt induction, and are likely to be internalized only to the level of introjection.

- the suggestions that principles of interpersonal morality are likely to be valued extrinsically, used instrumentally, and as a result be a source of moral hypocrisy. In contrast, propriety principles are more likely to be valued intrinsically, endorsed automatically and uncritically, and be a source of moral integrity (and dumbfounding).

Relating these suggestions to specific research paradigms, we need to know whether children (and adults) rationalize their failure to uphold propriety principles less readily than their failure to uphold interpersonal principles. This is what the proposed differences in valuing (intrinsic vs. extrinsic) and motivation (integrity vs. hypocrisy) imply. We also need to know whether we're motivated to uphold propriety principles even when provided with wiggle room that would allow us to appear to uphold them without actually doing so. Conversely, we need to know whether

Table 5.1 Summary of Differences Between Interpersonal and Propriety Morality

Feature	Interpersonal morality	Propriety morality
Problem addressed	Interest conflict	Coherence
What the principles specify	Consideration given to others' interests when those interests conflict with our own	Maintenance of natural and social order
Some core principles	Fairness (justice), no harm, care, honesty	Purity, loyalty, honor, respect
How acquired	Reward and punishment, didactic instruction, guilt induction	Practice, modeling, imitation, didactic instruction; reward and punishment are minor
Level of internalization	Introjection likely, integration rare; experienced as ought but not want	Integration likely; experienced as both ought and want
Type of valuing of principles	Likely to be extrinsic (valued as means to promote other values)	Likely to be intrinsic (valued as ends in themselves)
Type of motivation	Likely to be instrumental moral motivation, including moral hypocrisy	Likely to be moral integrity (principlism)
Moral emotion felt at someone's violation of principles	Moral emotion likely rare; emotion felt (e.g., anger, guilt) isn't moral, but evoked by the threat to other values	Moral emotion likely common, especially feelings of moral disgust

interpersonal principles are less subject to restriction by taboo trade-offs than are propriety principles. And we need to know whether propriety principles are treated as sacred (unconditional and inviolable) values, whereas interpersonal principles aren't.

Although we need new data related to each of these possibilities, there's one key implication of the suggestion that interpersonal morality is likely to be used instrumentally in the service of moral hypocrisy on which data have recently become available. This is the implication that—contrary to current wisdom—threats to interpersonal morality standards should evoke little moral emotion (see the last row of Table 5.1). Tests of this implication are considered in the next chapter.

6

MORAL EMOTION

I suggested in Chapter 5 that interpersonal morality is likely to be internalized only to the level of introjection, where it's valued extrinsically rather than intrinsically. If this is true, violation of interpersonal standards should evoke little moral emotion. Such a lack would help explain the scarcity of interpersonal moral integrity found in the research reported in Chapter 4.

But surely this expectation is wrong. Violation of interpersonal interest-conflict principles often evokes strong emotion. Even the thought of violation does. Recall the adolescent Ursie's horror at the suggestion that she might consider keeping someone else's money. Like Ursie, many of us would face a flood of anxiety, shame, and guilt were we to go against our standards regarding stealing. The thought sets off emotional alarm bells that help us avoid the social and self-censure we've learned to anticipate (Bandura, 1990; Blair, 2007; Cohen, Panter, & Turan, 2012; Damasio, 1994).

Prinz (2007, pp. 21–22) cited a dramatic example of the emotion elicited by such a violation. The example comes from a biography of Stanley Milgram by Thomas Blass (2004). In order to study the power of everyday norms for right conduct, Milgram once suggested to students in his research seminar that each of them try asking strangers on the New York City subway to give up their seat and let the student sit instead. His suggestion was greeted with nervous laughter and no volunteers. Finally, one student accepted the challenge. In class the next week, the student reported that about half of the passengers he asked gave him their seat. He also reported that to make the request was so emotionally upsetting he couldn't complete the planned 20 trials. Thinking the request surely wasn't that hard to make, Milgram decided everyone in the seminar should try it—including himself. He discovered firsthand the strong emotion that anticipation and execution of this minor standard violation could evoke:

> I approached a seated passenger and was about to utter the magical phrase. But the words seemed lodged in my trachea and would simply not emerge. I stood there frozen, then retreated, the mission unfulfilled. ... I was overwhelmed by paralyzing inhibition. I argued to myself: "What kind of a craven coward are you? You told your class to do it. How can you go back to them without carrying out your own assignment?" Finally, after several unsuccessful tries, I went up to

a passenger and choked out the request, "Excuse me sir, may I have your seat?" A moment of stark anomic panic overcame me. But the man got right up and gave me the seat. A second blow was yet to come. Taking the man's seat, I was overwhelmed by the need to behave in a way that would justify my request. My head sank between my knees, and I could feel my face blanching. I was not role-playing. I actually felt as if I were going to perish. (Blass, 2004, p. 174)

In a more systematic study of emotional reaction to moral violation, Teper, Inzlicht, and Page-Gould (2011) compared the responses of undergraduates given the chance to cheat on a math test (action condition) with the responses of other undergraduates asked to predict whether they would themselves cheat in the same situation (forecasting condition). Those in the action condition actually cheated significantly less than the forecasters said they themselves would. Importantly, Teper et al. found that the reduced cheating in the action condition was a result of increased emotional arousal as measured by skin conductance and respiratory sinus arrhythmia. This finding echoes that of Dienstbier and Munter (1971), whose misattribution study (described in Chapter 2) also demonstrated the power of anxiety and anticipatory guilt to inhibit cheating.

Not only can our own moral violations evoke emotion in us, so can the violations of others. Numerous neuroimaging and lesion studies have found that reading about or seeing a violation—or even thinking about a moral dilemma—can activate neurological sites associated with emotion and emotion-linked decisions. These sites include the insula, anterior cingulate cortex, medial and ventromedial prefrontal cortex, and orbitofrontal cortex. (See Anderson, Bechara, Damasio, Tranel, & Damasio, 1999; Berthoz, Armony, Blair, & Dolan, 2002; Damasio, 1994; Decety, Michalska, & Kinzler, 2012; Greene, Nystrom, Engell, Darley, & Cohen, 2004; Greene, Sommerville, Nystrom, Darley, & Cohen, 2001; Heckeren, Wartenburger, Schmidt, Schwintowski, & Villringer, 2003; Moll & de Oliveira-Souza, 2007; Moll, de Oliveira-Souza, Bramati, & Grafman, 2002; Moll, de Oliveira-Souza, & Eslinger, 2003; Moll, de Oliveira-Souza, Eslinger et al., 2002; Sanfey et al., 2003.)

Further, it has been suggested that learning about violation of different types of moral standards can evoke distinct patterns of emotion (Horberg, Oveis, & Keltner, 2011). Rozin et al. (1999) provided preliminary evidence that undergraduates in both the United States and Japan were most likely to report *anger* after reading about someone acting unfairly (e.g., edging ahead of others in a long line)—a violation of interpersonal, interest-conflict morality—and to report *disgust* after reading about someone engaging in "unnatural" sexual practices (e.g., consensual incestuous sex)—a violation of propriety morality. Working only with US undergraduates, Horberg, Oveis, Keltner, and Cohen (2009) found additional evidence of these links.

Unfortunately, in both the Rozin et al. (1999) and Horberg et al. (2009) studies, the moral relevance of some of the supposed moral violations was questionable (e.g., eating a piece of rotten meat, used by Rozin et al., 1999; keeping an untidy and dirty living space, used by Horberg et al., 2009). Whether the standard violated was interpersonal or propriety was also at times questionable. As Horberg et al. (2009) noted, "Real world moral issues often cut across moral domains. For example, moral debates over gay marriage or drilling for oil in pristine natural settings can invoke concerns about purity, rights, freedom, or harm" (p. 973).

Horberg et al.'s (2009) first study provided their clearest evidence that interpersonal moral violations evoke anger whereas propriety violations evoke disgust. Participants in this study first read about two purity (propriety) violations—masturbating using a dead chicken and a brother and sister kissing passionately (both scenarios from Haidt et al., 1993). Then they read about two justice (interest-conflict) violations—failing to return a textbook so another student can prepare for an exam and interrupting a friend who's in an important meeting to ask a favor. After reading each scenario, participants rated the degree to which the violation made them feel various emotions. Some of the emotions tapped anger (e.g., *angry, mad*), others tapped disgust (e.g., *grossed out, disgusted*). Participants reported significantly more anger than disgust in response to the justice (interest-conflict) violations. They reported significantly more disgust than anger in response to the purity (propriety) violations.

Other research suggests that the links between interpersonal violations and anger on the one hand and between propriety violations and disgust on the other aren't exclusive. We can at times experience considerable disgust at violation of interpersonal standards (Chapman, Kim, Susskind, & Anderson, 2009; Hutcherson & Gross, 2011). We can also experience considerable anger at propriety violations (Gutierrez & Giner-Sorolla, 2007; Russell, Piazza, & Giner-Sorolla, 2013; Tetlock et al., 2000). Still, whether exclusive or not, it's clear that each type of violation can evoke considerable emotion. This seems to contradict the stated expectation that interpersonal violations evoke little moral emotion. We need to think more carefully about our emotional reactions to moral violations.

USING THE FRAMEWORK FROM CHAPTER 1 TO SHED SOME LIGHT ON MORAL EMOTION

In Chapter 1, I drew on Kurt Lewin's (1951) analysis of conditional-genetic psychological constructs to specify the relation of value, emotion, motivation, and behavior. I noted that our moral standards and principles can be valued either intrinsically as ends in themselves or extrinsically as means to other ends. We can, for example, value honesty itself. Or we can value honesty as a means to retain customers, gain esteem in the eyes of others, and avoid self-censure, shame, and guilt.

The distinction between these ways of valuing morality led to a distinction between two types of moral motivation. One type is instrumental. Morality is used as a means to self-serving ends such as those just mentioned. A second is truly moral (principlism/moral integrity), where to be moral is an ultimate goal. In Chapter 4, I identified a subtle yet important form of instrumental moral motivation—moral hypocrisy. And in Chapters 4 and 5, I also presented evidence and arguments that these distinctions in valuing and motivation are important for understanding our moral failures.

Whether morality is valued intrinsically or extrinsically needs to be taken into account not only when considering the nature of moral motivation but also when considering the nature of the emotion evoked by a moral violation. Specifically, this distinction raises questions of whether and when this emotion should be called *moral*.

An Overly Broad Definition

The past quarter-century has brought many assertions from moral psychologists and philosophers about the importance of moral emotion, often as a corrective to assertions of the previous quarter-century about the importance of moral reasoning (for example, Cohen et al., 2012; de Waal, 2006; Greene, 2008; Greene et al., 2001; Haidt, 2001, 2003; Kagan, 1984; Prinz, 2007; Rozin et al., 1999; Solomon, 1990; Tangney, Stuewig, & Mashek, 2007). Despite these frequent assertions, explicit statements about what qualifies as a moral emotion have been rare. Still, there seems to be implicit consensus: Moral emotions are ones that inhibit behavior considered immoral, promote behavior considered moral, or occur in response to immoral or moral behavior. If fear of punishment or anticipation of guilt leads you not to cheat, this fear or guilt is a moral emotion. If being treated unfairly evokes anger, this anger is moral. So is any disgust you feel on hearing about a case of sibling incest. And so on.

Making the implicit explicit, Haidt offered a "preliminary definition of the moral emotions" in his 2003 handbook chapter on the topic. He characterized them as "those emotions that are linked to the interests or welfare either of society as a whole or at least of persons other than the judge or agent" (Haidt, 2003, p. 853). Haidt went on to explain, "The puzzle of the moral emotions is that *Homo sapiens*, far more than any other animal, appears to devote a considerable portion of its emotional life to reacting to social events that do not directly affect the self" (2003, p. 853). Haidt then enumerated two key features of moral emotions: Disinterested elicitors—they are "triggered by triumphs, tragedies, and transgressions that do not directly touch the self" (Haidt, 2003, p. 854). Prosocial action tendencies—"they either benefit others or else uphold or benefit the social order" (p. 854).

Although Haidt's attempt to provide an explicit definition is commendable, the conditional-genetic framework provided in Chapter 1 leads me to think that his conception of moral emotions is overly broad and imprecise. Like virtually every other contemporary analyst, Haidt (2003) sought to identify moral emotions by their links to behavior and consequences rather than their links to values and motives. If an emotion increases some behavior judged moral, it's considered a moral emotion. But this criterion fails to take account of the fact that nonmoral emotions can motivate moral behavior.

In Chapter 1, I distinguished among valuing our own welfare (egoism), valuing another individual's welfare (altruism), valuing a group's welfare (collectivism), and valuing a moral standard, principle, or ideal (principlism). Each of these values and the motivation it evokes can lead a person to act in a way judged moral. A moral act can be an instrumental means to pursue self-interest, as when one is kind to court kindness in return. Or it can be designed to increase another individual's or a group's welfare. That is, it can be motivated by altruism or collectivism, with morality an unintended consequence. Only for principlism is acting morally intrinsically valued and an ultimate goal. Haidt's definition is overly broad in that it encompasses all forms of prosocial value and the emotions each evokes, not just moral values and emotions. It identifies the general class of *prosocial emotion* rather than the more specific class of moral emotion.

Haidt's definition is imprecise in that it fails to take account of the fact that one can respond emotionally to aspects of a moral violation other than the violation itself. Consider unfairness. An unfair act usually harms someone. That person or an observer may respond emotionally—with anger perhaps—at the threat to this particular person's welfare. If so, the emotion isn't evoked by violation of fairness principles themselves, but by concern for the victim's welfare. Depending on who the victim is, the emotion could be called egoistic or altruistic, but not moral.

A Value-Based Definition

From the perspective of the conditional-genetic framework, moral emotions should be defined by linking them to values and motives. I suggested in Chapter 1 that emotions are typically felt when we experience a change in our relation to a valued state. Of particular importance are changes that threaten these states. Such changes produce need-state emotions, which serve two functions. First, need-state emotions inform us about what our values are. Second, because the arousal component of these emotions activates many of the same neural circuits involved in motivation, they amplify goal-directed motives to have the valued states restored or preserved. Applying this framework to the moral domain, the strength of our emotional response to a violation of or threat to some moral standard informs us about how much we value that standard. It also amplifies the strength of our motivation to see the standard upheld.

This analysis suggests a more precise, Galilean definition of moral emotion to replace the Aristotelian definition offered by Haidt. (See Chapter 1 for the Aristotelian-Galilean distinction.) To be called moral, *emotion should arise in response to violation of or threat to some personally valued moral standard, principle, or ideal.* Such violations or threats might, for example, evoke anger, disgust, or contempt, as claimed by Rozin et al. (1999). They might also evoke concern, discomfort, or distress. These need-state moral emotions should in turn produce truly moral motivation to uphold the threatened standard, principle, or ideal (principlism). There are also end-state moral emotions. These include both positive emotions such as joy or admiration at the upholding of a valued moral standard, and negative emotions such as sorrow or grief at a moral violation that can't be rectified. But end-state emotions don't directly evoke motivation or produce moral behavior, so I won't consider them here.

Adopting this Galilean value-based definition of moral emotion, many emotions routinely considered moral need reexamination. For example, to the extent that *guilt* and *shame* are evoked by the threat to my self-image that comes from having violated one of my moral standards rather than being evoked by the standard violation itself, guilt and shame aren't moral emotions—contrary to common assumption. Similarly, to the extent that my feelings of *empathic concern, sympathy*, and *compassion* evoked by harm to a cared-for other are a response to the threat to the other's welfare not to the standard violation, they aren't moral emotions—again, contrary to common assumption.

Each of these sets of nonmoral emotions is capable of producing strong motivation. Guilt and shame can produce egoistic motivation to repair or maintain my self-image (Cohen et al., 2012; Cohen, Wolf, Panter, & Insko, 2011; de Hooge, Nelisson, Breugelmans, & Zeelenberg, 2011; Eisenberg, 2000; Tangney & Dearing, 2002; Tangney et al., 2007). Empathic concern, sympathy, and compassion can produce altruistic motivation to increase the welfare of the cared-for other (Batson, 2011). Each of these motives can in turn produce behavior judged moral. But as long as acting morally is an instrumental means or unintended consequence rather than an ultimate goal, the behavior isn't morally motivated.

So what? What difference does it make if these emotions and the motives they produce aren't moral? They're still emotions evoked by threat to a valued state. And even if the valued state isn't moral, these emotions can amplify motives that produce moral behavior. Indeed, in many situations these nonmoral emotions are more likely than moral emotions to produce moral behavior. If the adolescent Ursie refrains from stealing because she fears what her parents will think of her, or what she'll think of herself, she has acted as honestly as if she refrained because she values honesty itself.

The so-what is that in other situations these nonmoral values, and the emotions and motives they evoke, can lead to immoral action. If my concern is to avoid the disapproval of those in authority, then fear of their disapproval can lead me, when so ordered, to deliver severe shocks. Or to join in the massacre of mothers and babies at My Lai. If what's needed to protect my son's dream of college is for me to falsify preflight test results, then concern for his welfare can lead me to violate my standards of honesty. If to save the Fatherland it's necessary to solve the Jewish Problem, then patriotic fervor and loyalty can prompt me to do my part however personally distasteful the task. Emotions evoked by threats to nonmoral values and the motives these emotions amplify aren't reliable sources of moral behavior. In many circumstances, they permit or even produce moral failures.

In sum, a value-based analysis suggests that much of the emotion called moral has been mislabeled. It suggests that truly moral emotion, like truly moral motivation, may be far less common than has been thought. If so, the idea that violation of interpersonal standards evokes little moral emotion could be right after all. It at least deserves a closer look.

DIFFERENT EXPECTATIONS FOR EMOTIONAL RESPONSE TO INTERPERSONAL AND PROPRIETY VIOLATIONS

Earlier, I noted research indicating that interpersonal violations often evoke anger whereas propriety violations often evoke disgust, even though these pairings aren't exclusive. The analysis in Chapter 5 points to a more profound difference. There,

I suggested that propriety standards are likely to be learned easily and well. They become fully internalized and valued intrinsically. As a result, to hear of their violation should produce both moral emotion—especially feelings of disgust but sometimes anger as well—and truly moral motivation. Our own violation of propriety standards can produce feelings of guilt and shame so intense that we speak of being *mortified*, as did Milgram (Blass, 2004; Milgram & Sabini, 1978). The research by Haidt (2001) on moral dumbfounding and by Tetlock et al. (2000) on taboo trade-offs focused on violations of propriety standards. Most of us don't find it difficult to uphold these standards. They're so "natural" that their validity seems intuitively obvious: Avoid sex with a sibling. Don't sell body organs.

Acquisition of interpersonal standards is less straightforward. Because interpersonal standards often conflict with self-interest, their application to our own conduct is resisted. As a result, interpersonal standards and principles are likely to be internalized only to the level of introjection, not fully integrated. They're valued extrinsically and upheld instrumentally in the service of self-interest—specifically, in the service of being seen and seeing ourselves as moral. It's these characteristics of interpersonal morality that prompted the expectation that violation of these standards should evoke little moral emotion. We're not dumbfounded or shocked to learn that someone has acted unfairly or harmed someone else for personal gain. Nor are we dumbfounded to think we might be tempted to do so. Such acts are commonplace.

Of course, it's important not to jump too quickly to a conclusion about moral psychology that many moral psychologists and philosophers would doubt. As I noted at the start of this chapter, the suggestion that violation of interpersonal standards evokes little moral emotion is in direct conflict with widely accepted claims about the importance of moral emotion. And it seems to conflict with the evidence that witnessing an interpersonal-standard violation can evoke considerable emotion, most notably anger (Horberg et al., 2009; Gutierrez & Giner-Sorolla, 2007; Rozin et al., 1999; Russell et al., 2013). Before we grant this suggestion any credence, we need evidence that the anger evoked by violation of some interpersonal moral standard isn't moral emotion. That is, rather than the anger being evoked by the threat to a valued moral principle such as fairness or care, we need evidence that it's evoked by the threat to some other value.

ANGER EVOKED BY VIOLATION OF AN INTERPERSONAL STANDARD: IS IT MORAL?

"That's so unfair; I'm outraged!" Those angered by unfair treatment have often been described as feeling moral anger or outrage. This anger has been considered a prototypical moral emotion (Haidt, 2003). It's also claimed to be a potent source of moral motivation, prompting efforts to restore fairness and justice either by compensating the victim or by punishing the harm-doer (Carlsmith, Darley, & Robinson, 2002; Darley, 2002; Darley & Pittman, 2003; de Rivera, Gerstmann, & Maisels, 2002; de Waal, 1996; Haidt, 2003; Mikula, Scherer, & Athenstaedt, 1998; Montada

& Schneider, 1989; Salerno & Peter-Hagene, 2013; Schmitt & Maes, 1998; Solomon, 1990; Tetlock et al., 2000).

Should our anger at unfairness be called moral? Applying the value-based definition of moral emotion, *moral anger* is *anger provoked by the perception that a moral standard (principle, ideal) has been or will be violated.* By this definition, our anger after witnessing an unfair act shouldn't be called moral if it stems not from the standard violation itself but from the harm done by the unfairness. Depending on who's harmed, unfairness can evoke one of two other forms of anger.

Personal Anger and Empathic Anger

Most obviously, it's important to distinguish between moral anger and *personal anger*, the anger I feel when my own interests are thwarted. Such anger isn't the same as moral anger, even though I may call it that in order to give it legitimacy and the rhetorical power to call others to my defense (as discussed in the next chapter). Personal anger may also motivate action judged moral such as punishing the harm-doer. But if the ultimate goal is to get revenge or protect my personal interests rather than to promote principle, the motivation isn't moral. It's egoistic.

Recognizing this distinction, Frans de Waal (2006) followed the lead of Edward Westermark and concluded, "moral emotions ought to be disconnected from one's immediate situation: they deal with good and bad at a more abstract, disinterested level" (de Waal, 2006, p. 20). Or in Westermark's (1908) own words, "Moral emotions . . . differ from kindred nonmoral emotions by their disinterestedness, apparent impartiality, and flavor of generality" (p. 739).

As Westermark and de Waal imply, if I feel anger after seeing someone else treated unfairly, this can't plausibly be personal anger (unless I'm angered by implications that the other's treatment has for how I could be treated myself—"He could have done that to me!"; for possible examples of this kind of vicarious personal anger, see Fehr & Fischbacher, 2004; Martin, Brickman, & Murray, 1984). But when I see someone else treated unfairly, another distinction is needed. If I care about that person's welfare, then any anger I feel at seeing him or her treated unfairly could be *empathic anger* (Hoffman, 1989, 2000; Vitaglione & Barnett, 2003). I could feel anger because the interests of this person for whom I care have been harmed rather than because my fairness standards have been violated.

Westermark (1908) recognized this second possibility. He asked, "Why should we, quite disinterestedly, feel pain invoking indignation because our neighbor is hurt?" And he answered, "Sympathy aided by the altruistic sentiment—sympathy in the common sense of the word—tends to produce disinterested retributive emotions" (p. 739). Unfortunately, "disinterested" wasn't the best word choice here because although not self-interested we're not disinterested. We're interested in the welfare of the person for whom we feel sympathy. Martin Hoffman (2000) put it more clearly, "One may feel angry at the culprit because one sympathizes with the victim" (p. 96).

Like personal anger, empathic anger may be called moral anger to give it legitimacy and rhetorical power. But it shouldn't be considered a moral emotion or a source of moral motivation. It may motivate action judged moral such as punishing the harm-doer. Still, if the goal is to get revenge or to protect the interests of the cared-for other rather than promote some principle, the motivation is altruistic not moral.

So, reports of anger at unfairness don't necessarily reflect moral anger. They may instead express personal or empathic anger, neither of which is provoked by the moral violation itself.

Empirically Distinguishing Moral Anger from Personal and Empathic Anger

In the research claimed to provide evidence of moral anger, these three forms of anger have never been clearly distinguished. Montada and Schneider (1989) came closest. They conceptually distinguished the three but acknowledged that their correlational research couldn't differentiate them empirically. Before we accept that moral anger is a powerful moral emotion distinct from personal and empathic anger, clearer evidence is needed.

But how can we empirically distinguish these three forms of anger when each occurs in response to unfairness and when each is likely to lead to reports of irritation, anger, and outrage? Appraisal theories of emotion (Arnold, 1960; Frijda, 1988; Roseman, 1984; Scherer, 1984; Smith & Ellsworth, 1987) suggest that they can be distinguished by their eliciting conditions. As Forgas and Smith (2003) observed, "anger is elicited under conditions in which someone or something is thwarting one's goals" (p. 163). At least three distinct goals can be inhibited by unfairness. Threat to each evokes a different cognitive appraisal based on attention to a different aspect of the standard-violating situation, so each elicits a distinct form of anger. The appraisal producing moral anger is that a valued moral standard such as fairness has been thwarted. The appraisal evoking personal anger is that my own interests have been thwarted. The appraisal evoking empathic anger is that the interests of a person for whom I care have been thwarted.

If people report anger whenever an unfair act threatens one of these goals but report little or no anger when it doesn't, we have reason to think this goal elicited the anger. And we can identify the form of anger accordingly. If, for example, I report anger only when I'm the victim of the unfair treatment, my reports reflect personal anger. If I report anger when either I or a cared-for other is the victim, and not when someone else is the victim, my reports reflect personal anger and empathic anger but not moral anger. If I report anger regardless of whether I'm the victim, a cared-for other is the victim, or someone else is the victim, my reports reflect moral anger. Following this logic, if we're to disentangle moral anger from personal and empathic anger, we need to look at the pattern of anger evoked by unfair treatment of these different targets. Colleagues and I have done this in three experiments.

Unfair Redistribution of Resources

Batson et al. (2007) reported an experiment in which participants believed that they and two other same-sex participants (actually fictitious) were taking part in a study of reactions to outcomes in social situations. The outcomes were in the form of raffle tickets.

> Each of you will be given *10 raffle tickets*; each ticket is good for one chance at winning a *$30.00 gift certificate* from the store of the winner's choice. Depending on the result of the outcome situation, however, you may end up with more or less than 10 tickets. (Batson et al., 2007, p. 1277, italics in original)

The three participants were to remain anonymous and never meet. They were designated simply Participant A, B, and C, with the real participant always being Participant B. Ostensibly by random assignment, Participant A had the opportunity to change the outcomes by taking tickets from or giving tickets to one of the other participants. Participant A used this opportunity to take 9 of the other participant's tickets, which meant that A ended with 19 tickets and the other with only 1. Emotional reactions to this redistribution were then assessed, including feelings of anger.

Varying the person whom Participant A treated unfairly created the necessary appraisal conditions to determine whether any reported anger was moral, personal, or empathic. In two experimental conditions, Participant B (the real participant) observed Participant A take the 9 tickets from Participant C. To experimentally manipulate level of care for C, participants in these two conditions read a communication written by Participant C prior to the redistribution. The communication told of a recent romantic break-up and need for cheering up. (Ostensibly, Participant C wrote the communication, which was to describe "something interesting that happened to you recently," before knowing anything about the nature of the study.) Empathic concern—care for C—was manipulated by the perspective participants adopted while reading C's communication. Participants in a low-empathy condition were to remain objective. Those in a high-empathy condition were to imagine how Participant C felt as a result of the events described. (This procedure had been used successfully to induce care in a number of previous studies; see Batson, 2011.)

In a third experimental condition, Participant A took the 9 tickets from Participant B, the real participant (self-treated-unfairly condition). Finally, to provide a baseline assessment of anger when no fairness standard was violated, participants in a fourth condition learned that redistribution between Participants A and C was being made by chance rather than by Participant A and that by chance the distribution was unchanged. So in this condition all participants ended with the 10 tickets with which they began (all-treated-fairly condition). Participants in these last two conditions read no communication.

After the redistribution, participants were asked to report their emotional reactions and their perceptions. These measures provided a chance to assess both the perceived fairness of the ticket reallocation and any anger it produced. (Perceived fairness was measured after anger in order to avoid experimental demand; Orne, 1962.) Take a minute to think about how you would respond in each of the different experimental conditions if you were Participant B.

Here's how the participants in the experiment responded. First, on perceived fairness, participants in the all-treated-fairly condition, in which each participant retained 10 tickets, rated the redistribution quite fair ($M = 8.42$ on the $1 = not at all$ to $9 = totally$ scale). Those in the self-treated-unfairly condition, in which Participant A took 9 tickets from B, rated the redistribution much less fair ($M = 3.08$). Importantly, participants considered Participant A taking 9 tickets from Participant C to be as unfair as they considered A taking 9 tickets from themselves. And taking from C was considered unfair regardless of whether C was cared for (high empathy $M = 2.25$) or not (low empathy $M = 2.75$: see Column 1 of Table 6.1).

What about anger? Significantly more anger was reported in both the self-treated-unfairly condition ($M = 3.23$ on the $1 = not at all$ to $7 = extremely$ scale) and the high-empathy condition ($M = 2.94$) than in either of the other two conditions (all-treated-fairly $M = 1.42$; low-empathy $M = 1.78$). The difference between the means in the self-treated-unfairly and the high-empathy conditions wasn't reliable, nor was the difference between the means in the all-treated-fairly and the low-empathy conditions (see Column 2 of Table 6.1).

This pattern of anger suggested that, first, when participants were themselves the victim of Participant A's unfair reallocation, they felt personal anger. Reported anger was significantly higher in the self-treated-unfairly condition than in the all-treated-fairly condition. Second, when they had been led to care for Participant C and C was then treated unfairly, participants felt empathic anger. Reported anger was significantly higher in the high-empathy-C-treated-unfairly condition than in the low-empathy-C-treated-unfairly condition. Further supporting this interpretation, scores on an index of self-reported empathic concern felt for Participant C after reading the communication, which were significantly higher in the high-empathy condition than the low ($Ms = 5.60$ and 4.00, respectively, on a $1 = not at all$ to

Table 6.1 Perceived Fairness and Reported Anger After Tickets Were Taken from Other or Self (Batson et al., 2007)

Experimental condition	Perceived fairness	Reported anger
All treated fairly	8.42_a	1.42_a
Participant A takes 9 tickets from:		
Participant C—Low empathy	2.75_b	1.78_a
Participant C—High empathy	2.25_b	2.94_b
Participant B (Self)	3.08_b	3.23_b

Note: Fairness was assessed on a 1 (*not at all*) to 9 (*totally*) scale. Anger was assessed on a 1 (*not at all*) to 7 (*extremely*) scale. Means in a given column that don't share the same subscript differ significantly, $p < .05$, in a pairwise comparison.

7 = *extremely* scale), were positively correlated with anger reported after C was treated unfairly, $r = .53$.

There was no clear evidence of moral anger. Among participants not led to feel empathy, A's unfair treatment of C failed to produce a significant increase in anger relative to the all-treated-fairly condition. Anger increased only when participants were treated unfairly themselves or when someone for whom they had been led to care was treated unfairly.

Experiment 2: Anger at Unfair Exclusion

O'Mara, Jackson, Batson, and Gaertner (2011) extended the search for moral anger distinct from personal anger by assessing anger in response to a different type of unfairness, unfair exclusion from a pleasant experience. To do this, they adapted a research procedure developed by Gaertner, Iuzzini, and O'Mara (2008), creating a 2 (victim of exclusion: other vs. self) × 2 (method of exclusion: fair vs. unfair) experimental design. There was no manipulation of empathy in this experiment so it wasn't possible to test for empathic anger.

Participants believed they were one of four same-sex strangers taking part in an experiment concerning reactions to individual and shared pleasant and unpleasant experiences. (The other three participants were actually confederates.) The four were designated Participant A, B, C, and D, with the real participant always Participant C. One participant, either B or C, was assigned (ostensibly randomly) to have an individual pleasant experience—deep muscle-relaxation stimulation similar to a soothing massage. The other three were assigned to a shared pleasant experience—a virtual-reality vacation—which was described as follows:

> There are a wide range of pleasant experiences to enjoy on the vacation, includ-
> ing excerpts from movies, comedy routines, video games, adventure experiences
> (skiing, snow boarding, hang gliding, wake boarding), a beach experience, con-
> certs—the works! (O'Mara et al., 2011, p. 175)

After assignment, participants learned that due to a computer problem one of the three participants scheduled for the virtual-reality vacation would need to be reassigned to an individual unpleasant experience, a dull, tedious paper-and-pencil task. The experimenter introduced a fair method for determining who was to be reassigned. Index cards would be dealt face down to the three participants sched-uled for the vacation. Whoever got the card with an "X" would raise a hand and be assigned to the unpleasant task.

In the two fair conditions, the card draw determined reassignment. But, unknown to the real participant, all the cards had an X. So if Participant C (the real partici-pant) was scheduled to go on the vacation, he or she was dealt a card with an X, raised a hand, and was reassigned (self-excluded-fairly condition). If Participant C had been assigned the individual pleasant experience, he or she was dealt no card. In this case, the confederate designated Participant B raised a hand and was reassigned (other-excluded-fairly condition). In the two unfair conditions, just as the experimenter started to deal the cards, the confederate designated Participant A interrupted, pointed to either Participant C (self-excluded-unfairly condition) or Participant B (other-excluded-unfairly condition), whichever was scheduled to go on the vacation, and said, "I think *you* should be the one reassigned!" Looking a bit confused and flustered, the experimenter acquiesced.

Immediately after the exclusion, the participant and confederates were returned to their individual cubicles, and the participant completed a questionnaire that tapped his or her current feelings, including anger. Then he or she filled out a form to provide impressions of the other three participants, including a rating of the fairness of each.

As expected, Participant A was perceived to be less fair in the unfair conditions (Ms = 2.10 and 2.40 on the 1 = *not at all fair* to 9 = *totally fair* scale in the other- and self-excluded-unfairly conditions, respectively) than in the fair conditions (Ms = 4.70 and 4.00, respectively). Importantly, Participant A was perceived to be as unfair in the other-excluded-unfairly condition as in the self-excluded-unfairly condition (see Column 1 of Table 6.2).

Turning to anger, participants treated unfairly themselves reported significantly more anger (M = 2.68 on the 1 = *not at all* to 7 = *extremely* scale) than those who witnessed another participant (for whom they had not been led to care) suffer the same fate (M = 1.31). Participants excluded fairly (by receiving the X) also reported somewhat increased anger (M = 2.25) relative to when another participant was excluded fairly (M = 1.40), but this difference wasn't statistically significant (see Column 2 of Table 6.2).

Reported anger after the self was treated unfairly was somewhat lower in this experiment than in the previous one. But the level of anger was comparable to that reported in other experiments in which participants suffer unfair exclusion (see Buckley, Winkel, & Leary, 2004; Chow, Tiedens, & Govan, 2008). It has been suggested that participants in exclusion experiments under report their anger to downplay concern about being singled out for exclusion. Comments during debriefing certainly suggested that most participants in the self-excluded-unfairly condition

Table 6.2 Perceived Fairness and Reported Anger After Fair or Unfair Exclusion of Other or Self (O'Mara et al., 2011)

Experimental condition	Perceived fairness	Reported anger
Other excluded fairly	4.70$_a$	1.40$_a$
Self excluded fairly	4.00$_a$	2.25$_{a,b}$
Other excluded unfairly	2.10$_b$	1.31$_a$
Self excluded unfairly	2.40$_b$	2.68$_b$

Note: Fairness was assessed on a 1 (*not at all*) to 9 (*totally*) scale. Anger was assessed on a 1 (*not at all*) to 7 (*extremely*) scale. Means in a given column that don't share the same subscript differ significantly, $p < .05$, in a pairwise comparison.

of our experiment were more than a little surprised and angered at the unfair treatment. We heard words like "jerk" and "asshole."

Overall, results of this experiment cast further doubt on the prevalence of moral anger. Unfair exclusion of another person was judged to be as unfair as was unfair exclusion of oneself. Yet being unfairly excluded oneself produced significantly more anger than seeing another participant unfairly excluded, which evoked very little anger indeed. This is the pattern expected if the reported anger was personal anger at harm to self, not the pattern expected if the anger reported in the self-excluded-unfairly condition was moral. If it were moral, there should also to be anger in the other-excluded-unfairly condition, where the exclusion was perceived to be just as unfair.

Anger at Torture

Batson, Chao, and Givens (2009) assessed anger evoked by a more extreme moral violation—torture. Although few of us have suffered the agony and humiliation of torture, the distinction between moral and personal anger is still relevant. Hearing about harm to another member of a group with which we identify can produce a form of personal anger. Social-identity theorists have pointed out that we have a personal stake in what happens to other people in such a group (Tajfel, 1981; Tajfel & Turner, 1986). Anger at harm done to one of "us," even if not done to me or a known and cared-for other, might be called *identity-relevant personal anger*—anger at harm to someone from my group (Yzerbyt, Dumont, Wigboldus, & Gordijn, 2003). Batson et al. (2009) reasoned that for US undergraduates, reading about the torture of a US Marine could evoke identity-relevant personal anger.

Like direct personal anger and empathic anger, identity-relevant personal anger may be called moral anger to give it legitimacy and rhetorical power. Yet, such anger shouldn't be considered a moral emotion. It may motivate action described as moral, such as tracking down and punishing the torturer. But if the goal is to retaliate or to protect the interests of my group (e.g., Lickel, Miller, Stenstrom, Denson, & Schmader, 2006) rather than to promote a moral standard, the motivation isn't moral. If anger at torture is moral, it should be experienced even when I have no personal stake in the torture victim, as suggested by Westermark (1908) and de Waal (2006).

Building on this reasoning, Batson et al. (2009) conducted an experiment at the time of the US military involvement in Iraq. They had US university students (each seated alone in a research cubicle) read a news story (actually fictitious) describing a case of torture. Ostensibly, the purpose of the research was to study reactions to media reports of brutality. For half of the participants, the person tortured was a US Marine in Iraq (identity-relevant condition). For the other half, the torture victim was a Sri Lankan soldier in Sri Lanka (not-identity-relevant condition). A Sri Lankan soldier was chosen as the not-identity-relevant victim in order to parallel the situation of the identity-relevant victim in all respects except the absence of any national or other identity ties. None of the research participants had any connection with or much knowledge of Sri Lanka.

To assess the nature of the moral proscription against torture, consequences of the torture were varied too. In one condition, the information provided by the torture saved only property. In the other condition, it also saved lives. The Geneva Conventions and the UN Convention Against Torture consider torture wrong regardless of circumstance. If research participants embraced such standards, they should perceive the torture to be wrong even when it saves lives. Alternatively, participants might have more conditional standards. They might perceive torture less wrong if it saves lives than if it saves only property. Whichever form participants' standards took, if anger reported after reading about the torture was moral, it should follow the same pattern as the judgments of moral wrong.

Reading About a Case of Torture

For participants randomly assigned to the identity-relevant/saved-only-property condition, the article they read carried the headline "Torture Produces Information, Prevents Destruction." The story was as follows:

Baghdad, Iraq—Al Qaida in Iraq militants have admitted torturing a US Marine to gain information last Saturday. The information prevented destruction of an al Qaida in Iraq stronghold in the volatile Anbar province west of Baghdad. The information led to location and defusing of a bomb planted inside the stronghold building by commandos. Defusing occurred less than 5 minutes before the bomb would have exploded, completely destroying the building. No one would have been killed because the building was unoccupied at the time.

"We knew he had information about a planned bombing," said the militant commander who ordered the interrogation. "We tried to get it without using torture, but he wouldn't cooperate. So we used extreme measures." Further questioning revealed that the extreme measures used were, first, a severe beating that broke the captive's jaw and right arm, then "waterboarding" (being tied to a plank and submerged in a tank of water until almost drowned), and finally, ripping off three of the captive's fingernails with pliers. "He was tough, but the fingernails did it. After three, he was begging us to stop. He talked. We got the information just in time."

When asked whether the use of torture was authorized, the commander replied, "No, not really. But we're expected to get results—and we did. It's not what we want to do; it's what we have to do."

For participants in the identity-relevant/saved-lives condition, the headline was "Torture Produces Information, Prevents Destruction and Deaths." Content of the article was identical to that above except for two changes in the lead paragraph. First, following "stronghold" in the second sentence, "and the death of eight militants" was added. Second, the last sentence of the paragraph was replaced with one that read, "Eight militants were inside the building at the time and would have been killed."

In the two not-identity-relevant conditions (saved only property, saved lives), the headlines were the same as those above. But the by-line of the article was changed to "Columbo, Sri Lanka." Content of the two versions of the not-identity-relevant article was identical to that above, except the torture was by "Tamil rebels" of "a Sri Lankan soldier" to prevent the destruction of "a Tamil stronghold in the volatile Bangar province east of Columbo," and the quotes were from a "rebel commander."

After reading their randomly assigned version of the article, participants were asked to report their emotional response, including feelings of anger, and whether they thought the torture was morally wrong. In each experimental condition, the torture was judged to be quite wrong (overall $M = 7.52$ on the $1 = not$ at all morally wrong to $9 = yes$, totally morally wrong scale) with no reliable differences across conditions. Torture of a Sri Lankan soldier was judged no less morally wrong than torture of a US Marine, and torture that saved lives was judged no less wrong than torture that saved only property (see Column 1 of Table 6.3). But reported anger was significantly higher among participants reading about torture of a US Marine ($M = 4.17$ on the $1 = not$ at all to $7 = extremely$ scale) than those reading about the same torture of a Sri Lankan soldier ($M = 2.78$). This was true regardless whether the torture saved only property or also saved lives (see Column 2 of Table 6.3).

The identity-relevance effect on anger, coupled with the judgment that the torture was morally wrong in all conditions, suggested that the greater anger that participants expressed after reading about torture of a US Marine rather than a Sri Lankan soldier wasn't moral anger at the violation of their standards proscribing torture. Instead, it appeared to be evoked by harm done to one of "us"—identity-relevant personal anger.

Table 6.3 Judgment of Moral Wrong and Reported Anger After Reading About Torture of a Not-Identity-Relevant or Identity-Relevant Victim (Batson et al., 2009)

Experimental condition	Moral wrong	Reported anger
Victim not identity relevant (Sri Lankan soldier)		
Torture saved only property	6.92a	2.68a
Torture saved lives	7.92a	2.89a
Victim identity relevant (US Marine)		
Torture saved only property	7.83a	4.28b
Torture saved lives	7.42a	4.06b

Note: Moral wrong was assessed on a 1 (not at all) to 9 (yes, totally) scale. Anger was assessed on a 1 (not at all) to 7 (extremely) scale. Means in a given column that don't share the same subscript differ significantly, $p < .05$, in a pairwise comparison.

But there may also be some evidence of moral anger in this experiment. Although the level of anger reported after reading about torture of a Sri Lankan soldier was low ($M = 2.78$), it wasn't at the absolute bottom of the 1–7 scale. Nor was it as low as after unfair treatment of someone not especially cared for in the previous two experiments. Without knowing the amount of anger that would be reported in a comparison condition in which participants read a story that reported the same harm but involved no torture or other moral violation—for example, a story in which equivalent injury was inflicted by a natural disaster—it remains possible that some of the low level of anger reported in the not-identity-relevant conditions was moral. Accepting this possibility, it's still important to recognize that if present at all, moral anger was comparatively weak. Far more anger was expressed when the torture victim was a US Marine than a Sri Lankan soldier. It's also important to recognize that without data from the not-identity-relevant conditions, all of the considerable anger reported after reading about torture of a US Marine would likely have been thought to be moral anger.

Implications

Results of these three experiments lend support to the possibility that what has been called moral anger has often been mislabeled. The experiments varied the victim of immoral action, which made it possible to distinguish moral anger from personal and empathic anger. Reported anger tracked harm done to self or to a cared-for other, not the moral violation itself. This was true even though research participants in each experiment perceived the standard-violating act to have been as wrong when the victim was not a target of special interest. These experiments indicate that anger at unfairness is often personal or empathic anger at the harm done by the standard-violating behavior, not moral anger.

Still, it would be presumptuous to conclude from these three experiments that moral anger doesn't exist. Perhaps if the relevant moral standards were more central to research participants' sense of self, moral anger would be found (Aquino, Reed, Thau, & Freeman, 2007; Blasi, 1984). Perhaps it would be found among individuals especially sensitive to injustice (Fetchenhauer & Huang, 2004; Gollwitzer, Schmitt, Schalke, Maes, & Baer, 2005; Schmitt, Gollwitzer, Maes, & Arbach, 2005). Perhaps. Yet, given the very low mean levels of anger reported when participants in these experiments had no special interest in the victim of unfairness, it seems unlikely that even those participants who would score high on these individual difference variables reported much moral anger. Had they, the means wouldn't be so close to the bottom of the response scale.

But to persist, perhaps more moral anger would be found in different populations. For example, perhaps more would be found among moral philosophers or people from collectivist societies. Or perhaps more anger would be found in response to actions that violate standards on political issues such as abortion or capital punishment. Perhaps. For such issues, though, it would be important to distinguish anger at violation of moral standards themselves from anger at a threat to the respondent's political agenda. Applying Westermark's disinterest criterion, would I feel anger if the violation occurred in a less personally relevant society—such as Sri Lanka—or only in my own? If only in my own, the emotion would seem to be yet another variety of personal anger.

Consistent with this possibility, consider what's perhaps the most frequently cited evidence of moral anger. Montada and Schneider (1989) assessed the anger of German citizens at their government's failure to address the suffering of the society's disadvantaged. Green Party members reported the greatest anger, socialists reported moderate anger, and political conservatives reported very little. Although this pattern could reflect moral anger tuned to the different groups' judgments of how morally wrong the government's failure was, it could also reflect personal anger at the thwarting of the political agenda of different respondents. Or it could reflect empathic anger. Supporting this third possibility, Montada and Schneider found a high correlation between reported moral outrage and reported sympathy for the disadvantaged ($r = .66$). So, rather than evidence of moral anger, Montada and Schneider's results may reflect a combination of personal and empathic anger. Without experimental manipulation of the relevant appraisal conditions, we don't know.

Consider also another line of research that found anger in response to a moral violation that harmed an unknown other. Graham, Weiner, and Zucker (1997) found moderately high reports of anger toward a person accused of murder. This was true for both a hypothetical case and the actual case of former American football player O. J. Simpson. Mean ratings were sometimes above 5 on a 1 (*none*) to 7 (*a great deal*) scale, especially when the accused was perceived to have been in control of his actions at the time of the killing. But it's not clear whether the reported anger was in response to the interpersonal or the propriety implications of the killing. Nor is it clear whether the anger was in response to violation of relevant moral standards (e.g., "Thou shalt not kill") or the threat to the stability and safety of the society. Again, would the same anger be found if the murder occurred in a less personally relevant society?

The three anger-at-unfairness experiments I've described carry a clear methodological message for anyone wishing to understand the emotion evoked by an interpersonal moral violation: It's essential to disentangle moral emotion—emotion evoked by the violation itself—from emotion evoked by harm the violation caused to self or a cared-for other. And this disentangling is best done by experimental manipulation of the relevant appraisal conditions. Simply to measure emotion following a moral violation isn't enough.

Further, even if future research finds truly moral emotion in certain populations or in response to certain violations, there's also a clear substantive message that shouldn't be lost: Moral emotion in response to interpersonal interest-conflict violations seems to be far less common than has been thought.

WHAT ABOUT DISGUST EVOKED BY VIOLATION OF PROPRIETY STANDARDS: IS IT MORAL?

Even if violation of interest-conflict principles doesn't evoke much moral emotion, violation of propriety principles may. I noted earlier that there's evidence that violation of propriety standards often produces feelings of disgust (Gutierrez & Giner-Sorolla, 2007; Horberg et al., 2009; Rozin et al., 1999; Russell et al., 2013). I also suggested that these feelings might well reflect moral emotion. But as with the anger evoked by interpersonal violations, this possibility needs to be tested. Unfortunately, I know of only one study designed to test whether disgust evoked by a propriety violation is truly moral. Before I describe that study, some background information on morality and disgust may be useful.

Morality and Disgust

A conceptual distinction has often been made between physical disgust and moral disgust (Horberg et al., 2009; Marzillier & Davey, 2004; Russell & Giner-Sorolla, 2013). Physical disgust is a feeling of revulsion at bad tastes and smells, bodily waste, rotting flesh, and other physical contaminants. Paralleling the earlier definition of moral anger, *moral disgust* is *disgust evoked by the perception that a moral standard (principle, ideal) has been or will be violated*. In many contexts, what's labeled moral disgust co-occurs with other emotions such as anger, whereas physical disgust is more likely to occur alone (Marzillier & Davey, 2004; Russell & Giner-Sorolla, 2013).

Controversy exists over whether moral disgust involves actual emotion, or is only a metaphorical use of the word "disgust" to express strong disapproval (Chapman & Anderson, 2011, 2012; Lee & Schwarz, 2011; Royzman & Kurzban, 2011). Research in the misattribution-of-emotion tradition (see Chapter 2) and affect-as-information tradition (Schwarz & Clore, 1983, 1988) suggests that it involves actual emotion.

For example, Wheatley and Haidt (2005) provided highly hypnotizable individuals with a suggestion under hypnosis that on waking they would feel "a brief pang of disgust . . . a sickening feeling in your stomach" on reading a benign word—either the word "often" or the word "take." When these individuals later read the benign word embedded in descriptions of morally questionable acts, they reported more severe moral condemnation of these acts. The questionable acts included consensual sex between second cousins, cooking and eating one's already dead dog, a congressman espousing morality but taking bribes, an ambulance-chasing lawyer, shoplifting, and stealing library books. Eskine, Kacinik, and Prinz (2011) reported that swallowing a disgusting bitter drink prior to judging morally questionable acts produced the same effect.

Schnall, Haidt et al. (2008) found that a bad smell (Experiment 1), a dirty and messy work space (Experiment 2), recalling a physically disgusting experience (Experiment 3), and seeing a scene from the movie *Trainspotting* with a foul and unflushed toilet (Experiment 4) all led participants sensitive to their own bodily sensations subsequently to judge morally questionable acts more morally wrong. And Schnall, Benton, and Harvey (2008) found that participants who had just watched the disgust-inducing *Trainspotting* clip judged these same acts more wrong unless they had washed their hands between watching the clip and making the judgments. Presumably, in each of these experiments, participants reasoned backward from their actual feelings of physical disgust, which they incorrectly attributed to the morally questionable acts. Thinking their disgust was evoked by the acts they read about, they inferred that they must disapprove of them (Cameron, Payne, & Doris, 2013).

Other research has taken the immorality–disgust association an interesting step further. If moral violation evokes disgust and disgust is associated with filth and dirt, then moral violation should produce an increased desire for cleanliness. Consistent with this idea, Zhong and Liljenquist (2006) reported that recalling a past moral violation led to more thoughts about cleanliness, and it increased preference for an antiseptic wipe over a pencil as a free gift. Adding specificity, Lee and Schwarz (2010) found that participants induced to tell a lie using their mouth (via voice mail) showed an increased desire for mouthwash, whereas those who told the lie using their hands (via e-mail) showed an increased desire for hand sanitizer.

This research on the immorality–disgust association suggests that people in some sense equate or confuse feelings of physical disgust and their feelings evoked by a moral violation. Given that there's general agreement that physical disgust is an emotion, this substitutability supports the claim that our response to propriety violations involves actual emotion and this emotion deserves to be called disgust.

But the value-based definition of moral emotion proposed earlier suggests that we need to look more closely if we are to determine whether disgust at a moral violation is truly moral. As with anger at unfairness, we need to know that the disgust is evoked by the violation itself, not by harm done by the violation.

Is Disgust Evoked by the Moral Violation Itself or by the Harm Done?

How can we know? One context in which these two possibilities might be separated is when innocents not involved in an interest conflict are harmed. Think about military collateral damage. Most people believe that it's morally wrong to pursue military targets when doing so is likely to kill or harm noncombatants. Such collateral damage is considered a "crime against humanity" that threatens the social order. That is, it's considered a violation of propriety standards. So if propriety standard violations produce moral disgust, collateral damage should elicit moral disgust (and perhaps moral anger as well). Moreover—and important for research purposes—collateral damage violates propriety standards without involving exposure to anything pathogenic, unclean, distasteful, or "sick." There's no reason to think that hearing about such damage would evoke physical disgust. As a result, collateral damage has the potential to provide a clearer test for moral disgust than do the propriety violations used in past research, such as eating rotten meat (Rozin et al., 1999) or "filthy" sexual practices (Haidt et al., 1993).

But, even if collateral damage evokes disgust, how do we know it's moral disgust? According to the value-based definition, if the disgust is moral, it should occur even when those feeling it have no personal interest or stake in the events (unlike, for example, the disgust found by Skitka, Bauman, & Mullen, 2004, in the United States after the 9/11 attack on the World Trade Center). In addition, the disgust should occur in response to the moral violation rather than to the harm done by the violation.

Jackson, Batson, and Gaertner (2011) examined the disgust reported by a sample of US undergraduates to a case of collateral damage to see whether it satisfied these two criteria for value-based moral disgust. The undergraduates were asked to read a news article (actually fictitious) about the destruction of a primary school in rural Burma (Myanmar), a country in which none of the undergraduates had a personal interest and about which they knew very little. Half of the undergraduates read that the school had been destroyed by a preemptive Burmese military airstrike on a rebel stronghold in an effort to prevent impending rebel attacks on military outposts: "The Burmese military knew that hitting the school was likely, and that there was a very good chance that the school would be occupied at the time, but decided to go ahead with the strike."

To assess whether any disgust reported after reading about the attack was evoked by the perceived moral violation (collateral damage) rather than harm done, the remaining undergraduates read the same article except the school's destruction was caused by an earthquake. The harm done in the earthquake condition was identical to that in the airstrike condition. But without a perpetrator, this version of the article should produce no perception of moral wrong (as argued by Guglielmo & Malle, 2010). If the earthquake damage also evoked disgust, it couldn't be moral disgust.

There was a second, cross-cutting experimental manipulation: the type of harm done by the airstrike or earthquake. In a destruction-and-death condition, the last two sentences of the article read, "Unfortunately, 21 children and their teacher were inside the school. All were killed." In a destruction-only condition, these sentences read, "Fortunately, 21 children and their teacher had just evacuated the school. All were safe." If participants judged the morality of the airstrike on intent rather than consequences, these two conditions shouldn't differ in perception of moral wrong. Both involved pursuit of military action that had a good chance of killing innocent noncombatants. On the other hand, the two conditions differed dramatically in the actual harm done. If participants focused on consequences, they should perceive destruction-and-death to be more wrong than destruction only. And their reported disgust—if moral—should reflect this difference.

After reading the article, participants indicated the degree to which they were feeling a number of emotions, including disgust and anger. Then they indicated how morally right or wrong they judged the events described in the article. As expected, the airstrike was perceived to be more morally wrong ($M = 6.89$ on the 1 = *clearly morally right* to 9 = *clearly morally wrong* scale) than the earthquake ($M = 4.50$), which was judged close to the neutral midpoint of the scale (see Column 1 of Table 6.4). Further, at least some participants appeared to judge the morality of the airstrike consequentially. The strike was considered more morally wrong when it caused destruction and death ($M = 7.71$) than when it caused only destruction

Table 6.4 Judgment of Moral Wrong and Reported Disgust and Anger After Reading About Destruction of Primary School in Burma (Jackson et al., 2011)

Experimental condition	Moral wrong	Reported disgust	Reported anger
Destruction caused by earthquake			
Destruction only	4.29_a	1.07_a	1.09_a
Destruction and death	4.71_a	1.50_a	1.45_a
Destruction caused by airstrike			
Destruction only	6.07_b	2.86_b	2.43_b
Destruction and death	7.71_c	4.71_c	3.18_b

Note: Moral wrong was assessed on a 1 (*clearly morally right*) to 9 (*clearly morally wrong*) scale. Disgust and anger were assessed on 1 (*not at all*) to 7 (*extremely*) scales. Means in a given column that don't share the same subscript differ significantly, $p < .05$, in a pairwise comparison.

($M = 6.07$). There was no reliable difference in judgment of moral wrong between the two levels of harm when caused by the earthquake.

Unlike reports of anger in the three experiments that involved interpersonal moral violations, reports of disgust and anger in this experiment patterned much like the perceptions of immorality. The airstrike evoked more disgust than the earthquake ($Ms = 3.79$ and 1.29, respectively, on the 1 = *not at all* to 7 = *extremely* scale), and the airstrike that caused destruction and death evoked more disgust than the airstrike that caused only destruction ($Ms = 4.71$ and 2.86, respectively; Column 2 of Table 6.4). Across conditions, ratings of disgust were positively correlated with perceptions of moral wrong, $r = .65$. Ratings of anger were somewhat lower than ratings of disgust, but were highly correlated with them, $r = .70$, and showed a similar (although weaker) pattern of statistically significant differences across experimental conditions (Column 3 of Table 6.4).

Given that the US undergraduates in this experiment had no personal stake in Burma or in the people affected by destruction of the school, and given that their disgust and anger followed the same pattern as their perceptions of moral violation rather than the pattern of harm done, the reported disgust and anger met the criteria for moral emotions. They seemed to be evoked by the moral violation itself.

Of course, this is only one experiment. More research is needed, especially research that examines the motivational consequences of the emotion, before we can conclude that propriety violations such as collateral damage evoke truly moral emotion. All we can say at this point is that such a conclusion, if substantiated, would be entirely consistent with the proposed analysis of the value, motivation, and emotion difference between interpersonal and propriety morality.

CONCLUSION

Much evidence indicates that moral violations, whether our own or those of others, can evoke strong emotion. There's also much evidence that this emotion can produce powerful motivation. Such emotion has often been called moral emotion. But, in many cases, there's reason for doubt. In particular, there's reason to doubt that the emotion evoked by violation of interpersonal standards is truly moral. Due to the way they're acquired, interpersonal standards are likely to be valued only extrinsically. So valued, their violation should evoke little moral emotion. In contrast, propriety standards are acquired in a way likely to lead to intrinsic valuing, so their violation should evoke truly moral emotion.

Research that makes the distinctions necessary to identify the value violation that evoked a given emotion is rare. But what research there is provides data consistent with these expectations. Violation of collateral damage propriety principles—at least other people's violations—does seem to evoke truly moral emotion, especially feelings of disgust. Violation of interest-conflict principles of fairness, whether by others or by us, often evokes strong emotion. But it's not clear this emotion is moral. The anger frequently reported in response to another person's interpersonal violation seems to be evoked by the consequences for oneself or cared-for others. It's personal or empathic anger not moral anger.

Under some circumstances, personal and empathic anger may motivate us to act morally—to try to remove the unfairness and set things right. Under other circumstances, these nonmoral forms of anger may lead us to set morality aside. We may respond to harm done by inflicting harm in return. Indeed, these nonmoral forms of anger may lead to an escalation of moral violation. Rather than an eye for an eye, we may take a life for an eye. Or, as resources dwindle, these forms of anger may lead us to grab all we can, which may harm not only the standard violator but innocents as well (Schroeder, Steel, Woodell, & Bembenek, 2003). Personal and empathic anger amplify egoistic and altruistic motives, respectively, not moral ones. Lack of truly moral anger at interpersonal moral violations may further explain the scarcity of interpersonal moral integrity.

In addition to raising doubt about the moral status of anger at unfairness, I suggested that compassion and sympathy shouldn't be considered moral emotions. They're evoked by threats to the welfare of cared-for others rather than by violation of moral standards (Batson, 2011; Batson et al., 2007). And often, the guilt and shame we experience at violation of our own moral standards, whether propriety or interpersonal standards, shouldn't be considered moral emotions. Evidence indicates that guilt and shame are evoked by the harm to our social or self-esteem caused by a failure to live up to standards—an egoistic concern (Batson et al., 1988; Baumeister, Stilwell, & Heatherton, 1994; Cohen et al., 2011, 2012; de Hooge et al., 2011; Tangney & Dearing, 2002; Tangney et al., 2007). It's not clear that any of these emotions—all of which have been called prototypical moral emotions (Haidt, 2003)—should be considered moral.

To the degree that these emotions aren't truly moral, the motivation they produce isn't truly moral. That is, the motivation isn't directed toward the ultimate goal of upholding some moral principle (principlism). Instead, it's directed toward promoting or preserving the threatened intrinsic value—our own welfare (egoism), the welfare of one or more cared-for others (altruism), or the welfare of one or more cared-for groups (collectivism). Once again, such motives will produce moral behavior only to the degree that the action that most effectively promotes their ultimate goals happens to accord with principle. They're only tangentially and unreliably moral.

Absence of a reliable link between these nonmoral motives and moral action may help explain why what's thought to be moral motivation often proves weak, inconsistent, and fickle. It may be because motivation thought moral often isn't. And we can now add, the associated emotion, also thought moral, often isn't. The implausible expectation with which this chapter began has become more plausible. Lack of moral emotion may indeed be an important contributor to failure to act in accord with our interpersonal moral standards, principles, and ideals.

PART III

So What

7

MORAL COMBAT

Growing more pressing over preceding chapters has been the question of why we have morality. Moral principles and ideals are often assumed to be intrinsically motivating and "designed to regulate behavior" (Prinz, 2006, p. 41). We're said to have them because they provide a counterforce to our self-interested desires. They enable us to live in harmony with those around us, to take our place in the cultural chorus. "Beliefs about wrongness carry the motivational force that we experience as being under obligation. Consequently, moral judgments vie for control of the will. When they occur, we are thereby motivated to act" (Prinz, 2006, p. 36; also see Damasio, 1994; Haidt, 2001; Hauser, 2006).

The argument I've been developing casts doubt on any straightforward, optimistic view that moral judgments lead to motivation to uphold them and, thereby, to moral behavior (see also Stocker, 1976). As the quick review at the start of Chapter 1 underscored, allegiance to moral standards—even devout allegiance—often doesn't lead to moral action. And in subsequent chapters, I suggested it's not simply that we've failed to learn the right principles or that we lack the cognitive or emotional tools to judge what's right (Chapter 2). Nor is it simply that we're overwhelmed by situational pressure (Chapter 3). There's more.

Chapter 4 provided evidence that our ultimate goal when acting to uphold interpersonal moral principles is often either to avoid social and self-punishments or to gain social and self-rewards, especially the rewards of being seen by both others and ourselves as moral. Rather than being motivated by moral integrity, we're motivated by moral hypocrisy. This motivation draws us into a masquerade in which the link between our moral judgments and our behavior is unreliable. If given wiggle room so that we can appear moral without incurring the personal costs of acting as we judge moral, we pursue appearance.

Unreliable behavior regulation by interpersonal, interest-conflict principles seems to be a consequence of the way we acquire these principles. In recent years, it has become popular to suggest that our evolution as a species has prepared us to embrace morality naturally with little need for training, discipline, and instruction. If this were true, we should see full internalization of core principles such as fairness, care, and honesty. The developmental observations in Chapter 5 revealed a different scene.

From the outset, interpersonal principles are often at odds with our desires. So we have reason to resist their dictates. To be sure, we learn early on that these principles are an important part of life and must be reckoned with. It's necessary for me to act in accord, or at least be seen to do so, lest I suffer serious social and self-sanctions. But the conflict with self-interest is likely to lead to internalization only to the level of introjection. I value my interpersonal principles extrinsically, out of concern for the consequences of noncompliance.

In contrast, propriety principles are likely to be acquired relatively easily. We crave the coherence and comfort such principles provide so there's little reason to resist. Through practice, modeling, and instruction, our propriety principles become deeply ingrained and intrinsically valued. They may be questioned in later years, but they're apt to be accepted in childhood as the way things are and ought to be. Table 5.1 provided a summary of these differences between interpersonal and propriety morality.

IS THERE NO ROLE FOR INTERPERSONAL MORALITY?

So, the question: If interpersonal principles and the judgments they produce don't reliably motivate and guide our moral behavior, why do we have them? There's no doubt that we have them, at least most of us do. As noted in previous chapters, principles of fairness, justice, and care are often considered the essence if not the totality of morality. They're a defining attribute of our species. But if the raison d'être of interpersonal morality is to curb our self-interested desires and keep us from using everyone and everything for our own ends, it doesn't seem to be doing a very good job. Perhaps we would be better off to accept Thomas Hobbes's blunt analysis and turn to the State, his *Leviathan*, instead.

According to Hobbes, the natural human condition is a war "of every man against every man," in which life is "solitary, poor, nasty, brutish, and short" (1651, Chapter 13). The only hope of happiness lies in mutual agreement to curb everyone's natural passions. This social contract produces the State. Through its laws, the State can enforce the peace and security that the interpersonal morality embodied in "the laws of nature" dictates but can't deliver (Hobbes, 1651, Chapter 15):

> For the laws of nature, as *justice, equity, modesty, mercy,* and, in sum, *doing to others as we would have done to,* of themselves, without the terror of some power to cause them to be observed, are contrary to our natural passions, that carry us to partiality, pride, revenge, and the like. And covenants, without the sword, are but words and of no strength to secure a man at all. . . . If there be no power erected, or not great enough for our security, every man will and may lawfully rely on his own strength and art for caution against all other men. (Hobbes, 1651, Chapter 17, italics in original)

Without the State, morality can't control our self-interested passions. And with the State, we have its laws to keep the peace. There's no need for morality, at least not interpersonal morality. So again, why have it?

USING MORALITY TO CONTROL OTHERS' BEHAVIOR

Unlike Hobbes, I wish to argue that interpersonal morality plays an important role in our lives. Hobbes lived in the shadow of the English Civil War, which led him to look to an all-powerful State to keep the peace between the warring factions of society. My focus is on the more mundane and immediate person-to-person interest conflicts that fly below the radar of the State and its laws. I believe interpersonal morality plays a major role in such conflicts. But it's a different role from the one typically assumed.

As suggested in Chapter 5, person-to-person interpersonal conflicts begin in the first few years of life, where they're often addressed in quasi-judicial proceedings involving parents, siblings, playmates, and teachers. The relevant behavioral standards aren't laws but moral rules, principles, and ideals. Sometimes the child is the accused and sometimes the accuser. When accused, morality is an enemy. The child wants to break free from its grip. When accuser, morality is an ally that can overpower an adversary and bring his or her behavior in line with the child's desires. These proceedings suggest a use for interpersonal morality different from self-regulation: Rather than to evaluate and control our own behavior, we use interpersonal morality to evaluate and control *others'* behavior. We want to be treated morally, not to be moral ourselves.

Such a suggestion runs into an immediate challenge. How can we possibly expect to get away with imposing moral restrictions on others that we're not willing to accept for ourselves? Surely others won't let us get away with such self-serving partiality, just as we won't let them. Surely we must pledge allegiance to the same behavior-regulating principles and conditions we apply to others. We must show ourselves to be as moral as we expect them to be. But we don't want our own behavior constrained by our principles. Here's a moral dilemma of a very different kind from the hypothetical dilemmas posed in the moral judgment research described in Chapter 2.

Some of the experiments reviewed in Chapter 4 uncovered a promising way to reconcile these seemingly incompatible goals. Self-deception. Blatant hypocrisy, in which we preach morality but clearly practice otherwise, is doomed. Others are on guard for any failure by us to live up to avowed standards, for any sign of insincerity or deception, even as we're on guard for any failure by them. But if we can manage to deceive ourselves, we should be better able to deceive others. If we can not only appear to have acted morally but can also honestly believe we've done so when we haven't, we can avoid both social and self-accusation yet still remain free from moral regulation. Of course, the same is true for others. Unknown even to ourselves, we each seek to substitute the appearance of morality for its reality. The result is a form of moral combat in which in the name of what's right we try to bind our adversaries with moral restraints even as they, like us, struggle to break free.

And use of morality to control others' behavior may not be limited to interpersonal morality. It may apply to propriety morality as well. Self-deception plays a less important role in propriety battles because we typically don't seek to avoid adherence to our propriety principles. We want to act in accord with them. But, as noted in Chapter 1, we don't need to invoke principles to get us to do what we already want to do, such as avoid incest. So we must also ask of propriety principles why we have them. Are they unnecessary? Once again, perhaps we use them more to control others' behavior than to control our own.

Most of us feel it's important to keep others from violating our propriety standards. These standards protect the natural and social order, the structure that makes our life meaningful, good, and right. Their violation threatens the stability of this structure, casting doubt on our convictions about the way things are and should be. For someone to disrespect or defile a sacred object challenges its special meaning. I can't allow that. Unnatural sexual practices threaten my sense of what it means to be human. To debunk cherished traditions shakes the foundations of society. Propriety principles—and epithets—are wielded to prevent and punish such attacks: No sex outside marriage. Don't harm innocents. Don't take God's name in vain. Respect your elders, and the flag. Once again, moral combat. (For a somewhat similar view of why we have morality, but from the perspective of evolutionary psychology, see Kurzban, 2010.)

PRECEDENCE

The suggestion that we use morality to control others' behavior rather than our own isn't new. It has been around for well over 2,000 years.

Callicles

In *Gorgias*, one of Plato's Socratic dialogues (written around 385 BC), Callicles argued that the weak in society employ morality to constrain the actions of those who are naturally stronger and more capable. Moral standards are created, said Callicles,

> by the weaklings who form the majority of mankind. They establish them and apportion praise and blame with an eye to themselves and their own interests, and—in an endeavor to frighten those who are stronger and capable of getting the upper hand—they say that taking an excess of things is shameful and wrong, and that wrongdoing consists in trying to have more than others. (Plato, 1960, Section 483b–c)

Socrates disagreed with Callicles about why we have morality and about what it means to be strong. Socrates thought that true strength lies not in mastery over others but in self-mastery. Only through moderation and self-control is true happiness found. Socrates thus provided early expression of what was to become the dominant Western view: We use morality to control our own behavior.

Nietzsche

Nietzsche held a view similar to that of Callicles, except instead of the weak using morality to curb the ability of the strong to pursue pleasure, Nietzsche (1887/1967b) saw a battle of two distinct moralities. The herd or slave morality of pity, compassion, and altruism—the morality of good versus evil (right versus wrong)—opposes the more ancient morality of conquest and mastery—of good versus bad (strong versus weak). Specifically in Western history, Judeo-Christian morality opposes Roman morality. To control their Roman masters and bring them low, Christians castigated as evil the self-assertion and dominance that Roman morality valued as good. Although Nietzsche clearly sided with the earlier morality of mastery in this struggle, he sought to move beyond both of these polarities to a "revaluation of all values," the subtitle of his posthumous classic *The Will to Power*. Nietzsche's most vitriolic criticism of contemporary Christian, herd morality was that it constrained the creative genius and flourishing of "higher men" (Leiter, 2011):

> Moral judgments and condemnations constitute the favorite revenge of the spiritually limited against those less limited. . . . It pleases them deep down in their hearts that there are standards before which those overflowing with the wealth and privileges of the spirit are their equals. (Nietzsche, 1886/1967a, Section 219)

Nietzsche sought to alert the noble few to the constraints imposed on them by the herd. These higher men must free themselves from the fetters of morality as we know it in order to create the human future:

> The noble type of man experiences *itself* as determining values; it does not need approval; it judges, "what is harmful to me is harmful in itself"; it knows itself to be that which first accords honor to things; it is *value creating*. (Nietzsche, 1886/1967a, Section 260, italics in original)

Freud

Freud (1930/1961) also depicted morality as an imposed constraint to control behavior. But he believed the constraint is felt by us all, not just a noble few. And morality's constraint has a different purpose. Faced with a world full of dangers and threats even more frightening than Hobbes imagined, we turn to civilization and the constraints it imposes as a defense:

> We are threatened with suffering from three directions: from our own body, which is doomed to decay and dissolution and which cannot even do without pain and anxiety as warning signals; from the external world, which may rage against us with overwhelming and merciless forces of destruction; and finally

from our relations to other men. The suffering which comes from this last source is perhaps more painful to us than any other. ... Civilized man has exchanged a portion of his possibilities of happiness for a portion of security. (Freud, 1930/1961, pp. 24, 62)

The power that we want civilization to wield to protect us and control the behavior of others, it also uses to control us. Our defense is also an offense, a source of pervasive discontent. Freud considered this an astonishing contention.

What we call our civilization is largely responsible for our misery. ... I call this contention astonishing because, in whatever way we may define the concept of civilization, it is a certain fact that all the things with which we seek to protect ourselves against the threats that emanate from the sources of suffering are part of that very civilization. (Freud, 1930/1961, p. 33)

For Freud, control wasn't by the State and its laws as it was for Hobbes. Nor was it, as for Callicles and Nietzsche, by one class or type of people over another. According to Freud, civilization seeks to control each of us through moral ideals such as the commandment to love our neighbor as ourselves, "a commandment which is really justified by the fact that nothing else runs so strongly counter to the original nature of man. ... Anyone who follows such a precept in present-day civilization only puts himself at a disadvantage vis-à-vis the person who disregards it" (Freud, 1930/1961, pp. 59, 90).

How can civilization get us to pursue such unnatural ideals? Freud (1930/1961) didn't find the answer, as had Nietzsche, in the history of culture (which Freud addressed only by analogy) but "in the history of the development of the individual" (p. 70). As we saw in Chapter 2, Freud argued that this development involves formation of a superego, which uses the harsh constraints of self-censure and guilt to control us. The battleground is intrapsychic.

Civilization, therefore, obtains mastery over the individual's dangerous desire for aggression by weakening and disarming it and by setting up an agency within him to watch over it, like a garrison in a conquered city. ... The price we pay for our advance in civilization is a loss of happiness through the heightening of the sense of guilt. (Freud, 1930/1961, pp. 70–71, 81)

Civilization works through parents and other socializing agents to set up this moral garrison that controls our libidinal impulses with guilt. The result is discontent and misery.

Campbell

In his 1975 Presidential Address to the American Psychological Association, Donald Campbell employed the idea of social evolution to explain society's use of moralistic teaching and preaching in order to control our biologically inherited selfish impulses: "Human urban social complexity is a product of social evolution and has had to counter with inhibitory moral norms the biological selfishness which genetic competition has continually selected" (Campbell, 1975, p. 1123). Campbell suggested that moral constraints exist because they have survival value for the society relative to other societies. Accordingly, he cautioned against therapeutic models designed to free individuals from the neurotic anxiety and guilt produced by these controls. Any gains in individual happiness are apt to be at the expense of society as a whole. Whereas Freud was deeply troubled by the discontent produced by moral restrictions, and was ready to use psychoanalysis to loose the bonds, Campbell emphasized their positive value. He didn't attribute moral constraint to a punitive superego garrisoned within the psyche but to the need to accommodate both societal and personal interests.

According to Campbell, optimal resolution of the tension between societal and personal interests doesn't lie either in total subjugation of our biologically based selfish desires, or in total disregard for social standards and norms. The optimum is between the two. But because the biological pull is stronger, moralistic preaching must necessarily be extreme in order to move the individual toward the optimal compromise.

> The extremity of the preached ideal can be seen as an effort to overcome, to balance out, the biological bias in the opposite direction. . . . In Moses' day as in ours, there was indeed a valid functional commandment, "Look out for your own interests." But people then were so spontaneously complying with it that it did not need the continual social system preaching which "Thou shalt not covet" did. (Campbell, 1975, p. 1118)

If, as Campbell's analysis implies, people understand at some level that moral edicts are extreme and not to be taken at face value but subjected to compromise with personal interests, we have especially fertile ground for moral hypocrisy to grow.

Callicles, Neitzsche, Freud, and Campbell thought moral constraint is imposed either on one segment of society by another or on the individual by society as a whole. Their analyses are quite consistent with the suggestion that morality functions to regulate the behavior of individuals in order to produce action that promotes the welfare of the group (Haidt, 2003, 2012; Haidt & Kesebir, 2010). Although not at odds with this possibility, my proposal is different. I'm suggesting that morality is likely to be used by one individual to control another's behavior. It's used down in the trenches in hand-to-hand combat.

TWO CASES TO CONSIDER

To illustrate what I'm talking about, let me point to two quite different cases.

Tattling

As early as 14 months, children tattle. That is, they draw their parents' attention to the misdeeds of a sibling (Dunn & Munn, 1985; see Chapter 5). Ross and den Bak-Lammers (1998) conducted an extensive study of tattling by young siblings in 39 English-speaking Canadian families. Home observations were made when the siblings were 2 and 4 years old, then 2 years later when 4 and 6. Ross and den Bak-Lammers found that for both the younger and the older child tattling became more frequent, explicit, and evaluative as the child grew older. In part, these changes were due to improved verbal skills. But they also reflected increased understanding that "telling" is an effective means to get your way in sibling conflicts.

Initially, tattling was most likely to occur when the tattler wanted parental assistance in some specific interest conflict: "Suzie hit me!" "He won't give me the ball." "It's *my* turn." "She's cheating!" With time, it was also likely in the absence of direct conflict: "She's drawing on the wall." "Davy took a cookie after you said no." The reason for tattling to secure parental assistance seems clear. The reason for tattling in the absence of immediate conflict is less obvious, but it too appeared combative. Ross and den Bak-Lammers (1998) felt that children use such tattling to align themselves with the parent against their brother or sister. It was designed to better the child's position in ongoing sibling rivalry. "Through their tattling children actively solicit differential treatment favoring themselves, or redress from their parents' perceived favoring of the sibling" (p. 276).

Despite frequent popular media advice to parents that they should discourage tattling, Ross and den Bak-Lammers found that parents rarely reprimanded tattlers. Reprimands occurred less than 5 percent of the time, although they were somewhat more likely when children tattled simply to get a brother or sister in trouble. The researchers also found that tattlers (1) generally told the truth (over 90 percent of the time—perhaps because children learn early on that false accusations backfire), (2) were most likely to report physical aggression and property damage/possession, and (3) increasingly framed their tattling in moral terms.

Ross and den Bak-Lammers (1998) concluded that "tattling is clearly moral talk" (p. 298). To this conclusion, we might add that it's moral talk that promotes the child's own interests in the most central interpersonal conflict for many young children, sibling conflict. At this early age, moral standards aren't used to attack the offending sibling directly but indirectly through that great moral authority, the parent. Lack of direct moral attack may be because the children haven't yet internalized self-regulatory standards. And without internalization, guilt trips go nowhere. External control and sanctioning is required, and the parent can manage that far better than the child. Each child learns that if he or she can convince Mom or Dad that the other child has done something which violates a parental standard, the battle's won.

Thus, three roles are involved in tattling: accuser, accused, and audience. In later years, charges of moral violation are apt to be fired directly at the offender, seeking to elicit self-control rather than parental control. But the audience is still important.

Confrontation over Parking in a Handicapped Spot

Geoffrey Miller (2003) used computer searches of local newspapers in the United States and Canada to locate stories, gripe lines, and letters to the editor that provided either examples of or commentary on confrontations over parking in handicapped spots. These are cases in which a person who considers it wrong for an able-bodied person to park in a spot reserved for those with disabilities confronts someone believed to have violated this standard. There are laws against such behavior but violations are rarely handled by authorities. Instead, they're addressed on a more informal level. Individuals confront one another by appealing to social norms. Miller (2003) defined social norms as "extralegal rules and standards for conduct" (p. 896)—what I'm calling moral principles. Miller found thousands of cases.

The moral implications of parking in a handicapped spot are clear in this reflection from *Cincinnati Enquirer* columnist Laura Pulfer:

> When I am standing at the Pearly Gates and St. Peter is struggling to heft the enormous ledger of my sins, I will at least know that I never put my car in a parking space meant for handicapped people. Not ever. Not even when it was raining. Not even when I was sure nobody would notice. Not even when I was sure spaces designated for the handicapped outnumbered the people who are handicapped in the entire region. Perhaps in the entire hemisphere. I drove past those spaces, grateful that I do not qualify. (Miller, 2003, p. 916)

Confrontations over parking in a handicapped spot are almost always between adults. Thus, the accused is someone the accuser believes has internalized the relevant moral standards. Interest-conflict standards (fairness, care), propriety standards (law-breaking, norm violation), or both, may be invoked. Sometimes the accuser has a disability, sometimes not. Sometimes the confrontation is indirect—a note left on a windshield, a letter to the local newspaper, a key scratch along the side of the offending car, deflated or slashed tires. Sometimes the confrontation is direct and face-to-face—a cold stare, a question or comment ("Have you no shame?" "You don't look handicapped."), a negative judgment ("You have no right." "People like you disgust me!").

Among the moral epithets Miller cited as having been applied to violators are: egoist, lout, boor, creep, low-life, philistine, jerk, thoughtless, selfish, cruel, uncaring, self-centered, conscienceless, irresponsible, indecent, insensitive, inconsiderate, cheat, thief, moocher, stealer, ethically challenged, shameful, and morally handicapped (2003, pp. 921-923). These labels are used to shame the violator into a change of behavior. In addition, by calling attention to the behavior as wrong, the labels discourage others from acting similarly. Even when the accuser and accused are the only people on the scene, others in society still play a part:

> Enforcers regularly denigrate the morality, intelligence, and even basic humanity of people who knowingly violate the handicapped-parking rules. Through these shaming tactics, handicapped-parking enforcers implicitly assert the existence of a consensus against violating these rules. They claim that if others knew of the violator's conduct, they would condemn it. (Miller, 2003, p. 909)

Those accused aren't without moral weapons of their own. They can strike back with: "Don't be so obnoxious." "You ought to mind your own business." "How can you judge without knowing me and my situation?" "Look at the damage you've done!"

The confrontation isn't likely to be taken lightly by either side. Sometimes, it goes beyond a war of words and turns physical. Miller (2003) recounted the experience of a man in Ontario who followed three young men into a hair-dressing salon and accused them of parking in a handicap spot. Their response was to knock him down, punch and kick him, and threaten to beat up his wife. Nor do only the accused resort to violence.

> In Park Forest, Illinois, two men pulled into the handicapped space at the Stop & Shop to get some beer. A handicapped driver who pulled up at about the same time confronted them. After an exchange of words and collision of car doors, the handicapped driver grabbed a tire iron from his trunk and smashed it against the head of the passenger of the other car. The victim collapsed on the tarmac, with the disabled driver announcing, "*Now* you know how it feels to be handicapped." (Miller, 2003, p. 932, italics in original)

FIVE FEATURES OF MORAL COMBAT

These two cases are quite different, but together, they highlight five noteworthy features of our use of morality to control others' behavior.

1. As already suggested, three roles are important in moral combat, accuser (standard promoter), accused (standard violator), and audience. Persons in the audience can be of at least three types: *Sanctioners*, such as the parent to whom a child tattles, have the power to punish standard violators. *Endorsers* (or *opponents*) support (or oppose) the standard the accuser wishes upheld, as implied by appeals to societal norms in cases of handicapped parking. And there are *potential future standard violators* or *enforcers*. The accuser may confront the accused directly in an effort to change the latter's behavior. Or may seek to effect change indirectly through appeal either to a sanctioner for enforcement or to endorsers to join in proclaiming the violation wrong. Even if the accuser can't change the behavior of the accused, the accuser may seek to ensure that members of the audience don't become future violators.

2. Although the accuser wants to prevent violation of the standard, he or she often doesn't know a violation is coming until it occurs. So, is accusation too late to do any good? It seems not. Moral combat typically takes place in situations in which, if the violation is permitted to go unpunished, it may be expected to lead to subsequent violations by the accused. Further, violations typically occur in situations in which onlookers (audience) may be inclined to model the violator's behavior if it goes unchallenged. So to address the past is to address the future.

3. If the violation has harmed the accuser or those for whom the accuser cares, he or she may seek revenge by inflicting harm in return. Often, such a counterattack isn't morally motivated. It's motivated by a desire to make the violator suffer. Still, if retaliation can be cast as a moral crusade, it's lifted above simple tit-for-tat in which the accuser may be seen as acting no better than the accused. The accuser gains the high moral ground. And if others (audience) can be persuaded that the retaliation is moral, they should feel pressure not only to distance themselves from the accused but even to join in on the accuser's side. Tattling research indicates that children as young as two have some understanding of these dynamics of revenge. When practiced by adults, moral retaliation often involves more than inflicting material harm. As in the handicapped-parking cases, there's also the pain of stigma, guilt, and shame.

4. Combat over interest conflicts often involves three further complexities. First, as we saw in the courtrooms of childhood described in Chapter 5, when both parties have vested interests, each is likely to claim that the other is wrong. Both are at once accuser and accused. So, at the same time that each may wish to employ interpersonal moral standards to control the other's behavior, each also wishes to avoid allowing these standards to constrain his or her own behavior. Second, to the degree that each is motivated by hypocrisy rather than integrity, as the research reviewed in Chapters 4 through 6 suggests is likely in interest conflicts, we can expect deception (including self-deception) on both sides. Each combatant invokes standards, affirms their relevance, and shows adherence, yet if possible does so without paying the cost of true adherence. Third, each tries to invoke those standards and principles that best suit his or her own cause. If, for example, a fair procedure permits a distribution of resources that favors me, I'm likely to proclaim the relevance and importance of procedural fairness and disregard distributive fairness: "I was randomly chosen to divide the profits, so it's fair for me to take more." The person who gets less is likely to do the reverse: "I did just as much work, so I should get half." We each pick a battlefield on which our victory is assured.

5. As previously noted, many moral issues can be framed as either interpersonal concerns, propriety concerns, or both. If it's true that propriety principles are likely to be more fully internalized and so more apt to evoke moral emotion and motivation when violated, then a fruitful strategy when appealing to the audience in moral combat may be to *proprietize*. That is, direct your attack against threats to the natural and social order. Accuse the opposition of unnatural acts, breaking divine law, crimes against humanity, or violation of inalienable rights.

SOME RELEVANT RESEARCH

I know of no research explicitly designed to test the claim that we use morality to control other people's behavior rather than our own, but some findings are at least consistent with the idea. These findings provide evidence of plausibility. They also highlight the need for more direct tests.

Punishment of Moral Violators

First and most obviously, there's research that shows our readiness to incur costs to punish a person who treats us unfairly. For example, Sanfey et al. (2003) had participants play a series of Ultimatum Games—in which one player (the Proposer) makes an offer to the other player (the Responder) of how to split $10.00 between the two. If the Responder accepts the offer, the money is divided accordingly. If the Responder doesn't accept, neither player gets anything. From a purely monetary standpoint, it makes sense for the Responder always to accept any offer larger than zero because that's what he or she receives by rejecting.

All participants in the Sanfey et al. experiment were in the role of Responder. For some games the Proposer was another participant. For other games, the Proposer was a computer ostensibly programmed to make a randomly selected proposal. Actually, proposals in each case were preset so that half of the offers were fair ($5/5) and half favored the Proposer. Participants were far more likely to reject clearly unfair offers ($9/1 or $8/2 to the Proposer/Responder, respectively) when made by another participant than when made by the computer. Given the structure of the game, this rejection came at some cost—$1 or $2—but inflicted a much larger cost on the Proposer—$9 or $8. Further, greater likelihood of rejection was associated with neural activity in a brain region known to be involved in the experience of negative emotion, the anterior insula. Consistent with the research on anger at unfairness described in Chapter 6, this emotion was likely personal anger at the human Proposer's attempt to take advantage of the situation for personal gain at the participant's expense.

Heightening the perception of affront in this experiment, the participant had met each Proposer participant before the games began. Imagine how the Responder would react to an unfair offer by one of these Proposers. I can imagine my reaction: "So that's what you think of me. I'll show you, you won't get anything!" Because Responders played only once with each human Proposer, and because their response to one Proposer wasn't revealed to others, rejection didn't seem to be an attempt to control either this Proposer's or other Proposers' future behavior in the experiment. More likely, it was a past-oriented act of revenge intended to punish the personal affront and abuse of power.

Carlsmith and Sood (2009) reported a similar readiness to punish immoral behavior, but in a very different context—the so-called War on Terror. They found that an online sample of US adults recommended more severe, painful techniques be used when interrogating a 26-year-old Afghan man who had little or no current contact with enemies of US forces if instead of being given no information about his past they were told that several years earlier he had been a member of an extremist Muslim group, a supporter of the Taliban, and an insurgent involved in setting roadside bombs and lethal ambushes of US Marines. Tellingly, the difference in recommended severity of interrogation existed even when there was very little chance that the man had any useful information. Recommended severity was instead associated with reported desire to see the man punished ($r = .65$), which was in turn associated with judgment of the man's immorality ($r = .63$). So this study, like the previous one, provides evidence of retaliation for past harm done, not future-oriented promotion of principle.

Those Harmed (Accusers) Punish More Severely than Third-Party Sanctioners (Audience)

Research also shows—again predictably—that although third-party sanctioners who haven't themselves been harmed by the violation will punish moral violators, those harmed are likely to punish more severely. Fehr and Fishbacher (2004) reported the results of four relevant experiments. Experiments 1 and 3 involved a one-trial anonymous Dictator Game, in which one of two players is randomly selected to divide a monetary sum, giving the other player whatever portion the first chooses and keeping the rest. (So, unlike the Ultimatum Game described earlier, in a Dictator Game the second player has no say at all.) Most people consider the morally right division in a Dictator Game to be an even split. Experiments 2 and 4 involved a one-trial anonymous Prisoner's Dilemma, in which each of two players makes a choice to either cooperate or defect, with defection always the most profitable choice for self but cooperation the most profitable both for the other player and for the two players combined. Most people consider the morally right choice in a Prisoner's Dilemma to be cooperation.

Experiments 1 and 2 added the possibility of third-party punishment to the Dictator Game and Prisoner's Dilemma, respectively. In each of these experiments, the two participants affected by the decision(s) knew that a third participant had the opportunity (at some monetary cost to self) to punish the Decider. Each experiment provided evidence that individuals who aren't harmed by an unfair, self-favoring division or choice are willing to incur cost to punish the self-favorer. These third-party punishers may have felt obliged to responsibly fulfill their role as police.

Experiments 3 (Dictator Game) and 4 (Prisoner's Dilemma) each included two repeated-measures conditions. One condition allowed for second-party punishment, punishment of a self-favoring Decider by the person harmed. The other condition allowed for third-party punishment. Results of these experiments revealed that second-party punishment was considerably more severe than third-party punishment. Experiment 4 included a post-experimental questionnaire to assess emotions felt by third-party punishers. Responses suggested that their decisions to punish were associated with negative emotion. Unfortunately, the nature of this emotion wasn't specified. Referring back to Chapter 6, it could have been moral anger, empathic anger at the harm done to the victim of the violation, or personal anger at the thought that the violator—if given the chance—would have treated the punisher as badly.

Results of one of the experiments reported in Chapter 6 suggest that the emotion in the Fehr and Fishbacher (2004) studies was not moral anger. Although not mentioned in Chapter 6, O'Mara et al. (2011) in their experiment on unfair exclusion provided the chance for both second-party and third-party punishment. They found that participants who were themselves unfairly excluded punished the excluder more severely than did participants who witnessed another person be unfairly excluded, paralleling the results of Fehr and Fishbacher (2004). Further, as you may recall, O'Mara et al. found evidence of personal anger among participants unfairly excluded but not of moral anger. So, in their experiment, the punishment seemed to be anger-based vengeance for the unfair treatment.

Possibility of Punishment Inhibits Moral Violation

Turning to the effect of punishment on potential violators, research shows that the possibility of punishment, when sufficiently severe, can control people's impulse to take unfair advantage. Fehr and Gächter (2002) placed participants in an anonymous four-person public-goods dilemma. On each of 12 trials, each of the four persons could either keep a monetary endowment or could contribute some of it to the group for the benefit of all. Group composition changed from trial to trial, and no two participants were ever in the same group on more than one trial. For one set of six trials there was no opportunity to punish other participants for low contributions to the group. For the other set, there was an opportunity to punish by paying to inflict a monetary penalty for low contribution. The amount of the penalty was always three times what the punisher paid. Whether the six no-punishment trials occurred first and the six punishment trails second, or the reverse, was counterbalanced. This variation had no effect.

Fehr and Gächter (2002) found that across the six no-punishment trials, contributions to the group declined to near zero. On the sixth no-punishment trial, over half of the participants contributed nothing. In contrast, across the six punishment trials, contributions over trials stabilized at a high level. On the sixth punishment trial over 70 percent contributed three-fourths or more of their endowment, and almost 40 percent contributed it all. Further, post-experimental assessment revealed that decisions to punish were associated with feelings of anger and annoyance. Assessment also revealed that participants expected a low contribution to elicit such feelings from other group members.

Because punishment couldn't directly benefit the punisher but might benefit members of future groups containing the punished participant, Fehr and Gächter called the punishment altruistic. But it seems more likely that, as in the Sanfey et al. (2003) experiment, punishment of those trying to take unfair advantage was vengeful and the negative emotion was personal anger. Due to the structure of the situation—encountering multiple dilemmas with different group members—vengeance had an "altruistic" effect. Consistent with this interpretation, when Rand and Nowak (2011) changed the situation to one in which cooperation made non-cooperators look bad, they found "antisocial" punishment of cooperators by non-cooperators. Again, vengeance.

Yamagishi (1986) provided evidence not only of negative reactions to unfairness but also of a readiness to pay to support a sanctioning system to control it. Like the Fehr and Fischbacher experiment, Yamagishi's experiment involved an anonymous four-person public-goods dilemma. But unlike the Fehr and Fischbacher experiment, Yamagishi's participants remained in the same group for all 12 trials. (Participants weren't told until the end how many trials there would be.) For some groups, there was no opportunity to sanction or punish other group members (no-sanctioning condition). For other groups, after contributions to the group had been made on a trial each member was given the opportunity to contribute anonymously to a punishment fund. The amount in this fund was to be deducted from the earnings of the member who made the smallest contribution to the group on that trial (low-sanctioning condition). For still other groups, the procedure was the same as for low-sanctioning except that the deduction was to be twice the amount in the punishment fund (high-sanctioning condition). Once all decisions were made for a given trial, participants were informed of the total amount contributed to the group on that trial (but not individual contributions) and, in the low and high-sanctioning conditions, the total amount contributed to the punishment fund. They were also told the amount of punishment received by the lowest contributor (or lowest contributors if there was a tie for low-contribution).

For simplicity in reporting results over the 12 trials, data were aggregated into three blocks of four trials each. In all blocks, even the first, contributions to the group were higher in the two sanctioning conditions than in the no-sanctioning condition. As Yamagishi (1986) explained, these results "suggest that the mere existence of the sanctioning opportunity was enough to scare subjects about the possible punishment" (p. 114). Further, in both the no- and low-sanctioning conditions, contributions to the group decreased over time. But in the high-sanctioning condition, contributions increased. This last effect was most apparent for participants who had scored relatively low on a pre-experimental assessment of interpersonal trust. Apparently, those low in trust, who were less likely to contribute in the no-sanctioning condition, needed the possibility of severe punishment to coerce them. In contrast, punishment didn't seem necessary to get those high in trust to contribute. They contributed at a relatively high rate even in the no-sanctioning condition.

By the third block in the high-sanctioning condition, contributions had risen to over 80 percent and punishment had dropped by almost a third, to about 10 percent. It seems that the threat of severe punishment was sufficiently effective that the need to actually punish was reduced. Remember that—unlike the experiments by Fehr and Fischbacher (2004), Fehr and Gächter (2002), O'Mara et al. (2011), and Sanfey et al. (2004)—this experiment included on-going interaction with the group members a participant could punish. Because of this, punishment could be used as a future-oriented strategy to benefit self by forcing others in the group to comply with standards of cooperation, not merely used to inflict past-oriented vengeance. Participants in the high-sanctioning condition seemed to take advantage of this opportunity to control each other's behavior.

But, as you may recall from Chapter 2, there's a potential problem with using punishment as a future-oriented control strategy. In that chapter, I reviewed research indicating that the use of threat of punishment to get people to comply with moral standards, especially severe punishment, has only a limited effect. Once the threat is removed, compliance disappears. Consistent with this possibility, Chen, Pillutla, and Yao (2009) found that while in place, sanctions (either promised rewards or threatened punishments) increased contributions to the common good in a four-person public-goods dilemma. But once the sanctions were removed, the increase vanished.

Punishment Can Be in the Form of Imagined Moral Disapprobation Rather Than Monetary Costs

The research considered thus far provides evidence that moral violations can be constrained by the threat of punishment in the form of monetary costs to the violator, as long as the threat is in place. But to use morality to control others' behavior involves more than this. It involves constraint of potential violators by the anticipated moral disapproval of either the accuser (the person harmed) or the audience (a third-party sanctioner). Is there any evidence that concern about other people's moral judgments can control our behavior? Outside of the developmental literature reviewed in Chapters 2 and 5, there's disappointingly little, but some.

Effect of an Authority's Moral Appeal

In the research by Chen et al. (2009) just mentioned, one experiment included a condition in which, rather than a monetary sanction, participants received a message from the project supervisor encouraging each participant to make a fair contribution to the common good. This moral appeal increased contribution as much as did the monetary sanctions. Moreover, unlike monetary sanctions, the appeal significantly increased participants' trust in the willingness of other group members to contribute, an important factor in promoting future cooperation. This experiment indicates that an explicit moral appeal from an authority can increase standard compliance. What about imagined moral approval or disapproval by an authority or by our peers? Can it also increase compliance?

Effect of Others' Imagined Moral Approval or Disapproval

An experiment conducted a number of years ago by Reis and Gruzen (1976) suggests it can. Their experiment is the one of which I am aware that comes closest to offering direct evidence that concern about others' moral approval or disapproval can control adults' behavior.

The procedure of the experiment was rather complex, but the results were clear. Ostensibly as part of a study concerning the effects of noise on task performance, male introductory psychology students were designated as Person B in a four-person group of Persons A-D. Each group member or "partner" was to work alone on a proofreading task while listening to moderately distracting noise. Performance would then be evaluated and paid for at the group level: "The amount the whole group will get will depend on how well all of you do; that is, the amount of work and the number of errors" (Reis & Gruzen, 1976, p. 492). Participants were told that payment was included to simulate realistic working conditions and to motivate group members to work at their highest level of effort and ability. Division of the group's earnings among the group members was to be made by one of the four partners. "That person will be allowed to distribute the money among you in any way he wishes" (p. 492). Ostensibly by a random drawing, Person B—the actual participant—was always chosen to be the allocator for the group. In essence then, the participant was the Decider in a four-person version of a Dictator Game.

After performing the proofreading task (and after an appropriate delay for scoring) the participant was given four scored booklets, his own and one for each of his three partners. Scoring revealed that Person C's performance was roughly 50 percent better than the participant's. Person D's was roughly 50 percent worse. And Person A's was close to the participant's performance. As the group's payment, the participant was given $5.00 in change, "the money the four of you have earned" (p. 493). He was also given four change purses, one for each partner's earnings.

Instructions for how to proceed with the allocation were varied to introduce two experimental manipulations: (a) whether the partners would be aware of the allocation and so could be anticipated to judge it, and (b) whether the experimenter would be aware. In the *partners-aware condition*, the instructions explained, "After you've left, I'll send the others out to the secretary as a group. She'll give them their purses along with a report form for each summarizing how you've divided the payment." In the *partners-not-aware condition*, the others were to be sent to the secretary one at a time, so she could give them their purses separately. "In this way, they'll only know what they themselves received. . . . They won't know what anyone else received, or the total amount" (p. 494).

Cross-cutting this manipulation was the manipulation of experimenter awareness. In the *experimenter-aware condition*, the allocator was to fill out a form titled, "Payment Summary: Report to Experimenter," "which will indicate to us how you've divided the money" (p. 493). This form was to be handed to the experimenter before leaving. In the *experimenter-not-aware condition*, the form was titled "Confidential Report," and participants read that they should seal the form in an envelope, mark it "Moderate Noise," and give it to the secretary on the way out. "She'll put it in a box so that at the end of the experiment, we'll have twenty moderate-, twenty high-, and twenty low-noise envelopes. In this way, we'll know what effect the noise has without knowing anything about how you, as an individual, have divided the payment" (p. 494).

Reis and Gruzen (1976) assumed that participants would expect their partners, who didn't know about the performance difference between group members, to consider "share and share alike" (equality) to be the appropriate standard for a fair allocation of the earnings and to disapprove of any major deviation from this standard. In contrast, participants would expect the experimenter, who knew the performance of each group member, to consider payment in proportion to performance (equity) to be the appropriate standard and to disapprove of deviation from it. Accordingly, Reis and Gruzen predicted that relative to the condition in which neither the partners nor the experimenter would know how the pay was distributed, partner awareness would move participants in the direction of equal payment whereas experimenter awareness would move them toward proportional payment.

Importantly, note that these effects were predicted for a situation in which participants had no reason to fear monetary punishment from awareness of either type. Nor was there the prospect of direct social censure. The only coercive force was the participant's imagination about how an aware party would judge his action.

Results conformed to Reis and Gruzen's predictions. First, participants paid themselves significantly more when no one else would know how the pay was allocated compared to when there was either form of awareness. Second, partner awareness significantly diminished the difference in payment across group members, leading to greater equality. This was accomplished primarily by increasing the payment for low-performing Person D and decreasing the payment for high-performing Person C (relative to the no-awareness condition). Third, experimenter awareness widened the payment difference, primarily by increasing pay for Person C and decreasing the enhanced payment to self (again, relative to the no-awareness condition). These results are quite consistent with the idea that imagining others' moral approval or disapproval of our actions, either others who suffer the effects of our actions (the partners) or an audience (the experimenter), can lead us to act more in line with those others' imagined standards.

Effect on Potential Punishers of Others' Imagined Moral Approval or Disapproval

Kurzban, DeScioli, and O'Brien (2007; also see DeScioli & Kurzban, 2009) provided evidence of an interesting variation on this theme. Across two experiments, they manipulated whether participants thought that other people would know if the participant, who was in the role of third-party punisher, chose to punish someone who failed to show trust in a Trust Game (Experiment 1) or to cooperate in a Prisoner's Dilemma (Experiment 2). Participants in Experiment 1 thought that the experimenter either would know or wouldn't know what they did. In Experiment 2, some participants thought no one would know whether they chose to punish, some thought the experimenter would know, and some thought both the experimenter and other participants (also in the role of third-party punishers, but for different players) would know. Given the structure of the experiments, participants could reasonably assume that both the experimenter and the other potential punishers thought moral violations—lack of trust (Experiment 1), lack of cooperation (Experiment 2)—should be punished. Results revealed that participants were more likely to pay to punish their violator when either the experimenter or the experimenter and other third-party punishers would know what they did compared to when no one would know. Thus, sanctioners' readiness to promote standard compliance also seems to be sensitive to the anticipated moral approbation or disapprobation of an audience.

Imagined Self-Approval or -Disapproval

Another variation already considered in some detail is that we can be sensitive to the power of self-sanctioning and self-censure (see Chapters 2 and 5). Once standards are internalized, even if only to the level of introjection, we're likely to sanction our own violations. Aware of this possibility, we adjust our behavior to avoid self-censure (e.g., Bandura, 1991; Mischel & Mischel, 1976). Several findings are consistent with such a prediction. For example, (a) making participants self-aware by placing them in front of a mirror eliminated the moral hypocrisy effect (Batson, Thompson et al., 1999; see Chapter 4). Apparently, these participants had to be fair to appear fair. (b) Giving participants time to think before making a decision of whether or not to cheat led to more honesty (Shalvi, Eldar, & Bereby-Meyer, 2012).

But we have also seen considerable evidence that self-sanctioning can be quite ineffective when we have sufficient wiggle room to avoid evaluating our behavior in light of relevant moral standards (Chapter 4). Indeed, it was in large part the evidence of lack of reliable self-regulation that led to the suggestion that interpersonal morality is used to control others' behavior rather than our own.

What's Missing

I haven't reported any experiments testing the idea that people actively use moral standards, like they do monetary sanctions, to control others' behavior in interest-conflict situations. The reason I haven't is that, as far as I know, no such experiments exist. The only evidence I can cite for this key proposition are the observations noted in Chapter 5 and cases such as tattling and confrontation over parking in a handicapped spot. It may take a little cleverness to create such experiments, but clearly they're needed.

Fighting over Frames

As noted earlier, an implication of the suggestion that we use morality to control others' behavior rather than our own is that we should try to frame morally relevant situations in ways that minimally restrict our behavior but promote our efforts to control the behavior of others.

Might Versus Morality

In economic games and dilemmas such as those described above, people typically face a choice between doing what's smart from the perspective of personal monetary self-interest and doing what's morally right in the sense of being best for everyone involved. The problem posed by these games and dilemmas echoes Nietzsche's (1887/1967b) depiction of the battle between two ways of thinking about what's good: We can think about good versus bad, the Roman morality of mastery, where to display the necessary personal dominance and strength to favor myself is good and weakness is bad. Or we can think about good versus evil, the Christian morality of compassion, where to promote the interests of others is good and self-interest and self-assertion are evil.

Consistent with these two dichotomies, there's evidence that some players tend to frame economic games in terms of might, while others frame in terms of morality (Liebrand, Jansen, Rijken, & Suhre, 1986; van Lange & Kuhlman, 1994). Not surprisingly, those who adopt a might frame tend to act competitively. Those who adopt a morality frame tend to act cooperatively. Moreover, these frames can be induced. Sattler and Kerr (1991) found that listening to a message highlighting the importance of being strong, strategic, and in control—a power message— prior to being placed in a social dilemma decreased cooperation. Listening to a message that highlighted mutual obligation and cooperation—a moral message—increased it. In a trust game, Gunia, Wang, Huang, Wang, and Murnigan (2012) found much the same. These findings suggest that it would be personally profitable in interest-conflict situations to induce others to frame morally while maintaining a might frame yourself.

Moralization

Whether a given action is framed morally or not is also central to Paul Rozin's (1997; Rozin, Markwith, & Stoess, 1997) concept of *moralization*. This term refers to the process whereby objects or activities that were previously morally neutral come to be seen as morally relevant. Prime examples of moralization offered by Rozin are the reaction to eating meat by many vegetarians and the changed attitudes toward cigarette smoking over the past half century. Rozin (1997) also noted that a reverse process can occur—*amoralization*—whereby behavior once judged moral ceases to be. He cited divorce, marijuana smoking, and homosexuality as recent examples.

Moralization is often employed in moral combat. As Rozin emphasized, "If something is in the moral domain for person A, then A is concerned that other people hold and behave according to the position held by A" (1997, p. 380). And moralization can be used to rally public support for political and institutional change in society (Effron & Miller, 2012). But there can also be amoralizing resistance. For example, meat eaters may accuse moralizing vegetarians of being overly strict and judgmental (Minson & Monin, 2012).

Competing Moralities

In the might-versus-morality and moralization literatures, the issue is whether the activity in question is framed as morally relevant or not. But the struggle can be between two different moral frames, as was the case for participants in Milgram's (1963, 1974) obedience studies described in Chapter 3. Is the morally right course of action to stop delivering the potentially harmful shocks, or to obey the experimenter and keep going? And recall the deeply disturbing conflict of competing moralities that faced Nazi doctors at Auschwitz (Lifton, 1986) and the men of Reserve Police Battalion 101 (Browning, 1998) described in Chapter 1. Is morality what I learned as a child, or the new morality of the Third Reich? Hitler worked hard to build a new frame.

As I suggested earlier, one strategy that may be especially effective when trying to control others' behavior is to frame the situation in terms of propriety morality. If, as it seems, propriety standards are likely to be fully internalized, intrinsically valued, emotionally evocative, and motivationally potent (see Table 5.1), such a frame should carry particular force. Consistent with this possibility, appeals to the necessity of promoting the natural and social order were central to the new Nazi morality. The focus was on in-group loyalty, respect for authority, and purification of the sacred Aryan race. Similar proprietization seems to have played a major role in other cases of genocide as well (Staub, 1989). In more benign forms, proprietization has also been used to promote support for a range of social issues, environmental protection for one (Feinberg & Willer, 2013). And all of the examples of moralization cited by Rozin (1997) seem to involve proprietization.

CULTURE WARS

Culture wars are a prominent feature of modern life. Liberals and conservatives fight over gun control, minority rights, immigration, welfare programs, health care, affirmative action, abortion, embryonic stem-cell research, the death penalty, assisted suicide, extreme interrogation techniques—the list goes on and on.

Most of these culture wars are fought on moral battlefields. And it's often moral combat of a particularly frustrating and unproductive kind. Not unlike the trench warfare of 1914-1917, there can be intense battles that produce little change. A few of the issues under dispute focus on interest conflicts, such as affirmative action to address systemic injustice: Should we totally ignore racial, ethnic, and socioeconomic background when making admission decisions and judge every applicant purely on academic performance and potential? Or should we seek to promote diversity and ameliorate the disadvantages created by past injustices? And most culture-war issues at least touch interest conflicts. But virtually all are framed in propriety terms. For example, depending on your side of the issue, gay marriage is removing discrimination and extending inalienable rights. Or it's an oxymoron, a violation of God's Law, and a threat to the very foundation of the society. Abortion concerns a woman's right to make decisions regarding her body, her life, and the life of her potential offspring. Or it's murder of an unborn baby.

Although both liberals and conservatives in society have standards that specify the way things ought to be, there are clear differences in the importance they place on certain propriety standards. Liberals are likely to judge the natural order from the perspective of science, and to judge the social order in terms of distributive justice and the right of everyone to a decent life. Conservatives are more likely to judge the natural order from the perspective of religion, as God's creation and subject to His law, and the social order in terms of procedural justice and every individual's right to free and unfettered pursuit of personal advantage with minimal restraint. In addition to emphasizing different standards of justice and human rights, conservatives are likely to place more emphasis on respect for tradition and authority than are liberals. Liberals are more likely to emphasize the need for creation of a better world.

Documenting these differences, Haidt and Graham (2007) found in a large internet survey that both liberals and conservatives felt justice and care considerations were of clear relevance to moral decisions. But conservatives also felt that in-group loyalty, respect for authority, and purity/sanctity were of clear relevance. Liberals thought these factors were only moderately relevant. Comparing the extremes of the liberal-conservative continuum, Haidt and Graham found a cross-over pattern. Respondents who self-identified as extremely liberal rated harm and fairness of greater moral relevance than did extreme conservatives. Extreme conservatives rated loyalty, authority, and purity of greater relevance than did extreme liberals (also see Graham, Haidt, & Nosek, 2009; Haidt, 2012).

It may seem from these findings that liberals care more about interpersonal interest-conflict issues and conservatives care more about propriety issues. That seems unlikely. A more appropriate conclusion is, I think, that each group cares about issues of each kind but liberals and conservatives differ in what circumstances raise these issues and what interpersonal and propriety standards they feel should be applied. Liberals, for example, may be quite concerned about threats to the purity of the natural environment, a propriety concern. And conservatives may be quite concerned that everyone is treated equally before the law, an interpersonal concern. Still, as a rough rule of thumb, Haidt and Graham's (2007) depiction of the relative concerns of the two groups seems useful. It certainly presents a situation ripe for moral combat. (Janoff-Bulman & Carnes, 2013, offer a somewhat different but also useful depiction. And note that culture wars can be fought across class as well as political lines; Trautmann, van de Kuilen, & Zeckhauser, 2013—and across ethnic, racial, and religious lines.)

Reflecting on the liberal-conservative difference in judged moral relevance, Haidt (2012) attributed the impasse in cultural debates to liberals' failure to understand and appreciate where conservatives are coming from. The argument I've been developing in this chapter suggests that there's more involved than misperception of others' convictions. As in one-on-one moral combat, the moral rhetoric in our broader cultural wars may not simply be an expression of the speaker's own convictions but an attempt to control others' behavior.

In culture wars, the others whose behavior we seek to control are likely to be of three types. Most obviously, there's the opposition. We want them to stop doing wrong and opposing right. To this end, we fire moral salvos in their direction. Those in favor of allowing abortion challenge restriction of a woman's right to privacy and to decide about her own body and welfare, a restriction that in the abstract few would think morally right. Those opposed describe abortion as killing babies, which even fewer would think morally right.

Of course, with each side entrenched in its own position, and often with each knowing God is on its side, these attacks have little effect. As Bandura (1991) noted with regard to reactions to international violence, terrorism, and counterterrorism,

> Moral appeals against violence usually fall on deaf ears. Adversaries sanctify their own militant actions but condemn those of their antagonists . . . . Terrorists invoke moral principles to justify human atrocities. Moral justification is also brought into play in selecting counterterrorist measures. . . . It is hard to find nations that categorically condemn terrorism. Rather, they usually back some terrorists and oppose others. (pp. 75, 81)

If the only targets of our moral attacks in culture wars were the opposition, the attacks would make little sense. But there are two additional targets. First, there are those on our side of the issue, our comrades in arms. Raising our own moral standards high helps rally the troops and keep them committed and loyal to the cause. As Skitka, Bauman, and Sargis (2005) observed, morally-based support for a cause is likely to increase activism. And intractability.

Second, there are those in the society who haven't enlisted in either army. By invoking morality, we encourage them to join our righteous cause. Thus, when moral combat takes place at the broader cultural level, as when it's one-on-one, it involves accuser, accused, and audience. And, once the battle lines are drawn, the audience is perhaps the most important target.

Framing is a particularly important strategy in culture wars. Among the many moral standards we endorse, we're likely to see issues in terms of the ones that support our side. Consistent with this suggestion, Uhlmann et al. (2009) found that politically liberal US undergraduates but not their conservative peers were more likely to endorse a given standard when that standard would protect a racial minority. In contrast, conservatives but not liberals were more likely to endorse a standard when it would protect American rather than Iraqi citizens (also see Ditto, Pizarro, & Tannenbaum, 2009). Again, the abortion issue provides a clear example. Each side marches forth under its carefully chosen standard: Free choice. Right to life.

Finally, as in one-on-one moral combat, proprietization plays a prominent role in culture wars. Even on issues that touch heavily on interpersonal interest conflicts, such as affirmative action, my attack is likely to gain more ground with those not immediately involved in the conflict if I can appeal to the natural and social order. Quotas violate individual rights. Diversity enriches a society. The conflict may not be about morality at all, as when each side aligns to defend the particular economic policy that best serves its interests. Yet the battle ground is still likely to be moral and the issue proprietized.

CONCLUSION

If we can discern the morally right thing to do and if situational pressure isn't too great, we'll be motivated to act morally. Previous chapters have provided a number of reasons to doubt this optimistic assumption. Especially when faced with interpersonal interest conflicts, our goal is often to appear rather than be moral. And when it is and we're provided sufficient wiggle room, we won't act morally even when we know what's right and there's no strong situational pressure.

So, of what use is morality? The present chapter builds on the preceding ones to suggest that we often use it to control other people's behavior rather than our own. Others do the same, using their morality (and ours) to control us. Precedent for such a view was found in the writings of Plato (who presented the view to reject it), Nietzsche, Freud, and Campbell. Unlike them, I focused on the use of morality to control others' behavior in one-on-one combat over specific issues, not to exert control at a societal level. I was able to offer some apparent examples of the use of morality to control others' behavior, and to cite evidence consistent with the argument, but not to report any direct empirical tests. Such tests await future research, especially research in which participants have the opportunity to use morality rather than money to control others' behavior.

Despite the provisional status of the argument, it may be worthwhile to consider some implications of a claim that we invoke morality to control others' behavior. The first and most obvious implication is that when we hear people advocate some moral stance we shouldn't assume they're talking about what they ought to do. More likely, they're talking about what they want others to do. It isn't that people lack moral self-regulatory standards or fail to feel guilt and shame when they violate these standards. It's that our moral discourse is more likely to be other-directed than self-directed. More precisely, our discourse is likely to be directed not only at those we accuse of a moral violation but also at those who might be tempted to violate in the future and those who are or could become our allies in the control effort.

A second, related implication is that we shouldn't expect a person's moral discourse to be an accurate reflection of his or her personal moral standards. At best, it's likely to reflect only a subset. If my moral pronouncements are a response to others' actual or possible behavior, what I say will depend on who is doing, has done, or could do what. It will also depend on who else is present. Often, we have multiple standards that are relevant to a given situation, and the ones we proclaim are selected to serve nonmoral ends. Recall the young hockey players in Chapter 5. The oldest boy invoked a standard that would give him the extra slice of pizza. The boy with the smallest slice did the same. Our moral arsenal is well stocked, and only those weapons best suited for the present battle are deployed.

Third, whether we invoke morality at all is likely to depend on our stake in the issue at hand. As suggested in Chapter 6, a moral violation that doesn't affect us or those we care about may prompt little response. But a violation that does is cause for attack.

Fourth, as already noted, if our moral suasion is to have credibility, we must show ourselves to be as compliant with our standards as we expect others to be. The cynicism evoked by pedophilic priests and promiscuous preachers underscores how essential this is. But when our standards are at odds with our personal desires, we're likely to rely if possible on deception, including self-deception, to enable us to appear compliant yet not be. A risky strategy, but one at which we can become quite adept. Indeed, when such deceit is discovered, it's often because the person was so adept that he or she ceased to recognize the risk and got careless.

Finally, consider the implications of the argument for those who have internalized their moral standards beyond the level of introjection to full integration. Valuing their standards intrinsically rather than extrinsically, these people should experience compliance as a want not simply as an ought. Like Aristotle's virtuous persons and Colby and Damon's (1992) moral exemplars, their behavior should conform to their standards without any need for coercion and control. For them, we might speak of moral self-expression rather than moral self-regulation. If this characterization is accurate, these people have no reason to resist application of their standards to themselves. But interestingly, Colby and Damon's exemplars didn't seem to talk or think much about the morality of their own actions. Perhaps because their morality flowed naturally, they didn't have to.

Do moral exemplars engage in moral combat, using moral discourse to control other's behavior? Or have they beaten their moral swords into ploughshares and turned their back on moral combat altogether? These are intriguing and potentially important questions to which we lack good answers.

8

TREATING OUR MORAL MALADIES

Moral failures of the sort cataloged in Chapter 1 make it clear that neither Hobbes's State with its laws nor the confrontations discussed in Chapter 7 are sufficient to coerce us to consistently live up to our espoused moral standards. And to intensify either form of coercion isn't likely to improve matters. It's apt to add to our discontent, spurring us to new heights of self-deception and moral hypocrisy.

Diagnosing the source of an ailment doesn't guarantee a cure, but it should enable us to prescribe treatments if any exist. We've considered three major diagnoses for our moral maladies, each of which sheds important light—personal deficiency (Chapter 2), situational pressure (Chapter 3), and motivational and emotional limitations (Chapters 4–6). What treatments can we offer to address each?

PRESCRIPTIONS TO ADDRESS PERSONAL DEFICIENCY

The first diagnosis is that moral maladies can arise from failure to acquire the right moral standards, principles, and ideals. Or failure to apply them appropriately when faced with a particular moral problem. Beyond the standard nostrums to "be good," "take responsibility," and "think good thoughts" (or "feel good feelings"), what prescriptions are possible? Clearly, it isn't easy to change our moral character or our ways of thinking and feeling about moral issues. And no single prescription will be effective for all people in all situations. Still, Chapter 2 did suggest some ideas, many with the ring of common sense.

Make Regular Exercise a Habit

Aristotle believed that the process of building good character begins from the earliest age by regularly acting virtuously so that it becomes a habit: "We must give our activities a certain quality, because their characteristics determine the resulting dispositions" (Aristotle, 1976, p. 92). Consistent with Aristotle's prescription, Colby and Damon (1992) reported that people identified as moral exemplars thought and acted morally "in a spontaneous and non-reflective manner, as if by force of habit" (p. 308).

Early parental modeling may be especially important for development of moral habits. David Rosenhan (1970) interviewed people who had been active in the US civil rights movement during the 1950s, before such activity was widely supported in the society. He found that for almost all activists who made an enduring commitment to the movement (those who participated for more than a year in projects like voter registration and education of the underprivileged) at least one parent was committed to a moral cause over an extended period during the activist's formative years. This wasn't true for activists whose commitment was limited to less than a year (those who went, for example, on one or two freedom rides). Their parents were "concerned with moral issues, but there was evidence of a discrepancy between what they preached and actually practiced" (Rosenhan, 1970, p. 263).

Three warnings should probably accompany the prescription to develop moral habits. First, habits can lead to inappropriate action. To the degree that a habit becomes automatic and mindless, it can be unresponsive to the nuance of the situation. For Aristotle, virtues were formed as habits but had to be pursued thoughtfully and wisely.

Second, early modeling and practice are doubtless important in character development, but aren't sufficient to guarantee success. As a case in point, Samuel and Pearl Oliner (1988) reported the following statement from a nonrescuer of Jews in Nazi Europe:

> My parents were loving and kind. I learned from them to be helpful and considerate. There was a Jewish family living in our apartment building, but I hardly noticed when they left. Later, when I was working in the hospital as a doctor, a Jewish man was brought to the emergency room by his wife. I knew that he would die unless he was treated immediately. But we were not allowed to treat Jews; they could only be treated at the Jewish hospital. I could do nothing. (Oliner & Oliner, 1988, p. 187)

Third, the research on character development by Hartshorne and May, and the subsequent research by social learning theorists on the acquisition of self-regulatory standards, provided much evidence that the morality most of us develop in childhood isn't as broad as Aristotle's virtues. Rather than general moral dispositions, we acquire more concrete and qualified standards. This research suggests a different prescription—internalize specific self-regulatory standards. Or more colloquially, develop self-control.

Develop Self-Control

Children learn early on, like Ursie in Chapter 5, which behaviors are censured and discouraged (taking what isn't yours) and which are encouraged and praised (returning others' property). As a child's cognitive, verbal, and interpersonal skills develop, his or her parents soon move beyond physical to social rewards and punishments. The child is praised for being nice and faces displeasure when naughty. If the parent–child relationship is warm and supportive, parental praise and disappointment carry heavy weight.

It's only a short step from these social rewards and punishments to where the child models the parent and passes similar judgment on his or her own actions. The child experiences pride and pleasure at doing right, and guilt and shame at doing wrong. Although the standards are still valued extrinsically—upheld in order to gain praise and avoid censure—the praise and censure now come not only from parents and other socializing agents but also from the self. Moral self-regulatory standards are internalized to the level of introjection.

Introjected morality can be quite important for a person's self-image, as it was for John Dashwood. Aquino and Reed (2002) developed a popular self-report measure of the importance of moral identity. The key subscale of their measure assesses the importance of seeing oneself as moral. As might be expected, individuals scoring relatively high on this subscale are more likely than those scoring low to adhere to their moral standards without having to be primed to think about morality (presumably, high scorers are chronically concerned about their moral standing). And when primed to think about morality, high scorers are more likely to resist when tempted to violate their standards (presumably, they anticipate feeling more guilt; Aquino, Freeman, Reed, Lim, & Felps, 2009). You might think this subscale measures internalization beyond introjection to integration (Deci et al., 1994), but it probably doesn't. If the depiction by Aquino et al. (2009) is correct, it measures introjection.

Internalization to the level of introjection can lead us to act in accord with our standards and ideals even in the absence of surveillance. At least it can do so if our standards are primed or chronically salient, and if countervailing pressures aren't too strong. But introjected standards are still valued extrinsically and experienced as oughts. We adhere to them to maintain a positive social and self-image, to be seen by others and see ourselves as moral. As the research reviewed in Chapter 4 reveals, this instrumental moral motivation is unreliable. It's vulnerable to rationalization and self-deception.

If we're to effectively treat our moral ills that arise from limited character development, we need to find a way to move beyond introjection to integration. Rather than our principles operating as controls that stand over against us in the manner of Freud's superego or social learning theorists' self-regulatory standards, we need to fully internalize them so they become valued intrinsically as ends in themselves. There's no guarantee that the principles we integrate are good ones (the normative issue), but there's reason to believe that we'll try to act in accord with them across a range of situations. Integration is the level of internalization required for Aristotle's (1976) virtuous person and Colby and Damon's (1992) moral exemplars, people who don't struggle to do right but from whom it flows naturally.

What prescriptions are available to help us reach the point where our moral standards and ideals are valued intrinsically as part of our core self? Disappointingly few I fear, but two deserve mention.

No Pain, No Gain

Philip Brickman (1987) offered an intriguing analysis of how value commitments can be transformed from extrinsic to intrinsic. That is, how they can be transformed from being introjected to integrated. His analysis was based primarily on the theory of cognitive dissonance (Festinger, 1957). As discussed in Chapter 2, dissonance theory predicts that if I act on some moral principle despite strong inducement to violate it, doing so should increase my experience of the principle as intrinsically valued. But if I adhere to principle under strong extrinsic pressure to comply, doing so is likely to increase extrinsic valuing.

Brickman applied the first of these dissonance predictions to the experience of intrinsic commitment that Mihaly Csikszentmihalyi (1990) called "flow":

> There are negative elements even in the most totally absorbing of commitments. Surgeons, mountain climbers, and chess players make heavy sacrifices for their skills and run risks—both material and psychological—in the exercise of these skills. Patients can die, climbers can fall, and chess players can be defeated. . . . The presence of these negative elements is not accidental but essential to the experience of flow. (Brickman, 1987, p. 7)

Brickman (1987) believed that the negative elements of a commitment—the costs and risks involved—are critical if the commitment is to deepen to the level of integration. In an echo of Aristotle, he suggested that "intrinsic value comes from actions" (p. 59). But Brickman was more specific than Aristotle about the process of intrinsic value creation.

> Intrinsic value derives from a choice (positive element), an awareness of the negative features of such a choice (negative element), and responsibility for any negative consequences that occur (link between the positive and negative elements). The positive features of the choice tell us only that we are attracted to it. It is the negative features of a choice—the concomitant uncertainties, sacrifices, and oppositional forces—that transform actions into intrinsic values. (p. 59)
>
> The end product of this integration represents a stronger form of commitment, accompanied by stronger motivation than was present prior to the appearance of the opposing forces. (Brickman, 1987, p. 145)

Brickman (1987) went on to consider the implications of his analysis for internalization of culturally endorsed moral values (which he called collective values), such as justice and care:

> Collective values become personal values only through the same process of work, effort, and sacrifice that, under the right circumstances, makes anything a personal value. We may make a mistake in trying to teach people to appreciate the heritage of the past without allowing them to experience something of the effort that went into creating that heritage. (p. 103)

Turning to the second dissonance prediction, Brickman (1987) noted a paradox that makes gaining intrinsic moral values especially hard.

The paradox is that things that society labels as having intrinsic value have, by definition, extrinsic pressure on them. Because people are under pressure to attain these values, it is harder for people to see their attainment as the result of personal choice. This is especially threatening to adolescents who have not yet established their own identity. (p. 103)

And there's another problem. Not only are culturally valued standards and ideals especially difficult to fully internalize due to the extrinsic pressure to comply. But also, even when fully internalized, they can be eroded by extrinsic pressure in the form of societal and personal expectations that we should act in accord with them. These expectations can lead to loss of commitment, self-doubt, and cynicism. They can undermine intrinsic valuing of our moral principles in the same way that the pressure of expectations can undermine intrinsic valuing of a person's profession or marriage (Brickman, 1987, pp. 173, 200–208).

So, Brickman's prescription for movement from extrinsic to intrinsic moral valuing—from introjection to integration—was to act on principle in the face of as much countervailing pressure as possible, and to keep acting under countervailing pressure. No pain, no gain.

Emulation

The steep climb Brickman prescribed may not be the only route to intrinsic value. A second, less difficult path may be through emulation of an inspiring person, a "moral hero." Emulated figures may be close at hand in the person of a parent, teacher, or friend. Or they may be more remote, such as Dr. Martin Luther King Jr., Mother Teresa, Nelson Mandela, or the Dalai Lama. A moral hero may even be fictional. Moral emulation is often spoken of as *identification*, as it was by historian Lynn Hunt.

Hunt (2007) presented a persuasive argument that an important consequence of the great popularity of epistolary novels in eighteenth-century Britain, France, and America—novels in which a story is told through letters written by one or more characters—was the promotion of moral principles and ideals, especially principles of human rights. Supporting her argument, Hunt recounted Thomas Jefferson's response when a relative wrote to him in 1771 requesting a list of recommended books. Jefferson began his list with poetry, plays, and novels, including the epistolary novels of Samuel Richardson (*Pamela: or, Virtue Rewarded*, 1740/2011; *Clarissa: or, The History of a Young Lady*, 1747/1971) and Jean-Jacques Rousseau (*Julie, or the New Héloise*, 1761/1997). Jefferson thought that such fiction "produces the desire for moral emulation even more effectively than reading history" (Hunt, 2007, p. 57).

How do we know that emulation of a moral hero, whether real or fictional, reflects an intrinsic desire to uphold standards, principles, and ideals instead of an extrinsic desire to feel good about ourselves for living up to a particular image of the kind of person we should be? As far as I know, we have no clear evidence which it is. The thought that through identification with a moral hero we might be able to leap to the level of moral integration without the conflict-laden process prescribed by Brickman is certainly appealing. But at this point, it's only a tantalizing thought.

A different and perhaps more plausible thought is that emulation and Brickman's pain–gain process can work in tandem. Identification-based emulation may prompt the kind of costly moral action that starts us on the challenging road that Brickman prescribed as necessary to reach integration of intrinsic moral values.

Use Better Judgment

Turning attention from prescriptions to overcome deficiencies in the acquisition of moral standards to prescriptions to remedy deficiencies in moral judgment, there have been several attempts to develop treatments to improve moral reasoning. Best known is the +1 *disequilibrium strategy* proposed by Kohlberg and his colleagues (e.g., Kohlberg, 1984; Turiel, 1966). This strategy involves creating dissatisfaction with my level of moral reasoning—disequilibrium—by discussing the right course of action in a moral dilemma with someone who presents reasoning one stage above my current stage in Kohlberg's scheme. The +1 strategy is based on two assumptions: Without the challenge of more mature reasoning than mine, there's no impetus for change. If the challenge is too far above my current stage, I won't be able to appreciate and accommodate to it.

Although there's some empirical evidence that a +1 strategy can be effective (e.g., Turiel, 1966), there's also evidence that cognitive disequilibrium may not be the best way to stimulate more sophisticated moral reasoning. A study reported by Norma Haan (1985) suggested this possibility. Haan compared the effectiveness of a cognitive disequilibrium strategy (unfortunately, not a carefully calibrated +1 strategy) and what she called a social disequilibrium strategy. This second strategy was based on the assumption that more mature moral judgment emerges out of

> a social, emotional dialectic of practical reasoning among people. Its distinctive feature—and its ground—is the attempt people make to equalize their relations during disputes. . . . Social disequilibrium is a holistic, emotional, and interactive experience wherein participants expose themselves to others' complaints and even to the possibility that they themselves may be found morally wanting or even wrong. (Haan, 1985, pp. 996–997)

Haan's social disequilibrium seems quite reminiscent of Piaget's description of the conditions for developing autonomous moral judgment: "Ideal equilibrium, dimly felt on the occasion of every quarrel and every peace-making" in a "long reciprocal education of the children by each other" (Piaget, 1932/1965, p. 318; see Chapter 2).

To assess the effect of cognitive and social disequilibrium on moral reasoning, Haan (1985) recruited 15 first-year undergraduate friendship groups from dormitories at Berkeley to take part in "an investigation of young adults' moral-social problem-solving." Each group was made up of four women and four men, and each met for five three-hour sessions, one session a week for five weeks. At the meetings of ten of the groups—the social-disequilibrium groups—members played games that provoked moral conflict (e.g., a survivor game, a group-level Prisoner's Dilemma, and StarPower, a game designed to simulate a hierarchically arranged and unjust society). These 10 groups played a different game each week. The other five groups—randomly chosen to be the cognitive-disequilibrium groups—discussed three hypothetical moral dilemmas at each session.

Effect of the different group experiences on level of moral reasoning and behavior was measured in two ways. First, each undergraduate was interviewed individually shortly before and after the 5 weeks of group sessions, as well as 3 months after the last session. Second, all group sessions were observed and the observations subsequently rated for the level of moral thought and action displayed by each individual in each session.

Cognitive disequilibrium (reflected in rational disagreement and attempts to sharpen differences in moral judgment) had relatively little effect on moral reasoning and behavior. Social disequilibrium (reflected in interpersonal conflict) was associated with positive changes in both moral reasoning and behavior. But these positive changes were statistically significant only among those individuals who came into the study with good skills for coping with conflict.

Haan (1985) summarized the results as follows: "Students developed [morally] if they were the sort of people who characteristically handle conflict by coping *and* if they faced socially turbulent experiences in these group sessions" (p. 1002, italics in original). Development due to social disequilibrium was found not only on a measure of concrete interpersonal moral reasoning and conflict resolution but also on a Kohlberg-type measure of abstract moral reasoning. Apparently, striving to overcome interpersonal interest conflicts led both to improved conflict-resolution skills and to more principled moral reasoning. It appears that Haan's social disequilibrium strategy may be a Piagetian means to a Kohlbergian end, at least for those who can handle conflict.

Broaden Your Outlook

A second prescription for evoking more mature moral judgment, and one that could have been operating in Haan's (1985) friendship groups, is perspective taking. In Chapter 4, I noted that there are two major forms of perspective taking: imagine how you would think and feel in some other person's situation (an imagine-self perspective) and imagine how the other thinks and feels in that situation (an imagine-other perspective). Before we can reasonably apply our principles of right conduct to interest-conflict situations, we must recognize and appreciate what others' interests are. Imagining their thoughts and feelings can promote this appreciation. (At times, imagining our own thoughts and feelings in the other's situation can be an important stepping stone to imagining his or her thoughts and feelings, but imagine-other seems to be the form of perspective taking that promotes appreciation of the other's interests; see Chapter 4 and Batson, 2009.) There are several ways that imagine-other perspective taking might be used to improve moral judgment.

Think About How Others Are Affected by Your Actions

John Gibbs (2003, 2014) built on the ideas of Kohlberg and his colleagues (e.g., Kohlberg, 1976, 1984; Selman, 1980) to create a program called EQUIP, which was designed to reduce aggressive and antisocial behavior of male juvenile offenders. EQUIP involves having the juveniles meet together in groups directed by trained leaders. The groups discuss problem situations related to antisocial behavior. The situations are "designed to stimulate ethical discussion and perspective taking and thereby promote a deeper understanding of the reasons for moral values or decisions such as telling the truth, not stealing or cheating" (Gibbs, 2014, p. 191).

Perspective taking is stimulated in EQUIP groups by use of the "you're the victim" technique developed by Vickie Agee (1979). This technique gets juvenile offenders to put themselves in the position of those affected by their actions. Initially, the focus is on actions that affect someone the juvenile cares about. Then it's extended to actions affecting strangers.

> If a violent offender has a sister and cares about her, . . . that is an opening. The therapist might frame a female victim as someone's sister and appeal to moral reciprocity: "If it's okay for you to do that to someone else's sister, is it okay for them to do it to your sister?" (Gibbs, 2014, p. 178)

An evaluation study that compared participation in an EQUIP group with participation in either of two control groups, one a no-program baseline and one that received motivational messages, found evidence of "substantial institutional and post-release conduct gains" for EQUIP participants. "The recidivism rate for EQUIP participants remained low and stable, whereas the likelihood of recidivism for untreated [control-group] participants climbed" (Gibbs, 2003, p. 188). At 12 months, the EQUIP recidivism rate was 15.0 percent. For the control groups, recidivism had risen to 40.5 percent.

But contrary to Gibbs's Kohlbergian assumptions, there was only limited evidence that the beneficial effects of the EQUIP experience were the result of higher-level moral reasoning. In retrospect, it seems possible that the effects were instead a consequence of the ability of imagine-other perspective taking to produce increased empathic concern for potential victims (see Chapters 1 and 4). Perhaps perspective taking affects moral behavior through other-oriented emotion more than through reason.

Dive Into a Good Novel

Hunt (2007) argued that eighteenth-century epistolary novels did more than provide targets for moral emulation. They also played a major role in the development of moral standards regarding human rights, rights that extend to all people not just the privileged. The novels did this, Hunt suggested, by inducing readers to embrace the thoughts and feelings of the protagonists and to care for them. That is, the novels induced imagine-other perspective taking. Through the fictional exchange of letters

> epistolary novels taught their readers nothing less than a new psychology and in the process laid the foundations for a new social and political order. Novels made the middle-class Julie [Rousseau, 1761/1997] and even servants like Pamela [Richardson, 1740/2011] . . . the equal and even the better of rich men such as Mr. B, Pamela's employer and would-be seducer. Novels made the point that all people are fundamentally similar because of their inner feelings. (Hunt, 2007, pp. 38–39)

The perspective taking induced by epistolary novels forced recognition that the disadvantaged of society think, feel, and suffer too. They're as human as the reader, so to treat them as lesser beings is morally wrong.

The mid-nineteenth century produced even clearer examples of the potential of novels to change moral judgment via perspective taking. Dickens introduced his readers to London's poor children (e.g., *Oliver Twist*, 1837–1839/1970). Harriet Beecher Stowe presented the lives, including the inner lives, of slaves (*Uncle Tom's Cabin*, 1852/2005). In each case, to imagine the thoughts and feelings of these "lowly" characters sparked a deep conviction that, "This is wrong!" Hunt concluded, much as Prinz (2007) might have said (see Chapter 2), "You know the meaning of human rights because you feel distressed when they are violated" (2007, p. 214).

Get Away

Travel is another means whereby perspective taking can improve moral judgment. Of course, not all travel broadens perspective. If we travel to conquer, colonize, or convert—or to tick off yet another tourist destination—we're likely to remain encapsulated in our own cultural cocoon. But sometimes travel leads us to see things differently, including morality. Paralleling Hunt's (2007) argument about the effect of epistolary novels, Steven Pinker (2011) suggested that the development of commerce and trade since the late Middle Ages has increased perspective taking and in turn changed our morality. By exposing us to alternative worldviews, it has encouraged "a more ecumenical morality, which gravitates to the rights of individuals rather than chauvinistic veneration of the group" (Pinker, 2011, p. 640).

For someone raised on Western views of human rights, moral perspective can be broadened in the opposite direction as well, from individual rights to veneration of the group, as Jonathan Haidt (2012) discovered when he lived for 3 months in Bhubaneswar, India.

> My first few weeks in Bhubaneswar were . . . filled with feelings of shock and dissonance. I dined with men whose wives silently served us and then retreated

to the kitchen, not speaking to me the entire evening. I was told to be stricter with my servants, and to stop thanking them for serving me. I watched people bathe in and cook with visibly polluted water that was held to be sacred. In short, I was immersed in a sex-segregated, hierarchically stratified, devoutly religious society . . . .

It only took a few weeks for my dissonance to disappear . . . because the normal human capacity for empathy kicked in. I *liked* these people who were hosting me, helping me, and teaching me. Wherever I went, people were kind to me. And when you're grateful to people, it's easier to adopt their perspective. . . . I began to see a moral world in which families, not individuals, are the basic unit of society, and the members of each extended family (including its servants) are intensely interdependent. (Haidt, 2012, pp. 101–102, italics in the original)

this seems dangerous! ↗

Such an experience may not lead a person to abandon ingrained views regarding the natural and social order. But it can increase understanding and tolerance of alien propriety standards. Moral judgments are likely to be tempered accordingly. It becomes harder to deny that there's more in heaven and earth than dreamt of in our philosophy.

Does this mean that all moralities lie alongside one another, each judged to be as good as every other? Or when compared, are some likely to be preferred? Pinker (2011) saw a directional trend across the centuries. Based on an extensive review of the historical evidence, he concluded that there has been a general movement from tribal, authoritarian, religion-based moralities toward individual human rights:

When cosmopolitan currents bring diverse people into discussion, when freedom of speech allows the discussion to go where it pleases, and when history's failed experiments are held up to the light, the evidence suggests that value systems evolve in the direction of liberal humanism. . . . Many liberalizing reforms that originated in Western Europe or on the American coasts have been emulated, after a time lag, by the more conservative parts of the world. (Pinker, 2011, pp. 691–692)

Yet Pinker (2011) was careful to point out that we can't know if this trend will continue. Recent anti-Western sentiment reminds us that the spread of liberal humanism can be violently resisted. Does this resistance reflect a rear-guard action? Or a new trend?

Summary

Most prescriptions for overcoming deficiencies of moral character, internalization, and judgment seem quite reasonable. Yet it's important to note that in almost every case, the empirical support is more suggestive than conclusive. It's also important to note that the earlier in life the prescribed treatment begins the better, which places heavy responsibility on creative, effective parenting. Finally, many of the treatments are complex and take time. Most also involve discomfort and sacrifice. They require us to confront challenges and to change. Personal change can be very hard to realize, especially when the person changed is the same person who must bring about the change. We're asked to be physicians who heal ourselves.

Clearly, such treatments are easier to prescribe than carry out. Yet there seems little doubt that if these treatments can successfully integrate intrinsic moral values into our core personality as deeply felt desires rather than simply obligations, and if they can enable us to make sound and sensitive judgments about when and how to promote these values, the risk of failure to live up to our principles would be greatly reduced. These are big ifs, but certainly ones worth investing considerable effort to pursue.

Or are they? Perhaps all the effort is unnecessary.

PRESCRIPTIONS TO ADDRESS SITUATIONAL PRESSURE

Prescriptions designed to address the situational pressures that inhibit moral action are often much easier to implement than prescriptions designed to treat personal deficiencies. We can change situations directly, removing or adding features, whereas to change people's core values is far more difficult. So, should we focus our efforts on situational change? Although clearly important and at times effective, I think there's reason to doubt that situational treatments alone will suffice. To see why, let me briefly catalog a sample of the myriad ways that have been suggested for treating moral maladies by means of situational change.

Increase Recognition of Moral Relevance

In Chapter 3, I identified five steps necessary to progress from a moral disposition to moral action along the value→emotion→motivation→behavior sequence. The first is to recognize that one or more of my moral principles (values) is relevant to the current situation. A number of strategies to increase awareness of moral relevance have been proposed and tested. For example, moral standards have been made more salient by seating research participants in a room with a conspicuous poster displaying a moral message (Gibbons & Wicklund, 1982), by prompting them to think about the Ten Commandments (Aquino et al., 2009) or other biblical texts (Carpenter & Marshall, 2009) or God or nonreligious moral concepts (Shariff & Norenzayan, 2007), and by providing cues for fairness or for care (Bersoff, 1999). Such strategies have been found to increase a range of moral behaviors.

But these increases were found in controlled laboratory environments and over short periods of time. Effects may attenuate in more complex, stimulus-rich natural environments. And as time of exposure to a moral-salience cue increases from minutes to hours, days, and longer, the cue is likely to become part of the background and lose its power. As a result, prescriptions based on such cues may have a short shelf life.

Stimulus overload was noted in Chapter 3 as a situational pressure that makes it easy to miss the moral relevance of events. So perhaps we need to cut back, slow down, and stay fresh. Perhaps we should move to the countryside. There's certainly reason to believe that a lighter stimulus load might allow us to attend to events and to their moral relevance more carefully (e.g., Gunia et al., 2012). But how many of us are willing to undergo such treatment? If anything, the multitasking nature of modern life has added to the pace and pressure. And unless you decide to live like Thoreau at Walden Pond, life in the country is likely to bring its own forms of stimulus overload. To live the simple life can be quite complex.

Turning to the business world, where stimulus load can be especially heavy and where quick decisions are required, some corporations have tried to make the moral relevance of employee's actions salient by introducing a formal code of ethical conduct. All employees are required to read the code and sign a certificate of compliance. They may also be required to attend ethical training seminars.

To provide a code of conduct and require ethical training are relatively easy treatments to implement. But as Bazerman and Tenbrunsel (2011, pp. 117–127) pointed out, these practices appear to increase awareness of the moral implications of employees' actions in some businesses (Johnson & Johnson) but not in others (Enron). Bazerman and Tenbrunsel suggested that the difference in moral practice at these two companies wasn't the result of their respective codes and training, which were quite similar, but of the informal corporate culture in which the formal procedures were embedded. Bazerman and Tenbrunsel went on to propose several steps that might be taken to improve the informal culture. But these steps involved efforts to change institutional atmosphere. Such change is likely to be at least as difficult to accomplish as the personal change discussed in the first section of this chapter. In the social world as in the physical, prescriptions for improving the atmosphere often drift toward vague exhortation and soon evaporate.

Increase Perception of an Opportunity to Act

The major prescription for combating the sense that although the situation is morally relevant there's nothing I can do is to limit the scope of the action required. If less is asked of me, to act should be less daunting. Consider, for example, the identified-victim effect. It increases action by focusing our attention and obligation on the needs of a single individual rather than on the needs of many (see Chapter 3). Or consider the strategy of soliciting donations for a good cause by assuring us that "even a penny would help" (Cialdini & Schroeder, 1976) or by asking for a one-time-only act rather than for action that might lead to future obligation (Miller, 1977). Each of these strategies has been shown to increase moral behavior. But the effectiveness of such strategies is bounded by the true scope of the problem, which may be too pervasive and persistent to frame in these ways. Poverty and economic inequities, whether at home or abroad, can't be made all better with a one-time contribution of pennies.

We can also increase our availability for action by avoiding other commitments. But this prescription seems self-defeating. Every new opportunity to act can be viewed as an "other commitment" to be avoided in order to remain free to act. Always on the ready, we would never do anything.

Increase Moral Motivation

In Chapter 3, I noted that the experience of moral motivation can be undermined by misattribution of the emotion evoked when encountering or contemplating a moral violation. It may seem we should be able to combat such misattribution by providing impactful exposure to the morally threatening situation, thereby making the source of our emotion clear. But, as with cues of relevance, exposure repeated over time is likely to lose impact. And controlling situations to prevent the ambiguity that allows for misattribution of emotion (as did Dientsbier & Munter, 1971; Schnall et al., 2008; Snyder et al., 1979; Wheatley & Haidt, 2005) can be extremely difficult if not impossible outside the lab.

Diffusion of responsibility can also undermine moral motivation. If I believe that someone else has already addressed the problem, or should, there's no need for me to mobilize for action. This source of malady has been treated with one of the more feasible and effective situational prescriptions: Pointedly designate responsibility. Thomas Moriarty (1975) found that designating responsibility led people on a crowded beach to act to stop the apparent theft of a person's belongings. Over 90 percent of bystanders who had been asked to keep an eye on the person's stuff intervened. Less than 25 percent did so when no one had been asked. An encouraging finding, but when it comes to moral hot-potatoes like care for the homeless, who will accept designation?

Increase Likelihood of Deciding to Act on Moral Motivation

We may be motivated to promote some moral standard or ideal, either as an ultimate goal or instrumentally, yet the motivation may not be sufficiently strong to produce action. This can be due either to strength of competing motives or to weakness of the moral motive. So, either decreasing the strength of competing motives or increasing the strength of the moral one should increase the likelihood that a person will decide to act morally.

Decrease Competing Motives

Decreasing competing motives is best accomplished by satisfying them. And to the degree that we can do this, it seems a good strategy. Motivation to promote interpersonal moral standards (those that address interest conflicts) should be especially sensitive to satisfaction of self-interests because conflict with others' interests is thereby reduced. But satisfaction of our interests isn't always possible. And even when it is, the effect can be surprising. When we get what we want, we often want more. Satisfaction of desire leads to more desire.

Strengthen Moral Motivation

A number of prescriptions seek to increase the strength of instrumental moral motivation by increasing the costs to self of a failure to act morally. The costs can be material, as when fines or penalties are imposed. They can be social, as when we know others will censure a moral violation (Reis & Gruzen, 1976; Chapter 7). They can be self-administered, as when we anticipate feeling guilt. Various accountability practices in business and government are designed to introduce costs of each of these kinds (Lerner & Tetlock, 1999).

But accountability can backfire. Adelberg and Batson (1978) created a situation in which research participants were given the task of making what they believed were real allocations of financial assistance to students who needed varying levels of aid to enroll for the next semester. Some participants were told their allocations would be entirely confidential. Others, that they would report their allocations in person to the aid applicants. Still others, that they would report their allocations to a supervisor. If participants had enough money in their budget to meet all applicants' needs, performance was close to optimal regardless of accountability. But when the budget was insufficient to enable all applicants to enroll, accountability of either type hurt performance. Accountable participants were more likely to make a seemingly fair distribution—such as treating all applicants equally—even though this meant that fewer applicants would have sufficient funds to enroll. Those not accountable were better able to give some applicants nothing in order to promote the greatest good overall. Accountability and the associated concern about social evaluation shifted the motivational balance away from doing the most good toward doing what could be most easily justified.

Melissa Bateson, Daniel Nettle, and Gilbert Roberts (2006) used a more subtle strategy to increase the social-evaluation cost of a failure to act responsibly. Every other week during a 10-week period, they placed a picture on the payment notice over the coffee room "honesty" box in the Psychology Department at the University of Newcastle. The picture showed a person's eyes looking directly at the viewer. (The eyes were of a different person each week, and the sex of the person varied.) For intervening weeks, the picture on the notice was of flowers. (Again, a different picture each week.) Members of staff were supposed to drop their money to pay for coffee and tea into the box. But the layout of the coffee room was such that payment (or nonpayment) was likely to go unobserved.

Bateson et al. found nearly three times as much money was put in the box when the picture showed eyes than when it showed flowers. Presumably, this was because the eyes created a sense of being watched and socially evaluated. Again, encouraging results. But again, there's a complication. The effect of the eyes was considerably stronger during the first week than in later weeks. Apparently, the eyes began to recede into the background over time. As with other situational prescriptions, the shelf life of this one may be short.

Perhaps the best-known strategy for improving standard compliance by increasing self-sanctions for moral failure is to induce self-awareness. In Chapter 4, I noted that placing people in front of a mirror effectively decreased cheating on a test (Diener & Wallbom, 1976) and increased use of a fair procedure to assign tasks (Batson, Thompson et al., 1999). But once more, the practical feasibility of this strategy is limited. We can't put mirrors everywhere in order to make people self-aware whenever their personal interests conflict with principle. And even if we could, the effect would likely diminish over time.

Lisa Shu, Nina Mazar, Francesca Gino, Dan Ariely, and Max Bazerman (2012) proposed and tested the effectiveness of a much simpler technique for inducing moral self-awareness. Their technique applies to situations in which we're tempted to make a dishonest report, such as when we fill out tax returns or insurance claims. These forms typically require us to sign a statement at the bottom testifying to the accuracy of the information provided. Shu et al. suggested that the statement to be signed be put at the top instead, so we promise accuracy before completing the form. To attest that all information provided will be accurate and complete should heighten our awareness of any subsequent standard-behavior discrepancy—and of the self-censure it would produce. Whereas, in the words of Shu et al., "When signing comes after reporting, the morality train has already left the station" (Shu et al., 2012, p. 15198).

In support of this reasoning, Shu et al. (2012) found that signing at the top of a form significantly reduced both the frequency and size of dishonest reports. In one laboratory study, 37 percent of research participants who signed at the top over-reported their performance on math problems solved for money. In contrast, 79 percent of those who signed the exact same form at the bottom over-reported, and 64 percent of those not asked to sign at all over-reported. In an unobtrusive field experiment conducted in cooperation with a large auto insurance company, Shu et al. found that policy holders who signed at the top of a form on which they reported how many miles they had driven their car (driving more would mean payment of a higher premium) reported driving 10.25 percent more miles on average than did those who signed the same form at the bottom.

Back to Hobbes

These results are impressive, and Shu et al. (2012; also see Ariely, 2012) used them to tout signing at the top as a simple and powerful technique to improve the honesty of self-reporting. But Shu et al. also sounded an important note of caution: If signing at the top becomes widely practiced and therefore routine, its effectiveness is likely to drop. Again, what seems a promising situation-change treatment for our moral ills may only be effective while its novelty lasts.

Consistent with this caution, consider the effect of having witnesses in court swear, prior to testifying, "to tell the truth, the whole truth, and nothing but the truth." Perjury laws exist because such swearing hasn't proved sufficient. With prior promise to tell the truth unable to keep witnesses from lying, society has turned to the power of the State manifest in laws to do the job. We're back to Hobbes in Chapter 7.

A similar evolution has occurred in business ethics, where compliance watchdogs are increasingly relied on to ensure that corporations meet government regulations. As Bazerman and Tenbrunsel (2011) noted,

> In response to the ethics scandals of the 1990s, . . . the Sarbanes-Oxley Act of 2002 requires all 9,000 publicly held corporations in the United States to employ "in-house watchdogs," or compliance officers—a position almost unheard of prior to 2002. (p. 102)

In university athletics, too, compliance rules backed by the force of law have increasingly become the means of producing ethical behavior.

But these Hobbesian strategies don't seem to work well. As Bazerman and Tenbrunsel (2011) also noted, "Despite all of the time and money that has been spent on these efforts, and all of the laws and regulations that have been enacted, unethical behavior appears to be on the rise" (pp. 102–103). Bazerman and Tenbrunsel went on to observe that this seemingly paradoxical result should have been expected. When coerced to comply with standards by threats of legal action, fines, and jail, we're likely to infer that our compliance is due to the pressure rather than to a concern to act morally. We focus on the pressure rather than the relevant moral standards (Shu & Gino, 2012; also see Gneezy & Rustichini, 2000). And even when the standards are salient, we're likely to look for ways to satisfy the letter of the law (or at least to avoid getting caught) yet still manage to bend if not break the rules. Finding such ways can be easy when the rules are complex, when many people are involved in the action, and when judgment calls are necessary. The situation morphs from moral to pragmatic. Bending or breaking the rules while appearing to comply becomes a game that must be played and played well to get ahead. Moral hypocrisy flourishes, not integrity.

Summary

Prescriptions based on a situational-pressure diagnosis of our moral ills, whether prescriptions designed to remove pressure to violate our standards or add pressure to comply with them, often seem straightforward. It's easier to change features of situations than to change people. But this ease is deceiving. Situational changes that have dramatic effects in the short term are likely to lose their potency over time. And adding pressure to comply can backfire. Even when effective in inducing compliance, coercion is likely to undermine moral values and motivation.

Most prescriptions based on situational pressure focus on controlling behavior without attending to the nature of the motivation underlying the behavior. But, as long as an individual's moral values are extrinsic and moral motivation instrumental, the effects of such situational pressure are apt to be limited and perverse.

Pressure to do what we ought becomes just one more aspect of the situation we must negotiate to pursue self-interest.

I said at the end of the first section of this chapter that effective treatment to overcome personal deficiencies is difficult and challenging. It appears that effective treatment to overcome the situational pressures producing moral failures isn't easy either, despite suggestions by some that it is (see Ariely, 2012; Haidt, 2012). For more effective treatment, perhaps we need to move beyond the person and the situation as causes of our moral ills. Perhaps we need to attend to the interplay of values, emotions, and motives that underlie our behavior.

PRESCRIPTIONS TO ADDRESS MOTIVATIONAL AND EMOTIONAL LIMITATIONS

In Chapter 1, I identified four general classes of motives that can lead a person to act morally: egoism, altruism, collectivism, and principlism. Each is based on a distinct intrinsic value, has a distinct ultimate goal, and distinct emotional antecedents. Each also has distinct strengths and weaknesses as a source of moral action. At the risk of being needlessly repetitive, let me summarize what was said in Chapter 1 about each of these classes of motivation.

Motivation with the ultimate goal of increasing our own welfare—egoism—is powerful and prevalent. It comes in many forms. The ultimate goal of acting morally can be to gain material, social, or self-rewards, as well as to avoid material, social, or self-punishments. When we think beyond the current situation, our self-interest becomes enlightened. Egoism can then motivate us to act in ways that go against our immediate self-interest, as moral principles often ask us to do, in order to promote self-interest in the long run. Egoism has a strong emotional base that includes feelings of pleasure, pain, fear, and frustration with which we are born, as well as more complex acquired emotions such as pride, guilt, and shame.

These are important strengths. But egoism also has an important weakness. Its relation to morality is unreliable. Egoistic motives promote morality only as an instrumental means to promote self-interest or as an unintended consequence of doing so. Given sufficient wiggle room, these motives are likely to produce a desire to appear moral rather than actually be moral.

Motivation with the ultimate goal of increasing the welfare of one or more others—altruism—is also a powerful motive (Batson, 2011). It has a strong emotional base in feelings of empathic concern (sympathy, compassion, tenderness, etc.) for cared-for others perceived to be in need. Parallel to egoism, altruism can be enlightened by consideration of the other's long-term welfare (Sibicky, Schroeder, & Dovidio, 1995). But also parallel to egoism, altruism is unreliable as a motivational basis for moral conduct. Its ultimate goal is to promote the other's welfare, not to act morally. At times, pursuing the former leads me to do the latter, as when I feel empathic concern for someone who has been treated unjustly. This feeling may prompt me to act to remove the injustice, an act I or others may judge moral. But at other times, acting on empathy-induced altruistic motivation can lead me to act immorally. It can lead me to benefit a cared-for other in violation of my standards of fairness and the greatest good for all (Batson, Batson et al., 1995; Batson, Klein et al., 1995).

Motivation with the ultimate goal of increasing some group's welfare—collectivism—can be powerful too, although its status distinct from egoism is yet to be clearly established. Collectivism has a strong emotional base in feelings of group pride, loyalty, team spirit, patriotic fervor, and the like. Yet it can be unreliable in a manner parallel to egoism and altruism. If promoting the cared-for group's welfare promotes a moral standard I hold, as when it leads me to set aside self-interest to do what's best for the group, fine. But collectivism can also lead me to pursue the group's interest in violation of what I think is fair and best for everyone across groups.

Motivation with the ultimate goal of promoting some moral standard, principle, or ideal—principlism—has an important advantage over the previous three motives. Because its ultimate goal is to be moral, principlism has a more reliable relation to moral action than do egoism, altruism, and collectivism. But it also has a serious problem.

Principlism is much less common than has been assumed. Often, moral behavior thought to be motivated by a desire to uphold some moral principle turns out on closer inspection to be a product of one of the other motives. In particular, moral hypocrisy seems more common (Chapters 4 and 5). At least this is true for interpersonal morality. Even though violations of interpersonal standards of fairness and care may evoke considerable emotion, this emotion is often produced by the implications of the violations for nonmoral valued states—our own welfare or the welfare of cared-for others or groups. Violations of interpersonal standards seem to evoke little truly moral emotion (Chapter 6).

This quick review suggests the need for a treatment that addresses the motivational and emotional limitations of interpersonal, interest-conflict morality. A first step toward prescribing such a treatment is to remember a further complication. As noted in Chapter 1, the four forms of motivation for acting morally can and often do co-occur. When they occur together, they don't always work in harmony. They can undercut and compete with one another.

Motives for Acting Morally Can Conflict

Well-intentioned attempts to encourage moral behavior by appeals to self-interest, even enlightened self-interest, can backfire by undermining other motives for moral action. As noted when considering situational treatments, use of monetary incentives (e.g., tax breaks), laws, normative pressure, and other inducements can lead people to believe that the reason they act morally is to get the inducement. They interpret their motivation as egoistic even if it originally was not (Batson, Coke, Jasnoski, & Hanson, 1978; Batson, Harris, McCaul, Davis, & Schmidt, 1979; Bowles, 2008; Thomas & Batson, 1981). As a result, the behavior becomes dependent on the inducement. When inducement is no longer present, the behavior vanishes. This is seen, for example, in the effect of required volunteerism on subsequent volunteerism (Stukas, Snyder, & Clary, 1999). More generally, this undermining effect can lead us to believe that egoism exhausts our motivational repertoire (Batson, Fultz, Schoenrade, & Paduano, 1987), leading to the further belief that our motivation *should be* self-interested (Miller, 1999).

Nor do altruism, collectivism, and moral motivation (whether principlism or instrumental moral motivation) always work in harmony. They too can conflict. For example, as mentioned above, altruism can lead us to act against our principles of fairness. Consider the results of three sets of experiments. Batson, Batson et al. (1995) found that empathy-induced altruism can prompt action to benefit a person for whom we care at the expense of our standards of fairness and what's best overall. Batson, Ahmad et al. (1999) found that participants who benefited a cared-for individual to the detriment of what was best for all considered their action to be less moral than those who acted to promote the greatest good. Batson, Klein et al. (1995, Experiment 1) found that many research participants in the role of Supervisor, when induced to feel empathic concern for one of two Workers, were willing to show partiality to that Worker even though they thought this unfair. These findings are reminiscent of Huck Finn's decision to do wrong and "go to Hell then" rather than turn in Jim, the runaway slave for whom he had come to care (Twain, 1884/1959).

Motives for Acting Morally Can Also Cooperate

Different forms of motivation for acting morally can also cooperate. And the fact that each form has strengths as well as weaknesses suggests a strategy for addressing our moral maladies that arise from motivational and emotional limitations. Perhaps we can combine different motives in such a way that the strengths of one can overcome the weaknesses of another. Specifically, perhaps we can create a combination that overcomes the weaknesses of interpersonal, interest-conflict moral motivation.

Especially promising as a strategy may be to combine an appeal to principle with either altruism or collectivism. Think about the widely acclaimed interpersonal principles of justice and care. If the evidence and argument in preceding chapters is correct, violation of these cherished interest-conflict principles evokes little truly moral emotion and motivation. As a result, we're likely to act in accord only when it's in our best interest to do so.

Empathy-induced altruism and collectivism are potentially powerful motives, each with a strong emotional base. But they're limited in scope. They produce special concern for particular persons or particular groups. Perhaps if we can be led to feel empathy for the victims of injustice, or if we can perceive ourselves in a common group with them (Gaertner & Dovidio, 2000), this will combine the unique strengths of two motives. Our principles will provide perspective and reason. Altruism or collectivism will provide emotional fire and motivational force directed specifically toward seeing the victims' suffering end. Perhaps the combination will produce even in those of us for whom concern for justice is introjected and instrumental what Robert Solomon (1990) called "a passion for justice." A want to accompany the moral ought.

Orchestration, Not Embedding

The proposal to combine empathy-induced altruism and instrumental moral motivation may seem to echo Martin Hoffman's (2000) idea of empathy-based morality, especially when he says:

> My hypothesis is that abstract moral principles, learned in "cool" didactic contexts (lectures, sermons), lack motive force. Empathy's contribution to moral principles is to transform them into prosocial hot cognitions—cognitive representations charged with empathic affect, thus giving them motive force. (p. 239)

My proposal does parallel Hoffman's hypothesis (except that I believe interpersonal principles are often learned in conflict contexts rather than cool ones—see Chapter 5). Still, I think his view of the empathy–morality relation and mine are importantly different. Hoffman (2000) speaks of empathy being "embedded in relevant moral principles" (p. 216) and "congruent with them" (p. 221), and of the "bonding of empathy and moral principles" (p. 221). Such language suggests that empathy becomes inextricably linked to the principles. For him, rather than empathy producing an altruistic motive that may cooperate or conflict with moral motivation, empathy and morality become joined. To evoke one evokes the other.

I believe the research on motivational conflict cited earlier, which indicates that empathy-induced altruistic motivation can prompt us to violate our moral standards, contradicts Hoffman's optimistic assumption (also see the research of van Lange, 2008). Although empathy-induced altruism can lead us to act in ways judged moral, it can also lead us to act immorally. Altruism and morality have no necessary connection (Batson, 2014). The challenge is to orchestrate altruistic motivation and instrumental moral motivation so they don't conflict but complement one another. That is, so the strengths of one motive overcome the weaknesses of the other. Such a combination may provide an effective treatment for those moral ills that arise from motivational and emotional limitations.

Some Examples of Motivational Orchestration

I have no research to cite that has directly tested the efficacy of this orchestration strategy. But I can cite cases in which orchestration seems to have occurred and been effective. All of the cases involve a combination of empathy-induced altruism and interpersonal moral motivation.

Unplanned Orchestration

Data collected by the Oliners and their colleagues (Oliner & Oliner, 1988) suggest that such orchestration occurred in the lives of a number of rescuers of Jews in Nazi Europe. Involvement in rescue activity frequently began with concern for a specific individual or individuals for whom compassion was felt—often someone known previously. This initial involvement seems to have been motivated more by altruistic than moral concerns. But it subsequently led to further contacts and rescue activity. It produced a commitment to care for the victims of persecution that extended well beyond the bounds of the initial empathy-based altruism.

Such orchestration also seems to have occurred at the time of the bus boycott in Birmingham, Alabama, in the 1950s. The sight on TV news of a small black child being rolled down the street by water from a fire hose under the direction of local police, and the empathic feelings this sight evoked, seemed to do more to promote racial equality and justice than had hours of reasoned moral suasion about civil rights.

Planned

In the two examples just cited, the orchestration wasn't planned. It occurred as a result of unfolding events. But sometimes the orchestra has a human conductor. Both Mahatma Gandhi and Martin Luther King Jr. organized nonviolent protests and sit-ins in the face of entrenched injustice. These protests and sit-ins evoked empathic concern for the mistreated, which produced motivation to right the wrongs. The protests sparked a passion for justice.

Illustrative of the effect such confrontation can have is a case reported by Robert Coles (1986) that occurred in 1961 in one of the newly desegregated high schools in Atlanta, Georgia. Improbably, the moral actor was a 14-year-old white student from a "redneck" background—"a tough athlete, a poor student, not a well-read boy" (Coles, 1986, p. 27). Here's the report:

> The young man found himself, inexplicably and suddenly, without forethought (he later had to acknowledge this condition repeatedly, when asked by me and others), impelled to help out "a nigger" (the words of the helper!). He described the incident (and himself) in this way: "I didn't want any part of them here. They belong with their own, and we belong with our own—that's what we all said. Then those two kids came here, and they had a tough time. They were all by themselves. The school had to get police protection for them. We didn't want them, and they knew it. But we told them so, in case they were slow to get the message. I didn't hold back, no more than anyone else. I said, 'Go, nigger, go,' with all the others. I meant it. But after a few weeks, I began to see a kid, not a nigger—a guy who knew how to smile when it was tough going, and who walked straight and tall, and was polite. I told my parents, 'It's a real shame that some-one like him has to pay for the trouble caused by all those federal judges.'"
>
> "Then it happened. I saw a few people cuss him. 'The dirty nigger,' they kept on calling him, and soon they were pushing him in a corner, and it looked like trouble, bad trouble. I went over and broke it up. I said, 'Hey, cut it out.' They all looked at me as if I was crazy, my white buddies and the nigger, too. But my buddies stopped, and the nigger left. Before he left, though, I spoke to him. I didn't mean to, actually! It just came out of my mouth. I was surprised to hear the words

myself: 'I'm sorry.' As soon as he was gone, my friend gave it to me: 'What do you mean, "I'm sorry"!' I didn't know what to say. I was as silent as the nigger they stopped. After a few minutes, we went to basketball practice. That was the strangest moment of my life." (Coles, 1986, pp. 27–28)

This experience led the redneck teenager to further contact then friendship with the black youth. Eventually, it led him to support desegregation. An empathic response to the youth's plight combined with a sense of fairness led to a costly moral act that precipitated a fundamental value change of the sort described by Brickman (1987). In retrospect, the white student reflected,

> I'd be as I was, I guess, but for being there in school that year and seeing that kid—seeing him behave himself, no matter what we called him, and seeing him being insulted so bad, so real bad. Something in me just drew the line, and something in me began to change, I think. (Coles, 1986, 28)

As Coles's report makes clear, we don't have to witness events directly to feel the impact of motivational orchestration. We can feel it as we read.

The effects of orchestration of empathy-induced altruism and concern for fairness can also be found in the writing of Jonathan Kozol. Deeply troubled by the "savage inequalities" in public education between rich and poor communities in the United States, Kozol (1991) clearly documents the disparities and the injustice. But he does more. He takes us into the lives of individual children. We come to care about their welfare and, as a result, to care about setting things right. Kozol's goal isn't simply to get us to feel. He wants to get us involved in action to improve funding for schools in poor communities. He uses empathy-induced altruism to promote this moral goal.

Orchestration in Fiction

Harriet Beecher Stowe (1852/2005) used much the same orchestration strategy to galvanize opposition to slavery in the United States through her famous novel. It isn't clear that Abraham Lincoln actually said, "So this is the little woman who made this big war," when he met Stowe at the White House in November 1962. But there's little doubt that Uncle Tom's Cabin contributed importantly to the abolition of slavery in the United States (Morris, 2007).

How did Stowe, who wasn't exempt from the racial stereotypes of her day, manage to inspire effective opposition to so deeply engrained and financially profitable a practice as slavery? She outlined her strategy on the first page:

> The object of these sketches is to awaken sympathy and feeling for the African race, as they exist among us; to show their wrongs and sorrows, under a system so necessarily cruel and unjust as to defeat and do away the good effects of all that can be attempted for them, by their best friends, under it. (Stowe, 1852/2005, p. 1)

Stowe pursues this agenda by taking her readers into the lives and minds of slaves, humanizing the dehumanized and evoking strong empathic concern. At the same time, she hammers home with example and dialogue the clear immorality of one human owning another. She invokes principles of fairness, justice, care, personal dignity, human rights, and sanctity of the family. These principles are all ones that her readers held dear—but withheld from slaves.

She follows George and Eliza Harris, and their little son Harry, on a harrowing but successful flight to Canada where they could rest, free at last:

> Who can speak the blessings of that rest which comes down on the free man's pillow, under laws which insure to him the rights that God has given to man? How fair and precious to that mother was that sleeping child's face, endeared by the memory of a thousand dangers! How impossible was it to sleep, in the exuberant possession of such blessedness! And yet, these two had not one acre of ground,—not a roof that they could call their own,—they had spent their all, to the last dollar. They had nothing more than the birds of the air, or the flowers of the field,—yet they could not sleep for joy. "O ye who take freedom from man, with what words shall ye answer it to God?" (p. 328)

She follows devout and loyal Tom after he is sold away from his home, wife, and children down the river to New Orleans. There, he first serves kind but feckless Augustine St. Clare and his angelic daughter Evangeline. Then, with St. Clare's sudden death, Tom is sold to the heartless and vicious Simon Legree, who eventually has him beaten to death for refusing to betray other slaves. Here is how Stowe characterized Tom's fate:

> It is one of the bitterest apportionments of the lot of slavery, that the negro, sympathetic and assimilative, after acquiring, in a refined family, the tastes and feelings which form the atmosphere of such a place, is not the less liable to become the bond-slave of the coarsest and most brutal,—just as a chair or table, which once decorated the superb saloon, comes, at last, battered and defaced, to the bar-room of some filthy tavern, or some low haunt of vulgar debauchery. The great difference is, that the table and chair cannot feel, and the *man* can; for even a legal enactment that he shall be "taken, reputed, adjudged in law, to be chattel personal," cannot blot out his soul, with its own private little world of memories, hopes, loves, fears, and desires. (p. 285, italics in original)

Stowe's flowery yet unflinching call to men and women, North and South, to act for the abolition of slavery outsold every book except the Bible in the 19th century (Morris, 2007). Arguably, it had more impact on public policy and social reform than has any other piece of fiction written in English.

And on the Radio

Elizabeth Paluck (2009) conducted an ambitious year-long field experiment in Rwanda to test the effect of a radio soap opera designed to promote reconciliation between Tutsi and Hutu after the 1994 genocide. Along with didactic messages about the roots and prevention of prejudice, the program presented characters wrestling with problems known to all Rwandans—cross-group friendships, overbearing leaders, poverty, and memories of violence. The story line featured the struggles of a young cross-group couple as they pursue their love in the face of community disapproval, and as they start a youth coalition for peace and cooperation. Listeners were drawn into the young couple's struggles, evoking empathic concern. At the same time, the soap opera sought to model and express right conduct in the current Rwandan situation of cross-group tension and distrust, and to make moral norms and principles salient (Staub & Pearlman, 2009).

The program seemed to have a powerful effect, in large part through the social interaction it prompted. Listeners of both groups gathered around the single radio provided to a community, and often remarked on or discussed the content. For example, Paluck reported that one episode of the program "ended with a character's comment that tolerance and respect for one another's ideas are necessary, to which a male [listener] called out, 'We should repeat those words!'" (Paluck, 2009, p. 582). At the end of the year, those in communities that had listened to this reconciliation soap opera showed more ability to trust and cooperate with others in their community, including members of the other group, than did those in communities that listened to a soap opera focused on health issues (which served as a control).

A Brief Word About Propriety Morality

If, as suggested in Chapters 5 and 6, its motivational and emotional underpinnings are stronger than those of interpersonal morality, propriety morality may not require orchestration with other motives to be an effective guide to behavior. Instead, our propriety morality may need treatment to soften uncritical acceptance and certainty that what we consider the right order is right for everyone. Perhaps the best prescription here is the one followed by Jonathan Haidt that was described in the first section of this chapter—interact with people you care about whose propriety principles differ from your own. Your concern for them may lead you to recognize that "good people" can honestly disagree with you about such matters and that their principles shouldn't be summarily dismissed. Again, orchestration of moral motivation and empathy-induced altruism, but of a different form.

There's another situation in which propriety morality may need motivation-based treatment. As made clear by the moral justifications for slavery in the antebellum United States and for mass killings in Nazi Europe, propriety morality can be co-opted. When our interests or the interests of those we care about conflict with our moral principles, whether interpersonal or propriety principles, powerful motivational forces may arise to align our principles with those interests. We can come to accept situations and behaviors as right and proper that, were our interests not involved, we would consider deeply immoral. Careful orchestration of moral and nonmoral motives may be needed to oppose these forces, which are themselves the product of an orchestration of moral and nonmoral motives.

Summary

The cited examples of orchestration highlight the potential power of shifting attention from the moral behavior sought to the different motives that might encourage or discourage this behavior. The examples also underscore the importance of resisting an indiscriminate appeal to any and all possible motives for acting morally. Instead, we need to attend to detail so that rather than the motives conflicting with and undercutting one another, the strengths of one can be used to overcome the weaknesses of another. Although all of the cited examples involved empathy-induced altruism, strategies that combine appeals to either altruism or collectivism with appeals to principle seem especially promising as a way to treat the limitations of moral motivation.

CONCLUSION

If we want people to live up to the moral standards, principles, and ideals they espouse, the best treatment would seem to be one that leads them to fully internalize their principles, integrating them into their core self as intrinsic values. The resulting moral desires may still at times be overpowered by other core desires. And the ability to act on principle may be hindered by situational constraints. But for those who intrinsically value their principles, doing what they think right should be an ultimate goal. Instead of looking for ways to blunt the thrust of the principles in order to serve self-interest, these people should want to uphold them, not simply appear to do so.

Most of us haven't internalized our moral standards to such a degree, at least not our interpersonal standards that specify right conduct when our interests conflict with the interests of others. Treatment is needed to take us beyond extrinsic to intrinsic valuing of these moral standards. Yet is this realistic? Perhaps the most effective treatment is the one prescribed by Brickman that involves personal cost and requires self-administration. Not a propitious combination.

Treatments to address the situational pressures that inhibit moral action are easier to implement. But without the personal change that a shift from extrinsic to intrinsic valuing entails, treatments based on situational change are likely to have limited, short-term effects. And they can easily backfire. As long as our goal is to appear and not actually be moral, we're apt to find ways to circumvent situational inducements to act morally.

For those of us who haven't reached the level of moral excellence at which interpersonal, interest-conflict standards are valued intrinsically, treatments that address the limitations of our moral motivation and emotion by orchestrating motives seem promising. Such treatments don't require that our moral values, emotions, and motives do all the heavy lifting required to produce costly moral conduct. Orchestration can draw on the strengths of nonmoral motives to overcome the weaknesses of moral ones.

Especially effective may be the combination of instrumental moral motivation, a form of egoism, with either empathy-induced altruism or collectivism. Altruism and collectivism are both powerful motives with a strong emotional base, but they're narrow in focus. Our moral standards—even introjected, extrinsically valued ones—can combat the myopia of these nonmoral motives. At the same time, the nonmoral motives can provide the emotional fire needed to turn obligation into desire. With these motives combined, we may find ourselves, like the redneck high-school student who stood up for "a nigger," being better people than we really are.

We may also find ourselves, as did he, involved in the costly pain-gain transformation from extrinsic to intrinsic valuing needed to address personal moral deficiency. We too may be able to look back and say, "Something in me began to change."

REPRISE

To close, let me return to the examples of moral maladies with which we began. I can't pretend to know the constellation of values, emotions, motives, and situational factors that prompted the behavior of a given individual in a particular past situation. Still, it may be worthwhile to point out likely contributors to some conspicuous moral failures.

Consider first the men of German Reserve Police Battalion 101, the Nazi doctors at Auschwitz, and the US soldiers at My Lai. All found themselves under strong situational pressures. They were encouraged to frame the slaughter of noncombatant men, women, and children as a noble act. It was presented as a difficult but humane solution to a public health problem. Or as pacification of the countryside. There were powerful motives that opposed any moral objection to the killing. These motives included nonmoral ones such as avoidance of stigmatization as a shirker or coward, fear of demotion, redeployment, or court-martial. They also included moral ones, obligation to do your duty and support your comrades. There was the presence of others, which made it possible to diffuse responsibility. Further, others' compliance with orders exerted pressure to comply too, and to judge doing so morally right. Alcohol and misattribution of emotion served to suppress both thought and feeling about what was happening, allowing avoidance of moral implications. Gradual step-by-step escalation of involvement in killing led incrementally to more killing. And all of these pressures were brought to bear in a hierarchical organizational structure and justification-providing society. The result? Killing innocents became business as usual. It became morally permissible, even praiseworthy.

In less extreme form, similar situational pressures contributed to provision of the defective four-disk brakes for the A7-D airplane and to provision of the unsafe digital electronic control for the Kiowa helicopter. At least some of these pressures are also felt in those cases of cheating or fraud in which actors believe their future happiness and the happiness of loved ones hang in the balance.

The conspicuous pressures in such cases exert pressure on us as well. They can lead us to conclude that situational pressure alone accounts for our moral failures. We're good people in a bad world. But this answer is too simple. Our character, which is a product of the way we internalize and value our moral standards, principles, and ideals, also plays a key role. Interpersonal standards of fairness, care, and honesty are likely to be internalized only to the level of introjection, where they're valued extrinsically. As a result, they evoke little truly moral emotion and motivation. They're vulnerable to rationalization, self-deception, and moral hypocrisy.

The importance of both the level of internalization and the nature of the values, emotions, and motives that underlie our moral behavior comes clearly to light in those cases in which situational pressure is comparatively weak. Think of law-breaking and truth-denying politicians, of pedophilic priests, philandering preachers, and fraudulent scientists. Rather than strong pressure to violate principle, they faced opportunity. They had a chance to do wrong and get away with it, and that sufficed. The same seems true for most people who cheat on their taxes or engage in shoplifting and wardrobing. The role of nonmoral motives, especially moral hypocrisy, seems pronounced in these cases.

The part played by nonmoral motives, emotions, and values is easiest to recognize in the part with the least situational pressure, the case of John Dashwood. John was well aware of his relevant moral standards as he debated with himself and his wife how best to fulfill the promise to his dying father. Opportunity was no problem. He could easily provide for his stepmother and three stepsisters without affecting either his own very comfortable lifestyle or his son's financial security. And John was motivated to do right. But his motivation was instrumental not truly moral. His ultimate goal was to gain social and self-approbation for having fulfilled his promise and displayed his generosity. With a little time, some prompting from his wife, and a creative thought or two of his own, he was able to reach this goal. He managed to proudly see himself as moral—as strictly fulfilling his obligation—while doing virtually nothing. By removing situational pressure, Austen (1811/1995) unmasks John's hypocrisy. We see his true values, his character.

So too in our own lives. We're most apt to see our moral masquerades for what they are when we face moral decisions in the absence of strong situational pressure to violate principle. Provide us some wiggle room and we may learn how closely we can resemble John Dashwood. We may learn there's more wrong with our morality than we imagined. Despite what each of us knows, we're not simply good people in a bad world. Not a comfortable or convenient truth, but an important one.

REFERENCES

Adelberg, S., & Batson, C. D. (1978). Accountability and helping: When needs exceed resources. *Journal of Personality and Social Psychology, 36*, 343–350.

Agee, V. L. (1979). *Treatment of the violent incorrigible adolescent.* Lexington, MA: Lexington Books.

Alexander, R. D. (1987). *The biology of moral systems.* New York, NY: Aldine de Gruyter.

Alfano, G., & Marwell, G. (1980). Experiments on the provision of public goods by groups: III. Non-divisibility and free riding in "real" groups. *Social Psychology Quarterly, 43*, 300–309.

Alicke, M. D., & Govorun, O. (2005). The better than average effect. In M. D. Alicke, D. A. Dunning, & J. I. Krueger (Eds.), *The self in social judgment* (pp. 85–106). New York, NY: Psychology Press.

Allport, G. W. (1961). *Pattern and growth in personality.* New York, NY: Holt, Rinehart, & Winston.

Amato, P. R. (1983). Helping behavior in urban and rural environments: Field studies based on a taxonomic organization of helping episodes. *Journal of Personality and Social Psychology, 45*, 571–586.

Anderson, S. W., Bechara, A., Damasio, H., Tranel, D., & Damasio, A. R. (1999). Impairment of social and moral behavior related to early damage in human prefrontal cortex. *Nature Neuroscience, 2*, 1032–1037.

Annas, J. (2006). Virtue ethics. In D. Copp (Ed.), *The Oxford handbook of ethical theory* (pp. 515–536). Oxford, England: Oxford University Press.

Anscombe, G. E. M. (1958). Modern moral philosophy. *Philosophy, 33*, 1–19.

Aquino, K., Freeman, D., Reed, A., II, Lim, V. K. G., & Felps, W. (2009). Testing a social-cognitive model of moral behavior: The interactive influence of situations and moral identity centrality. *Journal of Personality and Social Psychology, 97*, 123–141.

Aquino, K., & Reed, A., II (2002). The self-importance of moral identity. *Journal of Personality and Social Psychology, 83*, 1423–1440.

Aquino, K., Reed, A., II, Thau, S., & Freeman, D. (2007). A grotesque and dark beauty: How moral identity and mechanisms of moral disengagement influence cognitive and emotional reactions to war. *Journal of Experimental Social Psychology, 43*, 385–392.

Arendt, H. (1963). *Eichmann in Jerusalem: A report on the banality of evil.* New York, NY: Viking.

Ariely, D. (2012). *The (honest) truth about dishonesty: How we lie to everyone—especially ourselves.* New York, NY: HarperCollins.

Aristotle. (1976). *Ethics* (J. A. K. Thomson, Trans.; Revised by H. Tredennick). London, England: Penguin.

Arnold, M. B. (1960). *Emotion and personality* (2 vols.). New York, NY: Columbia University Press.

Aronson, E., & Carlsmith, J. M. (1963). The effect of the severity of threat on the devaluation of forbidden behavior. *Journal of Abnormal and Social Psychology, 66*, 584–588.

Asma, S. T. (2013). *Against fairness*. Chicago, IL: University of Chicago Press.

Assor, A. (2012). Autonomous moral motivation: Consequences, socializing antecedents, and the unique role of integrated moral principles. In M. Mikulincer & P. R. Shaver (Eds.), *The social psychology of morality: Exploring the causes of good and evil* (pp. 239–255). Washington, DC: American Psychological Association.

Austen, J. (1995). *Sense and sensibility*. New York, NY: Tom Doherty. (Original work published in 1811.)

Axelrod, R. (1984). *The evolution of cooperation*. New York, NY: Basic.

Ayal, S., & Geno, F. (2012). Honest rationales for dishonest behavior. In M. Mikulincer & P. R. Shaver (Eds.), *The social psychology of morality: Exploring the causes of good and evil* (pp. 149–166). Washington, DC: American Psychological Association.

Ayer, A. J. (1936). *Language, truth, and logic*. London, England: Gollancz.

Balzac, H., de (1962). *Pere Goriot* (H. Reed, Trans.). New York, NY: New American Library. (Original work published in 1834.)

Bandura, A. (1977). *Social learning theory*. Englewood Cliffs, NJ: Prentice Hall.

Bandura, A. (1990). Selective activation and disengagement of moral control. *Journal of Social Issues, 46(1)*, 27–46.

Bandura, A. (1991). Social cognitive theory of moral thought and action. In W. M. Kurtines & J. L. Gewirtz (Eds.), *Handbook of moral behavior and development: Vol. 1. Theory* (pp. 45–103). Hillsdale, NJ: Erlbaum.

Bandura, A. (1999). Moral disengagement in the perpetration of inhumanities. *Personality and Social Psychology Review, 3*, 193–209.

Baron, J. (1996). Do no harm. In D. M. Messick & A. E. Tenbrunsel (Eds.), *Codes of conduct: Behavioral research into business ethics* (pp. 197–213). New York, NY: Russell Sage.

Bateson, M., Nettle, D., & Roberts, G. (2006). Cues of being watched enhance cooperation in a real-world setting. *Biology Letters, 2*, 412–414.

Batson, C. D. (1975). Rational processing or rationalization?: The effect of disconfirming information on a stated religious belief. *Journal of Personality and Social Psychology, 32*, 176–184.

Batson, C. D. (1991). *The altruism question: Toward a social-psychological answer*. Hillsdale, NJ: Erlbaum.

Batson, C. D. (1994). Why act for the public good? Four answers. *Personality and Social Psychology Bulletin, 20*, 603–610.

Batson, C. D. (2009). Two forms of perspective taking: Imagining how another feels and imagining how you would feel. In K. D. Markman, W. M. P. Klein, & J. A. Suhr (Eds.), *Handbook of imagination and mental simulation* (pp. 267–279). New York, NY: Psychology Press.

Batson, C. D. (2011). *Altruism in humans*. New York, NY: Oxford University Press.

Batson, C. D. (2014). Empathy-induced altruism and morality: No necessary connection. In H. L. Maibom (Ed.), *Empathy and morality* (pp. 41–58). New York, NY: Oxford University Press.

Batson, C. D., Ahmad, N., Yin, J., Bedell, S. J., Johnson, J. W., Templin, C. M., Whiteside, A. (1999). Two threats to the common good: Self-interested egoism and empathy-induced altruism. *Personality and Social Psychology Bulletin, 25*, 3–16.

Batson, C. D., Anderson, S. L., Padget, M., Burgert, E., Hurt, C., & Buscher, D. (2004). *Taking advantage of privileged information: More evidence of moral hypocrisy* (Unpublished manuscript). University of Kansas, Lawrence.

Batson, C. D., Batson, J. G., Todd, R. M., Brummett, B. H., Shaw, L. L., & Aldeguer, C. M. R. (1995). Empathy and the collective good: Caring for one of the others in a social dilemma. *Journal of Personality and Social Psychology, 68,* 619–631.

Batson, C. D., Chao, M. C., & Givens, J. M. (2009). Pursuing moral outrage: Anger at torture. *Journal of Experimental Social Psychology, 45,* 155–160.

Batson, C. D., Cochran, P. J., Biederman, M. F., Blosser, J. L., Ryan, M. J., & Vogt, B. (1978). Failure to help when in a hurry: Callousness or conflict? *Personality and Social Psychology Bulletin, 4,* 97–101.

Batson, C. D., Coke, J. S., Jasnoski, M. L., & Hanson, M. (1978). Buying kindness: Effect of an extrinsic incentive for helping on perceived altruism. *Personality and Social Psychology Bulletin, 4,* 86–91.

Batson, C. D., Collins, E. C., & Powell, A. (2006). Doing business after the Fall: The virtue of moral hypocrisy. *Journal of Business Ethics, 66,* 321–335.

Batson, C. D., Dyck, J. L., Brandt, J. R., Batson, J. G., Powell, A. L., McMaster, M. R., Griffitt, C. (1988). Five studies testing two new egoistic alternatives to the empathy-altruism hypothesis. *Journal of Personality and Social Psychology, 55,* 52–77.

Batson, C. D., Early, S., & Salvarani, G. (1997). Perspective taking: Imagining how another feels versus imagining how you would feel. *Personality and Social Psychology Bulletin, 23,* 751–758.

Batson, C. D., Fultz, J., Schoenrade, P. A., & Paduano, A. (1987). Critical self-reflection and self-perceived altruism: When self-reward fails. *Journal of Personality and Social Psychology, 53,* 594–602.

Batson, C. D., Harris, A. C., McCaul, K. D., Davis, M., & Schmidt, T. (1979). Compassion or compliance: Alternative dispositional attributions for one's helping behavior. *Social Psychology Quarterly, 42,* 405–409.

Batson, C. D., Kennedy, C. L., Nord, L.-A., Stocks, E. L., Fleming, D. A., Marzette, C. M., . . . Zerger, T. (2007). Anger at unfairness: Is it moral outrage? *European Journal of Social Psychology, 37,* 1272–1285.

Batson, C. D., Klein, T. R., Highberger, L., & Shaw, L. L. (1995). Immorality from empathy-induced altruism: When compassion and justice conflict. *Journal of Personality and Social Psychology, 68,* 1042–1054.

Batson, C. D., Kobrynowicz, D., Dinnerstein, J. L., Kampf, H. C., & Wilson, A. D. (1997). In a very different voice: Unmasking moral hypocrisy. *Journal of Personality and Social Psychology, 72,* 1335–1348.

Batson, C. D., Lishner, D. A., Carpenter, A., Dulin, L., Harjusola-Webb, S., Stocks, E. L., . . . Sampat, B. (2003). "As you would have them do unto you": Does imagining yourself in the other's place stimulate moral action? *Personality and Social Psychology Bulletin, 29,* 1190–1201.

Batson, C. D., & Moran, T. (1999). Empathy-induced altruism in a Prisoner's Dilemma. *European Journal of Social Psychology, 29,* 909–924.

Batson, C. D., Sampat, B., & Collins, E. (2005). *Moral hypocrisy: Even among those who say it is important to be fair* (Unpublished manuscript). University of Kansas, Lawrence.

Batson, C. D., Shaw, L. L., & Oleson, K. C. (1992). Differentiating affect, mood, and emotion: Toward functionally based conceptual distinctions. In M. S. Clark (Ed.),

Emotion: Review of personality and social psychology: Vol. 13. Emotion (pp. 294–326). Newbury Park, CA: Sage.

Batson, C. D., Thompson, E. R., & Chen, H. (2002). Moral hypocrisy: Addressing some alternatives. *Journal of Personality and Social Psychology, 83,* 330–339.

Batson, C. D., Thompson, E. R., Seuferling, G., Whitney, H., & Strongman, J. (1999). Moral hypocrisy: Appearing moral to oneself without being so. *Journal of Personality and Social Psychology, 77,* 525–537.

Batson, C. D., Tsang, J., & Thompson, E. R. (2001). *Overpowered integrity: A second source of moral lapses* (Unpublished manuscript). University of Kansas, Lawrence.

Baumeister, R. F., & Newman, L. S. (1994). Self-regulation of cognitive inference and decision processes. *Personality and Social Psychology Bulletin, 20,* 3–19.

Baumeister, R. F., Stillwell, A. M., & Heatherton, T. F. (1994). Guilt: An interpersonal approach. *Psychological Bulletin, 115,* 243–267.

Bazerman, M. H., & Tenbrunsel, A. E. (2011). *Blind spots: Why we fail to do what's right and what to do about it.* Princeton, NJ: Princeton University Press.

Becker, E. (1973). *The denial of death.* New York, NY: Free Press.

Bem, D. J. (1967). Self-perception: An alternative interpretation of cognitive dissonance phenomena. *Psychological Review, 74,* 183–200.

Bentham, J. (1876). *An introduction to the principles of morals and legislation.* Oxford, England: Clarendon Press. (Original work published in 1789.)

Berkowitz, L. (1964). *The development of motives and values in the child.* New York, NY: Basic.

Bersoff, D. M. (1999). Why good people sometimes do bad things: Motivated reasoning and unethical behavior. *Personality and Social Psychology Bulletin, 25,* 28–39.

Berthoz, S., Armony, J. L., Blair, R. J. R., & Dolan, R. J. (2002). An fMRI study of intentional and unintentional (embarrassing) violations of social norms. *Brain, 125,* 1696–1708.

Blair, R. J. R. (2007). The amygdala and ventromedial prefrontal cortex in morality and psychopathy. *Trends in Cognitive Sciences, 11,* 387–392.

Blair, R. J. R. (2009). Neuro-cognitive systems involved in moral reasoning. In J. Verplaetse, J. De Schrijver, S. Vanneste, & J. Braeckman (Eds.), *The moral brain: Essays on the evolutionary and neuroscientific aspects of morality* (pp. 87–105). New York, NY: Springer.

Blair, R. J. R., Jones, L., Clark, F., & Smith, M. (1997). The psychopathic individual: A lack of responsiveness to distress cues? *Psychophysiology, 34,* 192–198.

Blasi, A. (1980). Bridging moral cognition and moral action: A critical review of the literature. *Psychological Bulletin, 88,* 1–45.

Blasi, A. (1984). Moral identity: Its role in moral functioning. In W. M. Kurtines & J. L. Gewirtz (Eds.), *Morality, moral behavior, and moral development* (pp. 128–139). New York, NY: Wiley.

Blasi, A. (2004). Moral functioning: Moral understanding and personality. In D. K. Lapsley & D. Narvaez (Eds.), *Moral development, self, and identity* (pp. 335–347). Mahwah, NJ: Erlbaum.

Blass, T. (2004). *The man who shocked the world: The life and legacy of Stanley Milgram.* New York, NY: Basic.

Bloom, P. (2012). Moral nativism and moral psychology. In M. Mikulincer & P. R. Shaver (Eds.), *The social psychology of morality: Exploring the causes of good and evil* (pp. 71–89). Washington, DC: American Psychological Association.

Bloom, P. (2013). *Just babies: The origins of good and evil.* New York, NY: Crown.

Blum, L. A. (1980). *Friendship, altruism, and morality*. London, England: Routledge & Kegan Paul.

Blum, L. A. (1988). Gilligan and Kohlberg: Implications for moral theory. *Ethics, 98*, 472–491.

Bowles, S. (2008). Policies designed for self-interested citizens may undermine "the moral sentiments": Evidence from economic experiments. *Science, 320*, 1605–1609.

Bowles, S., & Gintis, H. (2011). *A cooperative species: Human reciprocity and its evolution*. Princeton, NJ: Princeton University Press.

Brewer, M. B., & Kramer, R. M. (1986). Choice behavior in social dilemmas: Effects of social identity, group size, and decision framing. *Journal of Personality and Social Psychology, 50*, 543–549.

Brickman, P. (1987). *Commitment, conflict, and caring*. (Published posthumously with the collaboration of A. Abbey, D. Coates, C. Dunkel-Schetter, R. Janoff-Bulman, J. Karuza, Jr., L. S. Perloff, V. C. Raminowitz, and C. Seligman; C. B. Wortman & R. Sorrentino, Eds.). Englewood Cliffs, NJ: Prentice-Hall.

Brosnan, S. F., & de Waal, F. B. M. (2003). Monkeys reject unequal pay. *Nature, 425*, 297–299.

Browning, C. R. (1998). *Ordinary men: Reserve Police Battalion 101 and the Final Solution in Poland (with a new Afterword)*. New York, NY: HarperCollins.

Buckley, K. E., Winkel, R. E., & Leary, M. E. (2004). Reactions to acceptance and rejection: Effects of level and sequence of relational evaluation. *Journal of Experimental Social Psychology, 40*, 14–28.

Burton, R. V. (1963). Generality of honesty reconsidered. *Psychological Review, 70*, 481–499.

Burton, R. V. (1984). A paradox in theories and research in moral development. In W. M. Kurtines & J. L. Gewirtz (Eds.), *Morality, moral behavior, and moral development* (pp. 193–207). New York, NY: Wiley.

Burton, R. V., & Kunce, L. (1995). Behavioral models of moral development: A brief history and integration. In W. M. Kurtines & J. L. Gewirtz (Eds.), *Moral development: An introduction* (pp. 141–171). Boston, MA: Allyn & Bacon.

Cameron, C. D., & Payne, B. K. (2011). Escaping affect: How motivated emotion regulation creates insensitivity to mass suffering. *Journal of Personality and Social Psychology, 100*, 1–15.

Cameron, C. D., Payne, B. K., & Doris, J. M. (2013). Morality in high definition: Emotion differentiation calibrates the influence of incidental disgust on moral judgment. *Journal of Experimental Social Psychology, 49*, 719–725.

Campbell, D. T. (1975). On the conflicts between biological and social evolution and between psychology and moral tradition. *American Psychologist, 30*, 1103–1126.

Campbell, E. Q. (1964). The internalization of moral norms. *Sociometry, 27*, 391–412.

Carey, B. (2011, November 3). Fraud case seen as red flag for psychology research. *New York Times*. Retrieved from www.nytimes.com/2011/11/3/health/research

Carlsmith, K. M., Darley, J. M., & Robinson, P. H. (2002). Why do we punish? Deterrence and just deserts as motives for punishment. *Journal of Personality and Social Psychology, 83*, 284–299.

Carlsmith, K. M., & Sood, A. M. (2009). The fine line between interrogation and retribution. *Journal of Experimental Social Psychology, 45*, 191–196.

Carpenter, T. P., & Marshall, M. A. (2009). An examination of religious priming and intrinsic religious motivation in the moral hypocrisy paradigm. *Journal for the Scientific Study of Religion, 48*, 386–393.

Carruthers, P., Laurence, S., & Stich, S. (Eds.). (2005). *The innate mind: Structure and contents*. New York, NY: Oxford University Press.

Cassirer, E. (1921). *Substance and function* (W. C. Swabey, Trans.). Chicago, IL: Open Court. (Original work published in 1910.)

Chaiken, S., & Trope, Y. (Eds.). (1999). *Dual process theories in social psychology*. New York, NY: Guilford.

Chapman, H. A., & Anderson, A. K. (2011). Response to Royzman and Kurzban. *Emotion Review, 3*, 272–273.

Chapman, H. A., & Anderson, A. K. (2012). Things rank and gross in nature: A review and synthesis of moral disgust. *Psychological Bulletin, 139*, 300–327.

Chapman, H. A., Kim, D. A., Susskind, J. M., & Anderson, A. K. (2009). In bad taste: Evidence for the oral origins of moral disgust. *Science, 323*, 1222–1226.

Chen, X.-P., Pillutla, M. M., & Yao, X. (2009). Unintended consequences of cooperation inducing and maintaining mechanisms in public goods dilemmas: Sanctions and moral appeals. *Group Processes and Intergroup Relations, 12*, 241–255.

Chow, R. M., Tiedens, L. Z., & Govan, C. L. (2008). Excluded emotions: The role of anger in antisocial responses to ostracism. *Journal of Experimental Social Psychology, 44*, 896–903.

Cialdini, R. B., & Schroeder, D. A. (1976). Increasing compliance by legitimizing paltry contributions: When even a penny helps. *Journal of Personality and Social Psychology, 34*, 599–604.

Cohen, T. R., Panter, A. T., & Turan, N. (2012). Guilt proneness and moral character. *Current Directions in Psychological Science, 21*, 355–359.

Cohen, T. R., Wolf, S. T., Panter, A. T., & Insko, C. A. (2011). Introducing the GASP scale: A new measure of guilt and shame proneness. *Journal of Personality and Social Psychology, 100*, 947–966.

Colby, A., & Damon, W. (1992). *Some do care: Contemporary lives of moral commitment*. New York, NY: Free Press.

Coles, R. (1986). *The moral life of children*. Boston, MA: Houghton-Mifflin.

Crisp, R., & Cowton, C. (1994). Hypocrisy and moral seriousness. *American Philosophical Quarterly, 31*, 343–349.

Csikszentmihalyi, M. (1990). *Flow: The psychology of optimal experience*. New York, NY: Harper & Row.

Damasio, A. R. (1994). *Descartes' error: Emotion, reason, and the human brain*. New York, NY: Avon.

Damon, W. (1977). *The social world of the mind*. San Francisco, CA: Jossey-Bass.

Damon, W. (1988). *The moral child: Nurturing children's natural moral growth*. New York, NY: Free Press.

Dana, J., Lowenstein, G., & Weber, R. (2012). Ethical immunity: How people violate their own moral standards without feeling they are doing so. In D. De Cremer & A. E. Tenbrunsel (Eds.), *Behavioral business ethics: Shaping an emerging field* (pp. 197–215). New York, NY: Routledge.

Dana, J., Weber, R. A., & Kuang, J. X. (2007). Exploiting moral wiggle room: Experiments demonstrating an illusory preference for fairness. *Economic Theory, 33*, 67–80.

Darley, J. M. (1992). Social organization for the production of evil. *Psychological Inquiry, 3*, 199–218.

Darley, J. M. (1996). How organizations socialize individuals into evildoing. In D. M. Messick & A. E. Tenbrunsel (Eds.), *Codes of conduct: Behavioral research into business ethics* (pp. 13–43). New York, NY: Russell Sage.

Darley, J. M. (2002). Just punishments: Research on retributional justice. In M. Ross & D. T. Miller (Eds.), *The justice motive in everyday life* (pp. 314–333). New York, NY: Cambridge University Press.

Darley, J. M., & Batson, C. D. (1973). From Jerusalem to Jericho: A study of situational and dispositional variables in helping behavior. *Journal of Personality and Social Psychology, 27,* 100–108.

Darley, J. M., & Latané, B. (1968). Bystander intervention in emergencies: Diffusion of responsibility. *Journal of Personality and Social Psychology, 8,* 377–383.

Darley, J. M., & Pittman, T. S. (2003). The psychology of compensatory and retributive justice. *Personality and Social Psychology Review, 7,* 324–336.

Darley, J. M., & Shultz, T. R. (1990). Moral rules: Their content and acquisition. *Annual Review of Psychology, 41,* 525–556.

Darwin, C. (1913). *The descent of man, and selection in relation to sex.* London, England: D. Appleton. (Original work published in 1871.)

Dawes, R. M., McTavish, J., & Shaklee, H. (1977). Behavior, communication, and assumptions about other people's behavior in a commons dilemma situation. *Journal of Personality and Social Psychology, 35,* 1–11.

Dawes, R., van de Kragt, A. J. C., & Orbell, J. M. (1990). Cooperation for the benefit of us—not me, or my conscience. In J. J. Mansbridge (Ed.), *Beyond self-interest* (pp. 97–110). Chicago, IL: University of Chicago Press.

Decety, J., Michalska, K. J., & Kinzler, K. D. (2012). The contribution of emotion and cognition to moral sensitivity: A neurodevelopmental study. *Cerebral Cortex, 22,* 209–220.

Deci, E. L., Eghrari, H., Patrick, B. C., & Leone, D. R. (1994). Facilitating internalization: The self-determination theory perspective. *Journal of Personality, 62,* 119–142.

Deci, E. L., & Ryan, R. M. (1985). *Intrinsic motivation and self-determination in human behavior.* New York, NY: Plenum.

Deci, E. L., & Ryan, R. M. (1991). A motivational approach to self: Integration in personality. In R. Dienstbier (Ed.), *Nebraska symposium on motivation: Perspectives on motivation* (Vol. 38, pp. 237–288). Lincoln: University of Nebraska Press.

de Hooge, I. E., Nelissen, R. M. A., Breugelmans, S. M., & Zeelenberg, M. (2011). What is moral about guilt? Acting "prosocially" at the disadvantage of others. *Journal of Personality and Social Psychology, 100,* 462–473.

Demos, R. (1960). Lying to oneself. *Journal of Philosophy, 57,* 588–595.

DePaulo, B. M., & Kashy, D. A. (1998). Everyday lies in close and casual relationships. *Journal of Personality and Social Psychology, 74,* 63–79.

DePaulo, B. M., Kashy, D. A., Kirkendol, S. E., Wyer, M. M., & Epstein, J. A. (1996). Lying in everyday life. *Journal of Personality and Social Psychology, 70,* 979–995.

de Rivera, J., Gersmann, E., & Maisels, L. (2002). Acting righteously: The influence of attitude, moral responsibility, and emotional involvement. In M. Ross & D. T. Miller (Eds.), *The justice motive in everyday life* (pp. 271–288). New York, NY: Cambridge University Press.

DeScioli, P., & Kurzban, R. (2009). Mysteries of morality. *Cognition, 112,* 281–299.

de Waal, F. (1996). *Good natured: The origins of rights and wrongs in humans and other animals.* Cambridge, MA: Harvard University Press.

de Waal, F. B. M. (2006). *Primates and philosophers: How morality evolved*. Princeton, NJ: Princeton University Press.

Dickens, C. (1970). *Oliver Twist, or, the parish boy's progress*. New York, NY: Oxford University Press. (Original work published in 1837–1839.)

Dickens, C. (1982). *Martin Chuzzlewit*. New York, NY: Oxford University Press. (Original work published in 1843–1844.)

Diener, E. (1980). Deindividuation: The absence of self-awareness and self-regulation in group members. In P. B. Paulus (Ed.), *The psychology of group influence* (pp. 209–243). Hillsdale, NJ: Erlbaum.

Diener, E., Fraser, S. C., Beaman, A. L., & Kelem, R. T. (1976). Effects of deindividuation variables on stealing among Halloween trick-or-treaters. *Journal of Personality and Social Psychology, 33,* 178–183.

Diener, E., & Wallbom, M. (1976). Effects of self-awareness on antinormative behavior. *Journal of Research in Personality, 10,* 107–111.

Dienstbier, R. A., & Munter, P. O. (1971). Cheating as a function of the labeling of natural arousal. *Journal of Personality and Social Psychology, 17,* 208–213.

Ditto, P. H., Pizarro, D. A., & Tannenbaum, D. (2009). Motivated moral reasoning. In D. M. Bartels, C. W. Bauman, L. J. Skitka, & D. L. Medin (Eds.), *Psychology of learning and motivation* (Vol. 50, pp. 307–338). Burlington, VT: Academic.

Dollard, J., & Miller, N. E. (1950). *Personality and psychotherapy: An analysis in terms of learning, thinking, and culture*. New York, NY: McGraw-Hill.

Doris, J. M. (2002). *Lack of character: Personality and moral behavior*. New York, NY: Cambridge University Press.

Dostoyevsky, F. (1950). *The brothers Karamazov* (C. Garnett, Trans.). New York, NY: Random House. (Original work published in 1879–1880.)

Dunn, J. (1987). The beginnings of moral understanding: Development in the second year. In J. Kagan & S. Lamb (Eds.), *The emergence of morality in young children* (pp. 91–112). Chicago, IL: University of Chicago Press.

Dunn, J. (1988). *The beginnings of social understanding*. Oxford, England: Blackwell.

Dunn, J. (2006). Moral development in early childhood and social interaction in the family. In M. Killen & J. G. Smetana (Eds.), *Handbook of moral development* (pp. 331–350). Mahwah, NJ: Erlbaum.

Dunn, J., & Munn, P. (1985). Becoming a family member: Family, conflict, and the development of social understanding in the second year. *Child Development, 56,* 480–492.

Dunn, J., & Munn, P. (1986a). Sibling quarrels and maternal intervention: Individual differences in understanding and aggression. *Journal of Child Psychology and Psychiatry, 27,* 583–595.

Dunn, J., & Munn, P. (1986b). Siblings and the development of prosocial behavior. *International Journal of Behavioral Development, 9,* 265–284.

Dunn, J., & Munn, P. (1987). Development of justification in disputes with mother and sibling. *Developmental Psychology, 23,* 791–798.

Effron, D. A., & Miller, D. T. (2012). How the moralization of issues grants social legitimacy to act on one's attitudes. *Personality and Social Psychology Bulletin, 38,* 690–701.

Eisenberg, A. R., & Garvey, C. (1981). Children's use of verbal strategies in resolving conflicts. *Discourse Processes, 4,* 149–170.

Eisenberg, N. (1991). Meta-analytic contributions to the literature on prosocial behavior. *Personality and Social Psychology Bulletin, 17,* 273–282.

Eisenberg, N. (2000). Emotion, regulation, and moral development. *Annual Review of Psychology, 51,* 665–697.

Eliot, G. (1956). *Middlemarch.* Boston, MA: Houghton Mifflin. (Original work published in 1874.)

Eliot, G. (1962). *Silas Marner.* New York, NY: Harcourt, Brace, & World. (Original work published in 1861.)

Emde, R., Johnson, W. F., & Easterbrooks, M. A. (1987). The do's and don'ts of early moral development: Psychoanalytic tradition and current research. In J. Kagan & S. Lamb (Eds.), *The emergence of morality in young children* (pp. 245–276). Chicago, IL: University of Chicago Press.

Epley, N., & Dunning, D. (2000). Feeling "holier than thou": Are self-serving assessments produced by errors in self- or social prediction? *Journal of Personality and Social Psychology, 79,* 861–875.

Eskine, K. J., Kacinik, N. A., & Prinz, J. J. (2011). A bad taste in the mouth: Gustatory disgust influences moral judgment. *Psychological Science, 22,* 295–299.

Falk, W. D. (1947). "Ought" and motivation. *Proceedings of the Aristotelian Society, 48,* 111–138.

Fehr, E., & Fischbacher, U. (2004). Third-party punishment and social norms. *Evolution and Human Behavior, 25,* 63–87.

Fehr, E., & Gächter, S. (2002). Altruistic punishment in humans. *Nature, 415,* 137–140.

Feinberg, M., & Willer, R. (2013). The moral roots of environmental attitudes. *Psychological Science, 24,* 56–62.

Fernandez-Dols, J.-M., Aguilar, P., Campo, S., Vallacher, R. R., Janowsky, A., Rabbia, H., . . . Lerner, M. J. (2010). Hypocrites or maligned cooperative participants? Experimenter induced normative conflict in zero-sum situations. *Journal of Experimental Social Psychology, 46,* 525–530.

Festinger, L. (1957). *A theory of cognitive dissonance.* Stanford, CA: Stanford University Press.

Festinger, L., & Freedman, J. L. (1964). Dissonance reduction and moral values. In P. Worchel & D. Byrne (Eds.), *Personality change* (pp. 220–243). New York, NY: Wiley.

Festinger, L., Riecken, H. W., & Schachter, S. (1956). *When prophecy fails: A social and psychological study of a modern group that predicted the destruction of the world.* Minneapolis: University of Minnesota Press.

Fetchenhauer, D., & Huang, X. (2004). Justice sensitivity and distributive decisions in experimental games. *Personality and Individual Differences, 36,* 1015–1029.

Fleeson, W., & Gallagher, P. (2009). The implications of Big Five standing for the distribution of trait manifestation in behavior: Fifteen experience-sampling studies and a meta-analysis. *Journal of Personality and Social Psychology, 97,* 1097–1114.

Foot, P. (1978). *Virtues and vices.* Oxford, England: Blackwell.

Forgas, J. P., & Smith, C. A. (2003). Affect and emotion. In M. A. Hogg & J. Cooper (Eds.), *The SAGE handbook of social psychology* (pp. 161–189). Thousand Oaks, CA: Sage.

Forman, D. R., Aksan, N., & Kochanska, G. (2004). Toddlers' responsive imitation predicts preschool-age conscience. *Psychological Science, 15,* 699–704.

Frank, R. H. (1988). *Passions within reason: The strategic role of the emotions.* New York, NY: Norton.

Frank, R. H. (2003). Adaptive rationality and the moral emotions. In R. J. Davidson, K. R. Scherer, & H. H. Goldsmith (Eds.), *Handbook of affective sciences* (pp. 891–896). New York, NY: Oxford University Press.

Freedman, J. L. (1965). Long-term behavioral effects of cognitive dissonance. *Journal of Experimental Social Psychology, 1*, 145–155.

Freud, S. (1960a). *A general introduction to psychoanalysis* (J. Riviere, Trans.) New York, NY: Washington Square. (Original work published in 1917.)

Freud, S. (1960b). *The ego and the id* (J. Riviere, Trans.). New York, NY: Norton. (Original work published in 1923.)

Freud, S. (1961). *Civilization and its discontents* (J. Strachey, Trans.). New York, NY: Norton. (Original work published in 1930.)

Frijda, N. (1988). The laws of emotion. *American Psychologist, 43*, 349–358.

Gaertner, L., Iuzzini, J., Witt, M. G., & Oriña, M. M. (2006). Us without them: Evidence for an intragroup origin of positive ingroup regard. *Journal of Personality and Social Psychology, 90*, 426–439.

Gaertner, L., Iuzzini, J., & O'Mara, E. (2008). When rejection by one fosters aggression against many: Multiple-victim aggression as a consequence of social rejection and perceived groupness. *Journal of Experimental Social Psychology, 44*, 958–970.

Gaertner, S. L., & Dovidio, J. F. (2000). *Reducing intergroup bias: The Common Ingroup Identity Model*. Philadelphia, PA: Psychology Press.

Gert, B. (2012). The definition of morality. In E. N. Zalta (Ed.), *The Stanford encyclopedia of philosophy*. Retrieved from http://plato.stanford.edu/archives/fall2012/entries/morality-definitions/

Gibbons, F. X., & Wicklund, R. A. (1982). Self-focused attention and helping behavior. *Journal of Personality and Social Psychology, 43*, 462–474.

Gibbs, J. C. (2003). *Moral development and reality: Beyond the theories of Kohlberg and Hoffman*. Thousand Oaks, CA: Sage.

Gibbs, J. C. (2014). *Moral development and reality: Beyond the theories of Kohlberg, Hoffman, and Haidt* (3rd ed.). New York, NY: Oxford University Press.

Gilligan, C. (1982). *In a different voice: Psychological theory and women's development*. Cambridge, MA: Harvard University Press.

Gilligan, C., Ward, J. V., & Taylor, J. M. (1988). *Mapping the moral domain: A contribution of women's thinking to psychological theory and education*. Cambridge, MA: Harvard University Press.

Gino, F., & Ariely, D. (2012). The dark side of creativity: Original thinkers can be more dishonest. *Journal of Personality and Social Psychology, 102*, 445–459.

Gino, F., Ayal, S., & Ariely, D. (2009). Contagion and differentiation in unethical behavior: The effect of one bad apple on the barrel. *Psychological Science, 20*, 393–398.

Gino, F., & Mogilner, C. (2014). Time, money, and morality. *Psychological Science, 25*, 414–421.

Gino, F., Schweitzer, M. E., Mead, N. L., & Ariely, D. (2011). Unable to resist temptation: How self-control depletion promotes unethical behavior. *Organizational Behavior and Human Decision Processes, 115*, 191–203.

Glover, J. (2000). *Humanity: A moral history of the twentieth century*. New Haven, CT: Yale University Press.

Gneezy, U., & Rustichini, A. (2000). A fine is a price. *Journal of Legal Studies, 29*, 1–17.

Goffman, E. (1969). *Strategic interaction*. New York, NY: Ballantine.

Golding, W. (1954). *Lord of the flies, a novel*. London, England: Faber & Faber.

Gollwitzer, M., Schmitt, M., Schalke, R., Maes, J., & Baer, A. (2005). Asymmetrical effects of justice sensitivity perspectives on prosocial and antisocial behavior. *Social Justice Research, 18*, 183–201.

Graham, J., Haidt, J., Koleva, S., Motyl, M., Iyer, R., Wojcik, S. P., & Ditto, P. H. (2013). Moral foundations theory: The pragmatic validity of moral pluralism. *Advances in Experimental Social Psychology, 47,* 55–130.

Graham, J., Haidt, J., & Nosek, B. A. (2009). Liberals and conservatives rely on different sets of moral foundations. *Journal of Personality and Social Psychology, 96,* 1029–1046.

Graham, J., Nosek, B. A., Haidt, J., Iyer, R., Koleva, S., & Ditto, P. H. (2011). Mapping the moral domain. *Journal of Personality and Social Psychology, 101,* 366–385.

Graham, S., Weiner, B., & Zucker, G. S. (1997). An attributional analysis of punishment goals and public reactions to O. J. Simpson. *Personality and Social Psychology Bulletin, 23,* 331–346.

Greenberg, J., Solomon, S., & Pyszczynski, T. (1997). Terror management theory of self-esteem and cultural worldviews: Empirical assessments and conceptual refinements. In M. P. Zanna (Ed.), *Advances in experimental social psychology* (Vol. 29, pp. 61–142). New York, NY: Academic.

Greene, J. D. (2008). The secret joke of Kant's soul. In W. Sinnott-Armstrong (Ed.), *Moral psychology: Vol. 3. The neuroscience of morality: Emotion, disease, and development* (pp. 35–79). Cambridge, MA: MIT Press.

Greene, J. D. (2013). *Moral tribes: Emotion, reason, and the gap between us and them.* New York, NY: Penguin.

Greene, J. D., Nystrom, L. E., Engell, A. D., Darley, J. M., & Cohen, J. D. (2004). The neural bases of cognitive conflict and control in moral judgment. *Neuron, 44,* 389–400.

Greene, J. D., & Paxton, J. M. (2009). Patterns of neural activity associated with honest and dishonest moral decisions. *Proceedings of the National Academy of Sciences USA, 106,* 12506–12511.

Greene, J. D., Sommerville, R. B., Nystrom, L. E., Darley, J. M., & Cohen, J. D. (2001). An fMRI investigation of emotional engagement in moral judgment. *Science, 293,* 2105–2108.

Grusec, J. E. (1991). The socialization of altruism. In M. S. Clark (Ed.), *Prosocial behavior* (pp. 9–33). Newbury Park, CA: Sage.

Grusec, J. E., Kuczynski, L., Rushton, J. P., & Simutis, Z. M. (1978). Modeling, direct instruction, and attributions: Effects on altruism. *Developmental Psychology, 14,* 51–57.

Guglielmo, S., & Malle, B. F. (2010). Can unintended side effect be intention? Resolving a controversy over intentionality and morality. *Personality and Social Psychology Bulletin, 36,* 1635–1647.

Gunia, B. C., Wang, L., Huang, L., Wang, H. & Murnigan, J. K. (2012). Contemplation and conversation: Subtle influences on moral decision making. *Academy of Management Journal, 55,* 13–33.

Gur, R. C., & Sackheim, H. A. (1979). Self-deception: A concept in search of a phenomenon. *Journal of Personality and Social Psychology, 37,* 147–169.

Gutierrez, R., & Giner-Sorolla, R. (2007). Anger, disgust, and presumption of harm as reactions to taboo-breaking behaviors. *Emotion, 7,* 853–868.

Haan, N. (1985). Process of moral development: Cognitive or social disequilibrium? *Developmental Psychology, 21,* 996–1006.

Haidt, J. (2001). The emotional dog and its rational tail: A social intuitionist approach to moral judgment. *Psychological Review, 108,* 814–834.

Haidt, J. (2003). The moral emotions. In R. J. Davidson, K. R. Scherer, & H. H. Goldsmith (Eds.), *Handbook of affective sciences* (pp. 852–870). New York, NY: Oxford University Press.

Haidt, J. (2012). *The righteous mind: Why good people are divided by politics and religion.* New York, NY: Pantheon.

Haidt, J., & Bjorklund, F. (2008a). Social intuitionists answer six questions about morality. In W. Sinnott-Armstrong (Ed.), *Moral psychology: Vol. 2. The cognitive science of morality* (pp. 181–217). Cambridge, MA: MIT Press.

Haidt, J., & Bjorklund, F. (2008b). Social intuitionists reason, in conversation. In W. Sinnott-Armstrong (Ed.), *Moral psychology: Vol. 2. The cognitive science of morality* (pp. 241–254). Cambridge, MA: MIT Press.

Haidt, J., & Graham, J. (2007). When morality opposes justice: Conservatives have moral intuitions that liberals may not recognize. *Social Justice Research, 20*, 98–116.

Haidt, J., & Kesebir, S. (2010). Morality. In S. Fiske, D. Gilbert, & G. Lindzey (Eds.), *Handbook of social psychology* (5th ed., Vol. 2, pp. 797–832). Hoboken, NJ: Wiley.

Haidt, J., Koller, S., & Dias, M. (1993). Affect, culture, and morality, or is it wrong to eat your dog? *Journal of Personality and Social Psychology, 65*, 613–628.

Hallie, P. P. (1979). *Lest innocent blood be shed: The story of Le Chambon and how goodness happened there.* New York, NY: Harper & Row.

Hamlin, J. K., Wynn, K., Bloom, P., & Mahajan, N. (2011). How infants and toddlers react to antisocial others. *Proceedings of the National Academy of Sciences, 108*, 19931–19936.

Harbaugh, W. T., Mayr, U., & Burghart, D. R. (2007). Neural responses to taxation and voluntary giving reveal motives for charitable donations. *Science, 316*, 1622–1625.

Hardyck, J. A., & Braden, M. (1962). Prophecy fails again: A report of a failure to replicate. *Journal of Abnormal and Social Psychology, 65*, 136–141.

Hare, R. M. (2001). Weakness of will. In L. Becker & C. Becker (Eds.), *The encyclopedia of ethics* (2nd ed., Vol. 3, pp. 1789–1792). New York, NY: Routledge.

Harman, G. (1999). Moral philosophy meets social psychology: Virtue ethics and the fundamental attribution error. *Proceedings of the Aristotelian Society, 99*, 315–331.

Hartshorne, H., & May, M. A. (1928). *Studies in the nature of character: Vol. 1. Studies in deceit.* New York, NY: Macmillan.

Hartshorne, H., May, M. A., & Maller, J. B. (1929). *Studies in the nature of character: Vol. 2. Studies in service and self-control.* New York, NY: Macmillan.

Hartshorne, H., May, M. A., & Shuttleworth, F. K. (1930). *Studies in the nature of character: Vol. 3. Studies in the organization of character.* New York, NY: Macmillan.

Hauser, M. D. (2006). *Moral minds: The nature of right and wrong.* New York, NY: Harper Collins.

Heckeren, H. R., Wartenburger, I., Schmidt, J., Schwintowski, H.-P., & Villringer, A. (2003). An fMRI study of simply ethical decision-making. *Neuroreport, 14*, 1215–1219.

Heider, F. (1958). *The psychology of interpersonal relations.* New York, NY: Wiley.

Hersh, S. (1969, November 25). Ex-GI tells of killing civilians at Pinkville. *St. Louis Post Dispatch.*

Hobbes, T. (1651). *Leviathan; or the matter, form, and power of a commonwealth, ecclesiastical and civil.* London, England: A. Crooke.

Hoffman, M. L. (1977). Moral internalization: Current theory and research. In L. Berkowitz (Ed.), *Advances in experimental social psychology* (Vol. 10, pp. 86–135). New York, NY: Academic.

Hoffman, M. L. (1984). Empathy, its limitations, and its role in a comprehensive moral theory. In W. M. Kurtines & J. L. Gewirtz (Eds.), *Morality, moral behavior, and moral development* (pp. 283–302). New York, NY: Wiley.

Hoffman, M. L. (1989). Empathic emotions and justice in society. *Social Justice Research*, 3, 283–311.

Hoffman, M. L. (2000). *Empathy and moral development: Implications for caring and justice*. New York, NY: Cambridge University Press.

Horberg, E. J., Oveis, C., & Keltner, D. (2011). Emotions as moral amplifiers: An appraisal tendency approach to the influences of distinct emotions upon moral judgment. *Emotion Review*, 3, 237–244.

Horberg, E. J., Oveis, C., Keltner, D., & Cohen, A. B. (2009). Disgust and the moralization of purity. *Journal of Personality and Social Psychology*, 97, 963–976.

Hugo, V. (1862). *Les miserables: A novel* (C. E. Wilbour, Trans; revised and edited by F. M. Cooper). New York, NY: A. L. Burt.

Hull, C. L. (1943). *Principles of behavior*. New York, NY: Appleton-Century.

Hume, D. (1975). *An enquiry concerning the principles of morals*. (L. A. Selby-Bigge, Ed.) Oxford, England: Oxford University Press. (Original work published in 1751.)

Hume, D. (1978). *A treatise of human nature* (L. A. Selby-Bigge, Ed.; 2nd ed., with text and notes revised by P. H. Nidditch). Oxford, England: Oxford University Press. (Original work published in 1739–1740.)

Hunt, L. (2007). *Inventing human rights: A history*. New York, NY: W. W. Norton.

Hursthouse, R. (2013). Virtue ethics. In E. N. Zalta (Ed.), *The Stanford encyclopedia of philosophy*. Retrieved from http://plato.stanford.edu/archives/fall2013/entries/ethics-virtue/

Hutcherson, C. A., & Gross, J. J. (2011). The moral emotions: A social-functionalist account of anger, disgust, and contempt. *Journal of Personality and Social Psychology*, 100, 719–737.

Jackson, L. E., Batson, C. D., & Gaertner, L. (2011, July). *Ew! That's terrible! Experimental evidence of moral disgust*. Poster presented at the 16th General Meeting of the European Association of Social Psychology, Stockholm, Sweden.

Jaffee, S., & Hyde, J. S. (2000). Gender differences in moral orientation: A meta-analysis. *Psychological Bulletin*, 126, 703–726.

Janoff-Bulman, R., & Carnes, N. C. (2013). Surveying the moral landscape: Moral motives and group-based moralities. *Personality and Social Psychology Review*, 17, 219–236.

Janoff-Bulman, R., Sheikh, S., & Hepp, S. (2009). Proscriptive versus prescriptive morality: Two faces of moral regulation. *Journal of Personality and Social Psychology*, 96, 521–537.

Jencks, C. (1990). Varieties of altruism. In J. J. Mansbridge (Ed.), *Beyond self-interest* (pp. 53–67). Chicago, IL: University of Chicago Press.

Johnson, M. (1993). *Moral imagination: Implications of cognitive science for ethics*. Chicago, IL: University of Chicago Press.

Jones, E. E., & Pittman, T. S. (1982). Toward a general theory of strategic self-presentation. In J. Suls (Ed.), *Psychological perspectives on the self* (pp. 231–262). Hillsdale, NJ: Erlbaum.

Kagan, J. (1984). *The nature of the child*. New York, NY: Basic.

Kagan, J. (1987). Introduction. In J. Kagan & S. Lamb (Eds.), *The emergence of morality in young children* (pp. ix–xx). Chicago, IL: University of Chicago Press.

Kagan, J., & Lamb, S. (Eds.). (1987). *The emergence of morality in young children*. Chicago, IL: University of Chicago Press.

Kant, I. (1898). Fundamental principles of the metaphysic of morals. In Kant's *Critique of Practical Reason and other works on the theory of ethics* (5th ed.; T. K. Abbott, Trans.). New York, NY: Longmans, Green. (Original work published in 1785.)

Kant, I. (1991). *The metaphysics of morals* (M. Gregor, Trans.). New York, NY: Cambridge University Press. (Original work published in 1797.)

Kelman, H. C., & Hamilton, V. C. (1989). *Crimes of obedience: Towards a social psychology of authority and responsibility*. New Haven, CT: Yale University Press.

Kittay, E. F. (1992). Hypocrisy. In L. C. Becker & C. B. Becker (Eds.), *Encyclopedia of ethics* (pp. 582–587). New York, NY: Garland.

Knoch, D., Pascual-Leone, A., Meyer, K., Treyer, V., & Fehr, E. (2006). Diminishing reciprocal fairness by disrupting the right prefrontal cortex. *Science, 314*, 829–832.

Kogut, T., & Ritov, I. (2005). The "identified victim" effect: An identified group, or just a single individual? *Journal of Behavioral Decision Making, 18*, 157–167.

Kohlberg, L. (1969). Stage and sequence: The cognitive-developmental approach to socialization. In D. Goslin (Ed.), *Handbook of socialization theory and research* (pp. 347–480). Chicago, IL: Rand McNally.

Kohlberg, L. (1976). Moral stages and moralization: The cognitive-developmental approach. In T. Lickona (Ed.), *Moral development and behavior: Theory, research, and social issues* (pp. 31–53). New York, NY: Holt, Rinehart, & Winston.

Kohlberg, L. (1981). *Essays on moral development: Vol. 1. The philosophy of moral development*. San Francisco, CA: Harper & Row.

Kohlberg, L. (1984). *Essays on moral development: Vol. 2. The psychology of moral development*. San Francisco, CA: Harper & Row.

Kohlberg, L., & Candee, D. (1984). The relationship of moral judgment to moral action. In W. M. Kurtines & J. L. Gewirtz (Eds.), *Morality, moral behavior, and moral development* (pp. 52–73). New York, NY: Wiley.

Komorita, S. S., & Parks, C. D. (1995). Interpersonal relations: Mixed-motive interaction. *Annual Review of Psychology, 46*, 183–207.

Korte, C. (1981). Constraints on helping behavior in an urban environment. In J. P. Rushton & R. M. Sorrentino (Eds.), *Altruism and helping behavior: Social, personality, and developmental perspectives* (pp. 315–329). Hillsdale, NJ: Erlbaum.

Korte, C., Ypma, I., & Toppen, A. (1975). Helpfulness in Dutch society as a function of urbanization and environmental input level. *Journal of Personality and Social Psychology, 32*, 996–1003.

Kozol, J. (1991). *Savage inequalities: Children in America's schools*. New York, NY: Crown.

Krebs, D. L., & Denton, K. (2005). Toward a more pragmatic approach to morality: A critical evaluation of Kohlberg's model. *Psychological Review, 112*, 629–649.

Krebs, D. L., & Denton, K. (2006). Explanatory limitations of cognitive-developmental approaches to morality. *Psychological Review, 113*, 672–675.

Krevans, J., & Gibbs, J. C. (1996). Parents' use of inductive discipline: Relations to children's empathy and prosocial behavior. *Child Development, 67*, 3263–3277.

Kunda, Z. (1990). The case for motivated reasoning. *Psychological Bulletin, 108*, 480–498.

Kurtines, W., & Greif, E. G. (1974). The development of moral thought: Review and evaluation of Kohlberg's approach. *Psychological Bulletin, 81*, 453–470.

Kurzban, R. (2010). *Why everyone (else) is a hypocrite*. Princeton, NJ: Princeton University Press.

Kurzban, R., DeScioli, P., & O'Brien, E. (2007). Audience effects on moralistic punishment. *Evolution and Human Behavior, 28*, 75–84.

Lamm, C., Batson, C. D., & Decety, J. (2007). The neural substrate of human empathy: Effects of perspective-taking and cognitive appraisal. *Journal of Cognitive Neuroscience, 19*, 1–17.

Lammers, J., Stapel, D. A., & Galinsky, A. D. (2010). Power increases hypocrisy: Moralizing in reasoning, immorality in behavior. *Psychological Science, 21*, 737–744.

Latané, B., & Darley, J. M. (1968). Group inhibition of bystander intervention. *Journal of Personality and Social Psychology, 10*, 215–221.

Latané, B., & Darley, J. M. (1970). *The unresponsive bystander: Why doesn't he help?* New York, NY: Appleton-Crofts.

Latané, B., & Rodin, J. A. (1969). A lady in distress: Inhibiting effects of friends and strangers on bystander intervention. *Journal of Experimental Social Psychology, 5*, 189–202.

Laursen, B., & Hartup, W. W. (2002). The origins of reciprocity and social exchange in friendships. *New Directions for Child and Adolescent Development, 95*, 27–40.

Lee, S. W. S., & Schwarz, N. (2010). Dirty hands and dirty mouths: Embodiment of the moral-purity metaphor is specific to the motor modality involved in moral transgression. *Psychological Science, 21*, 1423–1425.

Lee, S. W. S., & Schwarz, N. (2011). Wiping the slate clean: Psychological consequences of physical cleansing. *Current Directions in Psychology, 20*, 307–311.

Leiter, B. (2011). Nietzsche's moral and political philosophy. In E. N. Zalta (Ed.), *The Stanford encyclopedia of philosophy*. Retrieved from http://plato.stanford.edu/archives/sum2011/entries/nietzsche-moral-political/

Lepper, M. R. (1973). Dissonance, self-perception, and honesty in children. *Journal of Personality and Social Psychology, 25*, 65–74.

Lepper, M. R. (1983). Social-control processes and the internalization of social values: An attributional perspective. In E. T. Higgins, D. N. Ruble, & W. W. Hartup (Eds.), *Social cognition and social development* (pp. 294–330). New York, NY: Cambridge University Press.

Lerner, J. S., & Tetlock, P. E. (1999). Accounting for the effects of accountability. *Psychological Bulletin, 125*, 255–275.

Lerner, M. J. (1970). The desire for justice and reactions to victims. In J. Macaulay & L. Berkowitz (Eds.), *Altruism and helping behavior* (pp. 205–229). New York, NY: Academic.

Lerner, M. J. (1980). *The belief in a just world: A fundamental delusion*. New York, NY: Plenum.

Lerner, M. J. (1981). The justice motive in human relations: Some thoughts on what we know and need to know about justice. In M. J. Lerner & S. C. Lerner (Eds.), *The justice motive in social behavior: Adapting to times of scarcity and change* (pp. 11–35). New York, NY: Plenum.

Lerner, M. J., & Clayton, S. (2011). *Justice and self-interest: Two fundamental motives*. New York, NY: Cambridge University Press.

Lerner, M. J., Miller, D. T., & Holmes, J. G. (1976). Deserving and the emergence of forms of justice. In L. Berkowitz (Ed.), *Advances in experimental social psychology* (Vol. 9, pp. 133–162). New York, NY: Academic.

Lewin, K. (1935). *Dynamic theory of personality*. New York, NY: McGraw-Hill.

Lewin, K. (1938). The conceptual representation and measurement of psychological forces. *Contributions to Psychological Theory, 1*, 1–247.

Lewin, K. (1951). *Field theory in social science*. New York, NY: Harper.

Lewis, M. (1989). *Liar's poker: Rising through the wreckage on Wall Street*. New York, NY: Norton.

Lewis, M., Stanger, C., & Sullivan, M. W. (1989). Deception in 3-year-olds. *Developmental Psychology, 25*, 439–443.

Lickel, B., Miller, N., Stenstrom, D. M., Denson, T. F., & Schmader, T. (2006). Vicarious retribution: The role of collective blame in intergroup aggression. *Personality and Social Psychology Review, 10*, 372–390.

Liebrand, W. B. G., Jansen, R. W. T. L., Rijken, V. M., & Suhre, C. J. M. (1986). Might over morality: Social values and the perception of other players in experimental games. *Journal of Experimental Social Psychology, 22*, 203–215.

Lifton, R. J. (1973). *Home from the war: Vietnam veterans; Neither victims nor executioners.* New York, NY: Simon & Schuster.

Lifton, R. J. (1986). *The Nazi doctors: Medical killing and the psychology of genocide.* New York, NY: Basic.

List, J. A. (2007). On the interpretation of giving in dictator games. *Journal of Political Economy, 115*, 482–493.

Lönnqvist, J.-E., Irlenbusch, B., & Walkowitz, G. (2014). Moral hypocrisy: Impression management or self-deception? *Journal of Experimental Social Psychology, 55*, 53–62.

Louden, R. (2006). Virtue ethics. In D. M. Borchert (Ed.), *The encyclopedia of philosophy* (Vol. 9, pp. 687–689). Detroit, MI: Macmillan Reference.

MacIntyre, A. (1984). *After virtue* (2nd ed.). Notre Dame, IN: University of Notre Dame Press.

Manning, R., Levine, M., & Collins, A. (2007). The Kitty Genovese murder and the social psychology of helping: The parable of the 38 witnesses. *American Psychologist, 62*, 555–562.

Martin, J., Brickman, P., & Murray, A. (1984). Moral outrage and pragmatism: Explanations for collective action. *Journal of Experimental Social Psychology, 20*, 484–496.

Marzillier, S. L., & Davey, G. C. L. (2004). The emotional profiling of disgust-eliciting stimuli: Evidence for primary and complex disgusts. *Cognition and Emotion, 18*, 313–336.

Mazar, N., Amir, O., & Ariely, D. (2008). The dishonesty of honest people: A theory of self-concept maintenance. *Journal of Marketing Research, 45*, 633–644.

Mazar, N., & Zhong, C.-B. (2010). Do green products make us better people? *Psychological Science, 21*, 494–498.

McCrae, R. R., & Costa, P. T., Jr. (2003). *Personality in adulthood: A five-factor theory perspective* (2nd ed.). New York, NY: Guilford.

McFarland, S., Webb, M., & Brown, D. (2012). All humanity is my ingroup: A measure and studies of identification with all humanity. *Journal of Personality and Social Psychology, 103*, 830–853.

McKinnon, C. (1991). Hypocrisy, with a note on integrity. *American Philosophical Quarterly, 28*, 321–330.

Medin, D. L. (2012). Rigor without rigor mortis: The APS Board discusses research integrity. *APS Observer, 25(2)*, 5–8.

Mele, A. R. (1987). *Irrationality: An essay on akrasia, self-deception, and self-control.* New York, NY: Oxford University Press.

Mele, A. R. (1997). Real self-deception. *Behavioral and Brain Sciences, 20*, 91–136.

Mele, A. R. (2001). *Self-deception unmasked.* Princeton, NJ: Princeton University Press.

Messick, D. M., Bloom, S., Boldizar, J. P., & Samuelson, C. D. (1985). Why we are fairer than others. *Journal of Experimental Social Psychology, 21*, 480–500.

Mikhail, J. (2007). Universal moral grammar: Theory, evidence, and the future. *Trends in Cognitive Sciences, 11*, 143–152.

Mikhail, J. (2011). *Elements of moral cognition: Rawls' linguistic analogy and the cognitive science of moral and legal judgment.* New York, NY: Cambridge University Press.

Mikula, G., Scherer, K. R., & Athenstaedt, U. (1998). The role of injustice in the elicitation of differential emotional reactions. *Personality and Social Psychology Bulletin, 24,* 769–783.

Milgram, S. (1963). Behavioral study of obedience. *Journal of Abnormal and Social Psychology, 67,* 371–378.

Milgram, S. (1970). The experience of living in cities. *Science, 167,* 1461–1468.

Milgram, S. (1974). *Obedience to authority: An experimental view.* New York, NY: Harper & Row.

Milgram, S., & Sabini, J. (1978). On maintaining urban norms: A field experiment in the subway. In A. Baum, J. E. Singer, & S. Valins (Eds.), *Advances in environmental psychology* (Vol. 1, pp. 31–40). Hillsdale, NJ: Erlbaum.

Mill, J. S. (1987). Utilitarianism. In J. S. Mill & J. Bentham, *Utilitarianism and other essays* (pp. 272–338). London, England: Penguin. (Original work published in 1861.)

Miller, D. T. (1977). Altruism and threat to a belief in a just world. *Journal of Experimental Social Psychology, 13,* 113–124.

Miller, D. T. (1999). The norm of self-interest. *American Psychologist, 54,* 1053–1060.

Miller, D. T., & McFarland, C. (1987). Pluralistic ignorance: When similarity is interpreted as dissimilarity. *Journal of Personality and Social Psychology, 53,* 298–305.

Miller, G. P. (2003). Norm enforcement in the public sphere: The case of handicapped parking. *George Washington Law Review, 71,* 895–933.

Miller, N. E., & Dollard, J. (1941). *Social learning and imitation.* New Haven, CT: Yale University Press.

Minson, J. A., & Monin, B. (2012). Do-gooder derogation: Disparaging morally motivated minorities to defuse anticipated reproach. *Social Psychological and Personality Science, 3,* 200–207.

Mischel, W. (2014). *The marshmallow test: Mastering self-control.* New York: Little, Brown.

Mischel, W., & Mischel, H. N. (1976). A cognitive social-learning approach to morality and self-regulation. In T. Lickona (Ed.), *Moral development and behavior: Theory, research, and social issues* (pp. 84–107). New York, NY: Holt, Rinehart, & Winston.

Moll, J., & de Oliveira-Souza, R. (2007). Moral judgments, emotions, and the utilitarian brain. *Trends in Cognitive Sciences, 11,* 319–321.

Moll, J., de Oliveira-Souza, R., Bramati, I. E., & Grafman, J. (2002). Functional networks in emotional moral and nonmoral judgments. *Neuroimage, 16,* 696–703.

Moll, J., de Oliveira-Souza, R., & Eslinger, P. J. (2003). Morals and the human brain: A working model. *Neuroreport, 14,* 299–305.

Moll, J., de Oliveira-Souza, R., Eslinger, P. J., Bramati, I. E., Mourão-Miranda, J., Andreiuolo, P. A., & Pessoa, L. (2002). The neural correlates of moral sensitivity: A functional magnetic resonance imaging investigation of basis and moral emotions. *Journal of Neuroscience, 22,* 2730–2736.

Moll, J., de Oliveira-Souza, R., & Zahn, R. (2008). The neural basis of moral cognition: Sentiments, concepts, and values. *Annals of the New York Academy of Sciences, 1124,* 161–180.

Monin, B., & Miller, D. T. (2001). Moral credentials and the expression of prejudice. *Journal of Personality and Social Psychology, 81,* 33–43.

Monin, B., Sawyer, P. J., & Marquez, M. J. (2008). The rejection of moral rebels: Resenting those who do the right thing. *Journal of Personality and Social Psychology, 95,* 76–93.

Montada, L., & Schneider, A. (1989). Justice and emotional reactions to the disadvantaged. *Social Justice Research, 3,* 313–344.

Moriarty, T. (1975). Crime, commitment, and the responsive bystander: Two field experiments. *Journal of Personality and Social Psychology, 31,* 370–376.

Morris, R. (2007). Introduction. In D. B. Sachsman, S. K. Rushing, & R. Morris (Eds.), *Memory and myth: The Civil War in fiction and film from* Uncle Tom's Cabin *to* Cold Mountain (pp. 1–8). West Lafayette, IN: Purdue University Press.

Much, N. C., & Shweder, R. A. (1978). Speaking of rules: The analysis of culture in breach. In W. Damon (Ed.), *New directions for child development: Moral development* (Vol. 2, pp. 19–39). San Francisco, CA: Jossey-Bass.

Murray, H. A. (1938). *Explorations in personality.* New York, NY: Oxford University Press.

Nietzsche, F. W. (1967a). *Beyond good and evil* (W. Kaufmann, Trans.). In *Basic Writings of Nietzsche.* New York, NY: Modern Library. (Original work published in 1886.)

Nietzsche, F. W. (1967b). *On the genealogy of morals* (W. Kaufmann, Trans.). In *Basic Writings of Nietzsche.* New York, NY: Modern Library. (Original work published in 1887.)

Noddings, N. (1984). *Caring: A feminine approach to ethics and moral education.* Berkeley: University of California Press.

Nunner-Winkler, G. (1984). Two moralities? A critical discussion of an ethic of care and responsibility versus an ethic of rights and justice. In W. M. Kurtines & J. L. Gewirtz (Eds.), *Morality, moral behavior, and moral development* (pp. 348–361). New York, NY: Wiley.

Nussbaum, M. C. (2014). Compassion: Human and animal. In H. Putnam, S. Naiman, & J. P. Schloss (Eds.), *Understanding moral sentiments: Darwinian perspectives?* (pp. 123–150). New Brunswick, NJ: Transaction.

Oliner, S. P., & Oliner, P. M. (1988). *The altruistic personality: Rescuers of Jews in Nazi Europe.* New York, NY: Free Press.

O'Mara, E. M., Jackson, L. E., Batson, C. D., & Gaertner, L. (2011). Will moral outrage stand up? Distinguishing among emotional reactions to a moral violation. *European Journal of Social Psychology, 41,* 173–179.

Opotow, S. (1990). Moral exclusion and injustice: An introduction. *Journal of Social Issues, 46(1),* 1–20.

Orne, M. (1962). On the social psychology of the psychological experiment: With particular reference to demand characteristics and their implications. *American Psychologist, 17,* 776–783.

Paluck, E. L. (2009). Reducing intergroup prejudice and conflict using the media: A field experiment in Rwanda. *Journal of Personality and Social Psychology, 96,* 574–587.

Petrocelli, J. V., & Smith, E. R. (2005). Who am I, who are we, and why: Links between emotions and causal attributions for self and group-discrepancies. *Personality and Social Psychology Bulletin, 31,* 1628–1642.

Piaget, J. (1926). *The language and thought of the child.* New York, NY: Harcourt.

Piaget, J. (1953). *The origins of intelligence in the child.* New York, NY: International Universities Press.

Piaget, J. (1965). *The moral judgment of the child.* New York, NY: Free Press. (Original work published in 1932.)

Pillutla, M. M., & Murnighan, J. K. (2003). Fairness in bargaining. *Social Justice Research, 16,* 241–262.

Pinker, S. (2011). *The better angels of our nature: Why violence has declined.* New York, NY: Viking.

Plato. (1960). *Gorgias* (W. Hamilton & C. Emlyn-Jones, Trans.). London, England: Penguin.

Plato. (1999). *Complete works* (J. Cooper, Ed.). Indianapolis, IN: Hackett.

Polak, A., & Harris, P. L. (1999). Deception by young children following noncompliance. *Developmental Psychology, 35,* 561–568.

Prinz, J. (2006). The emotional basis of moral judgments. *Philosophical Explorations, 9,* 29–43.

Prinz, J. (2007). *The emotional construction of morals.* Oxford, England: Oxford University Press.

Prinz, J. (2008). Is morality innate? In W. Sinnott-Armstrong (Ed.), *Moral psychology: Vol. 1. The Evolution of morality: Adaptation and prevention* (pp. 367–406). Cambridge, MA: MIT Press.

Rand, D. G., & Nowak, M. A. (2011). The evolution of antisocial punishment in optional public goods games. *Nature Communications, 2,* 434.

Ratner, R. K., & Miller, D. T. (2001). The norm of self-interest and its effects on social action. *Journal of Personality and Social Psychology, 81,* 5–16.

Rawls, J. (1971). *A theory of justice.* Cambridge, MA: Harvard University Press.

Reis, H. T., & Gruzen, J. (1976). On mediating equity, equality, and self-interest: The role of self-presentation in social exchange. *Journal of Experimental Social Psychology, 12,* 487–503.

Richardson, S. (1971). *Clarissa; or, the history of a young lady.* San Francisco, CA: Richardson. (Original work published in 1747.)

Richardson, S. (2011). *Pamela; or, virtue rewarded.* New York, NY: Cambridge University Press. (Original work published in 1740.)

Rokeach, M. (1973). *The nature of human values.* New York, NY: Free Press.

Roseman, I. J. (1984). Cognitive determinants of emotions: A structural theory. In P. Shaver (Ed.), *Review of personality and social psychology* (Vol. 5, pp. 11–36). Newbury Park, CA: Sage.

Rosenhan, D. (1970). The natural socialization of altruistic autonomy. In J. Macaulay & L. Berkowitz (Eds.), *Altruism and helping behavior: Social psychological studies of some antecedents and consequences* (pp. 251–268). New York, NY: Academic.

Rosenthal, A. M. (1964). *Thirty-eight witnesses.* New York, NY: McGraw-Hill.

Ross, H. S., & den Bak-Lammers, I. M. (1998). Consistency and change in children's tattling on their siblings: Children's perspectives on the moral rules and procedures of family life. *Social Development, 7,* 275–300.

Ross, L., & Ward, A. (1996). Naive realism in everyday life: Implications for social conflict and misunderstanding. In E. S. Reed, E. Turiel, & T. Brown (Eds.), *Values and knowledge* (pp. 103–135). Mahwah, NJ: Erlbaum.

Rousseau, J.-J. (1997). *Julie, or the new Héloise.* Hanover, NH: University Press of New England, Dartmouth College. (Original work published in 1761.)

Royzman, E., & Kurzban, R. (2011). Minding the metaphor: The elusive character of moral disgust. *Emotion Review, 3,* 269–271.

Rozin, P. (1997). Moralization. In A. M. Brandt & P. Rozin (Eds.), *Morality and health* (pp. 379–401). New York, NY: Routledge.

Rozin, P., Markwith, M., & Stoess, C. (1997). Moralization and becoming a vegetarian: The transformation of preferences into values and the recruitment of disgust. *Psychological Science, 8,* 67–73.

Rozin, P., Lowery, L., Imada, S., & Haidt, J. (1999). The CAD triad hypothesis: A mapping between three moral emotions (contempt, anger, and disgust) and three moral codes (community, autonomy, divinity). *Journal of Personality and Social Psychology, 76,* 574–586.

Rubin, Z., & Peplau, L. A. (1973). Belief in a just world and reactions to another's lot: A study of participants in the national draft lottery. *Journal of Social Issues, 29,* 73–93.

Rushton, J. P. (1975). Generosity in children: Immediate and long-term effects of modeling, preaching, and moral judgment. *Journal of Personality and Social Psychology, 31,* 459–466.

Rushton, J. P. (1980). *Altruism, socialization, and society.* Englewood Cliffs, NJ: Prentice-Hall.

Russell, P. S., & Giner-Sorolla, R. (2013). Bodily moral disgust: What it is, how it is different from anger, and why it is an unreasoned emotion. *Psychological Bulletin, 139,* 328–351.

Russell, P. S., Piazza, J., & Giner-Sorolla, R. (2013). CAD revisited: Effects of the work *moral* on the moral relevance of disgust (and other emotions). *Social Psychological and Personality Science, 4,* 62–68.

Ryan, R. M., & Deci, E. L. (2000). Self-determination theory and the facilitation of intrinsic motivation, social development, and well-being. *American Psychologist, 55,* 68–78.

Sachdeva, S., Iliev, R., & Medin, D. L. (2009). Sinning saints and saintly sinners. *Psychological Science, 20,* 523–528.

Salerno, J. M., & Peter-Hagene, L. C. (2013). The interactive effect of anger and disgust on moral outrage and judgments. *Psychological Science, 24,* 2069–2078.

Sanfey, A. G., Rilling, J. K., Aronson, J. A., Nystrom, L. E., & Cohen, J. D. (2003). The neural basis of economic decision-making in the Ultimatum Game. *Science, 300,* 1755–1758.

Saroyan, W. (1951). *Rock Wagram.* Garden City, NY: Doubleday.

Sattler, D. N., & Kerr, N. L. (1991). Might versus morality explored: Motivational and cognitive bases for social motives. *Journal of Personality and Social Psychology, 60,* 756–765.

Schachter, S., & Latané, B. (1964). Crime, cognition, and the autonomic nervous system. *Nebraska Symposium on Motivation, 12,* 221–275.

Scherer, K. R. (1984). On the nature and function of emotion: A component process approach. In K. R. Scherer & P. Ekman (Eds.), *Approaches to emotion* (pp. 293–317). Hillsdale, NJ: Erlbaum.

Schmidt, M. F. H., & Tomasello, M. (2012). Young children enforce social norms. *Psychological Science, 21,* 232–236.

Schmitt, M., Gollwitzer, M., Maes, J., & Arbach, D. (2005). Justice sensitivity: Assessment and location in the personality space. *European Journal of Psychological Assessment, 21,* 202–211.

Schmitt, M., & Maes, J. (1998). Perceived injustice in unified Germany and mental health. *Social Justice Research, 11,* 59–78.

Schnall, S., Benton, J., & Harvey, S. (2008). With a clean conscience: Cleanliness reduces the severity of moral judgments. *Psychological Sciences, 19,* 2119–1222.

Schnall, S., Haidt, J., Clore, G. L., & Jordan, A. H. (2008). Disgust as embodied moral judgment. *Personality and Social Psychology Bulletin, 34,* 1096–1109.

Schroeder, D. A., Steel, J. E., Woodell, A. J., & Bembenek, A. E. (2003). Justice within social dilemmas. *Personality and Social Psychology Review, 7,* 374–387.

Schwarz, N., & Clore, G. J. (1983). Mood, misattribution, and judgments of well-being: Informative and directive functions of affective states. *Journal of Personality and Social Psychology, 45*, 513–523.

Schwarz, N., & Clore, G. J. (1988). How do I feel about it? Informative functions of affective states. In K. Fiedler & J. Forgas (Eds.), *Affect, cognition, and social behavior* (pp. 44–62). Toronto, Canada: Hogrefe.

Sedikides, C., & Strube, M. J. (1997). Self-evaluation: To thine own self be good, to thine own self be sure, to thine own self be true, and to thine own self be better. In M. P. Zanna (Ed.), *Advances in experimental social psychology* (Vol. 29, pp. 209–269). New York, NY: Academic.

Selman, R. L. (1980). *The growth of interpersonal understanding: Developmental and clinical analyses.* Orlando, FL: Academic.

Shalvi, S., Dana, J., Handgraaf, M. J. J., & De Dreu, C. K. W. (2011). Justified ethicality: Observing desired counterfactuals modifies ethical perceptions and behavior. *Organizational Behavior and Human Decision Processes, 115*, 181–190.

Shalvi, S., Eldar, O., & Bereby-Meyer, Y. (2012). Honesty requires time (and lack of justifications). *Psychological Science, 23*, 1264–1270.

Shariff, A. F., & Norenzayan, A. (2007). God is watching you: Priming God concepts increases prosocial behavior in an anonymous economic game. *Psychological Science, 18*, 803–809.

Shaw, A., Montinari, N., Piovesan, M., Olson, K. R., Gino, F., & Norton, M. J. (2014). Children develop a veil of fairness. *Journal of Experimental Psychology: General, 143*, 363–375.

Shaw, L. L., Batson, C. D., & Todd, R. M. (1994). Empathy avoidance: Forestalling feeling for another in order to escape the motivational consequences. *Journal of Personality and Social Psychology, 67*, 879–887.

Sheikh, S., & Janoff-Bulman, R. (2013). Paradoxical consequences of prohibitions. *Journal of Personality and Social Psychology, 105*, 301–315.

Shu, L. L., & Gino, F. (2012). Sweeping dishonesty under the rug: How unethical actions lead to forgetting moral rules. *Journal of Personality and Social Psychology, 102*, 1164–1177.

Shu, L. L., Gino, F., & Bazerman, M. H. (2011). Dishonest deed, clear conscience: When cheating leads to moral disengagement and motivated forgetting. *Personality and Social Psychology Bulletin, 37*, 330–349.

Shu, L. L., Mazar, N., Gino, F., Ariely, D., & Bazerman, M. H. (2012). Signing at the beginning makes ethics salient and decreases dishonest self-reports in comparison to signing at the end. *Proceedings of the National Academy of Sciences, 109*, 15197–15200.

Shultz, T. R., & Darley, J. M. (1991). An information-processing model of retributive moral judgments based on "legal reasoning." In W. M. Kurtines & J. L. Gewirtz (Eds.), *Handbook of moral behavior and development: Vol. 2. Research* (pp. 247–278). Hillsdale, NJ: Erlbaum.

Shweder, R. A., Mahapatra, M., & Miller, J. G. (1987). Culture and moral development. In J. Kagan & S. Lamb (Eds.), *The emergence of morality in young children* (pp. 1–83). Chicago, IL: University of Chicago Press.

Sibicky, M. E., Schroeder, D. A., & Dovidio, J. F. (1995). Empathy and helping: Considering the consequences of intervention. *Basic and Applied Social Psychology, 16*, 435–453.

Singer, P. (1981). *The expanding circle: Ethics and sociobiology.* New York, NY: Farrar, Straus, & Giroux.

Singer, P. (1999, September 5). The Singer solution to world poverty. *New York Times Magazine*, 60–63.

Sinnott-Armstrong, W., Young, L., & Cushman, F. (2010). Moral intuitions. In J. M. Doris & Moral Psychology Research Group (Eds.), *The moral psychology handbook* (pp. 245–271). Oxford, England: Oxford University Press.

Skitka, L. J. (2012). Moral convictions and moral courage: Common denominators of good and evil. In M. Mikulancer & P. R. Shaver (Eds.), *The social psychology of morality: Exploring the causes of good and evil* (pp. 349–365). Washington, DC: American Psychological Association.

Skitka, L. J., Bauman, C. W., & Mullen, E. (2004). Political tolerance and coming to psychological closure following the September 11, 2001, terrorist attacks: An integrative approach. *Personality and Social Psychology Bulletin, 30*, 743–756.

Skitka, L. J., Bauman, C. W., & Sargis, E. G. (2005). Moral conviction: Another contributor to attitude strength or something more? *Journal of Personality and Social Psychology, 88*, 895–917.

Slovic, P. (2007). "If I look at the mass I will never act": Psychic numbing and genocide. *Judgment and Decision Making, 2*, 1–17.

Small, D. A., Lowenstein, G., & Slovic, P. (2007). Sympathy and callousness: The impact of deliberative thought on donations to identifiable and statistical victims. *Organizational Behavior and Human Decision Processes, 102*, 143–153.

Smetana, J. G. (1989). Toddlers' social interactions in the context of moral and conventional transgressions in the home. *Developmental Psychology, 25*, 499–508.

Smith, A. (1976a). *An inquiry into the nature and causes of the wealth of nations.* Chicago, IL: University of Chicago Press. (Original work published in 1776.)

Smith, A. (1976b). *The theory of moral sentiments.* (D. D. Raphael & A. L. Macfie, Eds.). Oxford, England: Oxford University Press. (Original work published in 1759.)

Smith, C. A., & Ellsworth, P. C. (1987). Patterns of appraisal and emotion related to taking an exam. *Journal of Personality and Social Psychology, 52*, 475–488.

Smith, E. R., Seger, C. R., & Mackie, D. M. (2007). Can emotions be truly group level? Evidence regarding four conceptual criteria. *Journal of Personality and Social Psychology, 93*, 431–446.

Smith, G. (2012, March 14). Why I am leaving Goldman Sachs. *New York Times.*

Smith, M. (1994). *The moral problem.* Oxford, England: Basil Blackwell.

Snyder, M. L., Kleck, R. E., Strenta, A., & Mentzer, S. J. (1979). Avoidance of the handicapped: An attributional ambiguity analysis. *Journal of Personality and Social Psychology, 37*, 2297–2306.

Solomon, R. C. (1990). *A passion for justice: Emotions and the origins of the social contract.* Reading, MA: Addison-Wesley.

Solomon, S., Greenberg, J., & Pyszczynski, T. (1991). A terror-management theory of social behavior: The psychological functions of self-esteem and cultural worldviews. In M. P. Zanna (Ed.), *Advances in experimental social psychology* (Vol. 24, pp. 93–159). San Diego, CA: Academic.

Staub, E. (1985). The psychology of perpetrators and bystanders. *Political Psychology, 6*, 61–85.

Staub, E. (1989). *The roots of evil: The origins of genocide and other group violence.* New York, NY: Cambridge University Press.

Staub, E. (1990). Moral exclusion, personal goal theory, and extreme destructiveness. *Journal of Social Issues, 46(1)*, 47–64.

Staub, E., & Pearlman, L. A. (2009). Reducing intergroup prejudice and conflict: A commentary. *Journal of Personality and Social Psychology, 96*, 588–593.

Staw, B. M., & Ross, J. (1987). Behavior in escalation situations: Antecedents, prototypes, and solutions. *Research in Organizational Behavior, 9*, 39–78.

Steblay, N. M. (1987). Helping behavior in rural and urban environments: A meta-analysis. *Psychological Bulletin, 102*, 346–356.

Steinel, W., & De Dreu, C. K. W. (2004). Social motives and strategic misrepresentation in social decision making. *Journal of Personality and Social Psychology, 86*, 419–434.

Stendhal. (2003). *The red and the black: A chronicle of 1830* (B. Raffel, Trans.). New York, NY: Modern Library. (Original work published in 1830.)

Stocker, M. (1976). The schizophrenia of modern ethical theories. *Journal of Philosophy, 73*, 453–466.

Stotland, E. (1969). Exploratory investigations of empathy. In L. Berkowitz (Ed.), *Advances in experimental social psychology* (Vol. 4, pp. 271–313). New York, NY: Academic.

Stowe, H. B. (2005). *Uncle Tom's cabin*. Mineola, NY: Dover. (Original work published in 1852.)

Strobe, W., Postmes, T., & Spears, R. (2012). Scientific misconduct and the myth of self-correction in science. *Perspectives on Psychological Science, 7*, 670–688.

Stukas, A. A., Snyder, M., & Clary, E. G. (1999). The effects of "mandatory volunteerism" on intentions to volunteer. *Psychological Science, 10*, 59–64.

Sully, J. (1908). *Studies of childhood*. New York, NY: Appleton.

Tajfel, H. (1981). *Human groups and social categories: Studies in social psychology*. Cambridge, England: Cambridge University Press.

Tajfel, H., & Turner, J. C. (1986). The social identity theory of intergroup behavior. In S. Worchel & W. Austin (Eds.), *Psychology of intergroup relations* (pp. 7–24). Chicago, IL: Nelson-Hall.

Talwar, V., Lee, K., Bala, N., & Lindsay, R. C. L. (2002). Children's conceptual knowledge of lying and its relation to their actual behaviors: Implications for court competence examinations. *Law and Human Behavior, 26*, 395–415.

Tangney, J. P., & Dearing, R. L. (2002). *Shame and guilt*. New York, NY: Guilford.

Tangney, J. P., Stuewig, J., & Mashek, D. J. (2007). Moral emotions and moral behavior. *Annual Review of Psychology, 58*, 345–372.

Tavris, C., & Aronson, E. (2007). *Mistakes were made (but not by me): Why we justify foolish beliefs, bad decisions, and hurtful acts*. Orlando, FL: Harcourt.

Tenbrunsel, A. E., & Messick, D. M. (2004). Ethical fading: The role of self-deception in unethical behavior. *Social Justice Research, 17*, 223–236.

Teper, R., Inzlicht, M., & Page-Gould, E. (2011). Are we more moral than we think? Exploring the role of affect in moral behavior and moral forecasting. *Psychological Science, 22*, 553–558.

Tetlock, P. E., Kristel, O. V., Elson, S. B., Green, M. C., & Lerner, J. S. (2000). The psychology of the unthinkable: Taboo trade-offs, forbidden base rates, and heretical counterfactuals. *Journal of Personality and Social Psychology, 78*, 853–870.

Thomas, G., & Batson, C. D. (1981). Effect of helping under normative pressure on self-perceived altruism. *Social Psychology Quarterly, 44*, 127–131.

Thorndike, E. L. (1898). Animal intelligence: An experimental study of the associative process in animals. *Psychological Review, Monograph Supplement, 8.*

Todorov, T. (1996). *Facing the extreme: Moral life in the concentration camps* (A. Denner & A. Pollak, Trans.). New York, NY: Henry Holt.

Tolstoy, L. (2009). *The death of Ivan Ilyich, and other stories.* (R. Pevear & L. Volokhonsky, Trans.). New York, NY: Alfred A. Knopf. (Original work published in 1886.)

Tomasello, M., & Vaish, A. (2013). Origins of human cooperation and morality. *Annual Review of Psychology, 64,* 231–255.

Trautmann, S. T., van de Kuilen, G., & Zeckhauser, R. J. (2013). Social class and (un)ethical behavior: A framework, with evidence from a large population sample. *Perspectives on Psychological Science, 8,* 487–497.

Trivers, R. L. (1971). The evolution of reciprocal altruism. *Quarterly Review of Biology, 46,* 35–57.

Trivers, R. L. (1985). *Social evolution.* Menlo Park, CA: Benjamin/Cummings.

Tronto, J. (1987). Beyond gender differences to a theory of care. *Signs, 12,* 644–663.

Tsang, J. (2002). Moral rationalization and integration of situational factors and psychological processes in immoral behavior. *Review of General Psychology, 6,* 25–50.

Turiel, E. (1966). An experimental test of the sequentiality of developmental stages in the child's moral judgments. *Journal of Personality and Social Psychology, 3,* 611–618.

Turiel, E. (1983). *The development of social knowledge: Morality and convention.* Cambridge, England: Cambridge University Press.

Twain, M. (1959). *Adventures of Huckleberry Finn.* New York, NY: Penguin. (Original work published in 1884.)

Uhlmann, E. L., Pizarro, D. A., Tannenbaum, D., & Ditto, P. H. (2009). The motivated use of moral principles. *Judgment and Decision Making, 4,* 476–491.

Vaes, J., Paladino, M. P., Castelli, L., Leyens, J.-P., Giovanazzi, A. (2003). On the behavioral consequences of infrahumanization: The implicit role of uniquely human emotions in intergroup relations. *Journal of Personality and Social Psychology, 85,* 1016–1034.

Valdesolo, P., & DeSteno, D. (2007). Moral hypocrisy: Social groups and the flexibility of virtue. *Psychological Science, 18,* 689–690.

Valdesolo, P., & DeSteno, D. (2008). The duality of virtue: Deconstructing the moral hypocrite. *Journal of Experimental Social Psychology, 44,* 1334–1338.

Vandivier, K. (1972). Why should my conscience bother me? In R. L. Heilbroner et al., *In the name of profit* (pp. 3–31). Garden City, NY: Doubleday.

Van Lange, P. A. M. (2008). Does empathy trigger only altruistic motivation? How about selflessness or justice? *Emotion, 8,* 766–774.

Van Lange, P. A. M., & Kuhlman, D. M. (1994). Social value orientations and impressions of partner's honesty and intelligence: A test of the might versus morality effect. *Journal of Personality and Social Psychology, 67,* 126–141.

Verplanken, B., & Holland, R. W. (2002). Motivated decision making: Effects of activation and self-centrality of values on choices and behavior. *Journal of Personality and Social Psychology, 82,* 434–447.

Vincent, L. C., Emich, K. J., & Goncalo, J. A. (2013). Stretching the moral grey zone: Positive affect, moral disengagement, and dishonesty. *Psychological Science, 24,* 595–599.

Vitaglione, G. D., & Barnett, M. A. (2003). Assessing a new dimension of empathy: Empathic anger as a predictor of helping and punishing desires. *Motivation and Emotion, 27,* 301–325.

Voltaire. (1930). *Candide.* New York, NY: Modern Library. (Original work published in 1759.)

von Hippel, W., & Trivers, R. (2011). The evolution and psychology of self-deception. *Behavioral and Brain Sciences, 34,* 1–56.

Walker, L. J. (1991). Sex differences in moral reasoning. In W. M. Kurtines & J. L. Gewirtz (Eds.), *Handbook of moral behavior and development: Vol. 2. Research* (pp. 333–364). Hillsdale, NJ: Erlbaum.

Walker, L. J., & Hennig, K. H. (2004). Differing conceptions of moral exemplarity: Just, brave, and caring. *Journal of Personality and Social Psychology, 86,* 629–647.

Walton, M. D. (1985). Negotiation of responsibility: Judgments of blameworthiness in a natural setting. *Developmental Psychology, 21,* 725–736.

Walton, M. D., & Sedlak, A. J. (1982). Making amends: A grammar-based analysis of children's social interaction. *Merrill-Palmer Quarterly, 28,* 389–412.

Webster's desk dictionary of the English language. (1990). New York, NY: Portland House.

Weiner, B. (1980). A cognitive (attribution)-emotion-action model of motivated behavior: An analysis of judgments of help giving. *Journal of Personality and Social Psychology, 39,* 186–200.

Weiner, B. (1995). *Judgments of responsibility: A foundation for a theory of social conduct.* New York, NY: Guilford.

Weiner, F. H. (1976). Altruism, ambiance, and action: The effects of rural and urban rearing on helping behavior. *Journal of Personality and Social Psychology, 34,* 112–124.

Westermark, E. A. (1908). *The origin and development of the moral ideas* (Vol. 2). Freeport, NY: Libraries Press.

Wheatley, T., & Haidt, J. (2005). Hypnotic disgust makes moral judgments more severe. *Psychological Science, 16,* 780–784.

Wicklund, R. A. (1975). Objective self-awareness. In L. Berkowitz (Ed.), *Advances in experimental social psychology* (Vol. 8, pp. 233–275). New York, NY: Academic.

Wicklund, R. A., & Brehm, J. W. (1976). *Perspectives on cognitive dissonance.* Hillsdale, NJ: Erlbaum.

Wilson, J. Q. (1993). *The moral sense.* New York, NY: Free Press.

Wright, R. (1994). *The moral animal: Evolutionary psychology and everyday life.* New York, NY: Vintage.

Yamagishi, T. (1986). The provision of a sanctioning system as a public good. *Journal of Personality and Social Psychology, 51,* 110–116.

Yamagishi, T., & Sato, K. (1986). Motivational bases of the public goods problem. *Journal of Personality and Social Psychology, 50,* 67–73.

Youniss, J. (1980). *Parents and peers in social development: A Sullivan-Piaget perspective.* Chicago, IL: University of Chicago Press.

Yzerbyt, V., Dumont, M., Wigboldus, D., & Gordijn, E. (2003). I feel for us: The impact of categorization and identification on emotions and action tendencies. *British Journal of Social Psychology, 42,* 533–549.

Zajonc, R. B. (1980). Feeling and thinking: Preferences need no inferences. *American Psychologist, 35,* 151–175.

Zhong, C.-B., & Liljenquist, K. (2006). Washing away your sins: Threatened morality and physical cleansing. *Science, 313,* 1451–1452.

Zimbardo, P. G. (1970). The human choice: Individuation, reason, and order versus deindividuation, impulse, and chaos. In W. J. Arnold & D. Levine (Eds.), *1969 Nebraska symposium on motivation* (pp. 237–307). Lincoln: University of Nebraska Press.

Zimbardo, P. G. (2004). A situationist perspective on the psychology of evil: Understanding how good people are transformed into perpetrators. In A. G. Miller (Ed.), *The social psychology of good and evil* (pp. 21–50). New York, NY: Guilford.

Zimbardo, P. G. (2007). *The Lucifer effect: Understanding how good people turn evil.* New York, NY: Random House.

INDEX

Page numbers followed by "f" and "t" indicate figures and tables.